SAM SRINIVASULU

INTERNATIONAL ACCOUNTING AND MULTINATIONAL ENTERPRISES

2ND EDITION

Jeffrey S. Arpan
University of South Carolina

Lee H. Radebaugh
Brigham Young University

John Wiley & Sons
New York   Chichester   Brisbane   Toronto   Singapore

Library of Congress Cataloging in Publication Data:

Arpan, Jeffrey S.
  International Accounting and multinational enterprises.

  Includes index.
  1. International business enterprises—Accounting.
2. Comparative accounting.   I. Radebaugh, Lee H.
II. Title.
HF5686.I56A76   1985   657'.95   84-29159
ISBN 0-471-88231-3

Printed in the United States of America

10 9 8 7 6 5 4 3 2 1

ABOUT THE AUTHORS

Jeffrey S. Arpan (D.B.A., Indiana University) is professor of international business and director of both Asian/Pacific programs and the Center for Industry Policy and Strategy of the College of Business Administration at the University of South Carolina. From 1971 to 1980, he was a member of the accounting faculty and of the Institute of International Business at Georgia State University.

Dr. Arpan also serves as consulting editor for the *Journal of International Business Studies,* and is a member and former vice-president of the Academy of International Business and a member of the International Section of the American Accounting Association. His doctoral dissertation was selected as the most outstanding one of 1970–71 by the Academy of International Business.

Dr. Arpan annually participates in more than a dozen corporate training programs for IBM and other multinational companies, and along with Lee Radebaugh, conducts semiannual seminars in international accounting at the IBM education facility in New York. He also directed a project sponsored by the Touche Ross Foundation to develop a model for an internationalized accounting curriculum.

Lee H. Radebaugh (D.B.A., Indiana University) is associate dean and professor of accounting and international business at Brigham Young University. He has also been a member of the faculty of the Pennsylvania State University and a visiting professor at the Escuela de Administracion de Negocios para Graduados (ESAN) in Lima, Peru.

Dr. Radebaugh has published articles on international accounting and international business in such journals as *The Journal of Accounting Research, The Journal of International Business Studies,* and *The International Journal of Accounting Education and Research.* He coauthored *International Business: Environments and Operations* in addition to this text.

He is a past chairman of the International Accounting Section of the American Accounting Association and has also been a member of the advisory board of the section as well as the chairman of several different committees of the section. In addition to activity in the International Accounting Section, Dr. Radebaugh has served on several committees of the American Accounting Association. He is a member of the Academy of International Business and has served as treasurer of that association.

Along with Jeff Arpan, Dr. Radebaugh conducts seminars in international accounting at the IBM educational facility in New York and also conducts various executive education programs for Penn State University.

PREFACE

The main reasons for writing a second edition of this book are essentially the same as those for writing the first: increasing international business activity and the related need for better awareness and understanding of what international business is and what its implications are—specifically in and for the accounting field.

In addition, several major changes have occurred in the field of international accounting itself. In the United States, for example, there have been major changes in accounting for foreign exchange gains and losses and in the taxation of exports and of income of U.S. citizens working abroad. In the international arena, several new international accounting standards have been adopted, some new ones are under consideration, and many countries have unilaterally made changes in their own accounting standards and practices.

A marked increase in the internationalization of business schools curricula has also occurred: new international content in heretofore domestically oriented courses, new specialized courses in international business (including many more courses in international accounting), and a host of new international business programs at the undergraduate, graduate, and continuing education levels.

We are indebted to our many colleagues who, over the past four years, have given us useful suggestions for improvements along these lines, and we invite similar input about this edition.

For this edition, we are also once again indebted to many other scholars and colleagues whose work helped form the basis for this revision. We also acknowledge the constructive comments of the reviewers of this edition: Janice Shields, University of Maine at Orono, Helen Gernon, University of Oregon, and Kathleen Bindon, University of Alabama.

Special thanks also go to the typists for the seemingly endless drafts and final version of the manuscript: Dee Williams, Michel Bergen, and Robin Stringham of the University of South Carolina, and Lisa Carter of Brigham Young University and to typist-assistants Jan Kingston, Cindy Montgomery, and Brent Anderson of Brigham Young University.

We thank our publisher, John Wiley & Sons, not only for its wisdom in acquiring our book, but also for the high degree of professionalism it devoted to every phase of the publication process. Particularly, we acknowledge Lucille Sutton's continuous efforts to hold our feet to the deadline fires without burning us unduly, and we thank Dorothy Hoffman, our manuscript editor, whose journalistic and grammatical skills made the revision more intelligible.

Finally, our immeasurable gratitude goes to our wives and children who struggled vicariously with us throughout the revision process and whose penetrating questions—such as "Is a revision really necessary so soon?" and then, "Isn't the revision done yet?"—were a constant source of inspiration to us.

Even with the collective help and prodding of all these persons and our own best effort, there undoubtedly remain some errors and omissions in the second edition. As we said in the first edition, such is the imperfect nature of man—a condition unchanged since that time. As authors, we assume full responsibility. But as all accountants know, there inevitably comes a time when the books must be closed, and not all errors are caught. So we once again solicit our external auditors, those who use our book, to let us know how it can be improved further.

Jeffrey S. Arpan
Lee H. Radebaugh

November 1984

CONTENTS

CHAPTER 1

An Overview of International Accounting and International Business

Despite a few rumors to the contrary, the field of accounting has had a notable international history and promises to have an even better future. Like the other functional areas of business, accounting has changed as the environments it serves have changed, moving sequentially from the more rudimentary to the more complex and sophisticated. This chapter first traces the international development of accounting, and then highlights some of the critical factors that determine national differences in accounting systems, and finally provides an initial perspective on these differences and their importance for accountants in the modern world. It also discusses the evolution of world trade and investment patterns, together with some of the accounting implications of these developments.

THE INTERNATIONAL DEVELOPMENT OF THE ACCOUNTING DISCIPLINE

Record keeping, the foundation of accounting, has been traced back as far as 3600 B.C. Concepts such as depreciation were evident during the early Greek and Roman civilizations, where, for example, walls were depreciated at 1/80th per year. Yet most accounting historians agree that modern accounting dates from the fourteenth century, when the double-entry system began.

The first record of a complete system was found in Genoa, in what is now Italy, in 1340. The Genoan system assumed the concept of a business entity, and because it recorded items in money terms, it was the first to imply that unlike items could be compared in terms of a common monetary unit, in other words, that economic events were quantifiable. The Genoan system also implied some understanding of the distinction between capital and income, as it included both expenses and equity accounts.

The Italian domination of accounting was further cemented in 1494 with the publication of the first formal treatise on accounting, *Summa de Arithmetica, Geometria Proportioni et Proportionalita,* by Luca Pacioli, a Franciscan friar residing in Venice. His treatise was unique also because it was one of the earliest printed books (printed in fact on Gutenberg's printing press).

Although one might argue that accounting made little progress from 3600 B.C. to A.D. 1494, it must be recognized that several important antecedents had to take place—including the art of writing, the development of arithmetic, the widespread use of money, the development of business organizations such as partnerships, the concept of private property, the development of credit, and a significant accumulation of private capital.

Pacioli's accounting system represented a landmark in accounting development. Its major objective was to provide information for the owner, reporting on stewardship and serving as a basis for granting credit. However, little distinction was made between the entity and the owner, as Pacioli's system reported together all the personal and business affairs of the owner. In addition, there was no concept of an accounting period or the continuing nature of a business; profit was calculated only at the termination of a venture, with no accruals or deferrals.

The concept of an accounting period did not emerge until the seventeenth and eighteenth centuries, when end-of-the-year reconciliations became prominent. During this period, the center of commerce shifted sequentially from Italy to Spain, to Portugal, to Northern Europe. With this commercial shift was an accompanying shift in accounting development. In 1673, France adopted the first official accounting code, which required, among other things, that balance sheets be drawn up every two years. This period also saw the first personification of accounts (the practice of treating accounts as independent, living entities) and the standardization of debits on the left, credits on the right.

Although accounting took a long time to get rolling, its development surged in the nineteenth and early twentieth centuries. The major force in this development was the Industrial Revolution. As the scale of enterprises increased following technological breakthroughs such as mass production, and as fixed assets grew in importance, accounting had to accommodate for depreciation, allocating overhead, and inventory. In addition, the basic form of business organization shifted from proprietorships and partnerships to limited liability and stock companies and ultimately to full-blown corporations. Accounting had to accommodate to these new needs. Massive railroad and canal construction during this period once and for all forced the distinction between income and capital, and increased government regulation of business made new demands and generated new accounting systems, which were harbingers of bigger moves to come. Most notable was the increased taxation of businesses and individuals, which brought with it new tax accounting systems and procedures.

Since the early years of this century, the rapidity of change and the increasing complexity of the world's industrial economies necessitated still more changes in accounting. Mergers, acquisitions, and the growth of giant multinational corporations fostered new internal and external reporting and control systems. With widespread ownership of modern corporations came new audit and reporting procedures, and new agencies became involved in promulgating accounting standards: stock exchanges, securities regulating commissions, internal revenue agencies, and so on.

And finally, with the dramatic increase in foreign investments and world trade and the formation of regional economic groups such as the European Economic Community, problems arose concerning the international activities of business. This phenomenon remains particularly complex, for it involves reconciling the accounting practices of different nations in which each multinational operates, as well as dealing with accounting problems unique to international business.

NATIONAL DIFFERENCES IN ACCOUNTING SYSTEMS

One might infer that these developments had a uniform effect on accounting systems throughout the world, yet nothing could be further from the truth. Despite some similarities, there are at least as many accounting systems as there are countries, and no two systems are exactly alike. The underlying reasons for these differences are essentially environmental: accounting systems evolve from and reflect the environments they serve. The reality of the world is that environments have not evolved uniformly or simultaneously. Countries today are at stages of economic development ranging from subsistence, barter economies to highly complex industrial societies.

In some countries there is no private ownership; in others there is virtually no manufacturing. In some countries there have been inflation rates of 200 to 300% per year; in others there has been no significant economic growth in years. Given these differences in economic conditions, differences in accounting practices should not be surprising. Just as the accounting needs of a small proprietorship are different from those of a multinational giant, so are the accounting needs of an underdeveloped, agrarian country different from those of a highly developed industrial country.

Yet economic factors are not the only influences. Educational systems, legal systems, political systems, and sociocultural characteristics also influence the need for accounting and the direction and speed of its development. For example, in countries where religious doctrine does not permit the charging of interest, there are unlikely to be elaborate accounting procedures related to interest.

The ways in which environmental factors affect the evolution of accounting practices are covered in greater detail in Chapter 2. For the moment, it is sufficient to acknowledge their role and the fact that in each country their unique combination results in a unique system of accounting.

Pragmatic Implications
of National Differences in Accounting

There is some benefit in understanding how different nations do things. After all, there is always something to be learned from the experiences of others. As a case in point, consider inflation. Suppose a country has never experienced any significant inflation and has therefore never developed accounting procedures related to inflation. What would happen the first time the country experienced substantial and persistent inflation?

It could independently try to devise appropriate accounting procedures. It could also benefit from the experiences of other countries, which, having experienced significant inflation for some time, have developed inflation accounting procedures that work and make sense. However, it must also be acknowledged that another country's solution may not be appropriate or feasible for our hypothetical country. The nature of the inflation may be different, its effects may be different, and the other country's practices for dealing with inflation may be incompatible or inconsistent with our country's accounting system. On the other hand, if another country's practices are suitable and feasible, they could significantly shorten the time it would take a country to adapt its system so as to account properly for the effects of inflation. In this sense, accounting is a form of technology that can be borrowed or shared, depending on its suitability.

At the present time the most important reason for understanding different national accounting systems lies in the increasingly internalized world of business, in which people buy and sell, invest and disinvest from one country to another. If an enterprise is considering granting credit to or acquiring a company in another country, it must be able to assess the financial position of that company. This is easier said than done.

When the foreign company offers a balance sheet and income statement for analysis, several things become immediately evident. First, the language and the currency are different. Second, the terminology is different; certain terms (accounts) have no counterparts in the other language or accounting system, or they mean different things. Third, the types and amount of information disclosed are likely to be different. In addition, there are a host of less obvious but perhaps more important differences. For example, the procedures that were followed to arrive at the final figures are likely to be different and less likely to be explained. Differences in procedures, such as rules of valuation, recognition, or realization, render the financial statements meaningless unless the analyst is familiar with the foreign country's accounting system.

THE EVOLUTION AND SIGNIFICANCE OF
INTERNATIONAL BUSINESS

International business can be traced back to 300 B.C., give or take a few hundred years. And as far as anyone can tell, the reasons and motives were the same then as they are today: people wanted something they did not have in their own country, and they found someone in another country able to provide them with what they wanted—for a fee, of course. Yet this early trade was really a fetal stage, for trade on a major and planned scale did not really begin until the Greeks started exporting inexpensive, mass-produced goods around the fifth century B.C. By the end of the Greek period, there was sufficient trade to have permitted not only full-time professional traders but even some traders who specialized by area of the world or by commodities.

During the Roman period, traders roamed freely through the empire, and with better transportation, political stability, and few tariffs and trade restrictions, trade flourished. In fact, the Roman Empire established the feasibility and desirability of what is now known as the European Economic Community.

During the Middle Ages, international business flourished in some areas of the world, sputtered in others, died and was resurrected in still others. It flourished in Byzantium (present-day Constantinople) until the Crusades, facilitated by the development of banking and insurance and by the first large-scale international trade fairs. International trade did not fare as well in Europe until much later. Wars, plagues, and a generally anticommercial religious doctrine hindered commerce both domestically and internationally. Not until the twelfth century did commercial activity and trade break out of their comatose state. Yet with their resurgence came laws and regulations regarding commerce and trade. Initially developed by guilds, then by city states, and then much later by nation states, international commercial regulations have continued to proliferate to the present day.

The Preindustrial Period

As Europe emerged from the Dark Ages, merchants sought ways to increase international business. By this time, however, the right to trade had become a privilege granted by the states, a phenomenon that has persisted to modern times. The privilege was based on what was to be known as mercantilism, a concept by which each state sought to become more pervasive and powerful militarily, economically, and politically than its rivals. During this period of mercantilism, the state was the driving and controlling force behind domestic and international economic activity, a phenomenon that, like several others, seems to have come back into vogue during recent decades.

The sixteenth and seventeenth centuries saw the first major foreign investments, under the rubric of colonialism. Governments invested directly in colonies, or gave individuals the right to do so, with the express purpose of obtaining raw materials, and then products, in a near-monopoly control of trade. Finally, during this period of mercantilism the center of commercial and financial activity shifted steadily westward, from Byzantium to Italy, to Holland and Belgium, and ultimately to London. This dominating influence of Western Europe was to last until the twentieth century.

The Industrialization Period

The Industrial Revolution, which began in the latter half of the eighteenth century, continued to have a major impact on international business throughout the nineteenth and twentieth centuries. The industrial revolution and its accompanying technologies gave rise to mass production and standardization of products and required sizable capital investments on a scale theretofore unparalleled. The emergence of large-scale, limited-liability companies combined with large-scale infrastructure projects such as railroads, canals, and power generating systems often necessitated obtaining capital from other countries—a major form of international business that has continued to the present. To fully exploit scale economies of production, the exporting of mass-produced products became a necessity for many firms located in countries with small domestic markets. Simultaneously, industrialization often required an increase in the importation of raw materials and capital goods in many countries that did not possess sufficient quantities or quality of them. The multinational firm as it is known today had its emergence in this period, with early overseas expansion by firms such as Singer, Colt, and Ford.

The industrialization process also brought with it growing trade restrictions as many nations sought to protect their "infant industries." Although there was relatively little U.S. government interference or involvement with international trade or investment during this period, there was growing foreign government involvement, particularly in trade. This prompted many U.S. and foreign firms to begin displacing exports with direct investments in the more protectionist countries in order to keep their established markets. And despite the continued increase in both trade and investments, a trend was established: foreign investments were becoming more influential than international trade.

The Post-World War II Period

The Great Depression and World War II stunted the growth of international business. The reasons are fairly obvious: drastic reductions in income, the bankruptcy of individuals, companies, and governments, then war, the destruction of property, and an end to the stability of money. Throughout this period, trade protectionism and the regulation of capital flows were on the rise, which, when combined with the other factors just mentioned, put a significant damper on international business activity.

At the end of World War II, there was a tremendous pent-up demand for products and services. With some semblance of order restored in international politics and the international monetary system, both trade and investment increased sharply.

The remnants of the protectionism of the 1930s and early 1940s conspired to emphasize investment. The formation of the European Economic Community (EEC), with its surging demand and the elimination of its internal trade restrictions, resulted in an unparalleled growth of U.S. manufacturing investment abroad. By the 1970s this trend had abated considerably, but it was followed by an equally significant surge of foreign investments by foreign-based companies into the United States and other countries.

The Multinational Era

The proliferation of multinational enterprises and their activities has constituted perhaps the most significant development in international business—not only in the past three decades, but possibly in the entire span of international business history. Their wealth and influence are gargantuan, as suggested by the fact that by 1971, approximately 20% of the 50 largest economic entities in the world (companies, countries, states) were multinational companies, and nearly 40% of the top 100. Yet the impressive role that they now play is far from the whole story of the tremendous increase in international business. For virtually all the world's economies, trade has increased in importance as a percentage of all their economic activity. From 1965 to 1977, total trade expressed as a percentage of gross national product (GNP) rose from 7 to 14% for the United States, from 20 to 35% for France, from 30 to 42% for Germany, from 28 to 49% for the United Kingdom, from 23 to 46% for Italy, from 70 to 83% for The Netherlands, and from 74 to 94% for Belgium.

Even these statistics do not show the whole picture, because they say nothing about international investment flows. The total value of foreign direct investment (FDI) in the noncommunist world was estimated at $546 billion in 1981, compared with $108 billion in 1967. The United States remains the largest foreign investor, with nearly 48% of the total, followed by the United Kingdom (14%), Switzerland (7%), West Germany (6%), Japan, France, and The Netherlands (approximately 5% each). Data limitations and deficiencies and the fact that most fixed assets values are understated (particularly because of inflation) make a realistic estimate difficult, but total FDI today may be $700 billion to $800 billion.

Foreign direct investments by foreign-based companies have grown at higher rates than those for U.S.-based companies. Much of this investment by foreign companies has been in the United States, where the level of FDI has grown from $3.4 billion in 1950 to over $101 billion in 1983. In addition, FDIs by all nations have changed their emphasis from mining and petroleum to manufacturing. In 1976, manufacturing accounted for approximately 60% of foreign production, whereas mining and petroleum totaled about 30%, and the dominance of manufacturing has steadily increased since then, along with the emergence of foreign investments in the service sector. In addition, more and more countries have become international investors, the most significant of whom have been the Arab oil producing nations. This group's total foreign investments (direct and portfolio), fueled by surging national revenues resulting from the quadrupling of oil prices in the 1970s, reached $400 billion in 1984, and is expected to double by the end of 1985.

Taken together, these developments suggest that virtually all countries' involvement in and dependence on international business will continue to grow. Thus, anyone contemplating a career in business should prepare for the international aspects in addition to the domestic aspects. This prognostication applies not only to those in marketing, purchasing, finance, production, and management, but also to those in accounting.

ACCOUNTING ASPECTS OF INTERNATIONAL BUSINESS

A firm's first exposure to international accounting usually occurs as a result of an import or export opportunity. In the case of exports, a domestic company may receive an unsolicited inquiry or purchase order from a foreign buyer. Assuming the domestic company desires to make the sale, it needs to investigate the foreign buyer, particularly when the buyer asks for the extension of credit. This procedure is not often as easy as it appears.

First of all, the buyer may not be listed in any of the international credit rating directories, such as Standard & Poor's. If so, the seller may need to ask its bank to have its foreign affiliates check on the buyer's creditworthiness. Alternatively, it may ask the buyer to supply financial information. The buyer may be willing to supply financial statements, but these statements will probably be difficult for the domestic company to interpret. The statements may be in a foreign language and are undoubtedly based on accounting assumptions and procedures unfamiliar to the company's accountants. Most companies new to international business must then get help, either from a bank or from an accounting firm with international expertise. Even if the foreign buyer is willing to pay before receiving the shipment, if it wants to pay in its own currency, the selling company must become familiar with the gains and losses from changes in the exchange rate that may occur between the time the order is confirmed and the time the payment is received.

Then the selling company must deal with a host of other international details—special international shipping and insurance documents, customs declaration forms, international legal documents, and so on. Once again, the services of lawyers, shippers, bankers, and accountants with international expertise are needed.

In the case of a potential import, the international accounting aspects are not as involved because most of the details are the responsibility of the foreign seller. However, if the foreign seller requires payment in his or her nation's currency, or if the domestic buyer wants information about the reliability of the foreign supplier, he should consult his international bank, lawyer, or accounting firm.

Establishing an Internal International Accounting Capability

As the firm becomes increasingly involved in trade, the international accounting activity increases, and so do the costs of using outside expertise. At some point it becomes feasible for the company to develop the international capabilities of its own staff, including its own accountants.

The next major development that is likely to necessitate increased international accounting skills is the creation of a separate organization within the company to handle international trade. In its least complicated form, this may be an export department. In more complicated forms, it may be a special export company such as a foreign international sales corporation (FISC), which receives special tax treatments under U.S. tax law. (For more on these organizational forms, see Chapters 7 and 8.) Special accounting systems and procedures must be established for these new organizational firms in control, reporting, and taxation areas.

Typically, the next evolutionary step is the establishment of a foreign operation of some kind. In the minimal case, the company may decide to license a foreign manufacturer to produce its product or some part of its product. This involves selecting a potential licensee, analyzing its reliability and capability, and drawing up a contract. It also involves developing an accounting system to monitor contract performance and royalty and technical payments and to handle the foreign money flows into the company's tax and financial statements.

In the maximum case, the development entails establishing a wholly owned subsidiary in a foreign country. Accounting for the foreign subsidiary would include (1) meeting the requirements of the foreign government, which would be based on procedures and practices different from those in the parent company's country, (2) a management information system to monitor, control, and evaluate the foreign subsidiary, and (3) a system to consolidate the foreign subsidiary's operating results with those of the parent for financial and tax-reporting purposes.

Between these extremes are a host of alternatives: setting up a sales office, setting up a warehouse, forming a joint venture with another company, buying into an existing company. Each brings with it new international dimensions and requirements for management and, more specifically, for the company's accountants. It should also be pointed out that before any of this takes place, a thorough study of market conditions—legal, economic, political, and sociocultural—should be made, including detailed feasibility studies and risk analysis. All of these steps require the collection and appropriate analysis of information in both quantitative financial terms and qualitative terms.

In its first venture into any of these more advanced areas, the international expertise of outside groups is all but indispensable because of the money and risks involved in international trade. However, using outside international experts in no way lessens the need to develop in-house international capabilities, not only in accounting but in other functional areas as well.

Finally, some knowledge of international accounting may be necessary even if a firm is not involved in international business *per se*—for example, if the firm wishes to borrow money or to buy or sell stocks or bonds outside its home country. In some cases, it may be cheaper to borrow money or issue stocks or bonds abroad because interest rates are lower or exchange rate movements are favorable. In order to take advantage of these situations, the firm needs to know not only the relevant foreign laws, regulations, and customs, but also the domestic, legal, tax, and accounting treatments of any of these transactions. Alternatively, there may be better investment opportunities abroad for short-term liquid funds, due to higher returns, predicted exchange rate movements, or both.

From an investment standpoint, the firm must know exactly what it is doing as well as know all the attendant risks. This entails an understanding of the financial statements, the terms of the foreign offer, and foreign currency movements. And as was the case with raising capital abroad, the investing firm must understand both the foreign and domestic laws and the tax and accounting treatments of the transaction being considered.

Thus, there are potentially many situations that may require some understanding of international accounting. As the world's economies become increasingly interdependent, the frequency and importance of these occasions will also increase. What is more, there will be a greater need for public accountants to provide international accounting services to companies with international operations. Almost all users of financial statements will also need to understand something about international accounting in order to understand the financial reports of these companies. In sum, virtually everyone who prepares, audits, or uses financial statements of companies with international operations will need to know more and more about international accounting. Hence the importance of international accounting, and of this book.

OVERVIEW OF TEXT

To provide a background for more detailed discussion of the problems, issues, and dimensions of international accounting, Chapter 2 describes the major environmental influences that determine how accounting systems and practices develop. A conceptual framework is first presented with illustrative examples. This framework is applied on a simplified comparative basis to Egypt, Brazil, and The Netherlands and then, on a more detailed basis, to Japan and France. The remainder of the chapter is devoted to a discussion of some national differences in standards and practices related to corporate disclosure in financial statements, and how these differences are caused by certain key differences in the nations' environments.

Chapter 3 continues the environmental approach developed in Chapter 2 and examines the subject of inflation: its origins and extent, the ensuing accounting problems and issues for a multinational firm, and how and why various countries have attempted to develop accounting standards that reflect the impact of inflation on financial statements. Specific countries covered are the United States, the United Kingdom, The Netherlands, Brazil, and Chile.

Chapters 4, 5, and 6 deal with foreign exchange. What is the international monetary system and the nature of currency exchange rates and their movements (Chapter 4) and what are the accounting problems related to changes in currency exchange values: the treatment gains and losses from foreign currency denominated transactions and from translations of statements expressed in foreign currencies? Chapters 5 and 6 also contain brief discussions of how foreign exchange gains and losses can be eliminated or lessened.

Chapter 7 covers the major aspects of international taxation, with particular emphasis on U.S. taxation of foreign source income. Also covered are some major differences in taxation systems/approaches throughout the world, and how such differences give rise to the importance of international tax planning.

Chapter 8 deals with a variety of managerial accounting issues and problems of a multinational enterprise (MNE). Included are discussions of pricing (internal and external), costing, planning, budgeting, performance evaluation, and management information systems, each of which has special complications for an MNE.

Chapter 9 is concerned with issues, problems, and practices of auditing in an international context. Internal and external auditing are both covered, as are the special accounting implications of the U.S. Foreign Corrupt Practices Act.

Finally, Chapter 10 examines how accounting standards are set in various countries and what efforts and successes have been made to reduce national differences in accounting standards and practices.

Study Questions

1-1. In one sense accounting is a kind of language, a basic form of communication. But, although verbal languages date back to early history, accounting itself did not develop until much later. Why not?

1-2. Discuss the importance of the Industrial Revolution on the development of accounting practices.

1-3. Discuss how changes in the forms of business organizations (proprietorships, partnerships, corporations, etc.) have affected accounting practices.

1-4. Discuss the changes in accounting that were necessitated by multinational corporations.

1-5. Discuss the major reasons why accounting systems differ among individual countries in the world.

1-6. Leadership in accounting development often follows dominance in world economic activity. That is, a country that leads the world in business activity often also leads the world in accounting development. Why would this be true?

1-7. Even though international business has been conducted for centuries, it has become truly significant in terms of its importance in the twentieth century. Why?

1-8. Discuss the changing accounting needs of a firm as it progresses from a strictly domestic company to a multinational company.

1-9. It is sometimes argued that an understanding of international business is important only for multinational enterprises. Why might this argument be naive?

1-10. The same type of argument is often made with respect to the need for understanding international accounting. What reasons can you give to counter this argument?

CHAPTER 2

Environmental Influences on Accounting Systems and Practices

Like other business practices, accounting is to a large extent environmentally bound. That is, it is shaped by and reflects particular characteristics unique to each country's environment. The list of these characteristics is virtually infinite, ranging from personal traits and values to institutional arrangements, and can even extend to climatic and geographical factors.

This chapter first presents a conceptual framework for analyzing how a country's environment influences the development and sophistication of its accounting system. Next, it applies this framework to the accounting systems of several nations. Finally, it illustrates how differences in nations' environments affect several specific accounting practices related to disclosure.

ENVIRONMENTAL INFLUENCES ON ACCOUNTING

In what has become a classic conceptual framework for analyzing differences in business practices, Farmer and Richman organized environmental characteristics into four major groups: educational, sociocultural, legal and political, and economic.[1] In effect, these characteristics become constraints on a firm's ability to operate effectively and efficiently. For example, a firm operating in a country with high political and economic instability will have a difficult time planning, meeting schedules, keeping workers' minds on their jobs, and so on.

The various elements in each of the four groups explain the way business organizations in a particular country operate and, to a certain extent, make it possible to predict how they will operate in a given situation. For example, in a country with a high degree of illiteracy (one of the educational characteristics), business must rely to a greater extent on picturegrams or audio methods for advertising rather than printed messages. Similarly, in a country where people are not materialistically oriented (a

---

[1] R. Farmer and B. Richman, *International Business: An Operational Theory* (Homewood, Ill.: Irwin, 1966 and subsequent editions).

sociocultural characteristic), businesses will rely more on nonmonetary forms of reward, such as titles or job security, to attract and motivate their employees. The Farmer-Richman conceptual framework is presented in Figure 2.1.

This conceptual framework can also be used to explain differences in how business is conducted in one country versus another. That is, differences in the national environments can be used to explain differences in business operations. For example, if one country has a law that prohibits firing employees after a certain length of service whereas another country has no such law, then, other things being equal, hiring and particularly firing practices are likely to be different in the two countries. Similarly, if there is an extensive private capital market (for example, a large stock exchange) in one country but none in another country, the principal methods of obtaining capital for business ventures are likely to be different.

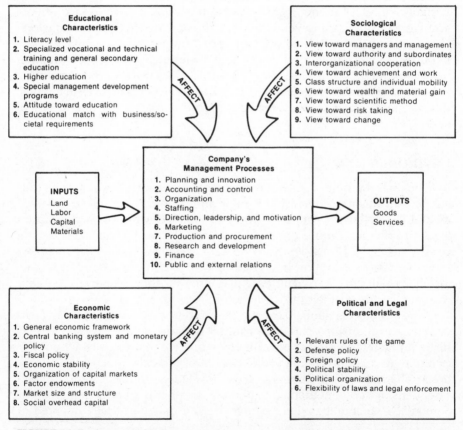

FIGURE 2.1 Environmental influence on the management process. (*Source:* Adapted from R. Farmer and B. Richman, *International Business: An Operational Theory*, Bloomington, Indiana: Cedarwood Press, 1974.)

In later modifications of the basic Farmer-Richman model, it was pointed out that several additional factors could have considerable effect on business practices. And perhaps most important, a firm need not passively adapt to the environment in which it operates.[2] The firm itself can modify or change the environmental characteristics of the country, thereby bringing about changes that would permit it to operate more efficiently and effectively. For example, if a law bans some desired business activity, the firm could bring about a change in that law by supporting candidates who would change it or by lobbying for the change.

Two essential points should be drawn from this opening section on environmental influences. First, environmental analysis can be a valuable tool in explaining and understanding differences in the way in which businesses operate in different countries and, more specifically and appropriately here, in which accounting principles and practices differ. The second point concerns cultural relativism, which means that the rationality of any behavior should be judged in terms of its own cultural context, and not from that of an outsider. Put another way, one cannot judge the rationality of behavior in Indonesia using the mores and values of the United States.

There are many practices around the world that appear from a U.S. viewpoint to be illogical and irrational—and, we should add, vice versa. Yet when you understand the culture in which the behavior takes place, you will usually find that the seemingly irrational behavior is in fact quite rational. More important, it may be the only true rational way of doing things in that country.

Too often the incorrect assumptions are made that the other people simply do not know any better, that our own ways are better than theirs, and that our ways, if transplanted to that country, would be more successful than theirs. In case after case, this assumption has been proven false at considerable financial loss to the companies involved.[3]

Let us now examine in greater detail how some of the environmental characteristics of a country affect the way accounting develops and is practiced.

Educational Factors

The educational characteristics of a country have a significant effect on accounting practices. These educational characteristics encompass (1) the degree of literacy, including the ability to use simple mathematics, (2) the percentage of people who have received formal schooling at various levels (elementary school, high school, college), (3) the basic orientation of the

[2]Anant Negandhi and Bernard Estafen, "A Research Model to Determine the Applicability of American Knowhow in Differing Cultures and/or Environments," *Academy of Management Journal*, December 1965, pp. 309–318.

[3]D. Ricks, M. Fu, and J. Arpan, *International Business Blunders* (Columbus, Ohio: Grid Inc., 1974). See also D. Ricks, *Big Business Blunders* (Homewood, Ill.: Irwin, 1983).

educational system (religion, vocational, liberal arts, scientific, professional), and (4) the educational match—the appropriateness of the educational system's output for the country's economic and societal needs.

Literacy

Because accounting takes a written and numerical form, it has relatively little use or significance in a society that is predominantly illiterate. Meticulous preparation and widespread circulation of corporate financial reports in such a society obviously would not be a judicious use of corporate time, money, and effort. Internally, the accounting planning and control system would be more difficult to use effectively because of the limited ability of employees to prepare and understand budgets and reports. At the same time, the need for budgeting and control tends to be greater in developing countries that have the highest level of illiteracy. Hence, the accountant can face many problems in designing an accounting system for either external or internal use.

As the educational level of the population improves, most of these accounting problems decrease, and more extensive and sophisticated accounting systems and reports become feasible. Whether they are put into practice depends on other factors to be discussed later.

It should also be pointed out that even in countries with a largely illiterate population there can be relatively sophisticated accounting systems. This paradox occurs most often when the industrial sector and government are run by well-educated individuals and the major external user of the accounting reports is the government—or when the government itself is the principal owner/manager of the firms. Egypt is an example of this situation. Egypt's literacy rate is not high, but its accounting system for large enterprises is relatively sophisticated because most of the major enterprises are government-owned and financial reports are prepared mainly for the government.

Orientation

The orientation of the educational system also plays a part in determining accounting practices. Perhaps the most obvious relationship is whether mathematics is taught sufficiently to permit compilation and analysis of numerical data. Further, the extent to which accounting itself is taught in the educational system will influence the number of people who have some training in and understanding of bookkeeping, budgeting, financial analysis, and auditing. And more specifically related to accounting, does an accounting curriculum exist, and if so, what does it entail? Is there a degree in accounting, and for what type of work does the degree qualify someone? More subtly, the teaching and acceptance of the scientific method (the basic law of causality) influences people's acceptance of, and adherence to, the process of planning, budgeting, and control. Stated another way, if people in the organization are fatalistic—if they believe that whatever happens will happen, regardless of their activities or efforts— they will not perceive any need for planning, budgeting, and control.

Educational Match

Finally, the educational match influences accounting system development to the extent that accountants and information users grow in number and sophistication as the economic and social systems need greater and more complex accounting information and procedures. In other words, as the country industrializes, there are more and bigger firms, more complex business arrangements (credit, leases, poolings, mergers), and usually an increased need for outside capital. Each requires more complex accounting procedures and more people who can use and understand them. The issue is whether the educational system is producing enough of these people at each stage of development.

Cultural Factors

Hundreds of cultural factors influence accounting practices. Among the most important are the society's degree of conservatism, secrecy, distrust, and fatalism, coupled with the people's attitudes toward business and the accounting profession itself.

Conservatism

The society's degree of conservatism influences a number of accounting principles and practices, especially valuation and profit determination. For example, the use of historical cost reflects a degree of conservatism, as do the lower-of-cost-or-market principles, the recording of contingent liabilities, the overallowance for bad debts, and the practice of using a wide variety of special reserves. These last two practices also generally result in lower reported profits, reflecting a higher level of conservatism, and often a desire to make a firm appear less profitable than it actually is.

Secrecy

The society's degree of secrecy most directly affects the amount of disclosure an enterprise is willing to make in its external reporting: the greater the level of secrecy or distrust of outsiders, the lower the level of disclosure. Internally, a high level of distrust makes it more difficult to implement a system of internal control and performance evaluation, because no one wants to have his or her activities scrutinized. Secrecy also affects the audit function, making it more difficult to obtain necessary support information, verification, and corroboration of the accounting data supplied by the enterprise. Curiously, in certain circumstances a high degree of trust may cause similar problems. In Japan, for example, to question someone's word is to question his or her honor—a serious insult and definitely bad form. Thus, an auditor who attempts to obtain proof of accounting information supplied by someone else will be in a difficult and uncomfortable position, and certainly one not likely to win friends.

Fatalism and its effect on accounting have already been described. Suffice it to say here that the stronger this conviction is, the less important will be the role of accounting in the enterprise, the economy, and the society.

Attitudes Toward Business

Societal attitudes toward business may range from distrust and antagonism to wholehearted support and trust. Distrust generates demands for more information and closer scrutiny of business operations, perhaps even regulation or nationalization. The information requested is likely to encompass far more than mere financial data and to include the enterprise's treatment of employees, societal and political activities and contributions, environmental impacts, and so on. However, whether or not firms actually make such disclosure depends largely on their need for public-source funds and their relationship with the government.

Government support of society's wishes can lead to establishing and regulating accounting procedures and practices. This appears to be the situation in countries such as Sweden and France, where social accounting is becoming the order of the day. At the other extreme, society and government may make few if any disclosure demands on enterprises. In this situation, accounting is likely to be more flexible and much more at the discretion of firms, resulting in considerably less pressure for disclosure. This was the case in the United States before the Great Depression and remains largely the case in Switzerland today.

Attitudes Toward Accounting

Finally, the attitude toward the accounting profession affects the status of the profession, the type of person who enters it, its credibility, and the work that accountants perform. In many countries, accounting is still regarded as a low-status occupation filled with thieves and people fit for no meaningful job. As can be expected, the best and brightest people in these countries do not aspire to become accountants. This may be a self-fulfilling prophecy; perhaps only thieves and other undesirables become accountants in these countries. In other countries, accountants occupy a highly respected place in society, and accounting attracts high-caliber individuals as a result. Accountants in these countries tend to lead the world in the development of accounting theory, procedures, and practices. Germany, The Netherlands, the United Kingdom, and the United States are representative examples.

Legal and Political Factors

At first blush the legal system may appear to have little influence on accounting systems. Yet in many countries, law, and particularly tax law, is the only reason accounting is done at all. In these countries, the accounting rules and practices are spelled out in laws, often called companies' acts, which also contain the general laws for all business operations and activities. In addition, tax laws in virtually all countries specify accounting procedures to be used in the tax area.

The Legalistic Approach

The countries in which laws determine accounting practices are commonly grouped in what can be called the legalistic approach. Their governments play an active, even dominant role in the economic sector, and their accounting profession is often relatively weak. In most of these countries, there is no difference between tax accounting and financial accounting: If a certain transaction is treated one way for tax purposes, it must be treated identically for financial reporting purposes. From a U.S. perspective, the legalistic approach to accounting has several major drawbacks and disadvantages. One is that accounting standards and practices are set by legislators who generally have little accounting background or training. Hence they may be unaware of the accounting implications for practitioners of the accounting legislation they pass—such as the amount of work required to comply with the laws. Perhaps more important, the legislators may ignore the validity and efficacy of the accounting practice in terms of either accounting theory or sound business practice.

The legalistic approach to accounting is found to some degree in all countries of the world, regardless of their stage of economic development or the level of their accounting profession's development. In the United States, for example, tax laws and the regulations promulgated by the Securities and Exchange Commission (SEC) are clearly representative of the legalistic approach to accounting. Thus the main distinctions among countries are the pervasiveness of the legal approach and whether other approaches are permitted.

In countries where the legalistic approach is dominant, the role and function of the auditor are also quite different, for example, from those in the United States and the United Kingdom. The main function of the auditor in the legalistic approach is to certify that the accounting books and related statements are in accordance with the law, down to the last detail. No assessment or comment is generally made in the audit report that a true and fair picture is presented by the statements. In addition, there are separate classifications of auditors into two groups: statutory auditors and all others. Statutory auditors are the only ones allowed to perform the official audit.

Apart from a legalistic approach to accounting (either in general or in the tax or securities area), certain laws not directly related to accounting may nonetheless have definite accounting implications. A recent U.S. example is the Foreign Corrupt Practices Act. Its main purpose is to prevent U.S. companies—or anyone acting on their behalf—from paying bribes to foreign government officials. Yet the accounting implications are considerable. The major accounting effect of the law is that U.S. multinational companies must establish a system of internal controls and an internal audit staff to make sure that bribes are not being made or being hidden. The outside auditor must also make sure that the internal control system is appropriately designed and implemented.

Political Factors

Certain political factors can also influence accounting systems and practices. In socialist countries it is often politically expedient and desirable to require certain information from companies about their social impact. For similar reasons, developing countries may require reports from companies on the balance of payments impact of their planned operations as a precondition to approving the investment. Changes in political direction—from right to left, for example—can bring about new accounting rules through new laws or, in the extreme case, can result in government takeovers. In this situation, the accountant may become involved in determining the fair value of the firm taken over, in hopes of receiving from the government fair compensation for the assets seized.

Economic Factors

A country's stage of economic development and basic economic orientation are two of the major economic factors that influence accounting development and practices. At extremely low levels of economic development, there is little economic activity and correspondingly little financial, tax, or managerial accounting. As the level of economic activity and the size of companies increase, there is a corresponding increase in accounting activity. This continues through each successive stage of development, albeit with certain lags. Direct wealth (income) taxation of both individuals and companies increases, managerial accounting develops, and so does financial reporting to creditors, investors, and so on. In addition, as business operations and relationships become more complex, new procedures are developed—accounting for mergers, acquisition, leases, foreign exchange gains and losses, and so on.

Degree of Government Involvement

The basic orientation of the economic system concerns the degree of government involvement in the economic sector. In Communist countries, for example, the state owns all production facilities, makes most of the economic and business decisions, and controls virtually all operations through a central planning and control system. These countries have a highly standardized and uniform accounting system to facilitate the government's planning and control function, and there are few users of accounting information other than the government. In market-capitalist economies, there is predominantly private ownership. With greater individual freedom in economic activity and decision making, a correspondingly greater diversity in accounting practices is permitted and practiced. There are also more users of accounting information—stockholders, auditors, suppliers, creditors— in addition to the government. Between these extremes are market socialist countries, which have considerable but not total government ownership, and countries with predominantly private ownership but some central planning and regulation by the government. Their accounting systems and practices fall somewhere between the other two systems.

A related economic characteristic is the type of monetary and fiscal policies employed by the government and their degree of use. For example, in order to stimulate economic activity, many countries have developed investment tax credit systems, which are accompanied by specific accounting rules. Other countries permit the accumulation of sizable reserves or permit income smoothing to provide pools of funds as a cushion during adverse times or for expansion. Through income smoothing, companies can report lower than actual income in good years and higher than actual income in bad years using inventory write downs or movement of funds in and out of reserves.

Sources of Funds

Another important economic characteristic is the source of funds for investment and working capital. First of all, the sources influence the degree of investor orientation versus creditor orientation of the accounting system. That is, if the major source of funds is loans from banks, financial intermediaries, or even wealthy individuals, then accounting standards, principles, and procedures will tend to be more conservative and reflective of creditor preferences and requirements. This creditor orientation remains predominant in the world, at least in terms of number of countries. On the other hand, if the major source of funds is of an equity orientation, then the accounting system will be similarly oriented and will include such important investor information as earnings per share and more extensive public disclosure. In countries where formally organized stock exchanges play an important role, even more complicated investor-oriented standards and procedures will be evident, such as the Securities and Exchange Commission's accounting regulations in the United States.

A company based in a creditor-oriented country that desires to raise equity funds in an investor-oriented country typically suffers considerable culture shock in terms of the amount of disclosure it must make in order to sell stock. For many such companies, the disclosure required becomes, in effect, a deterrent to seeking equity funds. In still other countries, banks have considerable freedom to take equity positions in corporations in addition to their more traditional creditor relationship. In Germany and Japan, for example, the banks are major shareholders in companies. In such countries, there is less public financial reporting and disclosure because the banks are the major investors and already have all the information they need from the companies because of their existing credit relationships with them.

Degree of International Activity

Another economic characteristic that influences accounting practices is the degree of international business activity. The greater the amount of a country's international trade, the greater is its need for accounting practices concerning foreign exchange transactions and translations.

Going a step further, the number and size of a country's multinational firms is directly related to the development of accounting rules for consolidation of foreign subsidiary reports, international transfer pricing, and taxation of foreign source income (income earned outside the parent company's country). As an example, the United States is the largest single trading country and also the one with the largest amount of foreign investment outside its own boundaries. As a result, the U.S. accounting system includes the most elaborate practices and requirements of accounting for foreign exchange gains and losses, global consolidation of financial reports, transfer prices, and taxation of worldwide income. At the other extreme, Afghanistan has little international trade or investment, no multinationals, and hence little if any accounting related to international business activity.

Inflation

Inflation is another economic characteristic that has an important influence on accounting practices in individual countries. Although inflation appears to be a worldwide phenomenon, its severity varies from single-digit to triple-digit and even quadruple-digit annual levels—often referred to as hyperinflation. Particularly in hyperinflationary countries, the cumulative effect of inflation over a number of years can render all accounting information meaningless unless it is appropriately adjusted. Chapter 3 describes in greater detail various countries' approaches to inflation accounting. Suffice it to say here that countries such as the United States and Germany, with relatively low levels of inflation, have been slower to develop inflation accounting rules than hyperinflationary countries such as Brazil, Argentina, and Chile.

Ties to Other Countries

One other economic factor deserving mention because of its influence on accounting system development is economic ties to and relationships with other countries. Historically, the first of such arrangements was colonialism. The colonies adopted or were forced to adopt the accounting system of their colonial power, even though it may not have been particularly appropriate at the colony's stage of development. Thus, the accounting systems in the British colonies were significantly influenced by British accounting, and the influence remains today, such as in the United States, Canada, Jamaica, and the Bahamas. The same can be said for former French colonies, Spanish colonies, and so on.

A second economic relationship worthy of note is formal regional economic groups such as the European Community (EC), the Andean Pact group, and the Central American Common Market (CACM). As these groups move toward full integration of their economic and political systems, they have recognized the need to integrate their accounting systems as well. This process is commonly referred to as regional harmonization. To date, only the EC has expended much effort or made much progress toward harmonizing the accounting systems of its member countries. Nevertheless, formal regional economic groups can significantly affect accounting development and practices as harmonization requires countries to modify their historical ways of accounting.

One final type of intercountry economic relationship that can affect accounting is the product cartel, such as the Organization of Petroleum Exporting Countries (OPEC), the copper cartel, and the bauxite cartel. In attempting to standardize world export prices, and in some cases to ensure equitable returns to its members, cartels often try to devise uniform costing and pricing systems among their members in addition to specific production or export quotas.

THE ENVIRONMENTAL ANALYSIS APPLIED

Of all the environmental factors that influence accounting system development, a strong case can be made that the economic characteristics are the most influential. The reason is that in addition to their direct effects on accounting, they also have significant indirect effects in terms of their influence on the other environmental areas. Economic development effects many sociocultural attitudes and brings about changes in legal, political, and educational objectives and sophistication, each of which in turn can affect accounting practices. Yet even the pervasive economic influences in isolation do not determine the development and practices of a country's accounting system. One need only examine the accounting systems and practices of the three dominant market economies of the world—the

United States, Germany, and Japan—to see that there are considerable differences in accounting among them despite great similarities in their economic sophistication and stature. Thus, there is a need to consider all the environmental factors in analyzing a country's accounting system. Some examples of the application of the environmental approach to different countries' accounting systems illustrate this point.

Egypt, Brazil, and The Netherlands

On a continuum of economic development, Egypt would be at one end (underdeveloped), Brazil would be in the middle (rapidly developing), and The Netherlands at the other end (highly developed). From the 1950s to the mid-1970s, most of Egypt's industrial sector—which is small compared with those of Brazil and The Netherlands—was owned, operated, and highly regulated by the government. Brazil, too, has many large government-owned companies and many regulations, but it also has a flourishing private sector. The Netherlands has a large and complex private sector with comparatively little government ownership and regulation.

The population in Egypt has comparatively low levels of literacy and education, The Netherlands has a highly literate and well-educated population, and Brazil falls somewhere in between. Egypt has virtually no multinational companies, Brazil has a few, The Netherlands many. Finally, Egypt is a socialist country politically and economically, although the private sector has begun to flourish in recent years. The Netherlands is basically democratic and capitalist; and Brazil, once again, is somewhere in between, it has a military junta but basically is capitalism oriented.

The environmental differences among these countries can be seen clearly in their different accounting systems. Egypt has a uniform, highly standardized accounting system whose main purpose is to provide information to the government for centralized planning and control. Because accounting skills are not widespread, accounting practices must be spelled out in fine detail. Standardization also permits intraindustry and interindustry comparisons on the efficiency and effectiveness of operations. Because there is virtually no domestic organized capital market, there is less need for financial reporting than in The Netherlands. On the other hand, Egypt's socialist orientation requires the reporting of certain social information that is not found to anywhere near the same extent in The Netherlands or Brazil.

At the other extreme, the Dutch accounting system is virtually tailored to each firm. As long as the accounting practices reflect sound business practice, they are essentially acceptable. The widespread, high levels of education and accounting skills in The Netherlands are the source of some of the most sophisticated examples of accounting practices—particularly in inflation accounting, for which many of the companies use replacement cost (current value) accounting. Because so many Dutch companies are multinational and need to tap international money and capital markets, Dutch financial reports are typically well disclosed and presented in segmented form and in several languages. The business community and the accounting profession are highly regarded and independent; and compared with Brazil and Egypt, the accounting profession is left relatively to its own devices by the Dutch government.

As should be expected at this point, the Brazilian accounting system falls somewhere between the Egyptian and the Dutch systems. In a sense, Brazil has a two-tiered system of accounting—one for the large, publicly owned companies, called open companies (many of which are subsidiaries of foreign companies), and a second one for virtually all other firms. The accounting system of the open companies is not much different from that of U.S. companies (e.g., fair presentation, independent audits), whereas that for other companies is considerably different. Privately held companies have much less disclosure and regulation, and generally their financial statements are not very reliable or indicative of their true financial position.

All major companies in Brazil share one special accounting aspect: both balance sheets and income statements must be adjusted for inflation, using official government indices. This requirement is necessitated by the rampant inflation in Brazil for the past several decades. Brazil's extremely rapid movement to an emerging industrialized status required different rules for different purposes and different economic entities. Hence, the need for the two-tiered accounting system.

As this perhaps oversimplified analysis shows, the differences in countries' environments are reflected in their accounting systems. One cannot say that any one system is absolutely or even comparatively better than the others. All that can be concluded is that each accounting system reflects and is tailored for the environment of which it is a part. To see in even more detail how the environment affects a country's accounting system, let us now focus on the environment and accounting practices of Japan and France.

Japan

The Japanese society is highly organized, disciplined, respectful, and perhaps above all cooperative and group oriented. It also has one of the world's highest literacy rates because of its strong emphasis on education for all its people. Japan is a classic example of what sociologists call a closed, geometric society, in which every person and organization is defined and fixed in position in relation to all others. The society is held together by a complex network of interrelationships and interdependencies based largely on an equally complex system of reciprocal obligations.

Japan's societal characteristics are mirrored in its economic and business system. There is a complex maze of interdependencies among firms, between firms and their employees, and between firms and the government, which operates most of the time in a reciprocally supportive and cooperative manner. Although most evident in the older industrial sectors (steel, chemicals, automotives, textiles), and to a lesser extent in almost all sectors, the web of interrelationships and obligations that comprise Japan's economy remains one of its most basic characteristics.

The complex pattern of cross-ownership and lending among members of a Japanese business group (such as the Mitsubishi group) virtually defies control analysis. It is seldom possible to say who really controls what and whom. A manufacturing concern may own stock in several supplying and purchasing companies (and even a bank or two), each of which may in turn own stock in the manufacturing company. Credit arrangements within the group can be equally complex and serve to further cement business relationships. When any group member gets into financial trouble, it is the obligation of the other members and, if necessary, the government to provide assistance to the ailing company. This may mean extending additional credit or delaying collections or providing technical or managerial assistance. Thus, short-term debt can become long-term, and long-term debt can become a form of equity investment in the company by its creditors. This is why the extremely high leverage of Japanese firms, which also has considerable tax advantages, is seldom as precarious and risky as it appears to an outsider.

With respect to business, the government adopts a sort of Calvin Coolidge philosophy: What is good for business is good for the country. The Japanese government plays an active supporting role in the economy, which has at its core the stable growth of enterprises and employment by means of domestic and international expansion of its companies. At times it has also pursued a stringent policy of protecting its domestic market from foreign business influences and activities. Yet overall, the government has sought ways to enhance the international competitiveness of its firms by encouraging and promoting mergers and consolidations, overseas market development, modernization of plants and equipment, and the development and implementation of new product and process technologies.

Accounting Practices

The influence of Japanese environmental characteristics can be clearly seen in its accounting practices. To facilitate the accumulation of funds in companies to achieve and maintain international competitiveness, the government permits a wide variety of reserve accounts. These reserves are for general purposes (bad debts, security price fluctuations, retirement allowances) and for specific purposes (overseas market development, export activities). The government also permits special depreciation allowances in excess of statutory limits for certain types of assets: computers, shipping vessels, company housing, and antipollution equipment. The reserves and allowances are pretax deductions, thereby lessening or postponing taxes. They also permit income smoothing, which has the effect of stabilizing income and inspiring societal confidence in the firms.

The government also provides a wide variety of tax credits, primarily for use by companies that are losing their international competitive position. These credits cover expenses for scrapping obsolete equipment, promoting mergers, and conducting experimental research and development. The tax credits can also have considerable impact on reported income and cash flows. Together with the use of reserves, Japanese companies generally show a lower level of profitability and pay less taxes than they would if they were operating under U.S. tax laws and generally accepted accounting principles.

Additional environmental characteristics of Japan are reflected in still other accounting practices. The general public confidence and trust in the business-government partnership results in no great desire for extensive disclosure of financial information by Japanese companies. For similar reasons, the audit function is largely perfunctory and ceremonial. Because Japanese society is oriented to both long-term growth and employment security, and because cross-ownership of firms is commonplace, there is less interest in such information as earnings per share or even current financial performance. Furthermore, neither kind of information would be particularly meaningful because of income smoothing. And although accountants enjoy a respected position in Japan, their role is largely passive; the government plays the dominant role in setting accounting standards, policies, and practices.

In recent years there have been noticeable changes in the Japanese accounting system, the most significant one concerning consolidation of corporate financial reports. Prior to the 1970s nonconsolidation was the rule; financial reports were typically prepared on a parent-company-only basis. This practice often hid losses in nonconsolidated subsidiary companies and showed artificially high profits in parent company reports because intracompany sales and profits were not eliminated. Prior to 1975 some of the major Japanese companies were compelled to prepare consolidated financial statements according to U.S. generally accepted accounting principles in order to obtain funds from U.S. or other international sources. However, a law passed in 1976 requires consolidated reports for most of Japan's major companies as well as considerably more disclosure in these reports.

France

Historically France was a nation of independent, self-reliant craftsmen, artists, and farmers who took pride in themselves and in their work. An elitist aristocracy governed France politically, and the aristocratic status quo orientation, combined with the society's Catholicism-based lower drive for achievement and materialism, caused France to fall behind as its neighbors and competitors industrialized.

Several forces made changes essential if France was to remain a world power. The agricultural revolution, which reduced employment in the agricultural sector from 44% in the 1940s to less than 10% in the 1970s, provided a large pool of labor for industry, new markets, and a middle class; but it also caused rising expectations and societal polarizations. The formation of the European Community brought increased competition to France, as did the influx of American and other foreign investments into France and the EC. It became evident that France's traditional business structure and traditional ways of doing business needed modification, yet the traditionalist, independent Frenchman was slow to recognize this and to make the necessary adaptations. The government, therefore, had to take action to restructure the policies, management, and activities of the French economy, industries, and firms.

The major government thrust was a renewed and strengthened policy of economic and sectoral planning. Tax incentives and political suasion were used to induce firms to move in ways that would improve not only their own financial and competitive position, but also that of the economy in general. And when and where such inducements or efforts were not successful, the French government itself became involved directly in the ownership of French companies.

Accounting Practices

To facilitate economic planning and analysis, France revamped an old uniform plan of accounting. Historically, the uniform plan had for the most part been restricted to nationalized industries (iron, coal, steel, railroads) and to the few largest publicly held companies. By successive government acts, however, the plan was made more comprehensive and extended to more and more enterprises, both publicly and privately held.

The main advantage of the uniform plan is that it facilitates and permits better government planning and decision making because all firms covered by the plan must follow identical procedures and formats for accounting reports. Thus interindustry comparisons are easier to make, and strengths and weaknesses, opportunities and bottlenecks are easier to identify. Once these are identified, the government can change the plan or change the inducements and more readily observe the impact of such changes.

The French government also embarked on a policy that had as its objective the development of national champions in the major French industries. This "contracts de croissance" policy included tax incentives (allowances and credits) to nurture the development of the selected national champions. The uniform plan made it easier to identify the best candidate firms, to determine what inducements would be best, and to assess the program and success of the policy.

The growing socialist movement in France has also been felt in the accounting sector. The society has made increased demands on the government to require firms to make more disclosure about their activities, particularly those which relate to workers and working conditions. In 1977 the government passed new legislation requiring certain large companies to prepare a *Bilan Social*, or social report, showing what actions they had taken with respect to their workers and working conditions. More about this social accounting is discussed later in this chapter.

In sum, the increased direct and indirect role of the French government in the economy of France strongly influenced the French accounting system even though the basic plan had existed for centuries. And as the economy and society changed in consequence of this intervention, new pressures brought about yet more changes in accounting. And the process goes on.

COMPARATIVE DISCLOSURE WORLDWIDE

As described earlier, environmental characteristics do influence the development, the general form, and the orientation of a country's accounting system. They also clearly affect the specific accounting standards and practices of each nation. However, it is well beyond the scope and length of this book to describe how differences in environmental characteristics affect all accounting standards and practices of all or even a few nations. Instead, the remainder of this chapter focuses on accounting standards and practices related to selected issues in disclosure. Other issues will be treated in Chapters 3–9.

The importance of disclosure should not be underestimated. In the absence of uniform accounting standards, many people believe that adequate disclosure of the basis of financial statements is essential for purposes of proper and useful analysis. However, good disclosure is not a substitute for good accounting standards; the two should work together. Even with good accounting, certain key information needs to be communicated to users.

In general, issuers of financial statements prefer to limit disclosure to avoid preparation costs and to preserve secrecy. On the other hand, users of financial statements generally prefer greater disclosure than issuers are willing to make. In the resulting tug-of-war, each group seeks to get its own way, so their respective power usually determines the outcome concerning disclosure: what items are disclosed, how much detail is provided, and how and when the disclosure is made. Thus disclosure standards and practices evolve from the educational, sociocultural, legal-political, and economic forces of each country. They may be minimal or extensive; be oriented toward investors, creditors, the government, or the society as a whole; or be uniform or highly flexible. One thing is clear, however. Without adequate disclosure, little practical use can be made of financial statements.

General Levels of Disclosure

Precisely how bad disclosure is worldwide is fairly difficult to assess because one must define the needs of the users in order to measure and compare disclosure. Most studies of disclosure have been conducted by U.S. researchers who were biased toward the investor orientation. However, even foreign analysts are aware of the general lack of disclosure. According to one Swiss analyst, "We [the Swiss] have no uniformity in financial reporting. Only a few legal requirements, like having to publish an annual report and a balance sheet. But it can be just three lines."[4] The article also points out that the Swiss hesitation over disclosure covers up some of the world's most conservative accounting. And a study by the French stock exchange revealed that 34.8% of the annual reports published in 1978 for listed firms carried "markedly insufficient" information and only 12% provided "excellent" reports to shareholders.

In an empirical study by Barrett, the disclosure practices of the 15 largest publicly held firms in the United States, United Kingdom, Japan, France, West Germany, The Netherlands, and Sweden were compared during the period 1963 to 1972. Given that firms might issue different financial statements for local investors, international investors, and so on, Barrett selected the most consolidated sets of financial statements and therefore the ones most relevant to international investors. He drew the following conclusions:

> The results of this study (1) . . . support the theme that the extent of financial disclosure in the annual reports of major, publicly held U.S. corporations was greater, on average, than that found in the annual reports of major publicly held corporations in Japan, Sweden, The Netherlands, Germany, and France during the 1963 to 1972·period; (2) indicate . . . that the U.S. annual reports were not uniformly better than those of these other five countries in terms of specific categories of disclosure; (3) imply that the extent of financial disclosure in the annual reports of major, publicly held U.S. corporations was no greater, on average, than that found in the annual reports of similar British corporations; and (4) provide evidence . . . that there is a relationship between the extent and quality of financial disclosure and the degree of efficiency of national equity markets.[5]

It should be noted that the time frame covered ended in 1972, and a review of recent annual reports of companies worldwide demonstrates a marked improvement in disclosure.

Local versus Transnational Disclosure

Transnational disclosure occurs when a firm needs to issue financial statements for foreign investors and other foreign users. For transnational re-

---

[4]"The New Chic-Swiss Stocks," *Forbes*, 5 March 1979, p. 34.
[5]M. Edgar Barrett, "The Extent of Disclosure in Annual Reports of Large Companies in Seven Countries," *The International Journal of Accounting*, Spring 1977, p. 19.

porting, many firms simply translate the narrative of the report into the language of the foreign users—often English. However, there may be no attempt to change the underlying standards on which the financial statements were prepared. In this case, extensive disclosure may be necessary to help the reader understand how the statements were prepared in order to facilitate decision making. Firms such as N.V. Philips' Gloeilampenfabrieken of The Netherlands include a section in the English-language version that delineates the major differences in Dutch and U.S. accounting principles and quantifies the impact on earnings.

Other firms change their entire financial statements to conform with a foreign or international reporting standard. In a recent study on the financial statements of Japanese firms, it was found that 10 to 92 firms prepared their statements according to generally accepted accounting principles (GAAP) in the United States.[6] In addition, all foreign firms seeking to list their shares on the New York Stock Exchange must file financial statements with the SEC prepared according to U.S. GAAP or at least reconciling to U.S. GAAP, as is done by Philips.

Social Responsibility and Social Accounting Disclosure

Social accounting[7] is inexorably intertwined with social responsibility. On a global scale, social responsibility and social accounting have basically encompassed three main areas:

1. Environmental quality (for example, pollution).
2. The impact of the firm on its employees and community (in ways other than pollution).
3. National income accounting.

Particularly since the 1960s, there has been renewed public awareness of some negative aspects and effects of industrialization and technology. A new social consciousness is emerging globally, although to different degrees in different countries. Intelligent and prudent managers in today's world should realize that their organization's success rests not only on profit performance but also on social achievement. Social responsibility accounting as discussed hereafter focuses primarily on the disclosure of such information.

[6]Hiroshi Yoshida, Kenji Shiba, and Lilia Teresa Sagara, "A Survey of Accounting Reports on Foreign Exchange Gains and Losses in Japan," Working Paper No. 49 (Kobe, Japan: Institute of Economics Research, Kobe University of Commerce, February 1979).
[7]We are particularly indebted to Professor Edmond Marques of CESA (France) for much of the material in this section on social responsibility. For more details, see Edmond Marques, "The Firm: Its Impact on Society; Introducing Societal Accounting," a paper presented at the Georgia World Congress Institute Conference on Exploring the Brave New Worlds of Accounting, Atlanta, Georgia, 8 September 1978.

The Content of a Social Report

The breadth and depth of information disclosed in a social report vary considerably from country to country, as does the medium selected for disclosing the information. For example, a firm may choose to report social responsibility information in its annual report (in the narrative section, in the financial data section, or in notes to the financial data section) or in a special, separate publication not part of the annual report. Regardless of the communication vehicle utilized, the most common topics having to do with social accounting are the following: environment, equal opportunity, personnel, community involvement, products, disclosure of codes of conduct, and business ethics. In a given country, social accounting may focus on only a few of these categories. Although several efforts are underway in the United Nations (UN), Organization for Economic Cooperation and Development, and EC to improve social disclosures, these efforts are still largely in the developmental stage.

There are wide variations in the qualitative versus quantitative presentation of inputs and outputs. Inputs refer to specific social programs put into effect, such as the installation of air pollution control equipment. Outputs refer to the impact of the programs, such as the reduction of specific pollutants in the atmosphere. The following possibilities are those most likely to be found in company disclosures:

1. Inputs and outputs are expressed in literal, nonquantitative form.
2. Inputs are stated in quantitative terms, generally in monetary form (expenses, investments) and outputs in quantitative but nonmonetary form (physical measures, social indices).
3. Inputs and outputs are expressed in quantitative, monetary terms.

Following are examples illustrating how the same information would be presented in these three kinds of reports:

1. The company spent considerable funds on a plan to reduce accidents in the plant and is happy to report that its efforts have been eminently successful.
2. The company spent $500,000 on a plan to reduce accidents in the plant and has achieved a 50% reduction in the accident rate.
3. The company spent $500,000 on a plan to reduce accidents in the plant and has saved $1 million in injury-related claims and expenses as a result.

The quantitative, nonmonetary approach is the basis of the law in France called the *Bilan Social* (which, roughly translated, means social balance sheet or social report) and is similar to the *Social Jaareslag*, prescribed in The Netherlands. French nationalized companies use some highly sophisticated methods in certain accounts, such as the *comptes de surplus*

(surplus accounts), to measure periodically how marginal productivity gains contributed to each constituency and in what proportion.

The Swedish social reports use monetary measures for social input and value added distribution among shareholders,·in combination with physical measures for outputs. One recent report by the Fortia Group included the results of a survey using social indicators as a measure of social achievement. In Germany's *Sozial Bilanz*, inputs are in monetary terms accompanied by comments on their achievement of social objectives.

Generally, only short statements about social responsiveness are found in the annual reports of large U.S. companies. However, one quite sophisticated approach is utilized by ABT, a Boston-based consulting group. In its American Social Audit it presents a balance sheet and income statement in which net social income is calculated for several constituencies: the company and its stockholders, its employees, its clients, the general public, and the community. In fact, ABT utilized a double-entry system to arrive at its net social income, or net contribution to society for the year.

As these examples show, there are really only two approaches to social reporting: one utilizing the terminology, procedures, and formats of accounting and the other employing methods that are not accounting based. The real advantage of the accounting approach is that it permits the distinction between social investment and social expenses and ultimately produces a balance sheet and income statement. As such, it facilitates managerial social accounting within traditional guidelines: setting objectives, plans, and budgets; allowing variance analysis; and facilitating corrective actions. In fact, some European companies have published their forecasts or plans in terms of social objectives and responses, and they follow up during the next year with a comparison of actual versus planned. Yet despite the natural appeal to accountants of this approach, the other approach remains closer to real life. The well-being of people both inside and outside the firm can rarely be expressed in quantitative terms. Thus, caution should be exercised in extending this monetary approach to the social area.

The French Law. On July 12, 1977, France adopted a law requiring all French firms with 300 or more employees to prepare a *bilan social*. The law covers all of the private sector (above the employment size minimum) and most of the public sector (including state-owned railways, utilities, and companies such as Air France and Renault). However, compliance with the new laws varies somewhat according to the size of the company and size of plants.

By 1984 all social balance sheets must encompass three years (the current year plus the two previous years), and enterprises that have more than one plant with more than 300 workers must prepare and submit one social balance sheet for the enterprise as a whole and one for each plant.

Every social balance sheet must provide information in seven areas:

1. Employment.
2. Wage-related costs (benefit packages).
3. Health and safety protection.
4. Other conditions of work.
5. Employee training.
6. Industrial relations.
7. Other conditions of life relating to the undertaking, including housing and transportation provided to employees by the company.

Each of these categories is further divided into subcategories. For example, "other conditions of work" is subdivided into (a) length and arrangement of the workweek, (b) organization and content of work, (c) physical working conditions, (d) changes in the organization of work, (e) expenditures on improving working conditions, (f) works doctors, and (g) unfit workers. These subcategories are, in turn, comprised of several quantifiable indicators. For example, under the "physical working conditions" subcategory are such numerical indicators as "the number of employees normally and regularly exposed to more than 85 decibels of sound on the job," "the number of employees . . . exposed to heat above the level specified in the Decree of May 10, 1976 . . ." and "number of samples, analysis of toxic substances and measurements thereof. . . ."

The French law is quite detailed and specific and is highly employee oriented and hence quite narrow in scope. Yet it is also consistent with the French environment: like other laws and accounting rules, it is legislated, codified, and standardized. It also reflects the growing discontent of French workers, who wield considerable political clout (enough, at least, to get such a law passed), and the growing socialist orientation of the French society.

It is evident from this discussion that social responsibility accounting is perceived as an increasingly important area of disclosure worldwide. The nature of the information being disclosed depends on what each country feels is most important, but the consensus seems to be that corporate accountability extends beyond the traditional profit measures of enterprise performance.

Value Added Statements

Another interesting version of social accounting is the value added statement. Value added accounting, which is seen more in Europe than elsewhere, is primarily a two-step process. First, the firm identifies the value it adds in the production and sales process by subtracting from sales all materials and services purchased by the firm. Then, the firm separates the value added into various constituencies, such as employees, government, providers of capital, and the business itself. Exhibit 2.1 is the value added statement of Imperial Chemical Industries PLC, the British multinational.

A study of annual reports published in 1979 by 200 major companies

Exhibit 2.1 Value Added Statement, Imperial Chemical Industries PLC, 1982 (sources and disposal of value added)

		1982 £m	1981 £m	Percentage Change
Sources of Income				
	Sales	7,358	6,581	+12
	Royalties and other trading income	99	82	+21
	Less: Materials and services used	5,272	4,551	+16
	Value added by manufacturing and trading activities	2,185	2,112	+3
	Share of profits less losses of principal associated companies and income from other trade investments	39	52	
	Total value added	2,224	2,164	+3
Disposal of Total Value Added				
	Employees[a]	1,444	1,362	+6
	—pay, plus pension and national insurance contributions, and severance payments	1,421	1,335	
	—profit sharing bonus[b]	23	27	
	Governments[c]	67	88	−24
	—corporate taxes	92	111	
	—less: grants	25	23	
	Providers of capital	283	287	−1
	—interest cost of net borrowings	146	142	
	—dividends to stockholders	115	113	
	—minority shareholders in subsidiaries	22	32	
	Reinvestment in the business[d]	430	427	+1
	—depreciation and provisions in respect of extraordinary items	400	354	
	—profit retained	30	73	
		2,224	2,164	

This table is based on the audited historical cost accounts; it shows the total value added to the cost of materials and services purchased from outside the Group and indicates how this increase in value has been disposed of.

[a] Average number of employees decreased by 6%.

[b] 1982 UK bonus rate 4·2p per £1 of remuneration (1981 4·8p).

[c] Does not include tax paid by employees on their pay. Income tax paid by UK employees under PAYE amounted to £136m in 1982 (1981 £136m).

[d] Contribution toward the total spent in the year on new fixed assets working capital and additional investments.

Exhibit 2.2 Publication of Value Added Statements

	Sample Size	Companies Publishing Value Added Statements
Europe		
France	15	2
Germany	15	8
United Kingdom	15	9
Netherlands	10	2
UK and NL[a]	2	2
Italy	10	1
Belgium	10	1
Switzerland	10	—
Sweden	7	1
Spain	5	—
Denmark	3	1
Rest of the World		
United States	30	—
Japan	15	—
Canada	15	1
Australia	15	3
South Africa	10	1
Singapore	5	—
Brazil	5	—
Hong Kong	3	—
	200	32

[a]Shell and Unilever are operating companies jointly owned by British and Dutch interests. Hence they are better classified under a joint United Kingdom–Netherlands grouping rather than in one country or the other.
Source: Stuart McLeay, "Value Added Statements: A Comparative Study," presented at the Third Congress of the European Accounting Association, Amsterdam, 24–26 March 1980.

from 18 countries revealed that European companies were most likely to provide value added statements. Exhibit 2.2 summarizes the results of the study. Note that no U.S. firm provides such information. The European firms provide the information because of the strength of employee groups. However, it is obvious from Exhibit 2.2 that the practice is still not uniformly widespread throughout Europe.

In more specific research targeting larger samples of firms from single countries, the value added performance does not appear as bleak as might be indicated here. In a survey of all listed companies in the *Times* 1977–1978 group, 18% of the 455 firms disclosed value added statements.[8] That is still

[8]S. J. Gray and K. T. Maunders, *Value Added Reporting: Uses and Measurement* (United Kingdom: The Association of Certified Accountants, June 1980), p. 55.

a relatively small group of firms, however. In a study of Dutch annual reports between 1980 and 1982, approximately 20 to 22% of the firms disclosed value added information.[9]

Disclosure of Forecasts

The debate about publishing forecasts has been around for years and seems to have no resolution. Obviously, managers use forecast information when they decide on future directions of the business. This information would be valuable for investors, creditors, government, and other users as well. However, forecasting is extremely difficult and imprecise, especially in the international arena. A multinational must forecast changing conditions in many countries for many product lines. In addition, it must forecast changes in exchange rates and the ways in which changes in one of its markets affect its operations in other markets. Thus, preparing a forecast is a lot more difficult and hazardous for a multinational than for a domestic company. Once again, however, the inherent risks and difficulties do not dissuade firms from preparing such forecasts for internal management purposes. Management is also concerned that it might be held liable by external users for imprecise forecasts. The key is to have assumptions properly identified so that users can evaluate forecasts based on those assumptions.

Auditing forecasts is a difficult but not insurmountable problem. A company's external auditors are generally well versed and knowledgeable about the company and its industry. This knowledge places them in a reasonable position to assess the forecast and its underlying assumptions. Admittedly, there may have to be a separate auditor's opinion stressing the cautionary nature of the forecast and perhaps attesting to its reasonableness and comprehensiveness. This second opinion would not be inordinately difficult to initiate, nor would it be too complicated to understand. Furthermore, auditors in many countries, including the United States, are already coping with price-level-adjusted statements (which also have a degree of imprecision inherent in them) and with some corporate reports that already do include management forecasts.

European Practices

Gray's study is perhaps the most comprehensive one on forecast disclosure in Europe.[10] His study examined the hundred largest industrial multinational companies based in the EC in 1973 (45 British, 23 German, 20 French, 4 Italian, 4 Dutch, 3 Belgian, and 1 Luxembourg). His results showed that

[9]Jan Dijksma and Robert van der Wal, "Value Added in Dutch Corporate Annual Reports," a paper presented at the Seventh Annual Congress of the European Accounting Association, St. Gallen, Switzerland, 12 April 1984.
[10]S. J. Gray, "Managerial Forecasts and European MNC Reporting," *Journal of International Business Studies*, Fall 1978, pp. 21–32.

overall the extent of disclosure was somewhat low and largely qualitative: 58% included a statement of business prospects, 56% included research and development data, 91% included actual expenditure data, and 51% included planned capital expenditure data. He also concluded that overall there was no statistically significant difference between British and Continental EC companies, although German firms exhibited significantly greater disclosure than did French firms, and British firms made the greatest disclosure of capital expenditure data.

In assessing the environmental forces that might have influenced forecast disclosure, Gray examined the stock exchange regulations, the professional accounting standards, and the statutory legal requirements in each of the countries included in the study. In terms of legal requirements, he found little stimulus to disclose forecast and related data, except for the item of capital expenditure. In this specific area, quantitative data relating to capital expenditure actually contracted for were required in Ireland, The Netherlands, and the United Kingdom. However, only in the United Kingdom was the requirement extended to include amounts authorized by directors. In no country were disclosure of forecasts related to profits, sales, or cash flows required. At the EC level, there were a number of requirements concerning forecasts, but only a very general and vague nature that information must be given in the management/directors report about the company's future development. No guidance was provided as to the form this report should take.

Professional Requirements.   Gray also found that there were no professional requirements at the national level relating to the disclosure of forecasts in annual reports. However, there has been some discussion of this topic by Britain's Accounting Standards (Steering) Committee. In its discussion paper, "The Corporate Report," a major recommendation was that annual reports include a "statement of future prospects" indicating "profit levels, employment levels and prospects, and investment levels," and also include the major assumptions on which such forecasts were based. At the wider EC level, however, there was little support from the profession for developments of this nature. At an even wider international level, the Accountants International Study Group (AISG), prior to its demise, called for an orderly progression toward the publication of profit forecasts.

Stock Exchange Requirements.   Finally, in examining the rules of stock exchanges, it appeared that only in the United Kingdom and Ireland were there any specific rules concerning forecasts. The Federation of Stock Exchanges permits them but does not require them. The only requirement is that a company report explain why actual results "shown by the accounts for the period under review differ materially from any published forecast made by the company (previously)."

The only other EC country whose stock exchange says something about forecast disclosure is France. The *Commission des Operations de Bourse* has made suggestions that are contained in its recommendations on information to be included in company reports. The Bourse recommends that a section of the report be headed Future Outlook and that information be provided on such subjects as corporate objectives, capital expenditure plans and expected returns, and anticipated financing arrangements. However, no mention is made of quantitative profit forecasts. And as Gray's study showed, French companies were among the worst in Europe about disclosing forecasts.

What can be concluded from all these studies and observations about publishing company forecasts? A prudent conclusion would be that the outlook for disclosing forecasts is more cloudy than clear. Although more and more groups are warming up to the idea, the majority remain cold to the prospect. And as is the case for most changes in accounting practice, until sufficient pressure is brought to bear, the likelihood of change is slight. In this sense, the barometer reading would show some pressure for change, but not much. However, as forecasting becomes less of an art and more of a science, and as pressures for external financing become greater, one can predict that there will be more disclosure of corporate forecasts in the future. It is clearly an area in which accounting has considerable room and opportunity to grow.

HARMONIZATION OF STANDARDS

In view of the different accounting standards and practices in existence worldwide, it is difficult to imagine that any kind of standardization could take place. Although complete standardization would be impossible, narrowing the options is within the realm of possibility. The process of harmonization, in fact, is one of narrowing down the variety of standards and practices into a narrow set of acceptable ones. This process is being carried out on a national, regional, and international basis.

This chapter listed the reasons for differences in worldwide standards. In subsequent chapters, we discuss various topics, such as inflation accounting and translation of foreign currency financial statements, where different national standards are discussed. At the same time, we mention various efforts to narrow those differences through the process of harmonization.

A more in-depth discussion of harmonization is given in Chapter 10 where we tie in the ideas developed in the earlier chapters. However, we describe the various efforts of harmonization here because they are referred to many times before Chapter 10. The major sources of regional and international standards are the International Accounting Standards Committee (IASC), the International Federation of Accountants (IFAC), and the European Economic Community (EEC). There are other organizations, such as the United Nations and the Organization for Economic Cooperation and Development, but they are not referred to as much as the other groups mentioned.

The IASC is an international organization made up of professional accounting organizations from around the world. It has issued a number of standards that are not binding on member nations, since the IASC has no enforcement power, but those standards tend to be of high quality and fairly consistent with standards already existing in the United States and United Kingdom. The U.S. representative to the IASC is the American Institute of Certified Public Accountants.

The IFAC is closely aligned to the IASC, and most of its member institutions are common to the IASC, but the IFAC's function is to work on accounting and auditing related issues rather than be concerned about setting financial accounting standards. The IFAC's role is described in detail in Chapter 9.

The European Economic Community includes Denmark, the United Kingdom, Ireland, West Germany, Belgium, The Netherlands, Luxembourg, France, Italy, and Greece. The next two members of the EEC are expected to be Spain and Portugal. One of the goals of the EEC is to facilitate the free flow of capital. In order to do this, the EEC has issued a number of directives that are to be incorporated into each country's law. These directives provide guidance in the format and content of financial statements, the consolidation of financial statements, and the nature of the audit, among other things.

SUMMARY

- Because no two countries are identical, no two countries' accounting system will be identical. Each will be shaped by a series of complex interactions among its educational, sociocultural, legal-political, and economic characteristics.

- To properly understand any country's accounting system, it is necessary to understand the country's environmental characteristics.

- Without adequate disclosure, limited use can be made of financial statements, no matter how good a country's accounting standards may be.

- Like other accounting standards and practices, those related to disclosure are influenced by each country's environmental characteristics. They influence why disclosure is done at all, what kinds of information is disclosed, and when and how much information is disclosed.

- In general terms, Scandinavian and British firms rank at the top in terms of disclosure, followed by the large Dutch firms, the United States, Germany, and France. The Swiss rank at the bottom of all developed nations—and near the bottom of all countries, developed or developing.

Study Questions

2-1. What is meant by the statement that accounting is culture-bound?

2-2. What accounting functions and practices would be affected by the following:

(a) A very low level of literacy in the population.
(b) A high degree of distrust in the society.
(c) A high degree of international business activity.
(d) A high degree of government planning and regulation.

2-3. Explain how the perceived status of accountants in a country affects the development of the country's accounting standards and practices.

2-4. Even though The Netherlands and France are neighbors in a geographic sense, their accounting systems are quite different. What factors explain these differences?

2-5. The United States, United Kingdom, Canada, and Australia are geographically distant, yet their accounting systems have many similarities. What factors explain these similarities?

2-6. Most of the accounting practices in Latin America are not as sophisticated as those in the United States or Canada, yet several Latin American countries have inflation accounting procedures that are as or more sophisticated than those in the United States or Canada. Explain the apparent paradox.

2-7. Explain how the Japanese accounting system contributes to Japan's international economic competitiveness.

2-8. Among the most important environmental influences on accounting are the country's stage of economic development, and companies' needs for external financing. Why are these factors so influential?

2-9. Inflation is a common problem in most countries. Explain how one country might learn something of benefit from studying how another country handles inflation (in an accounting sense).

2-10. What benefit can be derived from learning about other countries' accounting systems
(a) for an accountant of a multinational firm?
(b) for an accountant *not* employed by a multinational?

2-11. What are some of the factors that need to be considered in determining the nature and extent of disclosure in financial statements?

2-12. How similar do you think financial statement disclosure would be in Egypt (a socialist economy in which most enterprises are state-owned), the United States, and Switzerland? Why?

2-13. How useful would it be for an investor to read the financial statements of a foreign corporation translated into the language of the investor? What other possibilities are there?

2-14. How would you compare the general level of disclosure of U.S. and foreign corporations?

2-15. What are some ways of defining social accounting? How would you characterize social accounting in the United States compared to that in Europe?

2-16. What is a value added statement? Why is it useful?

Case 1

HOWE'S DILEMMA

Ross Howe stared at the two piles of documents on his desk and threw his hands up. He had been given the assignment of ascertaining the creditworthiness of two companies in the same industry, normally an easy task: simply apply the standard financial analysis ratios he had learned and see which company was in better financial shape. However, these companies were foreign—one Egyptian and one Dutch—and Ross knew that his trusted and reliable methods were not necessarily going to work.

First of all, the Egyptian statements were in Arabic and the monetary values were expressed in Egyptian pounds. Second, once he had obtained a translation, he realized that he had never seen such a confusing format. Nothing seemed to be in the right order, many accounts appeared to have no direct U.S. equivalents, and he was not sure of the meaning of the account numbers listed in the margin beside each account. Finally, the few notes to the statements generally did not help explain anything he was unsure about. Even the auditors' statement was not much help, since it merely referred in general to compliance with Egyptian legal statutes and codes.

The Dutch company's statements, by contrast, initially seemed easier and more straightforward, as the company's annual report was available in English and U.S. dollar equivalents. Even after Ross had realized that the Dutch balance sheet was upside down by U.S. standards (increasing order of liquidity rather than decreasing), he noticed several major similarities between U.S. and Dutch accounting terms. However, his early euphoria was dampened by the realization that Dutch accounting principles were quite different from those in the United States. He was also bothered by the fact that the company's financial statements were prepared according to "sound business practice," a term unfamiliar to him. He also noticed that replacement cost values were used throughout the statements and wondered about their objectivity and verifiability. On the other hand, Ross was impressed by the tremendous amount of disclosure in the company's report, which was even more extensive than in U.S. reports.

Questions

1. Why do you suppose there were such significant differences between the Egyptian and Dutch companies' reports?
2. What suggestions or sources of information would you give Ross to help him to a better understanding of the foreign statements?
3. If both companies' statements showed the same net income, in which would you place more confidence? Why?

Case 2

THE JAPANESE PUZZLE

Tim Griffen was puzzled. He had just completed a standard financial ratio analysis of the translated financial statements of a major Japanese manufacturing company. He knew that it was an acknowledged leader in its industry and one of the largest and most successful in terms of world market share. What puzzled him was that the company appeared to be on the verge of bankruptcy—at least according to his calculations of the various financial ratios and indicators commonly employed in the United States.

In comparing the financial statements of the Japanese firm to its counterpart U.S. firm with comparable sales, employment, and market share, he observed the following differences.

Balance Sheet Comparisons

The Japanese firm had two and a half times as much cash, deposits and securities, 50% more notes and accounts receivables, and overall 30% more current assets despite having 25% less inventory than the U.S. firm. In terms of fixed assets, operating fixed assets of the Japanese firm were only 23% of total assets versus 38% for the U.S. firm, while its long-term investments accounted for 11% of total assets versus only 6% for the U.S. firm.

As for liabilities, the Japanese firm had two and a half times more short-term borrowings, and its debt was nearly double that of the U.S. firm. Finally, the equity base of the Japanese firm was less than half that of the U.S. firm, whereas its debt to equity ratio was roughly three times larger.

Income Statement

Over a four-year period, the reported income of the Japanese firm was generally only about half that of its U.S. counterpart but had remained remarkably stable as a percentage of sales while that of the U.S. firm had fluctuated significantly from year to year. Its earnings per share were also consistently lower, despite having less equity.

Although Tim knew that there were significant differences between U.S. and Japanese cultures and business environments, he was not certain how these differences might be affecting the Japanese company's financial statements. Perhaps something was wrong with his use of the standard financial rates analysis.

Questions

1. In general, what are the problems with applying one country's standard financial analysis techniques to the analysis of financial statements of a company from another country or with making other comparisons to firms in other countries?
2. In this specific case, what conditions or factors in Japan might be causing the puzzling financial analysis results?
3. What might Tim do to assess the true financial position of this company?

Case 3

MATTERHORN AG

Jack Stone is in a real quandary. He has only two weeks in which to make a final recommendation on the acquisition of Matterhorn AG, a company that manufactures high-quality mountain climbing equipment. Jack is on the international acquisitions staff of Leisure, Inc., a large U.S. company that specializes in recreational consumer goods for an increasingly fitness-conscious U.S. population. Leisure, Inc., has little experience in the international market but feels that Western Europe is a possibility. Jock Hansen, president and founder of Leisure, Inc., heard about Matterhorn AG from a mutual friend while skiing in Switzerland and asked his acquisitions staff to look into the matter.

Matterhorn AG is a Swiss corporation with a large percentage of the stock owned by Hans Groberg and his family. Hans started the business 30 years ago and is anxious to sell so that he can retire. He has two sons and one daughter who manage various subsidiaries of Matterhorn, but none of them is anxious to take over the business. Since beginning the business, some of the stock has been offered publicly, so Hans's personal holdings are less than 15%. However his control over Matterhorn has never been questioned by other shareholders. The banks have provided substantial financing for Matterhorn and control most of the proxy votes of other shareholders at the annual meetings.

Part of Jack's dilemma is that he has no idea what to offer Matterhorn shareholders for their stock, which is currently selling for the equivalent of $1900 on the Swiss stock exchanges. The Swiss Code of Obligations requires that financial statements be prepared, but they are very sketchy and do not have to be disclosed to the public. Jack computed a price/earnings ratio for Matterhorn and discovered that it was four times that of a similar company in the United States, and he suspects that Matterhorn's earnings were understated in comparison with U.S. generally accepted accounting principles. On the balance sheet, he noticed that certain fixed assets were carried at a value of one Swiss franc, even though their insured value was several million Swiss francs. In talking with a CPA who had experience in Switzerland, Jack found out that hidden reserves, which tend to understate the value of assets and overstate expenses, were allowed. Jack tried to get Matterhorn's accountant to show him how the hidden reserves really affected the books, but the accountant was hesitant to do so.

Another problem is trying to get a picture of the whole corporation. Matterhorn's financial statements—such as they are—contain the results of only the parent. Jack knows that at least ten subsidiaries controlled by Hans's children were not consolidated with Matterhorn's operations. Jack has tried to get copies of the financial statements of the subsidiaries and a summary of intercompany transactions but has still not received a response.

One thing that really irks Jack is that he cannot get much financial data, but he can get all kinds of information from the company's social balance sheet about the quality of life of the workers. "Why would they go to such trouble for all that garbage?" muses Jack. He decides that it must be a public relations gimmick.

Jack knows he has to have an answer soon. He assumes that Jock wants the acquisition in order to write off his ski trip, but he does not want to recommend a lemon.

Questions

1. What are the major problems that Jack faces in trying to evaluate this investment opportunity?
2. Why is the consolidation issue so tricky here?
3. What are some major differences in disclosure between Switzerland and the United States as brought out in the case?
4. Why are the Swiss so conservative in their accounting? What role do the banks play in this conservatism? (For greater insight into this question, read The 1973 Annual Report of CIBA-GEIGY A.G.—Switzerland, in "Report of the AAA Committee on International Accounting," *Accounting Review*, supplement 1976.)

CHAPTER 3

Accounting for Changing Prices

At the mere mention of inflation, people conjure up images of the collapse of the world monetary system and the end of civilization, gold bugs complain about the presses that work overtime printing paper currencies in Latin America, and Europeans recall with horror how the German mark shriveled in value from 4 per dollar to 4.2 billion per dollar in the 1920s. Inflation is a focus of interest around the world among economists and government fiscal and monetary policy makers, and even accountants are getting into the act. This chapter discusses what inflation is and what it does to business, looks at alternative ways to account for inflation, examines specific guidelines for inflation accounting in several national and international settings, and highlights the difficulties facing a multinational enterprise that operates in a variety of inflationary environments and is subjected to myriad reporting regulations.

WHAT IS INFLATION?

Inflation, as defined from an economic standpoint, is an increase in the price of goods in terms of money. This implies that prices rise for reasons other than changes in the nature of the product, technological advances, and so forth. Thus, the supply of money is increasing in relation to the excess supply of products in the market. This would hold true on an international level rather than just a domestic level, as pointed out by Laffer and Miles.[1]

Although they are technically not correct, most people tend to look at inflation as a sustained increase in the price index from one period to the next. Because attitudes vary from country to country, it might be more accurate perceptually to say that inflation occurs when the price index rises above a tolerable level. For example, an increase in consumer prices of 100% in one year would be perceived very differently in the United States,

---

[1]Arthur B. Laffer and Marc A. Miles, *International Economics in an Integrated World* (Glenview, Ill.: Scott, Foresman and Company, 1982), pp. 258–259.

Exhibit 3.1 Annual Increase in the Consumer Price Index for Selected Years

	1970	1974	1976	1978	1980	1981	1982	1983
World	6.1	15.3	11.2	9.7	15.7	14.1	12.3	13.6
Industrial countries	5.6	13.3	8.3	7.2	11.9	9.9	7.5	5.5
Non-oil developing countries	8.6	24.8	25.1	23.5	32.4	31.6	34.3	44.5
Argentina[a]	13.6	23.5	443	176	101	105	165	245
Brazil[a]	22.3	27.6	42.0	38.7	82.8	106	98.0	108
Canada	3.3	10.9	7.5	9.0	10.2	12.4	10.8	7.6
Chile[a]	33.0	505	212	40.1	35.1	19.7	9.9	23.3
France	5.9	13.7	9.6	9.1	13.3	13.3	12.1	9.3
Japan	7.7	24.4	9.3	3.8	8.0	4.9	2.6	2.1
Mexico[a]	5.2	23.8	15.8	17.5	26.4	27.9	58.9	113
United Kingdom	6.4	16.0	16.5	8.3	18.0	11.9	8.6	5.0
United States	5.9	11.0	5.8	7.6	13.5	10.4	6.2	3.6
West Germany	3.3	7.0	4.3	2.7	5.5	5.9	5.3	3.7

[a]The inflation rate is rounded to the nearest percentage in the years when the rate of inflation is 100% or more.
Source: International Monetary Fund, *International Financial Statistics,* various issues.

where the increase in the consumer price index in 1983 was between 4 and 5%, and in Argentina, where consumer prices increased 430% during the same period. Most countries express inflation as the quarterly or annual change in the consumer price index, which is based on a broad basket of consumer goods. The wholesale price index and the gross national product (GNP) price deflator, and other indices, are also used in some countries.

Exhibit 3.1 compares rates of inflation worldwide using the consumer price index, the most widely used index for comparative purposes. As noted, inflation was at fairly low levels in the early 1970s, but it took off in 1973 and 1974, largely as a result of the oil price increases and the strains placed on the international monetary system during that period. Hardest hit were the non-oil developing countries where inflation increased by 24.8% in 1974 and then began a long upward climb.

As inflation began to heat up in the 1970s, economists noted some interesting things. In a study published by the International Monetary Fund,[2] it was pointed out that three things were clearly emerging in that decade from the standpoint of inflation: magnitude, diffusion, and dispersion. Magnitude implies the sheer increase in the consumer price index, as noted in Exhibit 3.1. That steady increase is dramatic in the industrial as well as developing countries, even though inflation began to moderate in the early 1980s. Diffusion implies that inflation was becoming more wide-

[2]*IMF Survey,* "Key Measures of Inflation Confirm Global Increase," 12 November 1979, pp. 349–356.

spread. During the 1960s, only 25 to 35% of the countries in the world were experiencing increases in the consumer price index of 5% or more; by 1974, more than 80% of the countries were experiencing inflation of 10% or more. From the standpoint of dispersion, there seemed to be greater variations around the mean in the 1970s. In 1974, for example, price increased in the world at large by 15.3%. However, Germany experienced increases of only 7%, whereas Chile was suffering under a staggering increase of 504.7%.

What are the major reasons for inflation? The explanation is that there is too much money chasing too few goods. In other words, the demand for products exceeds the supply. Sometimes the money supply expands too rapidly, putting plenty of money in people's hands when there are not enough goods for them to buy. This pushes up prices on available goods. Thus, government monetary policy is critical. Fiscal policy can also be important—if the government expands its service programs, for example, putting more purchasing power in people's hands without an expansion in the production of goods.

Argentina is a good example of how government fiscal and monetary policy can have a dramatic impact on inflation. As noted earlier, Argentina experienced inflation of 430% in 1983. However, its inflation rate has exceeded 100% every year since 1975. Most of the trouble can be traced to large increases in the money supply generated in the 1970s to pay for large government deficits instead of the government cutting spending as it should have. At the same time, the lame duck government in 1983 allowed wage increases of up to 20% a month for six months in an effort to appease labor.[3]

Sometimes, supply bottlenecks in one sector of the economy can create shortages in other sectors, leading to price increases as demand outstrips supply. This could occur in primary products such as raw materials as well as manufactured components. Or the unilateral price increase of an essential good, such as oil, may have a rippling effect. The quadrupling of oil prices in 1973 touched off an increase in inflation in 1974 that the world may never recover from. Although it would be unfair to blame worldwide inflation solely on oil prices, the effect is obvious.

A trade deficit can contribute to inflation. In a world of floating exchange rates, the currency of a deficit country is bound to weaken over time through a gradual depreciation or a formal devaluation. As explained in Chapter 4, it takes more of a country's currency to purchase one unit of foreign currency after a devaluation than it did before. Therefore, the local price of imported goods tends to rise over time, as does the price of locally competitive products. How much of this increase fuels inflation depends on how important imports are in the nation's consumption patterns.

Some of these examples relate to *cost-push inflation,* in which an in-

---

[3]"Salvaging an Economy after Seven Years of Chaos," *Business Week,* 6 February 1984, p. 67.

crease in the costs of production factors such as oil or labor tends to push up the price of products using those factors. Other examples relate to *demand-pull inflation*, in which excessive demand and purchasing power pull up the price of products that consumers want. As we look at ways to account for inflation, we will consider the distinction between a general rise in the price level and price increases in specific sectors of the economy or even for specific products.

Impact of Inflation of the Firm

Inflation affects both the balance sheet and the income statement, which results in some strange operating decisions both by managers who understand inflation and by those who do not. In terms of the balance sheet, financial assets such as cash lose value during inflation because their purchasing power diminishes. For example, if a business holds cash during a period when inflation rises by 10%, that cash buys 10% less goods at the end of the period than at the beginning. Conversely, holding financial liabilities such as trade payables is wise because the business would be paying its obligations in the future with cheaper cash. The one caveat here is that financial liabilities, such as short- and long-term bank notes, often carry very high interest rates in inflationary economies.

The effect of inflation on nonmonetary assets is reflected in the income statement as well as the balance sheet. During a period of rising prices, replacing inventory and fixed assets becomes increasingly expensive. This could lead to higher profits because current sales dollars are being matched against inventory that may have been purchased several months earlier and against depreciation that is computed on property, plant, and equipment that may have been purchased several years ago.

Those balance sheet and income statement effects could lead the firm into a liquidity crunch as the cash generated from revenues is consumed by the ever-increasing replacement cost of assets. The overstatement of profits that results from matching old costs with new revenues could lead to demands from shareholders for more dividends, even though the firm is watching its cash dwindle.

The tax consequence of inflation are also obvious. As profits rise, so does a firm's tax liability, causing a further outflow of cash. Much has been said in recent years about how inflated financial statements misrepresent a firm's real operating position. The concern is that analysts and investors cannot make wise financial decisions without understanding the impact of inflation. And what happens if the government decides to slow down inflation by raising interest rates, reducing the money supply, or imposing wage and price controls? The liquidity crisis becomes more severe and the operating problems are compounded as the firm complies with government regulations.

WAYS TO ACCOUNT FOR INFLATION

There are two philosophies on accounting for inflation: adjustment for general price level changes and adjustment for specific price changes. General price level or constant dollar accounting is concerned that the value of money has gone down, whereas specific price or current cost accounting is concerned that the cost of specific assets has gone up. It is possible to apply these approaches to all items in the financial statements that can be adjusted or to only some of the items. Also, the approaches can be used separately or in conjunction with each other. Whatever the approach, it is necessary to identify which accounts are to be adjusted, what is to be the basis for the adjustment (such as an index), and where the adjustment is to be reflected in the financial statements.

General Purchasing Power

The general philosophy supporting general purchasing power (*GPP*) accounting is to report assets, liabilities, revenues, and expenses in units of the same purchasing power. The attitude is that the unit of measure should be uniform but the basis for measuring the financial statements (e.g., historical cost) should not change.

In most countries of the world, financial statements are prepared on a historical cost–nominal currency basis. This means that the statements are not adjusted for changes in the general price level. Under GPP accounting the nonfinancial items in the financial statements (inventory, plant, and equipment), are restated to reflect a common purchasing power, usually at the ending balance sheet date. For example, assume that a firm purchased a machine on January 1, 1985, for $10,000 and that the general price level, as measured by the consumer price index, increased by 15% during the year. On December 31 the machine would appear on the balance sheet at $11,500 [10,000 + (10,000 × 0.15)] less accumulated depreciation. The amount implies that it would take $11,500 of end-of-year purchasing power to buy what $10,000 bought on January 1. For the year-end financial statements, the financial assets and liabilities (cash, receivables, payables) would not be adjusted because they are already stated in terms of December 31 purchasing power, but all other assets, liabilities, revenues, and expenses would be adjusted. When the 1984 and 1985 financial statements are compared, however, all of 1984's accounts—including the financial assets and liabilities—would be restated to December 31, 1985, purchasing power in order to compare with 1985's financial statements.

There is some feeling that GPP accounting should be applied to financial assets and liabilities as well. Cash, for example, loses purchasing power during an inflationary period because it cannot purchase as much at the end of the period as it did at the beginning. Debtors benefit during inflation, however, because they can pay their debts at the end of the period with cash whose purchasing power has fallen. Therefore, a firm that has increased its net financial asset position during an inflationary period suffers a loss in purchasing power, whereas a firm that has increased its net financial liability position enjoys a gain in purchasing power.

Under GPP accounting, a firm can realize a gain from holding an asset during an inflationary period, such as the $1500 gain in our example ($11,500 − $10,000). Where should that holding gain, as well as holding losses, be recognized? They could be reflected in the income statement as a holding gain or loss, or they could be reflected on the balance sheet as an adjustment to invested capital. Both approaches are used worldwide, as we shall see.

The last issue deals with the *index* to be used. As noted earlier, the consumer price index is the one most widely used to measure inflation around the world. It measures the changes in prices for a broad range of consumer goods and services that are purchased for final consumption. The index is very broad and may not reflect the direction and magnitude of the change in prices that directly affect a given firm; however, it does reflect the general change in prices and therefore in a currency's purchasing power.

Mechanics of GPP Accounting

Although the purpose of this chapter is to compare and contrast ways to account for inflation internationally rather than focus on the detailed procedures for making the adjustments, it might be useful to illustrate very simply how the restatement process works. Assume that an asset was purchased in Brazil at the beginning of 1981 for Cr$500,000 (cruzeiros) when the index was 100 and that the index at the end of the year was 205.6. The conversion of the asset to end-of-year cruzeiros would be done as follows:

$$\text{Nominal amount} \times \frac{\text{Price index converting to}}{\text{Price index converting from}} = \text{Constant dollar amount}$$

$$500,000 \times \frac{205.6}{100.0} = \text{Cr\$1,028,000}$$

In making the adjustments to the financial statements from a comprehensive standpoint, the historical cost values of nonmonetary items are adjusted for changes in the price level. Nonmonetary items, such as inventory, property, plant, and equipment, are defined as financial statement items that do not represent a right to receive or an obligation to pay a fixed sum of money. Income statement items are generally restated to constant dollars by using the average price index for the period in the denominator in the preceding formula. Depreciation expense and cost of sales would be restated using the index in effect when the assets were purchased.

Some countries also prefer to consider the impact of general inflation on monetary items. This is generally accomplished by doing the following, using dollars as an example:

1. The net monetary position at the beginning of the year is restated into end-of-year dollars using the formula above.

2. Transactions involving monetary items, such as sales, purchases, and other expenses, are restated into end-of-year dollars using an average index for the denominator and then are added to the restated net monetary position at the beginning of the year.

3. The sum of Steps 1 and 2 are reduced by the net monetary position at the end of the year. Since that amount is already stated in terms of end-of-year dollars, no restatement is necessary.

The result of this computation is a purchasing power gain or loss. The actual disclosure of that amount will be dealt with in the specific country sections.

Current Cost Accounting

As we have seen, *current cost accounting* is concerned with the rise in the cost of specific assets, not with the overall loss of purchasing power of a currency. Under this concept, income is not considered to be earned until the firm has maintained the replacement cost of its productive capacity. Under current cost accounting, a new basis for valuing assets replaces the traditional historical cost.

There are two major approaches to current cost accounting: current entry price (or replacement cost) and current exit price (or net realizable value). *Replacement cost accounting,* the most widely accepted method, is used for most classes of nonmonetary assets. Under this approach, assets are valued at what it would cost to replace them. Whether the value should reflect the same asset being replaced or a similar asset performing the same function but with a newer technology has been the subject of considerable discussion. The *current exit price approach* values assets, especially finished goods inventory, at what they could be sold for, less costs to complete and sell the items. In Dutch *exit value theory,* a further distinction is made between liquidation value and the going concern concept. Under *liquidation value,* the asset is valued at its estimated sales price on a forced sale assumption. Under the *going concern concept,* the asset is valued at the estimated sales price on normal completion of production.

Current cost accounting results in holding gains and losses when nonmonetary assets are revalued. The gains and losses in these holdings can either be taken into the income statement or be reflected on the balance sheet as a capital adjustment account. The final issue is the determination of current values. For inventory, suppliers' lists are most commonly used because they reflect the most current prices for the items. Fixed assets are more complex. Property and plant are usually revalued according to a specific index, such as a construction cost index. Equipment could be revalued on the basis of a supplier list or engineering estimates—especially for machinery that is custom designed and built. Appraisal values are also a possibility for fixed assets. It is obvious that current cost accounting is more complex to administer because it requires a mixture of actual prices, estimates, appraisal values, and indices for homogeneous groups of assets.

Current Cost Income—An Illustration

In order to see the impact that the use of current cost accounting can have on income, assume that the Mexican subsidiary of MultiCorp had sales revenues in Mexican pesos of Mex$1,000,000, current costs of goods sold of Mex$900,000, and historical cost of goods sold of Mex$700,000. Under current cost accounting, operating gross profit would be Mex$100,000 (the difference between sales revenues and current cost of goods sold). Under historical cost accounting, gross profit would be Mex$300,000 (the difference between sales revenues and historical cost of goods sold). However, some of the historical cost of goods sold was derived from holding inventory during a period when its specific cost was increasing. Thus, the difference between the current cost of goods sold and the historical cost of goods (Mex$900,000 − Mex$700,000 = Mex$200,000) can be considered a realized holding gain. It is realized because the asset was actually sold during the period.

Current Cost–GPP Accounting

Although GPP and current cost accounting have been discussed separately, many accountants and economists believe that the two should be combined. Assume, for example, that an asset was acquired at the beginning of the year for $150,000 and that at the end of the year the replacement cost of the assets was $190,000 but the value of the asset in end-of-year general purchasing power terms was $165,000. The total holding gain of the asset would be

$$\begin{array}{r} \$190,000 \\ \underline{150,000} \\ \$\ 40,000 \end{array}$$

However, the real holding gain (the gain net of the impact of inflation), would be only $25,000.

$$\begin{array}{r} \$190,000 \\ \underline{165,000} \\ \$\ 25,000 \end{array}$$

The inflation component of the holding gain would be $15,000.

$165,000
150,000
$ 15,000

THE UNITED STATES

Historical Perspectives

As noted in Concepts Statement No. 2 of the Financial Accounting Standards Board, a basic tenet of accounting is a stable monetary unit. As long ago as 1922, Professor Paton noted that comparisons of historical cost financial statements can be misleading during periods when the purchasing power of the dollar is changing. The first major comprehensive pronouncement concerning accounting for inflation was APB Statement No. 3, *Financial Statements Restated for General Price-Level Changes,* issued in June 1969. Although the Statement recommended historical cost–GPP financial statements, it did not require that those statements be presented to investors and creditors. As a result, few companies actually put those principles into practice.

The Securities and Exchange Commission

The SEC dropped a bombshell on the corporate world in 1976 with Accounting Series Release (ASR) 190 on replacement cost accounting. ASR 190 required disclosure of the following information in the 10-K report (an annual report that must be filed with the SEC):

1. The current replacement cost of inventories.
2. The cost of goods sold, using replacement costs of goods and services sold.
3. The current cost of replacing productive capacity (both gross and net of depreciation).
4. The amount of depreciation, depletion, and amortization of productive capacity carried at replacement cost.
5. The basis for determining the above values.
6. Other information of a qualitative nature (difficulties in generating data, usefulness of information, and so on).

This information was supplemental to the primary historical cost financial statements and needed to be disclosed only in the 10-K report, although reference to the effect that the information was in the 10-K had to be included in the annual report to shareholders.

ASR 190 was issued because of the relatively high levels of inflation experienced in the United States during the early 1970s and the fact that the accounting profession had not done anything substantive to provide information to users about the impact of inflation on the financial statements. However, ASR 190 met with significant negative reactions from a variety of sources.

ASR 190 had an important impact because firms were forced to experiment with collecting and reporting the data, and analysts had the use of the data. As noted in a study on ASR 190 by the Financial Executives Research Foundation, however, "management is almost unanimously opposed to present replacement cost disclosure," and "sophisticated investors and professional analysts do not believe that present disclosure of replacement costs is useful in making investment and credit decisions."[4]

The Financial Accounting Standards Board

The accounting profession has not been successful over the years at resolving accounting for inflation. The Financial Accounting Standard Board's (FASB's) initial attempt was an exposure draft that was issued in 1974 and then "deferred to future periods." However, the implementation of ASR 190 and the progress by FASB on the conceptual framework of accounting resulted in renewed actions. Finally in September 1979, the Board issued Statement 33, *Financial Reporting and Changing Prices*. In this Statement, the board expressed concern for management, creditors, current and prospective investors, and the general public. It then identified four ways that the statement should help users: (1) in assessing future cash flows, (2) in assessing enterprise performance, (3) in assessing the erosion of operating capability, and (4) in assessing the erosion of general purchasing power.[5]

Statement 33 applies to all public enterprises that have inventories and property or plant and equipment (before deducting accumulated depreciation) amounting to more than $125 million, or total assets amounting to more than $1 billion (after deducting accumulated depreciation). The inflation-adjusted information is to be published as supplementary financial information because the traditional historical cost statements are to remain as the primary financial statements. Statement 33 requires a combination of constant dollar and current cost information in order to encourage experimentation and help assess the impact of different kinds of information. The FASB noted that in response to its exposure draft issued in 1978, "many preparers and public accounting firms emphasized the need to deal with the effects of general inflation; users generally preferred information dealing with the effects of specific price changes."

In order to comply with Statement 33, the following supplementary information needs to be disclosed:

[4]Haskins and Sells, "The Week in Review," 22 December 1978, pp. 4–5.
[5]All quotes and references to the statement can be found in Financial Accounting Standards Board, *Statement of Financial Accounting Standards No. 33—Financial Reporting and Changing Prices* (Stamford, Conn.: FASB, September 1979).

1. Information on income from continuing operations on historical cost/constant dollar basis.
2. The purchasing power gain or loss on net monetary items (not to be included in income from continuing operations).
3. Information on income from continuing operations on a current cost basis:
   a. cost of goods sold at current cost and
      b. depreciation and amortization expense of property, plant, and equipment.
4. The current cost amounts of inventory and property, plant, and equipment.
5. Increases or decreases in the current amounts of inventory and property, plant, and equipment, net of inflation.
6. Summary information for the five most recent fiscal years:
   a. Net sales and other operating revenues.
   b. Historical cost/constant dollar information:
      (1) Income from continuing operations.
      (2) Income per common share from continuing operations.
      (3) Net assets at fiscal year-end.
   c. Current cost information:
      (1) Income from continuing operations.
      (2) Income per common share from continuing operations.
      (3) Net assets at fiscal year-end.
      (4) Increases or decreases in the current cost amounts of inventory and property, plant, and equipment, net of inflation.
   d. Other information:
      (1) Purchasing power gain or loss on net items.
      (2) Cash dividends declared per common share.
      (3) Market price per common share at fiscal year-end.

According to Statement 33, there are four major methods of determining replacement cost for productive capacity: direct pricing, indexing, unit pricing, and functional pricing. *Direct pricing* applies current prices to assets or homogeneous groups of assets. Direct pricing could come from actual invoices of items purchased recently, price lists of suppliers, or standard costs that reflect current prices.

Some firms prefer to use an *index*, which serves as a surrogate for specific price changes and can be applied to a homogeneous group of assets rather than to a specific asset. The assumption is that the specific prices of the assets move in the same direction and magnitude and can thus be represented by the index.

Unit pricing is a variation of direct pricing in which a current cost per unit (such as the cost per foot of building construction) is applied to the

EXHIBIT 3.2 Nabisco Brands Inc. Adjustments for Changing Prices

Consolidated Statement of Income Adjusted for the Effects of Changing Prices
Year Ended December 31, 1983

(in millions, except per share data)	Historical Basis	Adjusted for Changes in Specific Prices (Current Cost)
Net sales	$5985.2	$5985.2
Cost of sales	3650.8	3669.1
Depreciation expense	131.1	206.7
Other expenses	1560.4	1560.4
Interest expense	76.8	76.8
Provision for income taxes	243.5	243.5
Net income	$ 322.6	$ 228.7
Net income per common share	$4.86	$3.45
Gain from decline in purchasing power of net monetary liabilities		$34.4
Increase in specific prices of inventories and property, plant and equipment held during the year[a]		$ 34.2
Less effect of increase in general price level		(113.1)
Excess of increase in general price level over changes in specific prices		$ (78.9)
Foreign currency translation adjustment		$ (107.9)

[a] At 31 December 1983, the Current Cost of Inventory was $759.6 million and the Current Cost of Property, plant and equipment, net of accumulated depreciation was $2231.2 million.
Source: 1983 Annual Report, Nabisco Brands Inc., p. 46.

number of units being revalued. *Functional pricing* applies a current cost per unit of a processing function (such as in a food processing plant) times the number of units being processed. The FASB prefers the use of the direct pricing method in making adjustments.

A review of the annual reports of U.S. companies reveals a variety of approaches for disclosing the inflation-adjusted information, although most companies would fall within the guidelines set up by Statement No. 33.

An example of what the disclosures might look like is found in Exhibits 3.2 and 3.3 for Nabisco Brands Inc. Exhibit 3.2 contains the income statement adjusted for current costs. It is interesting to note that no infor-

Exhibit 3.3 Nabisco Brands Inc. Five-Year Summary of Accounting for Changing Prices

Five-Year Comparison of Selected Supplementary Financial Data Adjusted for the Effects of Changing Prices

(Dollars in millions, except per share data)	1983	1982	1981	1980	1979
Net sales—total					
Historical cost	**$5985.2**	$5871.1	$5819.2	$5587.2	$4975.3
Constant dollar	**5985.2**	6060.1	6377.1	6755.5	6829.2
Net sales—ongoing businesses					
Historical cost	**$5985.2**	5463.4	5049.7	4848.8	4349.7
Constant dollar	**5985.2**	5639.3	5533.8	5862.8	5970.6
Net income					
Historical cost	**$322.6**	$314.7	$266.3	$234.8	$186.5
Current cost	**228.7**	254.0	157.0	114.8	100.0
Net income per common share					
Historical cost	**$4.86**	$4.83	$4.21	$3.73	$2.97
Current cost	**3.45**	3.90	2.48	1.82	1.59
Net assets at year end					
Historical cost	**$1710.8**	$1835.9	$1522.8	$1344.1	$1200.3
Current cost	**2386.4**	2639.2	2579.5	2472.6	2483.5
Excess of increase in general price level over changes in specific prices	**$(78.9)**	$(196.6)	$(43.9)	$(110.4)	$(96.5)
Gain on net monetary liabilities	**$34.4**	$41.1	$88.7	$115.6	$134.5
Cash dividends declared per common share					
Historical cost	**$2.28**	$2.05	$1.77	$1.60	$1.45
Constant dollar	**2.28**	2.12	1.94	1.93	1.99
Market price per common share at year end					
Historical cost	**$41.00**	$36.75	$31.00		
Constant dollar	**40.31**	37.51	32.86		
Average consumer price index (1967 = 100)	**298.4**	289.1	272.3	246.8	217.4

Source: 1983 Annual Report, Nabisco Brands Inc., p. 47.

mation is provided in constant dollars except for the increase in general price level or changes in specific prices. Some companies provide both current cost and constant dollar information for cost of sales, depreciation expenses, and net income. Exhibit 3.3 contains the five-year summary.

THE UNITED KINGDOM

During the 1970s, the British accounting profession and the British government were active in generating proposals on methods to account for inflation in the annual accounts of British firms. The first major effort was a provisional standard issued in 1974 by the Accounting Standards Committee of the English Institute of Chartered Accountants, which recommended supplemental price-level-adjusted financial statements. However, the Sandilands Committee on inflation accounting, a government-sponsored committee, issued a recommendation in 1975 that favored eliminating historical cost statements completely and substituting current value accounting in their place. Revaluations were to be based on a set of government-published indices for 52 classes of capital assets and inventory.

In 1976 the Accounting Standards Committee of the Institute of Chartered Accountants of England and Wales responded with Exposure Draft 18 (ED 18) (better known as Son of Sandilands), which also recommended the adoption of current value accounting but with additional disclosure on the impact of inflation on monetary assets and liabilities. ED 18 was defeated by the members of the institute in 1977, because they were not ready for the mandatory retirement of historical cost accounting. The ASC released the *Hyde Guidelines* in 1977, which recommended three supplementary adjustments: a depreciation adjustment, a cost of sales adjustment, and a "gearing" adjustment.

SSAP 16

In May 1979, the ASC issued ED 24, "Current Cost Accounting," which reflected a transition from constant dollar accounting (1974) to current cost accounting (1975) to a mixture of the two (1976 and 1977). ED 24 became the foundation for Statement of Standard Accounting Practice 16, "Current Cost Accounting" (SSAP 16) issued by the ASC on March 31, 1980. It was adopted by firms whose accounting period started on or after January 1, 1980.

SSAP 16 must be followed by all listed companies, all nationalized companies, and all large, private companies whereas FASB Statement 33 relates only to the largest publicly listed companies. When the standards were first issued, approximately 5500 British and 1500 U.S. firms were required to report information on changing prices.

SSAP 16 requires that the following current cost information be presented in the annual report:

1. A current cost profit and loss account with
   a. Current cost operating profit derived after making depreciation, cost of sales, and monetary working capital adjustments and
   b. Current cost profit (after operations) attributable to shareholders derived after making a gearing adjustment.
2. A current cost balance sheet with
   a. Fixed assets and inventory at net current replacement cost and
   b. A capital maintenance reserve to reflect revaluation surplus and deficits, the monetary working capital adjustment, and the gearing adjustment.
3. Current cost earnings per share.[6]

In order to compute current cost operating profit, adjustments must be made to depreciation, cost of sales, and monetary working capital. Depreciation at current cost is determined by applying a depreciation rate to the current cost rather than historical cost of the asset. The major difference between the current cost and historical cost approaches would be the value of the asset rather than the depreciation rate. However, some firms may alter the depreciation rate at historical cost in order to more accurately reflect the charge to income for depreciation. The British firm ICI uses a shorter useful life for some assets under historical cost than it does for current cost accounting. Thus, the firm changes its depreciation rate as well as the value of the assets for determining depreciation.

The cost of sales adjustment is determined by using the current cost rather than historical cost for inventories. The *monetary working capital adjustment (MWCA)* is a fairly complex adjustment that reflects the impact of inflation on specific monetary items in working capital. The computation of that adjustment involves determining the following three items: the items to be included as working capital, the interval over which the calculations are to be made, and the indices to be used in adjusting the monetary working capital items.

Monetary working capital is defined in SSAP 16 as the aggregate of trade debtors, prepayments, and trade bills receivable, plus inventory not subject to a cost of sales adjustment as described briefly earlier, less trade creditors, accruals, and trade bills payable.[7] These items are intended to be involved in the day-to-day operating transactions of the business. Thus, operating income under historical cost is adjusted for the impact of inflation on certain monetary working capital items.

A major distinction between the inflation adjustment to monetary working capital items and adjustments under other methods is in the identification of the index. The British use different indices for trade receivables

---

[6]For a complete discussion, see "Statement of Standard Accounting Practice No. 16: Current Cost Accounting," *Accountancy*, April 1980, pp. 99–100.
[7]Ibid., paragraph 44.

and trade payables unless the difference between the two indices is immaterial. For trade receivables, the index reflects the current cost of goods sold, although a selling price index can be used as a surrogate. For trade payables, the index reflects price movements of goods purchased over the period of time during which the debt is carried. Thus, the index is far more specific than in most other systems in which the more general consumer price index is used.

Once the index and the items to be adjusted have been identified, the MWCA is computed. The adjustment is taken directly to operating income, and the balancing entry is made to reserves in the equity section of the balance sheet.

After current cost operating profit has been determined, a final adjustment must be made in order to come up with current cost profit or loss. That adjustment is called a *gearing adjustment*, which reflects the impact of inflation on the net borrowing of the company. Net borrowing, which becomes the foundation of the gearing adjustment, is basically net monetary assets and liabilities except those that have already been considered in the MWCA. In order to determine the gearing adjustment, the ratio of net borrowing, as defined previously, to average net operating assets is multiplied by the current cost adjustments defined previously (depreciation, cost of sales, and monetary working capital adjustments). The gearing adjustment is treated as an adjustment to interest expense, so that shareholders can see how their interest in the company has benefited from financing the business with debt. The adjustment is normally an increase

Exhibit 3.4 Income Statement (in thousands of pounds)

Turnover (sales)		£20,000
Profit before interest and taxation at historical cost		2,900
Less: current operating profit adjustment (see note)		1,510
Current cost operating profit		1,390
Gearing adjustment	370	
Interest	200	170
Current cost profit before taxation		1,560
Taxation		730
Current cost profit attributable to shareholders		830
Dividends		430
Retained current cost profit		400
Current cost earnings per share		27.7 pence

Note: Current adjustments

Cost of sales	£ 460	
Monetary working capital	100	
	560	
Additional depreciation	950	
	£1,510	

Source: *Accountancy*, May 1979, p. 43. Reprinted with permission.

Exhibit 3.5 Balance Sheet (in thousands of pounds)

Assets employed		
Fixed assets		£ 8,530
Net current assets		
Inventory	£4,000	
Trade debtors less trade creditors	800	
Other current liabilities	(1,000)	3,800
		£12,330
Financed by		
Capital and reserves		
Issued share capital	£3,000	
Capital maintenance reserve (see note)	3,030	
Retained profit	4,300	£10,330
Loan capital		2,000
		£12,330

Note: Capital maintenance reserve		
Balance at January 1		£1,180
Surplus on revaluations		
Land and buildings	£ 200	
Plant and machinery	1,430	
Inventory	490	£2,120
Monetary working capital adjustment		100
		2,220
Gearing adjustment		370
		1,850
Balance at December 31		£3,030

Source: Accountancy, May 1979, p. 43. Reprinted with permission.

to income. The offset to the income statement is taken to the same reserve account mentioned in the section on the MWCA.

Examples of what the British supplementary current cost reports might look like are shown in Exhibits 3.4 and 3.5. There are two notes to the statements that are necessary to determine what the adjustments were. The first explains the adjustments made to operating profit. Those are the cost of sales and monetary working capital adjustments. The second note explains the composition of the capital maintenance reserve. As noted, there are three major adjustments that need to be accounted for: adjustments to inventory and property, plant, and equipment on the balance sheet to reflect current costs; the monetary working capital adjustment; and the gearing adjustment.

SSAP 16 differs from FASB 33 in a number of ways. First, SSAP 16 separates the inflationary impact on monetary items into the MWCA and the gearing adjustments. Second, these adjustments become a part of profit rather than a separate figure. Third, the adjustments are comprehensive, involving both a balance sheet and an income statement. Fourth, more firms are involved, as mentioned earlier. Fifth, the current cost adjustments can be complied with in the following ways: "(a) presenting historical cost accounts as the main accounts which are prominently displayed; (b) presenting current cost accounts as the main accounts with supplementary historical cost accounts; or (c) presenting current cost accounts as the only accounts accompanied by adequate historical cost information."[8] Finally, SSAP 16 is concerned with current cost adjustments only, as opposed to general price level adjustments. The MWCA and gearing adjustments are not exactly general price level adjustments, as explained earlier.

Imperial Chemical Industries PLC—An Example

ICI is one of the largest chemical companies in the world, with sales revenues in 1982 of approximately $14 billion. In 1982, it provided supplementary current cost information consistent with SSAP 16. In addition, it provided 1981 financial statements adjusted for general price level changes in order to compare with 1982 financial statements. The following excerpts from the notes relating to the current cost group accounts reveal some interesting information about the application of current cost accounting in the United Kingdom.

> The accounts prepared on a Current Cost Accounting (CCA) basis include allowance for the impact of price changes on the funds needed to carry on the business and maintain its operating capability. Under the provisions of Statement of Standard Accounting Practice No. 16 (SSAP 16) this is achieved by making adjustments to the holding values of assets employed and to the historical cost trading profit to take into account the current levels of construction costs and of raw materials and other operating costs. The profit before taxation further includes a gearing adjustment which represents the inflationary benefit to the stockholders from loan finance, and partially offsets the cost of loan interest. The presentation of the accounts has been designed to separate trading items from items associated with finance and to demonstrate the relationship between the profit and loss account and the balance sheet.[9]

THE NETHERLANDS

The Dutch have been aware of current cost accounting for a long time. The extensive training of Dutch accountants in business economics has resulted in an accounting philosophy that is concerned with values and costs and with sound business-economic principles and practices. There are no set requirements for the use of current cost accounting, as either primary or supplementary information, but there is a clear preference for it. In a series of studies issued by the Tripartite Study Group beginning in 1974, the preference for current cost accounting was reemphasized with the com-

---

[8]Ibid., p. 102.
[9]*Annual Report*, Imperial Chemical Industries PLC, 1982, p. 36.

ment that current cost information on profit and equity should be contained in the footnotes to financial statements based on historical cost. Although a number of large firms use current cost statements as their primary statements, it is more common to see partial current cost statements or historical cost statements with supplementary disclosures.

If there are no requirements for current cost or constant dollar accounting, why be concerned about The Netherlands? First of all, Professor Theodore Limperg is often called the father of replacement value theory because of his pioneering works in The Netherlands in the early 1900s. He focused on the strong relationship between economics and accounting and felt that income should not be earned without maintaining the source of income of the business from a going-concern standpoint. Therefore, income is a function of revenues and replacement costs rather than historical costs. In addition, he felt that current cost information should be used by all decision makers—management as well as shareholders. The second reason for looking at The Netherlands is a large Dutch multinational called N. V. Philips, which uses current cost rather than historical cost financial statements.

N. V. Philips

Philips uses current cost with some constant dollar adjustments to monetary items. Under its current cost accounting system both balance sheet and income statement accounts are justified. For inventory, standard costs are determined at the start of each year. As prices change during the year, an index is developed by the purchasing department for homogeneous groups of assets and is applied to the standard cost to yield the current cost. The indices are prepared quarterly or bimonthly in situations in which inflation is more extreme. Current costs are determined by the purchasing department for fixed assets (either individually or in homogeneous groups), by the engineering department for specially designed pieces of equipment, and by the building design and plant engineering department for buildings. As is the case with inventory, indices are often used to update current values of homogeneous groups of assets. The increase (or decrease) in value to inventory and fixed assets due to specific price changes is credited to a *revaluation surplus* account in equity rather than to the income statement. The effect of inflation shows up in the income statement as a higher cost of goods sold (as a result of increases in inventory prices) and higher depreciation expense.

The 1982 Income Statement for Philips can be found in Exhibit 3.6. Trading profit for 1982 was computed at current cost. However, there is an adjusting item after trading profit in order to show what that profit would be at historical cost. This is an interesting departure from the procedure followed historically by Philips, which used to provide the financial statements at current cost and some supplementary information to show what income would have been under historical cost. The latter information was

Exhibit 3.6 1982 Income Statement for N. V. Philips[a]

	1982		1981	
Sales		42,991		42,411
Costs and expenses				
Cost of sales	−32,150		−32,209	
Selling and general expenses	−8,711	−40,861	−8,009	−40,218
Trading profit		2,130		2,193
Revaluation included in costs		745		710
Trading profit on the basis of historical cost		2,875		2,903
Financing charges		−1,773		−1,977
Miscellaneous income and charges		110		−21
Tax on profit		−376		−181
Profit after tax on the basis of historical cost		836		724
Addition to revaluation surplus realized, arising from financing with shareholders' interests		−364		−354
Profit after tax		472		370
Share in net result of nonconsolidated companies		70		86
Minority interests		−109		−134
Profit before exceptional items		433		322
Exceptional income and charges				
Elimination of provision for lifetime risks of fixed assets as from 1 January 1981		—		540
Restructuring provision		—		−525
Tax on exceptional income and charges		—		20
		—		35
Net profit		433		357

[a] Amounts in millions of guilders.
Source: 1982 Annual Report, p. 43.

generated primarily for U.S. financial statement users, but the 1982 current cost statements adjusted to historical cost are for all readers of the statements, not just those from the United States.

OTHER EXAMPLES

Brazil

Brazil has been recognized for years as having one of the highest inflation rates in the world. Rather than attempt to bring inflation down to the low levels experienced in most of the industrial countries, Brazil has learned to live with high rates of inflation. As part of the process of learning to live with inflation, Brazilians developed a complex system of indexing that involves maintaining purchasing power of certain monetary assets and liabilities as well as adjusting certain financial statement items for the effects of inflation.

In 1978, the monetary correction concept was changed so that currently an index, called the readjustable government treasury bond (ORTN) index, is applied to certain balance sheet accounts (permanent assets and shareholders' equity). *Permanent assets* are assumed to be property, plant, and equipment, accumulated depreciation, investments in equity securities, deferred charges, and related amortization. This is essentially the application of a general price level index to write up certain balance sheet accounts. Inventory, which is carried at the lower of first-in first-out (FIFO) or average cost or market, is not adjusted for general price level changes.

As the asset and equity accounts are adjusted, what happens to the balancing items? In the British case, as you will recall, the monetary working capital and gearing adjustments are treated as adjustments to profit in the supplementary statements, but the current cost adjustments are not, except as higher cost of sales and depreciation expense. In Brazil, the net monetary correction is charged to income for book and tax purposes if the equity position exceeds the permanent asset position. If it is the other way around, however, the net monetary correction is not charged to income for book and tax purposes unless the equity position exceeds the permanent asset position.[10]

Certain long-term liabilities are also adjusted to reflect the change in purchasing power, and these adjustments are considered charges to operating income in contrast with the net monetary correction, which is the last item reported before tax. The Brazilian experience, in a total business and economic context, is being carefully watched by many developing countries with similar problems and aspirations. The accounting experience is different from the others we have looked at because the adjusted statements are the primary statements, and yet not all accounts affected by inflation (such as inventory and certain monetary working capital items) are dealt with.

Chile

In Chile, firms are required for tax and financial purposes to adjust certain accounts for inflation. The system is called a monetary correction system, and it involves adjustments of nonmonetary assets and liabilities, as well as net worth. Inventory is adjusted to replacement cost, but the other adjustments all involve the use of the consumer price index. One of the interesting aspects of the Chilean system is that adjustments to asset and

[10]Ernst & Whinney, *E&W International Series—Brazil,* 1979, p. 5.

liability accounts are taken to the income statement rather than to an equity account, as is the case in the other integrated systems that we have examined.[11]

INTERNATIONAL APPROACHES TO ACCOUNTING FOR INFLATION

The International Accounting Standards Committee

The first reaction of the International Accounting Standards Committee (IASC) to inflation accounting came in IAS 6, "Accounting Responses to Changing Prices," in 1977. At that point, however, there was no definitive standard in either the United States or the United Kingdom, and there was substantial uncertainty as to how the inflation accounting issue would be resolved in those two countries. As a result, IAS 6 was very brief:

> In complying with International Accounting Standard 1, Disclosure of Accounting Policies, enterprises should present in their financial statements information that describes the procedures adopted to reflect the impact on the financial statements of specific price changes, changes in the general level of prices, or of both. If no such procedures have been adopted that fact should be disclosed.[12]

This standard appears to be very brief, and there is good reason for that. The IASC attempts to set standards that are essentially a narrowing of options available and must rely on a consensus of the member countries. In 1977, inflation accounting was a hot topic, but there clear-cut consensus emerged. Therefore, the IASC decided to do the next best thing—require good disclosure of the procedures being used.

A more definitive inflation standard did not emerge until 1981, with the issuance of IAS 15, "Information Reflecting the Effects of Changing Prices." The timing of that standard was better, because the FASB had issued Statement No. 33, "Financial Reporting and Changing Prices," in September 1979, and the Accounting Standards Committee (ASC) in the United Kingdom had issued Statement of Standard Accounting Practice No. 16, "Current Cost Accounting," in April 1980. With the influence and support of those two countries, the IASC was ready to issue a more definitive standard.

Rather than require one specific way to account for inflation, the IASC recognized that a difference of opinion still existed as to how inflation should be accounted for in the financial statements. As pointed out in the Standard:

[11]Langton Clarke y Cia. Ltd. [Coopers & Lybrand], *Chilean Tax Facts*, August 1981.
[12]International Accounting Standards Committee, "Accounting Responses to Changing Prices," *International Accounting Standard No. 6*, June 1977, paragraph 17.

. . . there is not yet an international consensus on the subject. Consequently, the International Accounting Standards Committee believes that further experimentation is necessary before consideration can be given to requiring enterprises to prepare primary financial statements using a comprehensive and uniform system for reflecting changing prices. Meanwhile, evolution of the subject would be assisted if enterprises that present primary financial statements on the historical cost basis also provide supplementary information reflecting the effects of price changes.[13]

The philosophy presented above is very similar to that of the United States, as noted earlier in the chapter.

The Standard discusses the merits of each of the two major philosophical approaches to accounting for inflation, the general purchasing power approach and the current cost approach, but it does not attempt to take a stand. The following major types of information reflecting the effects of changing prices must be disclosed:

1. the amounts of the adjustment to or the adjusted amount of depreciation of property, plant and equipment;

2. the amount of the adjustment to or the adjusted amount of cost of sales;

3. the adjustments relating to monetary items, the effect of borrowing, or equity interests when such adjustments have been taken into account in determining income under the accounting method adopted; and

4. the overall effect on results [income] of the adjustments described [above], as well as any other items reflecting the effects of changing prices that are reported under the accounting method adopted.

5. When a current cost method is adopted the current cost of property, plant and equipment, and of inventories, should be disclosed.

6. Enterprises should describe the methods adopted to compute the information called for above, including the nature of any indices used.

7. The information required above should be provided on a supplementary basis unless such information is presented in the primary financial statements.[14]

The importance of this standard is that it recognizes the need for information to be disclosed on inflation accounting and gives some specific guidelines that companies can follow to improve the quality of disclosure. The fact that the underlying information from country to country may differ is not too troublesome, because the profession in the United States cannot agree on one specific approach. However, better quality disclosure will assist financial statement users worldwide. The guidelines will be beneficial for countries that are concerned about inflation accounting but have

---

[13]International Accounting Standards Committee, "Information Reflecting the Effects of Changing Prices," *International Accounting Standard No. 15*, November 1981, paragraph 18.
[14]Ibid, paragraphs 23–27.

not yet developed their own standard. The guidelines are flexible enough to incorporate current cost or general purchasing power approaches but precise enough to guarantee high quality disclosure.

The European Economic Community

On July 25, 1978, the Council of Ministers of the EEC adopted the Fourth Directive on Company Law dealing with company accounts. That directive deals with the layout of annual financial statements, valuation methods, contents of the annual report, and provision concerning publication of the financial statements, and it also contains a section that deals with inflation accounting.

Although historical cost accounting is assumed by the directive to be the main basis for establishing account values, the directive allows for departure from historical cost in the following three instances: (1) revaluation of tangible fixed assets and financial fixed assets, (2) replacement value accounting for tangible fixed assets with limited useful lives and for inventories, (3) other accounting methods designed to take account of inflation.[15] The key is that national law must define what method of accounting for inflation is permissible in each member country. Then the firms must disclose the method used for accounting for inflation and which accounts are affected. Historical cost data must be presented if something other than historical cost is used in the financial statements. Any surpluses arising from the departure from historical cost accounting must be taken to a revaluation surplus account in the equity section of the balance sheet. This step is designed to keep firms from taking unrealized holding gains to the income statement.

The inflation dimension to the Fourth Directive is designed to improve disclosure rather than set a definitive standard on how to account for inflation.

THE DILEMMA OF THE MULTINATIONAL ENTERPRISE

The multinational enterprise that operates in multiple environments is subject to a variety of record-keeping requirements and must develop expertise in each of the countries. In addition, it needs to see whether home-country reporting requirements are applicable solely for domestic operations or for worldwide operations as well. Consolidated financial statements become laborious as firms need to keep multiple sets of books with multiple adjustments. A U.S. firm with a subsidiary in the United Kingdom is required to keep sufficient data to yield at least four sets of financial statements: (1) historical cost according to UK generally accepted account-

---

[15]Price Waterhouse, *Handbook on the EEC Fourth Directive* (Brussels: Price Waterhouse & Co., 1979), p. 6.

ing principles, (2) current cost supplementary financial statements to satisfy the requirements of SSAP 16, (3) historical cost financial information according to U.S. GAAP to facilitate consolidation, and (4) current cost and constant dollar information to satisfy the demands of Statement 33.

A major area of complexity involves the translation of inflation-adjusted information from the foreign currency to the reporting currency. That issue will be dealt with in Chapter 6 after we have discussed the process that one must follow to translate foreign currency financial statements into the reporting currency of the parent company. Until that time, it is sufficient to note that there is a real problem ahead of us.

SUMMARY

- Inflation is an increase in the price of goods in terms of money. It occurs when the supply of money is increasing relative to the excess supply of products in the market.

- During the 1970s, the magnitude, diffusion, and dispersion of inflation increased substantially worldwide. By the 1980s, however, world inflation began to moderate.

- The major factor influencing inflation is government monetary policy. Other contributing factors are government fiscal policy, supply bottlenecks, unilateral price changes, and a trade deficit.

- During periods of rising prices, financial assets lose value, and financial liabilities gain value. In addition, it may cost more to replace inventory and fixed assets.

- Constant dollar or general purchasing power accounting attempts to report assets, liabilities, revenues, and expenses in terms of units of the same purchasing power. Under this method, the basis for measuring assets and liabilities—historical cost—does not change. These adjustments are normally made to the nonmonetary accounts. However, it is also possible to compute a purchasing power gain or loss to net monetary items.

- Current cost accounting replaces the basis for measuring accounts from historical cost to some form of current cost. The most widely used method, replacement cost accounting, values assets at what it would cost to replace them.

- Current costs are determined by using suppliers lists, indices, estimates, and appraisals. Theoretically, holding gains and losses could be taken to income or deferred to the balance sheet.

- Current cost–constant dollar accounting attempts to separate the general inflation component from the rise in specific prices of assets.

- The first major standard for inflation accounting was Accounting Series Release 190 of the Securities and Exchange Commission, issued in 1976.

It required the use of replacement cost accounting as supplementary information.

- Statement No. 33 of the Financial Accounting Standards Board, issued in 1979, recommended that firms experiment with both current cost and constant dollar accounting as supplementary information in the annual report. Income from continuing operations is to be adjusted separately for current costs and general price level changes; purchasing power gains and losses on net monetary items is to be provided; and current costs of inventory, property, plant, and equipment is to be disclosed gross and net of inflation. Additional five-year summary information must be disclosed.

- SSAP 16, issued by the Institute of Chartered Accountants of England and Wales in 1980, requires the presentation of a current cost balance sheet and income statement. Included in the determination of current cost operating profit is a monetary working capital adjustment. A gearing adjustment, which reflects the impact of inflation on the net borrowing of the company, is treated as an adjustment to interest expense in order to determine net income after operations.

- According to SSAP 16, current cost financial statements can be supplementary to or in place of the historical cost financial statements.

- N. V. Philips, the Dutch company, uses current costs for its primary financial statements, although it provides a reconciling number to compute income at historical costs.

- Brazil requires the use of a government treasury bond index to adjust permanent assets for general price level changes. Some other accounts, such as certain long-term liabilities, are also adjusted for inflation, but others, such as inventory, are not.

- In Chile, a monetary correction system is used to adjust nonmonetary assets and liabilities for inflation.

- Because of a variety of inflation-reporting requirements at home and abroad, multinational companies are required to keep multiple sets of books.

- Standard No. 15 of the International Accounting Standards Committee recognizes both current cost and constant dollar accounting as viable ways to account for inflation but does not attempt to choose between the two. The Standard requires full disclosure of the effect of inflation on income and of the method or methods chosen to account for inflation.

- Although the Fourth Directive of the EEC does not require a specific method of accounting for inflation, it does permit a country to select a way to account for inflation and then requires adequate disclosure of the method selected and its impact on the financial statements.

Study Questions

3-1. Define inflation and describe some of the major reasons inflation occurs.

3-2. Using the consumer prices section at the beginning of a recent issue of *International Financial Statistics*, pick a country that has had a cumulative rate of inflation of approximately 100% over the past three years. Then try to find some current information to explain the source of inflation and its impact on business in the country.

3-3. How does inflation affect the financial statements of the firm? What operational problems does inflation create?

3-4. Compare the philosphies behind the following:
   a. Constant dollar accounting.
   b. Current cost accounting.
   c. Current cost–constant dollar accounting.

3-5. Assume that ABC Company buys a machine in 1980 for $150,000 when the index is 120. At the end of 1985, the index has risen to 205 and the replacement cost of the machine is now $275,000.
   a. What is the unrealized holding gain in constant dollars?
   b. What is the unrealized holding gain in current costs?
   c. What is the current cost gain or loss net of inflation?
   d. How would the holding gain on the machine be treated differently under FASB Statement No. 33 and SSAP 16?

3-6. If the current cost of the machine in Question 3-5 were $235,000 instead of $275,000, what would be the answers to Parts a through c?

3-7. What are the reporting requirements of FASB Statement No. 33?

3-8. Pick the annual report of a U.S. multinational and see if its supplementary inflation information is consistent with Statement No. 33. In its discussion of that information, does the firm mention anything about inflation outside of the United States?

3-9. What inflation accounting is required by the British in SSAP 16? How are those requirements similar to or different from FASB Statement No. 33?

3-10. How would you compare FASB Statement No. 33 and SSAP 16 with IAS No. 15?

3-11. Explain how N. V. Philips determines current costs for its financial reporting. How does its income differ from current cost income reported by a U.S. firm? by a British firm? More detail can be found in "The 1973 Annual Report of N. V. Philips—The Netherlands," in the Report of the AAA Committee on International Accounting, *Accounting Review*, Supplement 1976. Also, see the end of chapter references.

Case 1

ROYAL DUTCH SHELL GROUP

Some 75 years ago, the Dutch firm Royal Dutch Petroleum Company merged its interests with the British firm Shell Transport and Trading Company to form Royal Dutch/Shell Group of Companies. The group is 60% owned by the Royal Dutch Petroleum Company (RDPC) and 40% by the Shell Transport and Trading Com-

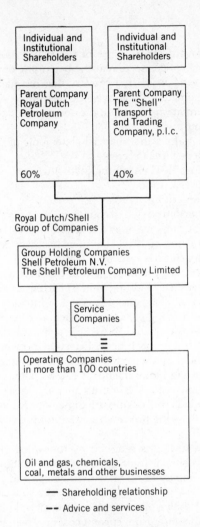

| Individual and Institutional Shareholders | Individual and Institutional Shareholders |

| Parent Company Royal Dutch Petroleum Company | Parent Company The "Shell" Transport and Trading Company, p.l.c. |
| 60% | 40% |

Royal Dutch/Shell Group of Companies

Group Holding Companies Shell Petroleum N.V. The Shell Petroleum Company Limited

Service Companies

Operating Companies in more than 100 countries

Oil and gas, chemicals, coal, metals and other businesses

— Shareholding relationship
-- Advice and services

The Structure of the Royal Dutch Shell Group of Companies

Source: Royal Dutch Petroleum Company, Annual Report 1982, p. 13.

pany PLC (STTC). Each of these holding companies is, in turn, owned by some 900,000 shareholders worldwide. The above diagram from RDPC's 1982 Annual Report illustrates this organizational relationship.

The following table illustrates the composition of shareholders of the two holding companies, with RDPC representing approximately 500,000 investors and STTC another 400,000 investors. One or both companies have stock listed on stock exchanges in eight European countries and the United States.

As noted in the organizational diagram, the group owns shares in the service companies and operating companies. There are 9 service companies located in The

Table 1 Shareholding in the Parent Companies

	Royal Dutch, %	Shell Transport, %	Combined, %
UK	8	98	44
Netherlands	33	—	19
USA	24	1	15
Switzerland	21	a	13
France	8	1	5
West Germany	3	—	2
Belgium	2	—	1
Luxembourg	1	—	1
Others	a	a	a
	100	100	100

aLess than 1%.
Source: Royal Dutch Petroleum Company, Annual Report 1982, p. 13.

Netherlands and the United Kingdom that provide advice and services to the group and associated companies. There are 15 major types of operating companies in over 100 countries involved in activities such as chemicals, coal, oil exploration, oil production, storage, and marketing. The United States alone provided over 27% of the 16.2 billion pounds sterling revenues of the group in 1982. The U.S. firm of Shell Oil Company has investments all over the world.

In its annual report, RDPC discloses supplementary current cost accounting information for the group. The current cost data is disclosed in the 1982 Annual Report in Table 2.1.

The discussion on the current cost data emphasizes that there is no internationally recognized way to account for inflation, especially for the oil industry, and that caution needs to be used in interpreting the current cost data. In addition, the following discussion concerning the adjustments is presented.

The present experimental nature of CCA is manifested in differing accounting practice in the Netherlands, the United Kingdom and the United States over the items which should be reflected in current cost accounts. These differences relate to the treatment of monetary items and taxation. The information shown [Table 2] has been presented to reflect the current cost adjustments common to the three countries. In addition, a gearing adjustment has been included to recognize the offsetting effect of borrowing on cost increases arising from changing prices. The basis of restatement for this purpose is set out [as follows]. Further details are provided under the heading "Additional information" [in Table 3] to facilitate the appreciation of the Group current cost data in the light of Netherlands, United Kingdom and United States practice.

Also included in the report is the following description on how the current cost restatements are made (see "Basis of Restatement," as follows).

Table 2 Current Cost Data

	1980[a] £ million	1981[a] £ million	1982 £ million
Summarized income data			
Historical cost net income	2,362	1,989	1,993
deduct current cost adjustments:			
Depreciation, depletion and amortization	804	1,105	1,319
Cost of sales	1,150	1,033	211
Earnings of associated companies	98	164	79
Income applicable to minority interests	(107)	(162)	(222)
Income/(loss) from continuing operations	417	(151)	606
Gearing adjustment	502	555	307
Current cost net income	919	404	913
Summarized statement of assets and liabilities			
Property, plant, and equipment—net	21,340	28,326	33,449
Investments in associated companies	2,202	2,564	3,382
Inventories	6,900	7,994	8,263
Other assets, less liabilities			
(other than long-term debt)	(3,850)	(4,757)	(5,923)
Capital employed	26,592	34,127	39,171
deduct:			
Long-term debt and capitalized lease obligations	4,215	5,518	6,858
Minority interests	2,594	3,815	4,361
Net assets	19,783	24,794	27,952

[a]Restated for comparative purposes.
Source: Royal Dutch Petroleum Company, Annual Report 1982, p. 53.

Basis of Restatement

The accounting policies used are the same as those applied in the Group financial statements except as modified. . . .

Property, plant and equipment of Group companies have been restated to year-end current cost by applying appropriate indices to historical local currency acquisition costs or by estimating the current cost of acquiring assets of approximately equivalent productive potential where technological change renders the use of an index inappropriate. Property, plant and equipment of associated companies has been restated on a basis as far as possible consistent with that of Group companies.

Inventories have been restated to their approximate year-end current cost.

Historical operating expenses have been adjusted to reflect the current cost of sales as at the date of sale.

Depreciation, depletion and amortization charges have been calculated as an appropriate proportion of the restated property, plant and equipment at current cost, on the basis of the same asset lives as those used for historical cost accounting.

Table 3 Additional Information

The following additional information is provided to assist in appraising the current cost data in the light of CCA practice in the Netherlands, United Kingdom and United States.

	1980[a]	1981[a]	1982 £ million
Netherlands			
If the provision for deferred taxation were to include the potential tax effects of current cost revaluations, net assets would become	16,083	19,594	22,552
If the historical tax charge were reduced to recognize tax effects related to the CCA additional depreciation and cost of sales adjustments and in addition the gearing adjustment (for which there is no standard practice in the Netherlands) were excluded, current cost net income would become	1,352	857	1,253
United Kingdom			
If the Group current cost data were to include only provisions for those taxes that are likely to be paid within the foreseeable future in conformity with the UK accounting practice:			
—the taxation charge would be reduced by	520	410	610
—the gearing adjustment would be reduced by	139	163	119
—current cost net income would become	1,300	651	1,404
United States			
If the Group adopted the LIFO basis of inventory accounting, which is common in the US, the tax charge would be reduced by	371	322	59
Adjustments for monetary items in the form of gearing are not recognized in the US, but companies disclose the gain on net monetary items arising from changes in purchasing power	1,030	1,015	539
After taking account of these two items, current cost net income would become	1,764	1,092	1,154

[a]Restated for comparative purposes.

Income tax and provisions for deferred tax included in the income statement are the same as those included in the historical cost financial statements.

A gearing adjustment has been made to quantify the proportion of the depreciation and cost of sales adjustments which relates to assets financed by borrowing. The proportion is calculated by reference to the ratio of average net borrowing to the average net operating assets over the year, taken at their current cost values. For this purpose net monetary working capital, which is not otherwise recognized in the current cost income statement, is included in the calculation of average net borrowing.

Comparative figures for 1980 and 1981 have been restated for changes in the method of accounting for currency translation. The restatement affects both the individual current cost adjustments and current cost net income, since the provisional adjustment for currency translation made in the 1981 presentation has now been superseded by the full application of current rate translation.

In addition to the above, the effect of gearing on the earnings of associated companies has now been taken into account and a modification has been made to the calculation of the gearing adjustment. All figures are expressed in pounds of the years to which they relate.

Of special interest is the report of the auditors reproduced here.

REPORT OF THE AUDITORS

on the Supplementary Information Current Cost Data

To Royal Dutch Petroleum Company and The Shell Transport and Trading Company, p.l.c.

We have reviewed the supplementary information—current cost data—of the Royal Dutch/Shell Group of Companies set out [in Tables 2 and 3].

In our opinion, the summarized data set out [in Table 2] has been properly prepared in accordance with the basis of restatement described [in Table 3].

Klynveld Kraayenhof & Co., The Hague
Ernst & Whinney, London
Price Waterhouse, New York

March 10, 1983

Questions

1. Why do you think it would be difficult for the group to account for inflation?
2. Compare the method adopted by the group with those we discussed in this chapter.
3. Discuss the nature of the audit report given the context of the group.
4. Evaluate the worth of IAS 15 and the international standard-setting process from the perspective of the accountants of the group.

Bibliography

Agami, Abdel M. and Felix P. Kollaritsch. *Annotated International Accounting Bibliography 1972–1981*. Sarasota, Fla.: International Accounting Section, American Accounting Association, 1983. There are numerous references in the section on inflation.

Ashton, R. K. *The Use and Extent of Replacement Value Accounting in The Netherlands*. London: The Institute of Chartered Accountants in England and Wales, 1981.

Enthoven, Adolf J. H. *Current Value Accounting: Its Concepts and Practice at N. V. Philips Industries, The Netherlands.* Richardson, Tex.: Center for International Accounting Development, The University of Texas at Dallas, 1982.

Enthoven, Adolf J. H. *Current Value Accounting: Its Concepts and Practice at N. V. Philips Industries, The Netherlands.* Richardson, Tex.: Center for International Accounting Development, The University of Texas at Dallas, 1982.

Sale, J. Timothy and Robert W. Scapens. "Accounting for the Effects of Changing Prices." *The Journal of Accountancy.* July 1980, pp. 82–87. Comparison between FASB Statement No. 33 and SSAP 16.

The Impact of Inflation on Accounting: A Global View. Urbana, Ill.: Center for International Education and Research in Accounting, University of Illinois, 1979.

CHAPTER 4

The World of Foreign Exchange

The past two decades have seen a lot of instability in foreign exchange markets. In 1971, the U.S. dollar was devalued (i.e., its value was lowered) against most major world currencies, and this process was repeated in 1973. During the rest of the 1970s, the dollar was generally weak, fluctuating between approximately 80 and 90% of its pre-1971 devaluation value, as illustrated in Figure 4.1.

In the early 1980s, however, the dollar began to strengthen. In 1980, there was a fairly steep rise in the value of the dollar during the first quarter but the steepest single-period decline in the value of the dollar was immediately thereafter in the second quarter. After a relatively flat third quarter, the dollar began a period of sustained strengthening, which culminated during the third quarter of 1981 at nearly 100% of its pre-1971 devaluation value. With the exception of moderate short-term decreases in value, the dollar remained relatively strong into the mid-1980s. All during 1983, experts were predicting a precipitous fall in the dollar by year-end, but that drop never materialized. Huge trading deficits (in which imports of merchandise exceeded exports of merchandise) in the United States vis-à-vis the rest of the world were not enough to push down the value of the dollar, but no one could accurately predict when and by how much the dollar would fall or against which currencies it would fall.

Similar scenarios of uncertainty could be written about literally every major currency of the world. For some currencies, such as the Mexican peso, the Brazilian cruzeiro, and the Argentine peso, the concern was about how far the currency could fall. For others, such as the yen and deutschemark, the question was when they would begin to rise against the U.S. dollar.

In order to understand the complexity surrounding the controller and treasury functions of the multinational enterprise, one must first understand the organization and dynamics of the foreign exchange market. This chapter explains the terminology of foreign exchange, describes the spot and forward markets, explains the forces that determine rates, and traces the history of currency movements up to the present time. It focuses more

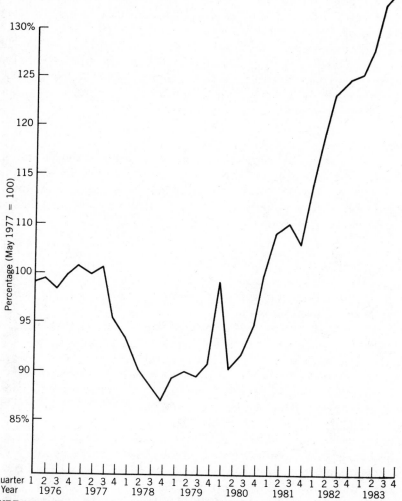

FIGURE 4.1 Indices of foreign currency price of the U.S. dollar against 22 OECD countries. (*Source:* Various issues of *Survey of Current Business.*)

on foreign exchange from the corporate and banking perspective than from a theoretical viewpoint. The usage of foreign exchange is fully developed in subsequent chapters on foreign currency transactions, translation of financial statements, and performance evaluation and control.

BASIC MARKETS

An *exchange rate* is the amount of one currency that must be given to acquire one unit of another currency. If the rate is quoted for current currency transactions—usually for delivery to be made two business days later—it is called the *spot rate*. Most currency transactions take place in the spot market. The *forward market* is for transactions that are to be completed at a later date. The majority of the transactions in the forward market are 30 to 180 days into the future, but contracts of other maturities are possible. The forward rate is a contractual rate between the foreign exchange trader and his or her client. It is seldom the same as the spot rate on the day the contract is made, and it may or may not be the same as the spot rate in effect when the forward contract is completed.

Spot Market

As is noted later in the chapter, most foreign currency transactions take place with the foreign traders of banks. Therefore, rates are quoted from the trader's perspective. Ordinarily, the trader will offer two quotes—the bid and offer price of a foreign currency. For example, the quote for British pounds sterling may appear as follows:

$$\$1.4525/35$$

which means that the trader will buy pounds for $1.4525 (bid) and sell pounds for $1.4535 (offer or ask). The difference between the two quotes is the profit margin for the trader and is often referred to as the *points* (10 points in the above example).

Exchange rate quotes can be obtained from a number of sources, such as *The Wall Street Journal*. In Exhibit 4.1 are quotes of a few currencies. Note that the rates listed in the table are the offer rather than bid price. Also note that two different rates are quoted for each day. The first two columns contain a *direct quote*, which is the amount of local currency equivalent to one unit of the foreign currency. Since the quote was made in the United States, the dollar is the local currency. The second two columns contain an *indirect quote*, which is the amount of foreign currency required for one unit of the local currency. For example, in Table 4.1 the exchange rate for U.S. dollars and Brazilian cruzeiros was as follows: $0.001079, or $\frac{1}{10}$ of 1 cent per cruzeiro (direct) or Cr$926.50 per U.S. dollar (indirect). Obviously, what is a direct quote in the United States would be considered an indirect quote in Brazil. Even if the direct quote were the only one provided, one could derive the indirect quote by taking the reciprocal of the direct quote. For example:

$$\frac{1}{\$0.001079} = \frac{Cr\$926.50 \text{ [the rounding of the denominator from } \$0.001079331}{\text{to } \$0.001079 \text{ yields } Cr926.78]}$$

The discussion thus far has centered on exchange rates between the U.S. dollar and other currencies. Rates are generally quoted this way because most foreign currency transactions take place in dollars, even when two currencies other than the dollar are directly involved. For example, a Japanese company selling goods to a Peruvian company may denominate the sale in dollars so that the Peruvian importer converts soles into dollars, and the Japanese exporter converts dollars into yen.

Exhibit 4.1 New York Foreign Exchange Selling Rates

Country	U.S. Dollar Equivalent		Currency per U.S. Dollar	
	Thurs.	Wed.	Thurs.	Wed.
Brazil (cruzeiro)	0.001079	0.001079	926.50	926.50
Britain (pound)	1.4525	1.4480	0.6885	0.6909
30-day forward	1.4534	1.4488	0.6880	0.6902
90-day forward	1.4552	1.4506	0.6872	0.6893
180-day forward	1.4574	1.4527	0.6861	0.6883
Canada (dollar)	0.8038	0.8034	1.2441	1.2446
30-day forward	0.8039	0.8039	1.2438	1.2438
90-day forward	0.8042	0.8042	1.2434	1.2434
180-day forward	0.8049	0.8049	1.2424	1.2423
France (franc)	0.1200	0.1199	8.3300	8.3400
30-day forward	0.1198	0.1196	8.3470	8.3570
90-day forward	0.1190	0.1189	8.4000	8.4080
180-day forward	0.1178	0.1176	8.4900	8.4975
Switzerland (franc)	0.4587	0.4585	2.1800	2.1810
30-day forward	0.4613	0.4610	2.1675	2.1690
90-day forward	0.4657	0.4656	2.1473	2.1477
180-day forward	0.4726	0.4723	2.1158	2.1170
Venezuela (bolivar)				
Official rate	0.1941	0.1941	5.15	5.15
Floating rate	0.07836	0.07836	12.76	12.76
West Germany (mark)	0.3676	0.3669	2.7205	2.7255
30-day forward	0.3688	0.3681	2.7111	2.7160
90-day forward	0.3713	0.3705	2.6934	2.6985
180-day forward	0.3747	0.3739	2.6689	2.6739

The Wall Street Journal, 3 January 1984, p. 53.

Sometimes, *cross rates* are quoted. Technically, a cross rate is an exchange rate that is computed from two other rates. Since most foreign currency transactions deal with dollars, it is common to use the dollar exchange rate to compute the cross rate, although any two currencies could be used. Using the U.S. dollar as the common currency to compute a cross rate, the spot rates for German marks and Swiss francs in Exhibit 4.1 were

DM 2.7205 per U.S. $

SwF 2.1800 per U.S. $

The cross rate would be

$$\frac{\text{DM } 2.7205}{\text{SwF } 2.1800} = \text{DM } 1.2479 \text{ per SwF}$$

which means that one Swiss franc equals 1.2479 German marks.

The cross rate is often stated as 124.8. German and Swiss businesspersons keep track of the cross rate because they trade extensively with each other. Any material shifts in the cross rate could change the local currency equivalent of foreign goods and thus alter trade flows. For example, at a cross rate of 1.2480, a Swiss product being sold to a German wholesaler for SwF 100 would cost DM 124.8. If the cross rate were to move to 1.2640, the same product would cost DM 126.4, which might be higher than the market is willing to bear.

Forward Market

As mentioned earlier, the forward rate is a contract rate between a foreign currency trader and customer for future sale or purchase of foreign currency. During a period of foreign exchange stability, there may be no difference between the current spot and forward rate. However, there normally is a difference, known as the *spread*, between the spot and forward rate. In Exhibit 4.1, for example, forward rates are quoted for several currencies. The spot and 90-day forward rates quoted for pounds and marks are as follows:

	British Pounds	French Francs
Spot	$1.4525	$0.1200
90-day forward	$1.4552	0.1190
Points	+ 27	− 10

The spread in pounds is 0.0027 [$1.4552 − $1.4525] or 27 points. Because the forward rate is more than the spot rate, the pound is selling at a *premium* of 27 points. The spread in French francs is 0.0010, or 10 points. Because the forward rate is less than the spot rate, the franc is selling at a *discount* of 10 points.

The premium or discount is normally quoted at the number of points above or below the spot rate, but it could also be expressed in annualized percentage terms. The formula used to determine the percentage is as follows:

$$\text{Premium (discount)} = \frac{F_0 - S_0}{S_0} \times \frac{12}{N} \times 100$$

where F_0 is the forward rate on the day that the contract is entered into, S_0 is the spot rate on that day, N is the number of months forward, and 100 is used to convert the decimal to percentages (i.e., $0.05 \times 100 = 5\%$).
Using pounds sterling,

$$\text{Premium} = \frac{\$1.4552 - \$1.4525}{\$1.4525} \times \frac{12}{3} \times 100 = 0.7435\% \text{ (less than 1\%)}$$

which means that the pound is selling at a premium of 0.7435% over the dollar spot rate.

Using the French franc example,

$$\text{Discount} = \frac{\$0.1190 - \$0.1200}{0.1200} \times \frac{12}{3} \times 100 = -3.3333\%$$

which means that the French franc is selling at a 3.3333% discount under the dollar spot rate.

FOREIGN EXCHANGE MARKETS AND INSTRUMENTS

Commercial Banks

Before discussing the major determinants of spot and forward rates, it would be useful to consider the actual market in which foreign currency is traded. There is no question that the U.S. dollar is the most important trading currency in the international monetary system. In addition, the dollar is the major reserve asset held by most countries. With respect to the U.S. market, it was determined in a 1983 survey conducted by the U.S. Federal Reserve Board that foreign exchange transactions had increased in volume in the United States by 50% to $998.4 billion over a survey conducted in 1980.[1] The majority of those transactions, 70.4%, was carried out by the commercial banks, with the rest being conducted by foreign exchange brokers. Brokers are specialists that facilitate transactions between banks rather than have the banks work directly with each other.

In terms of currencies traded, the German mark was the most popular in the U.S. with 32.7% of the market, followed by the Japanese yen with 22%, the British pound with 16.6%, the Swiss franc with 12.2%, and the Canadian dollar with 7.5%.

As mentioned earlier, the foreign exchange market is basically divided into spot and forward markets. Over 63% of all foreign exchange trading was in the spot market, primarily in the interbank market as opposed to transactions between banks and corporate clients. In fact, only 10% of the spot transactions fit in the latter category. Of the remainder of the trading, 33% was in foreign currency swaps, and only 4% in the forward and futures markets.

Earlier in the chapter, swaps were not discussed in detail, because those transactions almost exclusively involve the interbank market rather than the corporate market in foreign exchange. In a swap transaction, the

---

[1]Federal Reserve Bank of Chicago, "International Letter," No. 510, 7 October 1983, pp. 1–3. This is the reference for all of the data in the section on commercial banks.

bank sells (or buys) a specific amount of foreign currency that is to be delivered to another bank on a specific date, and then at the same time it buys (or sells) an equivalent amount of currency for delivery at a later date. Thus, the transaction involves a simultaneous buy and sell of foreign currency with a bank for some point in the future. This is different from the forward contract discussed previously, in which a corporate client agrees to buy or sell foreign currency at some point in the future.

Specialized Markets

Although most foreign exchange transactions take place in the commercial banking sector, it is possible to arrange foreign currency transactions in other ways. In some countries where the foreign exchange market is tightly controlled, a black market often exists. In that market, there is normally a large differential between the official rate and the black market rate, so that foreign currencies would sell at a substantial premium over the official rate. However, it is not always easy to arrange large transfers of money in the black market, and it is not usually wise for the corporate sector to operate in the black market because it is usually illegal.

There are other specialized, legitimate foreign exchange markets that are not a part of the commercial banking sector, however. For example, in the United States there is the *International Monetary Market (IMM)* of the Chicago Mercantile Exchange. The IMM deals in currency futures in the British pound, the Canadian dollar, the West German deutsche mark, the Dutch guilder, the French franc, the Japanese yen, the Swiss franc, and the Mexican peso. Even though this market is a good source of funds for the corporate sector, it is limited in its size and lack of flexibility. Very little trading is done in the French franc, the Mexican peso, or the Dutch guilder, and the maturity dates are fixed rather than flexible according to the cash needs of the corporate client. Also, currencies must be bought and sold in predetermined contract amounts in this market. In spite of its drawbacks, the IMM is increasing in importance in the currency futures market.

Another market that is just beginning to gain in importance is the foreign currency options market on the Philadelphia Exchange. In this market, one may enter into an option to deal in foreign currency (currently British pounds, the Canadian dollar, German marks, Japanese yen, and Swiss francs), but that option does not need to be exercised at maturity as is the case with a forward contract. The market started out at a fairly small level because of its novelty in the United States and relatively high cost, but many experts feel that foreign currency options could be the next major revolution in foreign currency trading.

Most of the discussion in the previous two sections has focused on the bank and corporate involvement in the foreign exchange market. However, *speculators* also play an important part in the psychology of the market as they attempt to profit on anticipated future trends. For example, a speculator who holds dollars and expects the German mark to strengthen vis-à-vis the dollar in the near future may sell dollars for marks. As the mark strengthens to a higher level in the future, the speculator will sell the marks for more dollars and earn a profit on the transaction. If enough speculators move into the market, they may play an active role in causing exchange rates to change.

In contrast to the speculator, the *arbitrageur* is one who takes advantage of differences in national money markets and foreign exchange markets. The arbitrageur is not "betting" on a currency moving in one direction or another but is able to borrow and invest currencies and take advantage of differences in interest rate yields that can result in profits as the yields are exchanged from one currency to another. This profit-opportunity will be discussed more fully in the section on the determinant of forward exchange rates.

Instruments of Payment

How does an importer transfer payment in foreign currency to an exporter in a foreign country? Most corporations do not keep large foreign currency deposits in each of their banks around the world; instead, they utilize commercial banks. The importer could receive a check in foreign currency from its bank, drawn on the bank's foreign branch or correspondent. Then the importer could mail the check directly to the exporter or simply give instructions to the bank and allow the bank to effect payment, or the bank could Telex instructions to its foreign branch or correspondent to effect payment, or send instructions by airmail.

In order to facilitate the flow of money, the exporter may send instructions to the importer in the form of a *commercial bill of exchange*. This instrument tells the importer how payment should be made. Normally, payment is made to the exporter's bank and added to the exporter's account. Payment can be required either at sight (when the importer receives the bill of exchange) or *on time* (a specified time after the importer is presented the bill of exchange). The importer then instructs his or her bank on how to transfer funds to the exporter.

A more formal document to facilitate the flow of money is a *letter of credit*. The importer may instruct his or her bank to issue a letter of credit to the exporter ensuring that the bank will effect payment. If the letter of credit is *irrevocable*, the importer's bank will honor the bill of exchange even if the importer defaults. If the letter of credit is *confirmed irrevocable*, the exporter's bank will honor the bill of exchange even if the importer's bank defaults. Thus, the letter of credit can be used to ensure that the bill of exchange is honored.

THE INTERNATIONAL MONETARY SYSTEM

Although foreign currencies are traded quite freely, there is a form of supranational influence that tries to encourage a certain amount of order.

The *International Monetary Fund* (*IMF*) was created in 1944 with the primary objective of promoting exchange stability. At that time, the currencies of 133 member countries were assigned a fixed exchange rate or par value based on gold and the U.S. dollar; gold was worth $35 an ounce, and currencies were quoted on that basis. Currencies were allowed to float freely in a band of 1% on either side of par value. However, stability did not last forever, and major changes began in the 1970s. Countries like Brazil were constantly devaluing their currency, permanently decreasing the par value in terms of gold and the dollar. Others were experiencing periodic changes, such as the British pound in 1967. But the major trading currencies were still adhering fairly well to par values. In December 1971, the IMF allowed the U.S. dollar to formally devalue and also allowed currencies to float 2¼% on either side of par value without a formal devaluation or revaluation.

Continued pressure on the dollar in early 1973 forced another devaluation, with subsequent instability finally forcing the major trading countries of the world to break loose from the fixed rate system into one of greater flexibility.

Exchange Rate Arrangements

As part of the move to greater flexibility, the IMF permitted countries to select and maintain an exchange arrangement of their choice, as long as they properly communicated their arrangement to the Fund. Each year, the Fund receives information from the member countries and classifies each country into one of three broad categories: (1) currencies that are pegged to a single currency or to a composite of currencies, (2) currencies whose exchange rates have displayed limited flexibility compared with either a single currency or group of currencies, and (3) currencies whose exchange rates are more flexible.[2] Exhibit 4.2 illustrates greater refinement of these breakdowns and includes the number of countries in each category as of March 31, 1983.

Pegged Rates

Countries that fit in the pegged category are so listed because they peg their currency with zero fluctuation margins (in the case of countries that peg to a single currency) or very narrow margins of 1% or less in the case of pegs to the *Special Drawing Right* (*SDR*) or other composite currency. An SDR is an international reserve asset created by the Fund to supplement existing reserve assets. The SDR can be used by member countries to trade for other currencies, or it can be retained as a reserve asset to be used at some point in the future. The SDR was originally linked to gold, but its value is now derived from a basket of currencies: the U.S. dollar, West

[2]International Monetary Fund, *Annual Report on Exchange Arrangements and Exchange Restrictions—1983* (Washington, D.C.: IMF, June 3, 1983), p. 7.

Exhibit 4.2 Exchange Rate Arrangements as of March 31, 1983

Type of Arrangement	Number of Countries	
Pegged	94	
To the U.S. dollar		38
To the French franc		13
To another currency		5
To the SDR		15
To another composite		23
Limited flexibility	18	
To a single currency		10
Cooperative arrangements		8
More flexible	33	
Adjusted according to a set of indicators		5
Other managed floating		20
Independently floating		8
	145	145

Source: Information from International Monetary Fund, *Annual Report* (Washington, D.C.: IMF, 1983), p. 8. This report includes information for all IMF countries except Democratic Kampuchea, for which no information was available.

German deutsche mark, the Japanese yen, the French franc, and the British pound sterling. The assumption behind pegging a currency to the SDR is that the SDR value of the currency should have less variability than would the currency if it were linked to only one currency, such as the U.S. dollar.

The "other composite" category means that the country has selected a basket of currencies that is different from the SDR. An example of this would be the renminbi, the currency of the People's Republic of China. The exchange rate is adjusted according to a basket of internationally traded currencies weighted with reference to their importance in China's external transactions and the trends in their relative values. The basket is composed of 23 currencies, including the U.S. dollar, the Canadian dollar, and the British pound.

Limited Flexibility

In the "limited flexibility" category, there are two subcategories. In the first of these, "limited flexibility to a single currency," the exchange rates fluctuate within a 2¼% margin. In all ten cases, the limited flexibility has been with respect to the U.S. dollar.

The other subcategory, "cooperative arrangements," refers to the *European Monetary System (EMS)*. The EMS was created in 1979 as an attempt to strengthen the old "snake" relationship that had been in existence for several years in the European Economic Community. The idea behind the snake was that the participating currencies would be held within a fairly narrow range of flexibility against each other, but the currencies as a group would float freely against outside currencies. The EMS links together the currencies of all European Economic Community members except the United Kingdom and Greece in two ways: through a European Currency Unit (ECU) and a parity grid.

The ECU is a basket of all EC currencies (except the Greek drachma, which is due to be introduced into the ECU by December 31, 1985) weighted by the importance of each economy. Once the value of one ECU is determined, a central exchange rate is determined for each currency in the basket, which results in the number of units of that currency for each ECU. At that point, the ECU becomes a numeraire, since each currency would have an established value per ECU. The parity grid is really a set of defined bilateral relationships between the various currencies of the EMS. For example, to find the bilateral central rate of the deutsche mark and French franc, one would simply divide the ECU central exchange rate of the DM with that of the FF to find the number of DM per FF. The bilateral central rate is then used to determine when intervention must occur. With the exception of the Italian lira, which allows a fluctuation of 6% from the bilateral central rates before intervention, bilateral rates are allowed to deviate from the central rates by only 2¼% before the respective central banks must intervene to protect the integrity of the central rate.

In addition to the use of the grid to determine intervention limits, there is a more complex process called the threshold divergence. Although that process is beyond the scope of this chapter, its purpose is to permit intervention even before the intervention limits just described are reached.

More Flexibility

The final major category of currencies is that of "more flexibility." Those currencies, including the currencies of Canada, Israel, Japan, Lebanon, South Africa, the United Kingdom, the United States, and Uruguay, float independently. That means that if government intervention does occur, it is only to influence but not neutralize the speed of movement of the exchange rate change. In the "other managed floating" category, governments usually set rates for short intervals, such as a week at a time, and buy and sell the currency at that rate for that period. The final subcategory includes currencies that are managed according to a set of indicators. The Brazilian cruzeiro, for example, is adjusted at relatively short intervals in terms of the U.S. dollar. The degree of adjustment depends on "the movement of prices in Brazil relative to that in its main trading partners, the level of foreign exchange reserves, export performance, and the overall balance of payments positioning."[3]

Multiple Exchange Rates

The foregoing discussion makes it appear that each exchange rate fits on a continuum of inflexibility to high flexibility. However, exchange rates are a bit more complex than that. According to the statutes of the IMF, member countries are not supposed to engage in multiple exchange rates without approval of the Fund. Multiple exchange rates, as defined by the Fund, include "separate exchange rates (through the mechanism of dual or multiple exchange markets, the establishment of separate official exchange rates for specified transactions, or the application of exchange measures, including exchange taxes or subsidies, and excessive exchange rate spreads), broken cross rates, or discriminatory currency arrangements."[4] About one third of the countries in the IMF practice some form of multiple rates, and most of these have been approved by the Fund.

DETERMINATION OF RATES

Spot Rate

The foreign exchange market has developed in recent years into a highly competitive market based primarily on the forces of supply and demand. The major actors in the market are foreign exchange traders of commercial banks, corporate treasurers, speculators, and national central banks. Their desire to buy or sell foreign currency is a combination of foreign currency balances they currently hold, anticipated changes in the spot rate, and anticipated future needs for foreign currency. Actors buy and sell foreign exchange for routine business transactions—trade, investment, working capital needs—as well as for profit seeking. What are the major determinants of rate changes?

Purchasing power parity (PPP) is one of the most important determinants of the value of a currency. PPP theory establishes a relationship between the relative rates of inflation of two countries and a change in the exchange rate. The theory maintains that if the prices of goods in two countries are not equalized by the exchange rate, the flow of trade will eventually force the exchange rate to change, in the absence of intervention or protectionism. For example, assume that an automobile sells for $10,000 in the United States and ¥2,327,000 in Japan when the exchange rate is ¥232.7 per dollar. If the price of the U.S. auto were to rise to $11,000 due to inflation while the price of the auto in Japan and the exchange rate were to

---

[3]Ibid., p. 111.
[4]Ibid., p. 40.

remain stable, U.S. consumers would begin to buy more Japanese autos, and U.S. autos would become even less competitive in Japan. The theory of PPP implies that the exchange rate would have to change to ¥211.55 per dollar in order to equalize the prices (¥2,327,000/$11,000 = ¥211.55). Thus, relatively higher inflation rates in one country vis-à-vis another are to be reflected by a weakening of that country's exchange rate. This makes sense in traditional economic theory, since an increase in demand for Japanese goods would lead to an increase in demand for its currency and thus an increase in price vis-à-vis the U.S. dollar.

Interest rates are also important determinants of a country's exchange rate, as can be seen in the value of the dollar during the early 1980s. As interest rates in the U.S. began to rise in late 1980 in relation to those of other countries, the value of the dollar began to rise. This was due to the fact that investors preferred to put their money into dollars in order to get a higher return. Of course, the lowering of inflation at that time in the United States yielded relatively high real interest rates, a key factor in the desire of others to hold dollars. The demand for dollars tended to push up the dollar's value.

An important determinant in a world of political and economic uncertainty is that of *confidence*. During times of turmoil, people would prefer to hold currencies that are considered safe haven currencies. During the early 1980s, the U.S. dollar was considered a safe haven currency, and this perception was an important source of strength for the currency. Conversely, when the Mexican peso began to slide, local investors were transferring large amounts of pesos out of Mexico by means of dollar transfers until the Mexican government clamped down. The investors had no confidence in the peso and preferred to hold dollar balances outside of Mexico.

In addition to the basic economic forces and confidence in leadership, a number of *technical factors* influence exchange rates, such as the release of national economic statistics, seasonal demands for a currency, and a slight strengthening of a currency following a prolonged weakness or vice versa. *Arbitrage* is another factor that causes rates to change, and it can occur in terms of exchange rates and interest rates. Arbitrage in the foreign exchange spot market occurs when an arbitrageur is able to make a profit by buying and selling currencies simultaneously in different markets. For example, assume the following rates in the following markets:

	Actual Rates	Equilibrium Rates
United States	$0.5366/DM	$0.5366/DM
West Germany	DM3.70/£	DM3.8021/£
United Kingdom	$2.0500/£	$2.0402/£

At the equilibrium rates, a speculator could trade $1000 for deutsche marks in the United States, trade marks for pounds in West Germany, trade pounds for dollars in the United Kingdom, and still end up with $1000. If the actual rates were quoted as listed, he or she could obtain a profit of $32.53 as shown below:

United States $1000 ÷ $0.5366 = DM1,863.5855

West Germany DM1,863.5855 ÷ 3.70 = £503.67175

United Kingdom £503.67175 × $2.0500 = $1032.53

Profit $1032.53 − $1000 = $32.53

However, the market would soon recognize such differences in rates, and as funds flow from one country to another, rates would quickly move back to an equilibrium position.

Foreign exchange traders are the ones who actually quote the rates that make up the spot market. What do they consider? Some of the major factors are (1) the price and size of recent transactions in the market, (2) trends by direction and time, (3) impending events concerning the economy and political stability of a country as brought out in news releases and elsewhere, (4) information from other currency centers when the market is especially volatile, (5) the time of day and day of the week, and (6) the currency position of the trader.[5] These factors are all closely related to the issues mentioned earlier.

Pressures can mount against a currency, and when they do, a number of things can occur, depending on the exchange arrangement its currency operates under, as discussed previously. A country may move to correct the fundamental imbalances in its economy by slowing down inflation and encouraging the development of export industries. The country may attempt to correct a run on its currency by rationing foreign exchange through licensing or through multiple exchange rates as described earlier.

In addition to these measures, a government may either intervene to support its currency or allow its currency to change in value. Intervention is usually accomplished by having the central bank of the country buy its currency in exchange for foreign currency (in order to create demand and therefore increase or stabilize the value) or sell its currency (in order to increase supply in foreign markets and depress or stabilize the price). Allowing a currency to change value depends on the exchange rate mechanism in use, as explained earlier in the chapter. A freely floating currency simply changes according to supply and demand. A strengthening of the currency is often called a revaluation, upvaluation, or appreciation, whereas a weakening of the currency is often called a devaluation or depreciation.

A currency that is pegged to another currency or to some type of composite in a narrow peg or limited flexibility is usually changed on a

[5]"An Inside View of the Foreign Exchange Market," Chase Manhattan Bank N.A., 1976, pp. 11–12.

formal basis with respect to its reference currency or currencies. This formal change is more accurately termed a devaluation or revaluation, depending on which direction the change occurs. The percentage change depends on whether one uses the direct or indirect method to quote exchange rates. For example, in February 1982, the Brazilian cruzeiro was changed by 23.3% against the dollar in what was termed a maxidevaluation. The Brazilian government had been using minidevaluations, or relatively small devaluations against the dollar at frequent intervals for a number of years. However, on February 21, 1982, the maxidevaluation was announced because the government felt that the minidevaluations were inadequate to accelerate the Brazilian balance of payments adjustment process. The percentage change can be determined as follows:

	Direct Quote[a] (in the U.S.)	Indirect Quote (in the U.S.)
Predevaluation	U.S.$0.003431709	Cr$291.4
Postdevaluation	U.S.$0.00263123	Cr$380.5

[a]The direct and indirect quotes are reciprocals of each other.

$$\text{Percentage change (direct)} = \frac{\text{Ending Rate} - \text{Beginning rate}}{\text{Beginning rate}} \times 100$$

$$= \frac{0.00263123 - 0.003431709}{0.003431709} \times 100 = -23.3\%$$

$$\text{Percentage change (indirect)} = \frac{\text{Beginning rate} - \text{Ending rate}}{\text{Ending rate}} \times 100$$

$$= \frac{291.4 - 380.5}{380.5} = -23.4\% \text{ (differences are due to rounding)}$$

Forward Rate

Someone who wants to buy or sell foreign currency in the future at a predetermined price can do it with a *forward contract*. Most forward contracts are entered into with a commercial bank at a contractual exchange rate called the *forward rate*. The accounting for and use of forward contracts are discussed in detail in subsequent chapters; however, one example of a contract would be useful at this point.

Assume that the British subsidiary of a U.S. company declares a dividend that will be paid to the parent in 90 days. The parent company, which deals in dollars, is concerned because the dividend will be received in British pounds. If the parent does nothing, the dollar equivalent of the dividend may fall over the next 90 days if the exchange rate changes. The parent could enter into a forward contract to deliver pounds to the bank in 90 days in return for dollars at a set forward contract rate. Thus, a fixed amount of dollars will be received no matter what the actual spot rate is when the dividend is received. For example, if a dividend of £1,000,000 is declared by a British subsidiary when the spot rate is $1.4525, the U.S.

parent could expect to receive $1,425,000. If the dividend is not to be paid for 90 days, however, there is no way of knowing what the dollar equivalent of the dividend will be. If the firm enters into a forward contract to deliver pounds for dollars in 90 days at $1.4552, it is guaranteed of receiving $1,455,200.

Forward markets do not exist for all currencies, and factors influencing the setting of rates vary from currency to currency. *The Wall Street Journal* lists forward rates for the British pound, Canadian dollar, French franc, Japanese yen, Swiss franc, and West German mark. Markets can be found for other currencies as well, but it could be that only the central banks of the specific countries will quote them, not commercial banks.

One of the most important determinants for the forward rate is the *interest rate differential,* as illustrated in the following example. Assume that the spot rate for pounds is $1.4525, the interest rate on a 90-day U.S. Treasury bill is 10% per annum, and the interest rate on a British debt instrument of similar risk and maturity is 9.3%. If investors were positive that the exchange rate would not change, they would always invest in the US debt instrument because it has a higher yield. But as more pounds were invested in the United States, it would become clear that in 90 days there would be a surplus of dollars on the market as the investors liquidated their U.S. dollar investments back into pounds.

This surplus of dollars would cause the spot rate to rise, and each investor would face the prospect of getting fewer pounds back for each dollar invested. Of course, no one knows precisely what the future spot rates will be, and thus the uncertainty and risk might prevent someone from investing in the US instrument.

This is where the forward rate comes in. At least in theory, the forward rate in the example would be the rate that exactly neutralizes the difference in interest rates between the United States and United Kingdom. This forward rate would be computed by the foreign trader as shown in Exhibit 4.3.

EXHIBIT 4.3 Determination of Forward Rates

$r_{us} = 10\%$ $S_0 = \$1.4525$

$r_{uk} = 9.3\%$ $F_0 = ?$

N = number of months for the T-bill

$$r_{us} - r_{uk} = \frac{F_0 - S_0}{S_0} \times \frac{12}{N}$$

$$S_0(r_{us} - r_{uk})\left(\frac{N}{12}\right) + S_0 = F_0$$

$$1.4525 \times (0.10 - 0.093) \times \frac{3}{12} + 1.4525 = F_0$$

$$\$1.4550 = F_0$$

Exhibit 4.4 Investment Yields I

1. Convert dollars to pounds at the spot rate.	$1000 ÷ $1.4525 = £688.468
2. Invest the pounds at 9.3% for three months.	688.468 + 688.468(0.093 × 3/12) = £704.475
3. At the same time, enter into a forward contract to deliver £704.475 for dollars.	
4. At the end of three months, deliver the pounds and receive dollars at the forward rate.	£704.475 × $1.4550 = $1025.01

At this forward rate, there is no incentive for someone to invest in the United States as opposed to the United Kingdom or vice versa. For example, if someone were to invest $1000 in the United States for three months, the yield would be

$$\$1000 + \$1000(0.10 \times 3/12) = \$1025$$

A similar investment of $1000 in the United Kingdom would yield $1025.01, as shown in Exhibit 4.4.

If investors were to move out of dollars and into pounds, for whatever reason, the demand would cause either interest rates or exchange rates to move to a new equilibrium level. Thus, the forward rate allows investors to freely trade currencies for future delivery at no exchange risk and without any differential in interest income. If a difference were to exist, traders would engage in *interest arbitrage*. This means that they would sell one currency for another and invest in the latter currency if the difference in interest rates exceeded the difference in exchange rates. Assume the same information as in the previous example except that the forward rate is $1.50. Exhibit 4.5 illustrates the possible yields of $1000 for a U.S. investor.

Exhibit 4.5 Investment Yields II

United States

Invest $1000 at 10% per annum for 90 days (¼ year)	$1000 + 1000 \times \dfrac{0.10}{4} = \$1025$

United Kingdom

1. Convert $1000 into pounds at the spot rate:	$1000 \times \dfrac{1}{1.4525} = £688.468$
2. Invest the pounds for 90 days:	$688.468 + 688.468\left(0.093 \times \dfrac{3}{12}\right) = £704.475$
3. Sell pounds forward for 90 days to cover the principle and interest:	£704.475 × $1.50 = $1056.71

In this situation it is obvious that investors would rather invest in the United Kingdom than in the United States. However, the flow of funds would cause the spot rate, the forward rate, or the interest rates to change to the equilibrium position.

Although the interest rate differential is the critical factor for a few of the most widely traded currencies, the expectation of future spot rates is also very important. Normally, a trader will automatically compute the forward rate through the interest rate differential and then adjust it for future expectations, where deemed necessary. Some forward rates are quoted strictly on future expectations rather than interest rate differentials. This would be especially true for currencies not traded very widely and for which total convertibility does not exist.

FORECASTING EXCHANGE RATE MOVEMENTS

There are a variety of factors that have an influence on exchange rate movements, and it is possible to analyze these factors in order to have a general idea of the timing, size, and direction of an exchange rate movement. However, prediction is not a precise science, and many things can cause the best of predictions to differ significantly from reality. Another problem with predictions is that different exchange rate regimes react differently. For example, a currency whose value is tied to another currency is very different from a currency whose value floats freely against all currencies. For currencies that are not floating relatively freely in currency markets, the political dimension is extremely important. Governments do not always allow rates to change according to pure economic reasons in the short run. This is especially crucial in the timing dimension of a rate change. In spite of the difficulties involved in forecasting, it is still important to look at some predictive indicators based on the discussion in the previous section on the determinants of exchange rates.

Relative Rates of Inflation

Purchasing power parity theory is one of the most important dimensions to consider in forecasting exchange rate changes, because inflation affects not only the relative costs and therefore competitiveness of goods worldwide but also the confidence that actors have in the government of a country. In looking at inflation, one must study the fundamentals that underly inflation, such as government fiscal and monetary policy, as well as the actual rates of inflation in an historical context.

In order to relate inflation to exchange rate changes, the following formula can be used:[6]

---

[6]A more detailed discussion of the determination of the following formula can be found in Alan C. Shapiro, *Multinational Financial Management* (Boston: Allyn & Bacon, Inc., 1982), pp. 39–41.

Inflation/Exchange Formula

$$\frac{e_t - e_0}{e_0} = \frac{i_{h,t} - i_{f,t}}{1 + i_{f,t}}$$

where e = the spot exchange quoted in terms of the number of units of the home currency for one unit of the foreign currency

i = the rate of inflation

h = the home currency

f = the foreign currency

0 = the base period

t = the end of a period

The anticipated future rate would equal

$$e_t = e_0 \times \left[1 + \frac{i_{h,t} - i_{f,t}}{1 + i_{f,t}}\right]$$

For example, on August 31, 1976, the Mexican peso was devalued from 12.5 pesos per dollar ($0.08 per peso) to 20.5 pesos per dollar (approximately $0.0488 per peso), the only devaluation to take place in the peso since 1954. In looking at some data, the consumer price index in Mexico went from 57.2 in 1955 to 176.8 in 1975; the same figures for the United States were 69.0 and 138.6. Using the formula given above,

$$i_{h,t} = \frac{138.6 - 69.0}{69.0} = 1.01$$

$$i_{f,t} = \frac{176.8 - 57.2}{57.2} = 2.09$$

$$e_t = 0.08 \times \left[1 + \frac{1.01 - 2.09}{1 + 2.09}\right]$$

$$= \$0.05204 \text{ per peso}$$

or 19.2 pesos per dollar compared with the actual amounts of $0.0488 per peso or 20.5 pesos per dollar.

It is difficult to pick a starting point when relative prices and exchange rates are in equilibrium, and it is also difficult to forecast inflation in order to predict exchange rate changes, but PPP can be a useful measure along with other inputs.

Balance of Payments Statistics

The *balance of payments* of a country summarizes the international transactions that take place in a given year. These transactions involve the flow of goods, services, and financial claims, and they affect and are affected by the value of currencies. Exhibit 4.6 summarizes the major categories of statistics collected annually for U.S. purposes.

Exhibit 4.6 U.S. International Transactions—1982

	1982
Exports of goods and services	*350,088*
Merchandise, adjusted, excluding military	211,013
Military	12,615
Services	126,460
Imports of goods and services	*−350,313*
Merchandise, adjusted, excluding military	−247,344
Military	−11,975
Services	−90,994
Unilateral transfers (excluding military grants of goods and services), net	*−7,868*
U.S. assets abroad, net [increase/capital outflow (−)]	*−118,265*
Foreign assets in the United States, net [increase/capital inflow (+)]	*84,494*
Statistical discrepancy (sum of above items with sign reversed)	*41,864*

Source: Survey of Current Business (Washington, D.C.: U.S. Department of Commerce, March 1983, p. 51).

Exports and imports are divided into two categories: merchandise trade and other goods and services. The first category features the trade most people are familiar with, such as grain exports and television imports. *Services* involve a variety of transactions such as foreign travel expenses, fees and royalties (such as earnings from showing U.S. movies and television shows abroad), and income from foreign investments. *Unilateral transfers* result from sending money or goods abroad without receiving anything in return, such as sending relief supplies to a country devastated by an earthquake. The transactions under *U.S. assets abroad* include changes in U.S. official reserve assets (such as gold, special drawing rights, and foreign currencies), foreign direct investment, and the purchase of foreign securities. The *foreign assets in the U.S.* category refers to foreign investment in the United States, the purchase of U.S. securities, and so on.

In analyzing the balance of payments for a country, it is important to understand the nature of the economy. It would be important to focus on the balance of trade for a country like Mexico because a large part of its foreign exchange earnings comes from oil exports. On the other hand, the services account is also important because tourism is an important factor for Mexico, and tourism transactions are accounted for in the services account. Thus, one must pay attention to trends in the balance of payments and the factors that may affect those trends in the future.

The impact of the balance of payments on a country's currency is obvious. If a country is constantly running a deficit in its balance of trade and current account balance, it is spending more than it is earning. This results in a drop in its foreign exchange assets or an increase in liabilities in the form of its currency being held abroad. As the world is flooded with more and more of the country's currency, the value of that currency must eventually fall.

Reserve Position

A country's international reserve position identifies how much the country has available in foreign currencies, monetary gold, and SDRs and how much it has available to borrow from the IMF. It is important to keep track of that position and any changes that may be occurring. For example, a large deficit in the balance of payments may indicate a future depreciation in the currency, but if the country has a large reserve position, it may be possible to forgo a depreciation in the short term.

Interest Rate Differentials

As mentioned earlier, a difference in real interest rates may imply that there will be a strong demand for the currency of the country with the higher interest rate, leading to an increase in price or at least continued strength. This has been a factor in the strength of the U.S. dollar in recent years. Thus, one would want to monitor trends in real interest rates and forecasts of those rates in the future. As one tries to forecast changes in interest rates, it would be important to keep track of the growth in money supply, fiscal policy, and similar economic indicators.

Trends in Spot Rates

Although it is always dangerous to forecast the future based strictly on the past, it would also be unwise to ignore past trends. These movements can be compared with other indicators, such as rates of inflation, to help predict future movements.

The Forward Rate

The forward rate is an unbiased predictor of the future spot rate, meaning that the forward rate is not systematically above or below the future spot rate. The forward rate also takes into account important economic fundamentals, such as interest rate differentials, so it is reasonable to assume that the forward spot rate would closely approximate the future spot rate.

SUMMARY

- An exchange rate is the amount of one currency that must be given to acquire one unit of another currency. The spot rate refers to a quote on current transactions; the forward rate is a contractual rate between the foreign exchange trader and his or her client for delivery of foreign exchange in the future.

- Exchange rates are typically quoted on a direct basis, which is the amount of local currency equivalent to one unit of the foreign currency. The indirect quote is the reciprocal of the direct quote.
- The difference between the forward rate and the spot rate is called the spread. If that difference is positive, the foreign currency is at a premium; if it is negative, the foreign currency is at a discount.
- Commercial banks handle the majority of foreign currency transactions worldwide, and most transactions take place in the spot market. The U.S. dollar is the most widely traded currency in the world, whereas the most important foreign currencies traded in the United States are the German mark, the Japanese yen, the British pound, the Swiss franc, and the Canadian dollar.
- In addition to the commercial banking sector, foreign currencies (especially foreign currency futures) can be bought and sold on the International Monetary Market of the Chicago Mercantile Exchange.
- Several instruments are used to facilitate the flow of foreign exchange, such as the commercial bill of exchange, which provides instructions on the method of payment, and the letter of credit, which is an even more formal document that links the flow of goods with the terms of payment.
- The International Monetary Fund was organized in 1944 by the United Nations to promote exchange rate stability in the world. Currently, the IMF classifies exchange rate regimens accordingly: currencies that are pegged to a single currency or to a composite of currencies, currencies whose exchange rates have displayed limited flexibility compared with either a single currency or group of currencies, and currencies whose exchange rates are more flexible. The U.S. dollar, British pound, and Canadian dollar fit the last category.
- The most important determinants of the spot exchange rate are purchasing power parity (the relationship between inflation and the exchange rate), interest rates, confidence in a country's government and economy, technical factors, and arbitrage. The forward rate for currencies that are dealt with in commercial banking sector are determined primarily by interest rate differentials between the two countries.
- When forecasting exchange rate movements, it is important to consider relative rates of inflation, balance of payments statistics, the international reserve position of the country, interest rate differentials, trends in the spot rate, and the forward rate.

Study Questions

4-1. Compute the direct and indirect rates between the Israeli shekel and the Lebanese pound given the U.S. dollar is equivalent to 107.53 shekels or 5.45 pounds.

4-2. The Italian lira closed the 1983 year at a 0.0006044 U.S. dollar equivalent and a

0.00119423 Chinese yuan equivalent. In direct terms, one dollar is worth how many yuan?

4-3. The spot and forward rates for the Swiss franc are as follows:

Country	U.S. $ Equivalent
Switzerland (franc)	
Spot rate	0.4602
30-day forward	0.4636
90-day forward	0.4813
180-day forward	0.4723

Compute the spread points for each forward contract and its respective annual percentage premium or discount.

4-4. The spot and forward rates for the British pound are as follows:

Country	U.S. $ Equivalent
Britain (pound)	
Spot rate	1.4501
30-day forward	1.3986
90-day forward	1.1212
180-day forward	0.9911

Compute the spread points for each forward contract and its respective annual percentage premium or discount.

4-5. What is the spot rate for the French franc if the franc was selling at a 4.5% premium on a 0.1314 U.S. dollar equivalent 30-day forward contract?

4-6. The German mark is selling at a 4.5% discount on a 180-day forward contract. What is the forward dollar equivalent rate given a spot rate of $0.3682?

4-7. Given the following currency changes in relation to the dollar answer the following:

a. What is the ending exchange rate in terms of local currency units per dollar?

b. What are the ending exchange rates in terms of number of dollars per unit of Brazilian cruzeiro and Swiss franc, respectively?

c. What are the exchange rates between the cruzeiro and franc before and after the changes?

Currency	Initial Exchange Rate per Dollar	Change Relative to Dollar
Brazilian cruzeiro	981.50	20% devaluation
Swiss franc	2.2180	5% revaluation

4-8. Assume the following initial exchange rates and changes in relation to the U.S. dollar:

Currency	Initial Exchange Rate per Dollar	Change Relative to Dollar
Saudi Arabian riyal	3.5000	32.4% revaluation
Irish punt	0.8810	13.8% devaluation

a. What are the ending exchange rates per dollar for the riyal and punt, respectively?
b. In terms of the dollar, what are the ending indirect rates for the riyal and punt?
c. What are the exchange rates between the riyal and punt before and after the changes?

4-9. Assume the following exchange rates:

Location	Actual Rates $/£	$/FF	FF/£
New York	2.1212	0.2231	—
Paris	—	0.2500	FF9.7134
London	2.0177	—	FF9.9435

What is the maximum profit in French francs that an arbitrager could earn by trading FF1000? Why is this a riskless profit?

4-10. Given the following exchange rates:

Location	Actual Rates $/DM	$/SF	SF/DM
Chicago	0.3679	0.1195	—
Frankfurt	—	0.1228	0.3248
Zurich	0.3704	—	0.3400

What is the maximum profit in German marks that an arbitrager could earn by trading DM1000?

4-11. Given the following rates:

Spot	$0.2513/FF
60-day forward	$0.2553/FF
Interest—U.S.	11%/year
Interest—France	8%/year

a. For someone who had $1000, what steps would be involved in interest rate arbitrage?
b. What is the total profit, assuming no transaction costs?
c. Assuming that the interest rates are current, what would be the equilibrium forward rate?
d. Assuming that the forward rate and the French interest rate are correct, what is the equilibrium U.S. interest rate?

4-12. Given the following rates:

Spot	$1.4525/£
90-day forward	$1.4552/£
Interest—U.S.	18%/year
Interest—Britain	12%/year

a. Assume a British friend just gave you £7000. What steps would be involved in an interest rate arbitrage?
b. What is the total profit, assuming no transaction costs?
c. What is the equilibrium forward rate?
d. What is the equilibrium UK interest rate?

Case 1

THE BRAZILIAN CRUZEIRO: TO MAXIDEVALUE OR NOT, THAT IS THE QUESTION

Georgia Romano, the new manager of Industrias Pesadas, S.A., the Brazilian subsidiary of a heavy equipment manufacturing company in the United States, was concerned about the deteriorating Brazilian environment. Georgia knew that her area manager was paranoid about the possibility of a large devaluation of the Brazilian cruzeiro against the dollar, so she decided to look more closely at what was going on and try to decide what to tell the area manager.

Introduction

In 1983, Brazil was falling deeper into industrial recession. The Brazilian finance minister was forecasting no growth for the year, and most bankers expected economic activity to drop by 3.5 to 5%. The predicted decline was partly based on a hangover from depressed world markets for Brazilian exports and partly a reaction to government measures designed to counter inflation, build a trade surplus, and meet debt payments.

The government's austerity program was also designed to satisfy the International Monetary Fund (IMF), which held up disbursements on a $4.9 billion loan agreement. When Brazilian inflation, forecast by the government at 70% for 1983, zoomed to a rate of more than 150%, the IMF stopped payments and sent a new team to Brazilia for more talks.

In response, the government cut back semiannual wage increases to only 80% of the rise in the cost of living from more than 100% previously mandated for most workers. It also promised still tougher curbs on spending by the huge state-owned companies and decreed interest-rate limits that bankers claimed paralyzed commercial lending.

As a result of these measures, the government claimed that "only formalities" remained to implement a new agreement whereby the IMF would resume its disbursement and enable billions of dollars to be raised from international commercial banks. From the IMF, however, there was no confirmation that things would be quite that simple.

Social Unrest

Austerity programs aside, Brazil's poorest were already in trouble. In major cities, slogans splashed on walls or or on placards carried in protest marches demanded "IMF Out." The president of the São Paulo Metalworkers Federation, which claims to be South America's biggest union, called for "a moratorium [on debt repayment] of one to five years or however long it takes to get the economy going again." The moratorium should be negotiated, but, if necessary, it should be unilateral, he said.

In the favelas, or slums, leftist Catholic priests, allied with the Workers Party, were active in organizing the general strike. "The debt shouldn't be paid, and it won't be paid," said a young seminarian who is part of the movement.

Still, the Brazilian masses ethically favor repayment of debts, say bankers, businesspersons, and pollsters. A nationwide Gallup poll in March 1983 asked Brazilians how the foreign debt should be handled. It found 40% in favor of paying it off "quickly"; 46% favored paying it off "more slowly"; 4% favored "postponing" it; and only 5% wanted to repudiate it. However, a follow-up poll in April found those favoring repudiation had grown to 10%, reported Carlos Matheus, head of the Gallup organization in Brazil.

The change in sentiment may reflect the deepening recession. In the state of São Paulo, which accounts for over half the nation's industrial output, industrial employment had fallen to 1973 levels, according to the State Industrial Federation. The São Paulo Metalworkers Federation said members' employment had fallen to 380,000 from 425,000 at the end of 1981. Bankruptcies in São Paulo were also up sharply.

A fierce debate has developed in the legislature, which cannot be counted on to rubber-stamp the austerity program suggested by the five-year-old government of Brazil's military rulers. Also, Brazil's 12 most prominent businesses, which control more than 200 companies and employ 215,000 workers, called for fundamental changes in government economic policy. Drawing freely on the theories of Celso Furtada, the planning minister in Brazil's last freely elected government, the opposition Brazilian Democratic Movement proposed an IMF-be-damned policy that would unilaterally declare a moratorium on Brazil's debts.

A Struggle to Refinance Debt

The IMF loan agreement covers a three-year, $4.9 billion standby facility to assist in meeting obligations for Brazil's $90 billion to $100 billion debt. In mid-September Brazil signed a letter of intent with the IMF that set new economic targets for the country. The fund had halted disbursal of credits in May because Brazil was not meeting economic targets set earlier.

In addition to the IMF credits, Brazil requested an immediate $3 billion in short-term credits as part of a $6.5 billion new loan it was seeking from commercial

Exhibit 1 Balance of Trade

Date	Exports US$ millions—FOB			Imports US$ millions—FOB			Balance US$ millions—FOB	
	On Date	Up to Date	Percentage Change Up to Date[a]	On Date	Up to Date	Percentage Change Up to Date[a]	On Date	Up to Date
1974	—	7,951	28.3	—	12,641	104.1	—	−4,690
1975	—	8,670	9.0	—	12,210	−3.4	—	−3,840
1976	—	10,128	16.8	—	12,383	1.4	—	−2,255
1977	—	12,120	19.7	—	12,023	−2.9	—	97
1978	—	12,659	4.4	—	13,683	13.8	—	−1,024
1979	—	15,244	20.4	—	18,084	32.2	—	−2,840
1980	—	20,132	32.1	—	22,955	26.9	—	−2,823
1981	—	23,293	15.7	—	22,091	−3.8	—	1,202
1982[b]								
Jan.	1,647	1,647	−2.9	1,653	1,653	−9.6	−6	−6
Feb.	1,439	3,086	−10.1	1,441	3,094	−16.9	−2	−5
March	1,767	4,853	−6.4	1,710	4,804	−14.3	57	29
April	1,569	6,422	−9.1	1,548	6,352	−15.8	21	70

May	1,713	8,135	−9.0	1,701	8,053	−14.3	12	82
June	1,690	9,825	−4.5	1,623	9,676	−13.4	67	149
July	1,757	11,582	−10.3	1,697	11,376	−13.4	60	209
Aug.	1,823	13,405	−10.2	1,725	13,098	−12.4	98	307
Sept.	1,698	15,103	−11.2	1,650	14,748	−12.1	48	356
Oct.	1,606	16,709	−12.6	1,548	16,296	−11.8	58	413
Nov.	1,713	18,422	−13.3	1,506	17,802	−12.1	207	620
Dec.	1,753	20,175	−13.4	1,593	19,395	−12.2	160	780
1983[b]								
Jan.	1,569	1,569	−4.7	1,412	1,412	−14.6	157	57
Feb.	1,376	2,945	−4.6	1,203	2,615	−15.5	173	380
March	1,707	4,652	−4.1	1,209	3,824	−20.7	498	826
April	1,832	6,484	1.0	1,239	5,063	−20.3	593	1,421
May	1,915	8,399	3.2	1,240	6,303	−21.7	675	2,096
June	2,002	10,401	5.9	1,173	7,476	−22.7	829	2,925
July	1,879	12,280	6.0	1,167	8,643	−24.0	712	3,537

[a]In relation to same period of previous year.
[b]Preliminary.
Sources: Cacex and CIEF.

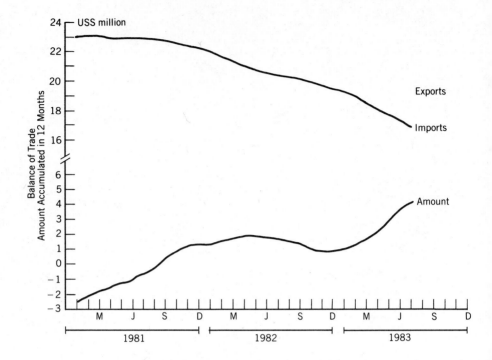

banks. The short-term credits would be used to erase about $2.8 billion in arrearages by the end of the year, allowing Brazil to meet an economic target contained in its IMF loan agreement.

The $6.5 billion in commercial loans would be part of an $11 billion package being assembled to meet Brazil's borrowing needs through 1984. That package would include $2.5 billion in financing from other governments, mostly in the form of trade credits. Governments also would refinance $2 billion already owed by Brazil, whose total foreign debt is about $90 billion.

Brazil in Profile

Once regarded as South America's miracle nation, Brazil is watching in despair as dreams of a golden future evaporate under the weight of social unrest, foreign debt, and economic crisis.

Brazilians normally are the most optimistic of people, with high confidence in themselves and their large country. Brazil's size of 3.3 million square miles is nine tenths the size of the United States. It is the sixth most populous nation in the world, with 131.3 million people.

Total output per person of $2215 is less than one fifth that of the United States. The major industries in Brazil are iron, steel, chemicals, petrochemicals, textiles, cement, and lumber. Exports in these products in 1982 amounted to $20.2 billion while total imports were $19.4 billion. Of Brazilian exports, 20.5% go to the United States, and 14.7% of imports come from the United States (see Exhibit 1).

Brazil is now in its third year of an economic recession. Consumer prices in May were 116.2% higher than a year earlier. The monthly rate for July, 13.3%, was the worst since officials began keeping records in 1944 (see Exhibit 2).

International Reserves

Position	US$ millions
1979	
Dec.	9,688.7
1980	
Dec.	6,912.6
1981	
Jan.	6,627.0
Feb.	6,584.3
March	6,474.5
April	6,272.3
May	6,369.7
June	6,150.2
July	6,232.0
Aug.	6,279.1
Sept.	6,345.6
Oct.	6,407.0
Nov.	6,574.4
Dec.	7,506.8
1982	
Jan.	7,280.1
Feb.	7,079.9
March	7,082.0
April[a]	7,024.9
May[a]	6,893.2
June[a]	6,941.1
July[a]	6,950.7
Aug.[a]	6,970.5

[a]Preliminary.
Source: "The Brazilian Economy," *Brazil Trade and Industry*, September 1983, pp. 41, 42.

Nature has added to the misery, unleashing the worst floods in a century on Brazil's southern states while searing the northeast with a drought that now is in its fifth year.

Brazilian officials contend, though, that the shocks of oil-price increases in the 1970s started the economic slide. At that time, Brazil imported 80% of its oil, and higher costs put a serious crimp on growth.

The jump in oil costs was followed by a surge in international interest rates on the vast amount of money Brazil had borrowed to finance development during the boom years.

Adding to the nation's weakening balance of payments was the sharp deterioration in markets for some of Brazil's key agricultural exports, particularly coffee, that provided a firm foundation for the economy.

Brazil's high level of inflation in relation to other countries has been a major factor in a series of minidevaluations of the Brazilian cruzeiro. Brazil has been announcing minidevaluations of its currency since 1978. Over the past few years

Exhibit 2 Price Indices for the United States and Brazil
(1980 = 100)

	United States		Brazil	
	Wholesale Prices	Consumer Prices	Wholesale Prices	Consumer Prices
1975	65.1	65.3	11.06	12.66
1976	68.1	69.1	15.85	17.98
1977	72.3	73.6	22.58	25.83
1978	77.9	79.2	31.07	35.83
1979	87.7	88.1	48.43	54.71
1980	100.0	100.0	100.00	100.00
1981	109.1	110.4	208.18	205.57
1982	111.4	117.1	399.79	407.00

Source: International Financial Statistics, 1983.

General Price Index–Goods and Services for Domestic Supply (GPI–DS)
Wholesale Price Index–Goods and Services for Domestic Supply (WPI–DS)
Percentage Changes

Months, 1983	Monthly GPI–DS	WPI–DS	Accumulated in Year GPI–DS	WPI–DS	In 12 Months GPI–DS	WPI–DS
Jan.	9.0	9.8	9.0	9.8	104.9	104.3
Feb.	6.5	5.6	16.2	16.0	104.3	102.7
March	10.1	10.7	27.9	28.4	109.7	109.0
April	9.2	10.3	39.6	41.7	117.4	119.0
May	6.7	6.6	49.0	51.0	118.6	121.2
June	12.3	13.7	67.3	71.7	127.2	130.3
July	13.3	14.4	89.6	96.5	142.8	149.5

Source: "The Brazilian Economy," *Brazil Trade and Industry,* September 1983, p. 45.

Exhibit 3 Exchange Value of the Cruzeiro in Number of
Units per U.S. Dollar

Market Rate, End of Year		Market Rate, End of Year	
1971	5.635	1977	16.050
1972	6.215	1978	20.920
1973	6.220	1979	42.530
1974	7.435	1980	65.500
1975	9.070	1981	127.800
1976	12.345	1982	252.670

Source: International Financial Statistics, 1983.

Exchange Rate Variations (Quotations in Relation to American Dollar)

Date	Term in Days	Rates		Percentage Change			
				On Purchase		On Sale	
		Purchase	Sale	Previous	December of Previous Year	Previous	December of Previous Year
12.21.82	6	247.580	248.820	1.6	94.7	1.6	94.7
12.27.82	10	251.410	252.670	1.5	97.7	1.5	97.7
01.06.83	5	255.980	257.260	1.8	1.8	1.8	1.8
01.11.83	8	259.680	260.990	1.4	3.3	1.4	3.3
01.19.83	5	284.780	266.100	2.0	5.3	2.0	5.3
01.24.83	4	269.280	270.630	1.7	7.1	1.7	7.1
01.28.83	6	273.910	275.280	1.7	8.9	1.7	8.9
02.03.83	8	278.700	280.090	1.7	10.9	1.7	10.9
02.11.83	6	288.110	286.540	2.3	13.4	2.3	13.4
02.17.83	4	291.950	293.410	2.4	16.1	2.4	16.1
02.21.83	9	379.540	381.440	30.0	51.0	30.0	51.0
03.02.83	7	386.710	388.640	1.9	53.5	1.9	53.5
03.09.83	7	394.060	346.030	1.9	56.7	1.9	56.7
03.16.83	9	403.320	405.340	2.4	60.4	2.4	60.4
03.25.83	11	415.460	417.540	3.0	65.3	3.0	65.3
04.05.83	8	423.980	426.100	2.1	68.6	2.1	68.6
04.13.83	7	432.290	434.450	2.0	71.9	2.0	71.9
04.20.83	8	440.550	442.750	1.9	75.2	1.9	75.2
04.28.83	7	452.670	454.930	2.8	80.0	2.8	80.0
05.05.83	7	462.000	464.310	2.1	83.8	2.1	83.8
05.12.83	7	471.930	474.290	2.1	87.7	2.1	87.7
05.19.83	8	481.470	483.880	2.0	91.5	2.0	91.5

Exchange Rate Variations (Quotations in Relation to American Dollar) *Continued*

| Date | Term in Days | Rates | | Percentage Change | | | |
| | | Purchase | Sale | On Purchase | | On Sale | |
				Previous	December of Previous Year	Previous	December of Previous Year
05.27.83	6	491.150	493.610	2.0	95.4	2.0	95.4
06.02.83	11	501.960	504.470	2.2	99.7	2.2	99.7
06.13.83	4	512.750	515.310	2.1	103.9	2.1	103.9
06.17.83	6	520.960	523.560	1.6	107.2	1.6	107.2
06.23.83	7	528.250	530.890	1.4	110.1	1.4	110.1
06.30.83	7	540.270	542.970	2.3	114.9	2.3	114.9
07.07.83	7	553.240	556.010	2.4	120.1	2.4	120.1
07.14.83	6	565.960	568.790	2.3	125.1	2.3	125.1
07.20.83	6	581.810	584.720	2.8	131.4	2.8	131.4
07.26.83	3	595.940	599.920	2.6	137.4	2.6	137.4
07.29.83	6	608.880	611.920	2.0	142.2	2.0	142.2
08.04.83	7	622.880	625.990	2.3	147.8	2.3	147.8
08.11.83	7	637.830	641.020	2.4	153.7	2.4	153.7
08.18.83	8	654.000	657.000	2.5	160.1	2.5	160.1
08.26.83	—	668.000	671.000	2.1	166.7	2.1	166.7

Source: "The Brazilian Economy," *Brazil Trade and Industry*, September 1983, p. 40.

these devaluations have averaged about 2% and have been made once every 10 days or so. A "maxidevaluation" of 30% in February was the biggest to have been made in Brazil since 1979 (see Exhibit 3).

The government said in a recent statement that the cruzeiro was devalued mainly because of the "need to accelerate the Brazilian balance-of-payments adjustment process in view of the adverse situation in international markets." The government offset the devaluation's benefits to foreign buyers by raising its export taxes 10 to 30% on a variety of products that the country does not want to make more competitive. Among these is coffee, exports of which are limited under an international agreement.

Brazilian officials had been denying that a major devaluation was in the works. Instead, they hoped to meet their balance of trade goal by continuing the minidevaluations and by holding down imports. After the 30% devaluation in February, the government once again has maintained that it will continue with its series of minidevaluations.

The Brazilian Economy

Brazil's monetary policy is one of expansion. Calculated on the basis of average daily balances, the money supply expanded by an estimated 11.2% in July, or 86.9% in the 12-month period ending in that same month. The monetary base, measured on the basis of the final monthly positions, expanded by 9.8% in July and 97.9% over the previous 12 months.

Bibliography

Eiteman, David K. and Arthur I. Stonehill. *Multinational Business Finance.* 3rd ed. Reading, Mass.: Addison-Wesley Publishing Company, 1983, Chapters 2–4.

George, Abraham M. and Ian H. Giddy, eds. *International Finance Handbook.* New York: John Wiley & Sons, 1983, Part 2.

International Monetary Fund. *Annual Report on Exchange Arrangements and Exchange Restrictions, 1983.* Washington, D.C.: IMF, 1983.

Riehl, Heinz and Rita M. Rodriguez. *Foreign Exchange Markets.* New York: McGraw-Hill Book Company, 1977.

Rodriguez, Rita M. and E. Eugene Carter. *International Financial Management,* 2nd ed. Englewood Cliffs, N.J.: Prentice-Hall, 1979, Chapters 3–5.

Shapiro, Alan C. *Multinational Financial Management.* Boston: Allyn & Bacon, 1982, Chapters 2–4.

Ungerer, Horst. "Main Developments in the European Monetary System," *Finance and Development,* June 1983, pp. 16–19.

Walmsley, Julian. *The Foreign Exchange Handbook: A User's Guide.* New York: John Wiley & Sons, 1983.

CHAPTER 5

Accounting in Foreign Currency: Transactions and Translation

The decade of the 1970s was a period of real turmoil for U.S. multinationals as they tried to cope with a gradually deteriorating dollar and eventually with a change in accounting standards to Statement No. 8 of the Financial Accounting Standards Board. The combination of both of these two elements resulted in a variety of reporting problems by firms that culminated in 1982 in a change of accounting standards.

In this chapter, we will discuss the major concepts involved in accounting for foreign currency transactions, including forward contracts, and we will also determine how to translate foreign currency financial statements. Although we will look at a variety of methods that could be used to translate financial statements, we will focus on the two major methods in use today: the temporal method and the current rate method. In the next chapter, we will discuss a variety of reporting issues. In the early part of Chapter 6, we will look at some specific issues involved in the translation process that build on the concepts developed in this chapter. In particular, we will look at accounting for inflation in foreign operations, some special problems in consolidation of foreign operations, disclosure of the impact of foreign exchange on the business, foreign exchange risk management in the context of new accounting standards, and non-U.S. translation practices.

FOREIGN CURRENCY TRANSACTIONS

The accounting standard under which the United States operates for the purposes of accounting for foreign currency is FASB Statement No. 52, hereafter referred to as Statement 52. That statement was issued in December 1981 with full implementation to take place for fiscal years beginning on or after December 15, 1982. In the discussion on foreign currency transactions that follows, there will be a general discussion of how one might account for foreign currency transactions as well as the specific requirements for Statement 52. However, some terminology involved in the statement is useful for even a general discussion.

According to Statement 52, the *functional currency* of an entity "is the currency of the primary economic environment in which the entity operates." Thus, the functional currency of a U.S. firm operating in the United States is normally the U.S. dollar. The functional currency of a Mexican firm operating in Mexico is normally the Mexican peso. In essence, the functional currency is the currency in which the entity generates and spends cash. This concept of the functional currency will be developed in more detail in the section discussing the translation of foreign currency financial statements.

Given this definition of the functional currency, it follows that a *foreign currency* is any currency that a firm deals in other than the functional currency. As pointed out in Statement 52, foreign currency transactions are

> transactions whose terms are denominated in a currency other than the entity's functional currency. Foreign currency transactions arise when an enterprise (a) buys or sells on credit goods or services whose prices are denominated in foreign currency, (b) borrows or lends funds and the amounts payable or receivable are denominated in foreign currency, (c) is a party to an unperformed forward exchange contract, or (d) for other reasons, acquires or disposes of assets, or incurs or settles liabilities denominated in foreign currency.[1]

No accounting problem arises as long as the transactions are denominated in the firm's domestic currency. However, when it is denominated in a foreign currency, the firm needs to resolve four accounting problems: (1) the initial recording of the transaction, (2) the recording of foreign currency balances at subsequent balance sheet dates, (3) the treatment of any foreign exchange gains and losses, and (4) the recording of the settlement of foreign currency receivables and payables when they come due.

These issues are obviously interactive. In addition, a firm may look at its transactions from two major perspectives, the one-transaction and the two-transactions perspectives. The latter perspective has two major options: the immediate recognition of gains and losses and the deferral of gains and losses until the financial side of the transaction is completed.

How these four issues are resolved depends on the perspective the firm chooses. For financial reporting purposes, U.S. firms subject to Statement 52 must select the two-transaction method, as will be explained shortly, but this method differs from the one required by the Internal Revenue Service, as will be explained more fully in Chapter 7.

One-Transaction Perspective

Under the one-transaction perspective, the transaction is not considered complete until the cash needed to liquidate the receivable or payable has

[1]Financial Accounting Standards Board, *Statement of Financial Accounting Standards No. 52*, "Foreign Currency Translation" (December 1981), p. 76.

actually been exchanged. Any gain or loss that arises from the transaction is considered an adjustment to the cost of the import or the revenue from the export.

To illustrate how to account for foreign currency transactions using the one-transaction perspective, assume that a U.S. firm imports equipment from West Germany on December 1 for DM 1 million when the exchange rate is $0.3525/DM. Payment in DM does not have to be made until January 31. Assume that on December 31 the exchange rate is $0.3500 and on January 31 it is $0.3510. Although the one-transaction perspective is not permitted by Statement 52, the entries under such a method would be as follows:

December 1	Equipment	352,500	
	Payable		352,500
	DM 1,000,000 × $0.3525		
December 31	Payable	2,500	
	Equipment		2,500
	DM 1,000,000 × ($0.3525 − $0.3500)		

The movement in the exchange rate causes the liability to decrease to $350,000. The resulting difference, normally considered a foreign exchange gain, is treated as an adjustment of the cost of the equipment.

January 31	Equipment	1,000	
	Payable	350,000	
	Cash		351,000
	DM 1,000,000 × $0.3510		

The movement of the exchange rate to $0.3510 means that the importer must pay $351,000 in order to get the DM necessary to liquidate the obligation. The difference between the amount of the payable on December 31 and the dollars converted into DM to settle the payable is considered as an adjustment of the equipment instead of a foreign exchange loss.

The result of the one-transaction perspective is that the impact of an exchange rate change is not recognized until the equipment is written off, and the gain or loss is treated as part of depreciation expense instead of as a separate financial item.

Two-Transaction Perspective

The two-transaction perspective treats foreign currency receivables and payables as separate from the sale or purchase that gave rise to them. Thus, the foreign exchange gain or loss that arises from translating the receivable or payable at the current exchange rate is not used to adjust the revenue from the export or the cost of the import.

Under the two-transaction perspective, the foreign exchange gain or loss could be handled in one of two ways. One possibility is to defer the gain or loss until it is actually realized when the payable or receivable is liquidated. The other possibility is to take the gain or loss directly to the income statement in the period incurred. This is the approach required by Statement 52. The following journal entries reflect the condition in which gains and losses are deferred:

December 1	Equipment	352,500	
	Payable		352,500
December 31	Payable	2,500	
	Deferred gain		2,500
January 31	Payable	350,000	
	Deferred gain	2,500	
	Gain		1,500
	Cash		351,000

A loss actually occurred on January 31, since the rate went from $0.3500 to $0.3510. This means that the value of the liability actually went from $350,000 to $351,000, a loss of $1000. However, that entry is not actually made, so the deferred gain of $2500 is offset by the $1000 difference between the payable and the cash expended. Thus, the gains of one period are offset by the losses of the next period, and the net amount is not recognized in income until the payable is liquidated. This is essentially the method required by the Internal Revenue Service in the United States.

The following entries illustrate the two-transaction perspective in which gains and losses are immediately recognized in income, the method required by Statement 52:

December 1	Equipment	352,500	
	Payable		352,500
December 31	Payable	2,500	
	Gain		2,500
January 31	Loss	1,000	
	Payable	350,000	
	Cash		351,000

This approach is consistent with the idea that gains or losses not deferred in the annual financial statements should not be deferred in the interim statements. Also, interim period recognition reflects the impact of the economic event (the exchange rate change) that occurred during the period.

Table 5.1 summarizes the differences between the three situations described above. As noted, these situations reflect the exchange rate changes but in different places in the financial statements and in different periods. The difference in the final value of the equipment is $1500, the same as the net foreign exchange gain. Therefore, the one-transaction per-

Table 5.1 Difference Between One- and Two-Transaction Perspective

	One Transaction	Two Transactions Recognize Gain/Loss	Two Transactions Defer Gain/Loss
Final value of purchase	351,000	352,500	352,500
Total cash disbursed	351,000	351,000	351,000
Gain (loss) on December 31	—	2,500	—
Gain (loss) on January 31	—	(1,000)	1,500

spective recognizes the foreign exchange gain when the equipment is depreciated at a lower amount than it would have been if it had been recorded at the original exchange rate. In the second and third situations, the issue is simply one of timing. The net gain is the same in both situations and is treated as a foreign exchange gain but in different periods.

Summary of Foreign Currency Transactions

Having looked at all the possibilities, it would be useful at this point to reiterate the position of Statement 52 as it relates to foreign currency transactions:

1. At the transaction date, each asset, liability, revenue, expense, gain, or loss arising from the transaction should be translated into the functional currency at the exchange rate in effect at that date.

2. At subsequent balance sheet dates, all assets and liabilities denominated in a currency other than the functional currency (such as a receivable or payable in a foreign currency) should be translated into the functional currency at the exchange rate in effect at that date.

As mentioned briefly in Chapter 2, the International Accounting Standards Committee is involved in setting accounting standards that it hopes can be adopted by its member countries. International Accounting Standard 21 (IAS 21), Accounting for the Effects of Changes in Foreign Exchange Rates, deals with the same issues covered in Statement 52. However, IAS 21, which was issued in March 1983, provides more options for accounting for foreign currency transactions than Statement 52. As does Statement 52, IAS 21 recommends the two-transactions perspective with immediate recognition of foreign exchange gains and losses for most situations. However, it does permit the following departures from that treatment:

1. The gain or loss on a long-term foreign currency monetary item (such as long-term debt) can be deferred and written off on a systematic basis over the life of the monetary item.

2. The gain or loss resulting from a severe devaluation that effects the value of debt incurred to purchase assets can be used to adjust the carrying value of the related asset and written off over the life of the asset, as long as the adjusted amount does not exceed the lower of replacement value or net realizable value.[2]

In May 1983, the Accounting Standards Committee of the United Kingdom issued Statement of Standard Accounting Practice 20 (SSAP 20), Foreign Currency Translation. SSAP 20 is very similar to Statement 52 in how it deals with foreign currency transactions. It does, however, permit the deferral and write-off of gains and losses that arise from long-term monetary items as does IAS 21. It is interesting to note that all three standards were issued within a short time of each other. The task force appointed to advise the FASB on the formulation of Statement 52 included representatives from the IASC and the ASC, so it is reasonable to expect that their standards would be fairly similar. It is interesting to note that IAS 21 was written so as to include elements that would be agreeable to both the United States and the United Kingdom. Thus, one could say that adherence to the standards in these countries would imply automatic adherence with IAS 21, the international standard.

ACCOUNTING FOR FORWARD CONTRACTS AND OTHER HEDGES

One of the areas in which Statement 52 resulted in a change in accounting for foreign currency transactions is the treatment of forward contracts and other transactions that can be considered hedges. The change was more in the liberalization of the definition of a hedge than in the accounting for a hedge once it has been so defined.

Although most of the numerical examples in this section deal with forward contracts, the term *hedge* can involve more than just a forward contract. As noted in Chapter 4, a forward contract is a contract with a foreign currency trader to deliver in the future one currency for another at a specific contract rate, known as the forward rate. As shown in an illustration later in this section, there are other foreign currency commitments that can also be considered hedges. One example is the creation of a foreign currency liability (such as borrowing a foreign currency) to offset a foreign currency asset.

As noted earlier in the chapter, gains and losses that arise from foreign currency transactions are to be taken into income at each balance sheet date. However, this does not necessarily hold for transactions that are entered into as a hedge. Therefore, it is important to examine such forward contracts and other transactions to see how they should be accounted for.

The costs of the contracts, excluding transaction costs that the foreign

[2]International Accounting Standards Committee, *International Accounting Standard No. 21*, "Accounting for the Effects of Foreign Exchange Rates" (July 1983), paragraphs 24–31.

exchange trader may charge, require knowledge of four exchange rates: the spot rate on the date the contract is entered into, the forward contract rate, the expected spot rate when the contract is to be completed, and the actual spot rate when the contract is completed. These rates are necessary when trying to determine whether to enter into a contract and in evaluating the contract decision once it is completed. In addition to these rates, the spot rates in effect at each financial statement date are used to determine the gains or losses on the contracts.

In trying to decide whether or not to enter into a contract, the financial manager may look at two costs, the premium or discount and opportunity cost. The premium or discount is simply the difference between the forward rate and the spot rate on the date the contract is entered into. The financial manager may look at this as an actual amount or as a percentage, as was computed in the illustrations in Chapter 4.

The opportunity cost (ex ante) is the difference between the forward rate and the expected spot rate. Although one would expect this rate to equal or approximate the expected spot rate, it may not in some situations, and thus may affect the decision of the financial manager to enter into a contract.

Another type of opportunity cost may be used to evaluate a contract after completion. This opportunity cost (ex post) is the difference between the forward rate and the actual spot rate in effect when the contract is completed. Here, the manager can evaluate what would have happened if no contract had been entered into. The first two costs are relevant for deciding whether to enter into a contract, and the third cost is for evaluation after the fact.

Before going into the accounting treatment of forward contracts as hedges against foreign exchange losses, it should be pointed out that a forward contract is an executory contract in which two parties agree to do something in the future. For example, a bank agrees to deliver foreign currency to a corporation, and the corporation agrees to deliver dollars to the bank in the future. Because neither party has fulfilled the commitment when they enter into the arrangement, this forward contract is recorded as a memorandum entry that is not normally reflected in the financial statements.

Hedging Foreign Currency Commitments

When a firm takes on a commitment, it enters into a contract to buy or sell assets with delivery to be made some time in the future. At that point, no transaction is recorded on the books because neither party has fulfilled any part of the contract; delivery has not taken place and payment has not been made. This is an executory contract.

Since this contract is a hedge of a commitment, the premium or discount and any gains or losses on the contract can be deferred until the transaction is recorded, and they are used to adjust the cost of the purchase or the revenue from the sale, assuming that the contract or other foreign currency transaction is designated and is effective as a hedge of the foreign currency commitment and that the foreign currency commitment is firm. The deferral applies only to that portion of the contract or transaction that covers the commitment on an after-tax basis. Anything over and above that amount must be taken immediately to income, as is the case in other foreign currency transactions.

Before considering a numerical example, we need to understand the actual goods and financial flow. Assume that a U.S. importer enters into a commitment to purchase merchandise from a British supplier and is to pay the supplier in deutsche marks on the transaction date. In order to hedge against a potential loss, the importer enters into a forward contract with its bank to deliver dollars for marks on the transaction date. Figure 5.1 illustrates in six sequential steps how the flow might take place.

Because the commitment is an executory contract, it is not officially recorded on the books until it becomes a transaction. The same is true of the forward contract as described earlier.

Assume in the illustration in Figure 5.1 that the U.S. importer agrees to pay £1,000,000 for the merchandise on the transaction date. The relevant exchange rates, journal entries, and explanations are as follows:

$1.4500—spot rate on March 1.

$1.4700—forward rate for contract due on April 30.

$1.4650—spot rate on March 31.

$1.4600—spot rate on April 30.

March 1	Contract receivable (£)	1,450,000	
	Premium expense	20,000	
	Contract payable ($)		1,470,000
	(Memorandum entry)		

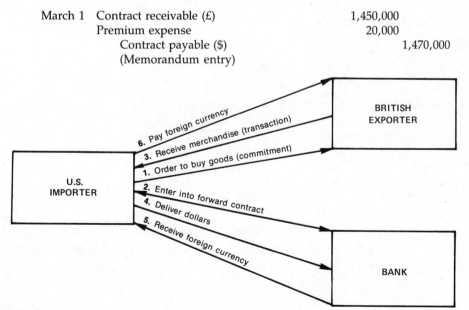

FIGURE 5.1. The use of a forward contract to hedge a commitment.

This entry represents step 2 in Figure 5.1. The importer will pay the bank in dollars at the forward rate ($1.4700) and will receive £1,000,000 when the contract is completed on April 30. The pound sterling receivable is translated at the spot rate ($1.4500) on the commitment date, consistent with the idea stated earlier that foreign currency receivables and payables are always translated at the spot rate on each balance sheet date. It is important to note that the dollar portion of the contract is always recorded at the forward rate and the foreign currency portion at the spot rate. In more precise terminology from Statement 52, it would be correct to say that the functional currency amount is always recorded at the forward rate and the foreign currency amount at the spot rate. The premium expense [£1,000,000 × (1.4500 − 1.4700)] is deferred until the transaction date. That entry could be recorded in the books as follows:

March 1	Deferred premium expense	20,000	
	Deferred charge		20,000

The deferred charge account is a suspense account that is created to offset the deferred premium expense and deferred gains and losses that will arise on the contract. The account is closed out as soon as the contract is fulfilled.

March 31	Deferred charge	15,000	
	Deferred gain		15,000

The contract receivable rises to a dollar equivalent of $1,465,000 (£1,000,000 × $1.4650) at the new balance sheet date, yielding a gain of $15,000. The gain is deferred until the transaction date.

April 30	Inventory	1,470,000	
	Deferred charge	5,000	
	Deferred gain	15,000	
	Deferred premium expense		20,000
	Cash		1,470,000

This combined entry reflects steps 3 through 6 in Figure 5.1. The cash reflects the amount of dollars given to the bank to satisfy the forward contract and receive sterling to pay the British exporter. The value of the inventory is set by the forward contract. We can also see its value as follows:

	$1,460,000	Value of inventory at April 30 spot rate, the rate in effect on the transaction date.
+	20,000	Premium expense deferred to transaction date.
−	15,000	Foreign exchange gain deferred to transaction date.
+	5,000	Reduction in value of the contract receivable between the transaction date (4/30) and the most recent balance sheet date (3/31).
=	$1,470,000	Carrying value of the inventory.

The value of the forward contract in this illustration is that it establishes the value of the merchandise purchases and the cash given up for the merchandise. If the importer had not entered into the contract, he or she would have had to pay $1,460,000, or $10,000 less than the contract price of $1,470,000. The additional cost is, in one sense, similar to an insurance premium in that it fixed the maximum price in dollars that the buyer would have to pay for the merchandise. This opportunity cost is reflected in the income statement as the higher cost of inventory flow through the cost of goods sold. Therefore, the premium expense net of the contract gain is treated as a product cost rather than a period cost.

Hedging Foreign Currency Transactions

The situation of hedging foreign currency transactions differs from the previous one in that a transaction has taken place which gives rise to a foreign currency receivable or payable. The event could be the sale or purchase of goods or services, the payment or receipt of dividends, or the payment or receipt of principal and interest on financial obligations. Statement 52 requires that foreign currency receivables or payables be translated at the current exchange rate at each balance sheet date, with the resulting gains or losses reflected in current income. For forward contracts entered into as a hedge for foreign currency receivables or payables, Statement 52 requires that the premium or discount be amortized over the life of the contract and that gains or losses on the contract be taken directly to income.

As an illustration, assume that a U.S. company purchases merchandise on March 1 for £1,000,000, with payment to be made on April 30. At the same time, the importer enters into a forward contract to deliver dollars for sterling on April 30 when payment is due. The exchange rates used in the commitment illustration still hold for this situation. The journal entries at each date with explanations are as follows:

| March 1 | Inventory | 1,450,000 | |
| | Accounts payable | | 1,450,000 |

To record the initial transaction at the spot rate.

	Contract receivable (£)	1,450,000	
	Premium expense	20,000	
	Contract payable ($)		1,470,000

Memorandum entry to record the receivable at the spot rate and the payable at the forward rate.

| | Deferred premium expense | 20,000 | |
| | Deferred charge | | 20,000 |

To set up the premium expense in the books so that it can be written off over the life of the contract.

| March 31 | Loss | 15,000 | |
| | Accounts payable | | 15,000 |

To reflect the new value of the liability at the current spot rate of $1.4650.

Deferred charge	15,000	
Gain		15,000

To reflect the fact that the contract receivable has increased in value due to the spot rate change from $1.4500 to $1.4650.

Premium expense	10,000	
Deferred premium expense		10,000

The amortization of half of the premium expense.

April 30	Premium expense	10,000	
	Deferred premium expense		10,000

The amortization of the remaining premium expense.

Accounts payable	1,465,000	
Deferred charge	5,000	
Cash		1,470,000

The final settlement of the liability. The cash amount reflects the cash given the bank to settle the forward contract in order for the importer to receive the pounds to send to the exporter.

From these entries we can see that a forward contract establishes the amount of cash given up for the merchandise ($1,470,000) but not the value of the merchandise ($1,450,000). The difference between these two ($20,000) is reflected as a premium expense in the income statement.

Hedging Net Investments

A third reason for entering into a forward contract is to hedge an exposed balance sheet position of a foreign branch or subsidiary. Although the discussion of this issue now might seem a little premature, since we have not precisely defined balance sheet exposure, we can still deal with the hedging concept. Very briefly, the concept of exposure means that the dollar equivalent of the foreign currency balance in an account changes when the exchange rate changes. The reason for the change will be discussed in the section of the chapter on translating foreign currency financial statements. However, let us assume for the purposes of this discussion that a U.S. firm has a subsidiary in the United Kingdom with a net exposed asset position (exposed assets exceed exposed liabilities) of £1,100,000. This means that the dollar equivalent of that position changes when the exchange rate between the dollar and pound changes. How can a firm protect itself against this exposure?

There are several methods, but let us examine two major ways: borrowing pounds to create a liability to offset the asset position and entering into a forward contract to deliver pounds to the foreign exchange trader and receive dollars in return.

In the first situation, let us assume that the parent in the United States borrows £1,000,000 to offset its net exposed asset position of £1,100,000. Assume that the spot rate at the time of borrowing was $1.46 and that the exchange rate at the balance sheet date had moved to $1.45, signaling a strengthening of the dollar. The loss in the exposed position would be offset by the gain on the borrowing, as illustrated below:

$$£1,100,000 \times (\$1.46 - \$1.45) = \$11,000 \text{ loss}$$
$$£1,000,000 \times (\$1.46 - \$1.45) = \underline{\$10,000}, \text{ gain}$$
$$\$ 1,000 \text{ net loss}$$

By the same token, the firm could enter into a forward contract to deliver pounds (thus creating a pound liability) and receive dollars on the balance sheet date. In this case, assume that the initial spot rate is $1.46, the forward rate is $1.44, and the spot rate on the balance sheet date is $1.45. As already noted, the exposed asset position would yield a loss of $11,000. If the firm were to enter into a contract to deliver £1,000,000, the journal entries would be as follows:

Contract receivable ($)	1,440,000	
Premium expense	20,000	
Contract payable (£)		1,460,000
Memorandum entry to show the contract.		

Deferred premium expense	20,000	
Deferred charge		20,000

Entry on books to set up the premium expense that will be recognized at the balance sheet date. In this case, assume that the contract will be fulfilled within one balance sheet period.

In the case of this forward contract, the U.S. firm is supposed to deliver pounds to the trader, so it must go into the market and buy pounds at the spot rate on the date that the contract is fulfilled and deliver the pounds to the bank in order to receive dollars at the forward rate. Thus, the entry to record the fulfilling of the contract is as follows:

Cash	1,440,000	
Deferred charge	20,000	
Premium expense	20,000	
Dollar value of pounds		1,450,000
Deferred premium expense		20,000
Gain		10,000

The premium expense represents the cost of entering into the contract. The dollar value of the pounds means that the firm bought pounds at the spot rate of $1.45 and delivered them to the bank. The gain is the difference between the old and new spot rates and reflects the fact that the value of the contract payable dropped from $1,460,000 to $1,450,000 over the life of the contract. It is this gain that offsets the loss on the exposed asset position of the British subsidiary, resulting in a net loss of only $1000. It is interesting that the firm had to give up $1,450,000 in cash to acquire the pounds to deliver to the trader in order to receive $1,440,000 back, a loss in cash of $10,000.

As will be pointed out later in the chapter, there are situations in which the gain or loss on an exposed foreign currency balance sheet will show up in a separate section in stockholders' equity rather than in income. In those situations, the gain or loss on the hedge will also be taken to stockholders' equity rather than income. Thus, the gains and losses will be treated in the same way.

Forward Contracts for Speculation

The final major use for a forward contract is for speculation in which the firm's major reason for entering into the contract is to make money on the contract rather than protect a business commitment, transaction, or exposed balance sheet position. A good example of the use of forward contracts for speculation involves Bankhaus I. D. Herstatt AG, a large West German bank that went bankrupt in June 1974. Apparently, Herstatt traders sold marks forward in late 1973 or early 1974 under the assumption that the mark would weaken in relation to the dollar. When the contracts matured, Herstatt would take its stronger dollars and buy back marks at a profit. However, the mark strengthened vis-à-vis the dollar by the time the contracts matured, so Herstatt had to pay more marks for dollars to fulfill the contracts than it could earn by reselling the dollars for marks. It ended up losing a sum estimated at more than $200 million, approximately six times it capital and reserves.[3]

A forward contract is accounted for much differently for speculation than it is for any other purpose. The data in Table 5.2 provides some exchange rates that can be used to illustrate the accounting for a speculative contract. Before going through the illustration, however, it is important to note the following: (1) in recording the contract, you ignore the premium or discount, (2) at each balance sheet date, you mark the value of the contract to its current market value, and (3) you recognize the gain or loss on the contract at each balance sheet date.

Table 5.2 Exchange Rates for a Speculative Contract

Date	Spot Rate	90-Day Forward Rate	60-Day Forward Rate	30-Day Forward Rate
March 1	$0.3903	$0.3923		
March 31	0.3937		$0.3950	
April 30	0.3944			$0.3952
May 29	0.3860			

The journal entries for a speculative contract are as follows:

March 1	Contract receivable (DM)	392,300	
	Contract payable ($)		392,300

[3]*The Wall Street Journal*, 27 June 1978, p. 5.

March 31	Contract receivable (DM)	2,700	
	Gain on contract		2,700
April 30	Contract receivable	200	
	Gain on contract		200
May 29	Contract payable	392,300	
	Cash		392,300
	Dollar value of DM	386,000	
	Loss on contract	9,200	
	Contract receivable		395,200

Given the huge loss on the contract on May 29, it is doubtful that the firm would have retained its rights to the contract to the bitter end. Instead, it probably would have sold the contract sometime when it felt its profit potential would be at the highest point. Assume, for example, that the firm sold the contract on May 5 for $3000. The entry on that date would have been:

May 5	Contract payable	392,300	
	Cash	3,000	
	Contract receivable		395,200
	Gain on sale		100

The cumulative gain in that case of $3000 was certainly better than the net loss in the original case of $6300 ($9200 − $2900). That loss of $6300 represents the difference between the cash given up to the trader ($392,300) in exchange for deutsche marks that were traded in the open spot market for $386,000.

TRANSLATION OF FOREIGN CURRENCY FINANCIAL STATEMENTS

The previous section dealt with amounts payable or receivable in foreign currency in which conversion would eventually take place. *Conversion* implies that one currency is changed into another currency, usually through the foreign currency section of the commercial bank that the firm deals with. *Translation* implies that one currency is expressed or restated in terms of another currency. For example, if a U.S. firm has an accounts receivable of DM 1 million when the exchange rate is $0.3903/DM, the account would be translated into dollars and carried on the financial statements at $390,300. If the firm were to receive DM 1 million and convert them into dollars, it would record cash of $390,300.

The situation becomes more complex when a firm's financial statements are expressed in one currency but need to be restated into another. Why should translation occur in the first place? Sometimes financial statements are restated or translated from one currency into another to assist the reader of the financial statements. For example, a U.S. investor desiring to invest in a British company may want to see the financial statements in dollars rather than pounds. The management of a multinational enterprise may wish to see the results of a foreign operation stated in the parent currency in order to facilitate cross-national comparisons. If a multinational enterprise is to prepare consolidated financial statements, it needs to express the statements of its different operations in a common currency before combination or consolidation can occur.

This discussion highlights the importance of making sure that we are consistent in terminology. So far in this chapter, we have defined two terms that are important to the discussion of translation: functional currency and foreign currency. The *functional currency* is the currency of the primary economic environment in which the firm operates. The *foreign currency* is any currency other than the functional currency. The *local currency* is the currency in the country where the firm is operating, and the *reporting currency* is the currency in which the parent company prepares its financial statements.

To illustrate these terms, let's assume that a U.S.-based multinational enterprise has an operating subsidiary in France that is relatively independent of the parent and that does some importing from Germany. Both the functional currency and local currency of the subsidiary would be the French franc; the German mark would be a foreign currency to the French subsidiary; and the U.S. dollar would be the reporting currency of the consolidated enterprise.

Because the French subsidiary imports merchandise from Germany, it may have accounts payable that are *denominated* in German marks. This implies that the amount of the liability is actually fixed in marks, because that is the currency in which the liability must be settled. For financial statement purposes, however, the mark liability must be *measured* in French francs, or it could not be included with the French franc liabilities on the balance sheet. A French franc liability would be both measured and denominated in French francs. The process of translation involves restating an account from one currency to another. If the exchange rate used to translate the account from one currency to another were the rate in effect when the original transaction took place (e.g., the acquisition of property, plant, and equipment), that rate would be called the *historical* exchange rate. If the exchange rate used were the one in effect at the balance sheet date, it would be considered the *current* or *closing* rate.

As will be pointed out in subsequent discussions in this chapter, the translation of financial statements involves dealing with two key issues: the exchange rates at which various accounts are translated from one currency into another (translation methods) and the subsequent treatment of gains and losses.

Translation Methodologies—An Overview

In the process of translation, all local currency balance sheet and income statement accounts are restated in terms of the reporting currency by mul-

Table 5.3 Exchange Rates Used to Translate Selected Assets and Liabilities

	Current– Noncurrent	Monetary– Nonmonetary	Current Rate	Temporal
Cash, current receivables and payables	C	C	C	C
Inventory	C	H	C	C or H
Fixed assets	H	H	C	H
Long-term receivables and payables	H	C	C	C

Note: C = current exchange rate; H = historical exchange rate.

tiplying the local currency amount times the appropriate exchange rate. The four major ways that have been used over the years in the translation process are the current–noncurrent, the monetary–nonmonetary, the temporal, and the current rate methods. In addition, slight variations of the first two methods have been used. No single method is used universally and all have been used in one or more countries around the world at one time. The adoption of Statement 52 in the United States and the subsequent release of IAS 21 and SSAP 20, as mentioned earlier in the chapter, should tend to narrow the options used worldwide to the temporal and current rate methods for financial reporting purposes.

Current–Noncurrent Method

Under the current–noncurrent method, as shown in Table 5.3, current assets and liabilities are translated at current exchange rates and noncurrent assets and liabilities and stockholders' equity are translated at historical exchange rates. This method was generally accepted in the United States from the early 1930s until FASB Statement 8 was issued in October 1975.

The current–noncurrent method is based on the assumption that accounts should be grouped according to maturity. Anything due to mature in one year or less or within the normal business cycle should be translated at the current rate, whereas everything else should be carried at the rate in effect when the transaction was originally recorded.

Monetary–Nonmonetary Method

The mood began to change in the 1950s as Hepworth[4] suggested that accounts be translated according to their nature rather than the date of maturity. He suggested that accounts be considered as either monetary or nonmonetary rather than current or noncurrent. Under this method, monetary assets and liabilities are translated at current rates, and nonmonetary

[4]Samuel R. Hepworth, *Reporting Foreign Operations* (Ann Arbor: University of Michigan, 1956).

assets and liabilities and stockholders' equity are translated at historical rates. The monetary–nonmonetary method was endorsed by the National Association of Accountants in 1960. This approach is a radical departure from the current–noncurrent method in the areas of inventory, long-term receivables, and long-term payables.

The philosophy behind this approach is that monetary or financial assets and liabilities have similar attributes in that their value represents a fixed amount of money whose reporting currency equivalent changes each time the exchange rate changes. Those accounts should therefore be translated at the current exchange rate. In the current–noncurrent method, some current assets are monetary (e.g., cash) and some are nonmonetary (e.g., inventory carried at cost), and yet all are translated at the current exchange rate. The proponents of the monetary–nonmonetary method consider it more meaningful to translate assets and liabilities on the basis of attributes instead of time. In 1965 the Accounting Principles Board of the American Institute of CPAs partially acknowledged this in APB 6 by allowing long-term debt to be translated at current rates. Under current generally accepted accounting principles of historical cost accounting in the United States, the monetary–nonmonetary method provides essentially the same results as the temporal approach.

Although these first two approaches seem fairly clear-cut, a number of firms were using variations prior to the issuance of Statement 8. Table 5.4

Table 5.4 Translation Methods Used by U.S. Multinational Corporations Prior to the Issuance of FASB 8

Translation Methods	Respondent Firms	
	Number	Percent
Current–noncurrent method	54	34.6
Current–noncurrent method with noncurrent receivables and payables translated at the current rate	10	6.4
Monetary–nonmonetary method	22	14.1
Monetary–nonmonetary method with inventories translated at the current rate	41	26.3
Temporal method	7	4.5
Current rate method	4	2.6
Other	3	1.9
No response	15	9.6
Total	156	100.0

Source: Thomas G. Evans, William R. Folks, Jr., and Michael Jilling. *The Impact of Statement of Financial Accounting Standards No. 8 on the Foreign Exchange Risk Management Practices of American Multinationals: An Economic Impact Study,* 1978, p. 147. Copyright by the Financial Accounting Standards Board, High Ridge Park, Stamford, Conn. 06905, U.S.A. Reprinted with permission. Copies of the complete document are available from the FASB.

summarizes the methods most widely used by U.S. firms prior to Statement 8. Some firms stated that they used the current–noncurrent method but that they translated long-term receivables and payables at current rates. Other firms stated that they used the monetary–nonmonetary method but translated inventories at current rates. These two variations yield essentially the same results. It is interesting to note from the table that only 2.6% of the firms were using the current rate method before the issuance of Statement 8.

Temporal Method

The temporal method was originally proposed in Accounting Research Study 12 by the AICPA[5] and formally required in Statement 8. According to the temporal method, cash, receivables, and payables (both current and noncurrent) are translated at the current rate. Other assets and liabilities may be translated at current or historical rates, depending on their characteristics. Assets and liabilities carried at past exchange prices are translated at historical rates. For example, a fixed asset carried at the local currency price at which it was purchased would be translated into the reporting currency at the exchange rate in effect when the asset was purchased. Assets and liabilities carried at current purchase or sales exchange prices or future exchange prices would be translated at current rates. For example, inventory carried at market would be translated at the current rather than the historical rate.[6]

The attractiveness of the temporal approach lies in its flexibility. If the United States were to change to current value accounting, the temporal method would automatically translate all assets and liabilities at current rates. The theoretical attractiveness of this approach is that the branches and subsidiaries of a U.S. company would be translated into dollars in such a way that the dollar would be the single unit of measure. Some have expressed the belief that this means the firm would be treating the transactions of foreign operations as if they had all taken place in dollars. Others disagree with this assessment but feel that the temporal method simply expresses in dollars the cost of foreign currency transactions.[7]

Current Rate Method

The current rate method is the easiest to apply because it requires that all assets and liabilities be translated at the current exchange rate. Only net worth would not be translated at the current rate. This approach is easier to

[5]Leonard Lorensen, *Accounting Research Study No. 12*, "Reporting Foreign Operations of U.S. Companies in U.S. Dollars" (New York: AICPA, 1972).
[6]Financial Accounting Standards Board, *Statement of Financial Accounting Standards No. 8*, "Accounting for the Translation of Foreign Currency Transactions and Foreign Currency Financial Statements" (October 1975), paragraphs 11 and 12.
[7]FASB Statement 52, pp. 20–21.

Table 5.5 Balance Sheet Effect of Translation

	Local Currency	Current–Noncurrent	Monetary–Nonmonetary	Variation	Current Rate
Cash	LC100	$ 100[a]	$ 100[a]	$ 100[a]	$100[a]
Inventory	200	200[a]	400[b]	200[a]	200[a]
Fixed assets	600	1200[b]	1200[b]	1200[b]	600[a]
	LC900	$1500	$1700	$1500	$900
Current liabilities	LC250	250[a]	250[a]	250[a]	250[a]
Long-term debt	150	300[b]	150[a]	150[a]	150[a]
Net worth	500	950	1300	1100	500
	LC900	$1500	$1700	$1500	$900

Note: Net worth is a plug figure.
[a]Translated at the current rate of 1LC = $1.
[b]Translated at the historical rate of 1LC = $2.

use than the others because a firm would not have to keep track of various historical exchange rates. The current rate approach results in translated statements that retain the same ratios and relationships that exist in the local currency. For example, the ratio of net income to sales in local currency is rarely the same in dollars under other translation approaches because a variety of current, historical, and average exchange rates are used to translate the income statement. Because all accounts would be translated at a single exchange rate under the current rate method, the ratio of net income to sales would remain the same in the reporting currency as in the local currency.

The simple example in Table 5.5 illustrates the balance sheet effect of financial statement translation. The variation in the illustration is the monetary–nonmonetary method, with inventory translated at the current rate. Note the difference in net worth depending on which approach is chosen.

Historical Development

Some of the evolutionary development of the translation standard in the United States has already been alluded to in the chapter. In 1934, the American Institute of Accountants, the forerunner of the AICPA, recommended that U.S. firms use the current–noncurrent method of translation. That method was reaffirmed in APB 43, Chapter 12, issued by the Accounting Principles Board (APB) in 1953. At that time, the APB permitted restatement of long-term debt if it were incurred prior to a major change in the value of a currency.

The movement to acceptance of the monetary–nonmonetary method began in 1956 when Professor Hepworth published his study, which was reinforced in 1960 by the National Association of Accountants. APB Opinion 6, which was issued in 1965, continued that move by permitting long-term debt to be translated at current rates.

In the late 1960s and early 1970s, the U.S. dollar came under severe pressure from other currencies, and in 1971 it was devalued approximately 10% against its official gold value. During that time, the APB was studying the translation issue, and in 1972, Accounting Research Study No. 12 was issued, which recommended the adoption of the temporal method of translation. However, the APB was being phased out and the FASB was being organized, so nothing was done with ARS 12.

In December 1973, the FASB issued Statement 1, Disclosure of Foreign Currency Translation Information, in an effort to stave off pressure while it deliberated on the more substantive issues of how to translate foreign currency financial statements. It is important to note that the dollar had been devalued another time in early 1973 and that it had finally been cut loose to float freely in the spring of 1973. Thus, the translation issue became much more critical than it had been when the dollar was fixed against most major currencies. In addition, the dollar was essentially floating down in value against most of the major currencies of the industrial world.

On February 21, 1974, the Board issued a discussion memorandum on translation, which addressed a number of important issues. After public hearings were held in June 1974, the issues in the discussion memorandum were consolidated and an exposure draft was issued in December 1974. After hearing responses to the exposure draft, the Board issued Statement 8 in October 1975.

Statement 8

According to Statement 8, the objective of translation was the following:

> For the purpose of preparing an enterprise's financial statements, the objective of translation is to measure and express (a) in dollars and (b) in conformity with U.S. generally accepted accounting principles (GAAP) the assets, liabilities, revenues, or expenses that are measured or denominated in foreign currency.[8]

The temporal method of translation has already been described briefly, but there are some important things about the temporal principle and Statement 8 that have not been addressed. In the income statement, for example, most revenues and expenses are translated at the average exchange rate during the year. In practice, the income statement is translated monthly, and the cumulative balance from prior months is added to the current month's balance to get the cumulative totals for the year. Accounts such as cost of sales and depreciation expense are translated at the exchange rate in effect when the assets were originally purchased. That is the

[8]FASB Statement 8, p. 3.

historical cost idea as it relates to inventory and other assets carried at past exchange prices (historical cost).

Another important feature is that Statement 8 required that all foreign exchange transactions and translation gains and losses be taken directly to the income statement. That meant that translated earnings were fluctuating widely depending on what was happening to the exchange rate, independent of the operations of the firm. This area became a source of real contention in the corporate world and was one of the major factors that led to the downfall of Statement 8.

Many firms complained about carrying inventory at historical rates in dollars for two reasons. The first reason was simply cost-benefit. The feeling was that inventory was turning over relatively rapidly, so that it was approximating current rates, and that it would be a lot easier to compute inventory values if the current rate could be used instead of having to keep track of the old historical exchange rates. The other reason was one of timing. Managers complained that because inventory was being translated at the historical rate, it was possible for an exchange rate change in one quarter to impact on earnings in a subsequent quarter when inventory flowed through the cost of goods sold. They felt that this was distorting the operating performance of each quarter. Thus, a number of critics of Statement 8 felt that the Statement would be improved if inventory could be carried at current rather than historical exchange rates.

A final major criticism related to the disposition of the gain or loss on long-term debt. Statement 8 required that firms translate long-term debt at current rates, a practice already followed by nearly half the U.S. multinationals prior to 1975. Because most of the foreign currency long-term debt in the 1970s was in currencies that were strengthening vis-à-vis the U.S. dollar, U.S. firms were recognizing sizable losses. Many firms felt that because the foreign currency debt was generally being liquidated by foreign currency earnings, there was really no dollar exposure. They also argued that the fixed assets purchased by the debt were a natural hedge or protection against loss, since they were constantly generating earnings. Thus, they felt they should have been able to write off the losses over the life of the assets or treat the losses as an adjustment to interest expense.

Movement to Statement 52

As a result of these and other criticisms, the Board decided in May 1978 to invite comments on Statements 1 through 12. Of the 200 letters received by the Board, most addressed the issues in Statement 8. In January 1979, the Board decided to add to its agenda a project to reconsider all or parts of Statement 8. In February 1979, a task force containing representatives of the IASC as well as the professional standard-setting bodies in the United Kingdom and Canada was appointed to advise the Board.

In August 1980, an exposure draft was issued after 18 public Board meetings and four public task force meetings. In December 1980, a public hearing was held on the exposure draft, which attracted 360 letters and 47 presentations. In an unprecedented move, the Board issued a revised exposure draft on June 30, 1981. This was followed by more public meetings and 260 letters of comment. Finally, in December 1981, Statement 52, Foreign Currency Translation, was issued.

Statement 52

The development of Statement 52 was not an easy thing. There were no clear-cut solutions to the problems raised from Statement 8, and the suggestions for change ranged from minor changes in the Statement to a major rethinking of the entire translation process. In the final analysis, the latter view prevailed, but the vote for both exposure drafts and the final standard was 4 to 3. The minority view held very strongly to Statement 8 and could not accept the changes inherent in Statement 52. Although the new standard has been issued, it is unlikely that the controversy surrounding the translation of financial statements will go away.

One major difference in the Statements is that Statement 52 has adopted new objectives of translation. The stated objectives are as follows:

a. Provide information that is generally compatible with the expected economic effects of a rate change on an enterprise's cash flows and equity.

b. Reflect in consolidated statements the financial results and relationships of the individual consolidated entities as measured in their functional currencies in conformity with U.S. generally accepted accounting principles.[9]

Selection of the Functional Currency

The term *functional currency* is used for the first time in the translation literature in conjunction with Statement 52. Although we have already defined and illustrated what is meant by functional currency, we need to refine our definition a little more. Exhibit 5.1 contains some information provided in Statement 52 on how a firm can choose the functional currency.

Conceptually, it is possible for a foreign operation to have more than one functional currency. For example, the operation could sell and distribute products manufactured by the parent company so that the functional currency might be that of the parent. However, it might also be manufacturing and selling products locally, in which case the functional currency for those functions would be the local currency. In practice, the Board expected that firms would pick only one functional currency for each operation abroad. Once the functional currency of the operation has been selected, it is possible to begin the translation process. It is important to

---

[9]FASB Statement 52, p. 3.

Exhibit 5.1 Determining the Functional Currency

a. Cash flow indicators
    (1) Foreign Currency—Cash flows related to the foreign entity's individual assets and liabilities are primarily in the foreign currency and do not directly impact the parent company's cash flows.
    (2) Parent's Currency—Cash flows related to the foreign entity's individual assets and liabilities directly impact the parent's cash flows on a current basis and are readily available for remittance to the parent company.
b. Sales price indicators
    (1) Foreign Currency—Sales prices for the foreign entity's products are not primarily responsive on a short-term basis to changes in exchange rates but are determined more by local competition or local government regulation.
    (2) Parent's Currency—Sales prices for the foreign entity's products are primarily responsive on a short-term basis to changes in exchange rates; for example, sales prices are determined more by worldwide competition or by international prices.
c. Sales market indicators
    (1) Foreign Currency—There is an active local sales market for the foreign entity's products, although there also might be significant amounts of exports
    (2) Parent's Currency—The sales market is mostly in the parent's country or sales contracts are denominated in the parent's currency.
d. Expense indicators
    (1) Foreign Currency—Labor, materials, and other costs for the foreign entity's products or services are primarily local costs, even though there also might be imports from other countries.
    (2) Parent's Currency—Labor, materials, and other costs for the foreign entity's products or services, on a continuing basis, are primarily costs for components obtained from the country in which the parent company is located.
e. Financing indicators
    (1) Foreign Currency—Financing is primarily denominated in foreign currency, and funds generated by the foreign entity's operations are sufficient to service existing and normally expected debt obligations.
    (2) Parent's Currency—Financing is primarily from the parent or other dollar-denominated obligations, or funds generated by the foreign entity's operations are not sufficient to service existing and normally expected debt obligations without the infusion of additional funds from the parent company. Infusion of additional funds from the parent company for expansion is not a factor, provided funds generated by the foreign entity's expanded operations are expected to be sufficient to service that additional financing.
f. Intercompany transactions and arrangements indicators
    (1) Foreign Currency—There is a low volume of intercompany transactions and there is not an extensive interrelationship between the operations of the foreign entity and the parent company. However, the foreign entity's operations may rely on the parent's or affiliates' competitive advantages, such as patents and trademarks.

Exhibit 5.1 *Continued*

---

(2) Parent's Currency—There is a high volume of intercompany transactions and there is an extensive interrelationship between the operations of the foreign entity and the parent company. Additionally, the parent's currency generally would be the functional currency if the foreign entity is a device or shell corporation for holding investments, obligations, intangible assets, etc., that could readily be carried on the parent's or affiliate's books.

Source: Financial Accounting Standard Board. *Statement of Financial Accounting Standards No. 52, Foreign Currency Translation* (Stamford, Conn.: FASB, December 1981), pp. 26–27.

remember that the functional currency is selected on the basis of operating criteria established by management. If the firm wishes to change the functional currency, it can do so only because the operating criteria used in the initial selection have changed. This is designed so that firms will not change functional currencies capriciously in order to take advantage of the differences in the financial statements that result from the different translation methods.

Translation Process

The Board defines the translation process in Statement 52 as "the process of expressing in the reporting currency of the enterprise those amounts that are denominated or measured in a different currency."[10] In the examples given in the balance of this chapter, the reporting currency is defined as the U.S. dollar.

The actual translation process depends on which currency the books and records of the foreign entity are kept in and on how the parent defines the functional currency of the foreign entity. Once those decisions have taken place, the translation process involves either the current rate method or the temporal method.

In a more precise discussion of the translation process, the Board refers to the processes of "translation" and "restatement." In order to understand the differences in these terms, refer to the conditions set forth in Exhibit 5.2. Notice that the books and records of the foreign entity can be kept in either the local currency or the reporting currency of the parent company (here assumed to be U.S. dollars). If the books and records are kept in dollars and the functional currency is defined as the dollar, no translation process is necessary.

If the books and records of the foreign entity are kept in the local currency, the translation process depends on the definition of the functional currency. If the functional currency is the local currency, the financial statements are translated into U.S. dollars using the current rate method.

[10]Ibid., p. 76.

Exhibit 5.2 Translation of Foreign Currency Financial Statements into U.S. Dollars

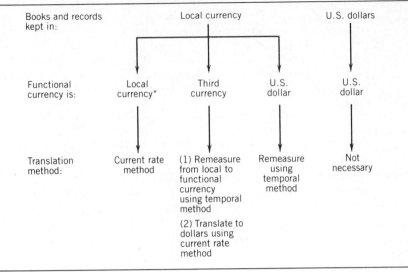

Books and records kept in:	Local currency			U.S. dollars
Functional currency is:	Local currency*	Third currency	U.S. dollar	U.S. dollar
Translation method:	Current rate method	(1) Remeasure from local to functional currency using temporal method (2) Translate to dollars using current rate method	Remeasure using temporal method	Not necessary

*In the case of a highly inflationary economy, the local currency may be the functional currency from an operating standpoint, but the dollar is considered the functional currency from a translation standpoint.

As noted in the exhibit, there is one exception to that rule—when the foreign entity is located in a highly inflationary economy. Highly inflationary economies are those that have a cumulative inflation rate of approximately 100% over a three-year period. In the early 1980s, when Statement 52 was being debated and implemented, this category included countries such as Mexico, Brazil, Argentina, and Israel. The determination of "highly inflationary countries" is subjective, because it depends on which three-year time period is selected and whether or not management is anticipating trends in the future or sticking to historical data.

The Board was concerned about using the current rate method to translate financial statements of highly inflationary countries because there is a tendency for the exchange rate of those countries to depreciate in relation to the dollar at approximately the same rate as the inflation differential, as discussed in Chapter 4. In a country like Brazil, where the rate of inflation exceeded 200% in 1984, this could lead to a rapid deterioration of the value of the currency. Fixed assets carried at historical cost in the local currency would rapidly lose dollar value to the point where they became insignificant on the financial statements. The Board considered permitting inflation adjustments of the primary financial statements before translation using the current rate method but rejected that approach because its inflation adjustments are not generally accepted in primary dollar financial statements. Thus, the best approach was to define the functional currency as the U.S. dollar and require remeasurement of the financial statements from the local currency to the dollar using the temporal method. As mentioned earlier in the chapter, this method requires that nonmonetary assets be translated at the historical rather than the current exchange rate. The method partially insulates the foreign entity from the impact of inflation on nonmonetary assets. Thus, even though the functional currency might be the local currency from an operational standpoint, the dollar is considered the functional currency from a translation standpoint.

Another possibility, although a very rare one, is that the books and records be kept in the local currency but the functional currency is a third currency. In this situation, the financial statements need to be remeasured from the local currency to the functional currency using the temporal method and then translated into dollars using the current rate method. The rationale behind the concept of remeasurement is to produce the same results as if the transactions had actually taken place in the functional currency. Thus, nonmonetary assets are restated in the functional currency at the exchange rate in effect when they were acquired in the local currency.

The last possibility is for the books and records to be kept in the local currency but the functional currency to be defined as the U.S. dollar. In this situation, the local currency financial statements are remeasured in U.S. dollars using the temporal method.

The important thing to note from this discussion is that Statement 52 uses both the current rate method and the temporal method of translating financial statements from a foreign currency to U.S. dollars. The key is to know in which currency the books and records are kept and how the functional currency of the foreign entity is defined. Thus, Statement 52 has not necessarily simplified the translation process, and we cannot forget all of the problems that occurred with Statement 8. Also, it is incorrect to refer to Statement 52 as the current rate method, as many people are prone to do, because it encompasses both methods.

Translation Process Illustrated

Earlier in this chapter, we mentioned that the translation process has to deal with two issues: which exchange rate (current or historical) must be used to translate each individual account in the financial statements and how the resulting translation gain or loss is to be recognized in the statements.

Table 5.6 contains the relevant exchange rates and basic assumptions that are necessary to translate the financial statements in Table 5.7 and Exhibit 5.3. Note that two different retained earnings figures are given for the current rate and temporal methods. That will be explained later in the chapter. Also, note that even though taxes were paid evenly throughout the year, dividends were paid only on June 30.

The Temporal Method.   Remember that the temporal method is used to restate financial statements from a foreign currency to the functional cur-

Table 5.6 Relevant Exchange Rates

Exchange Rates	Dollars/Pound
Rate in effect when capital stock was issued, the long-term notes payable were incurred, and fixed assets were acquired	1.90
December 31, 19X3	1.50
Average for 19X4	1.40
December 31, 19X4	1.30
Rate for December 31, 19X3 inventory	1.52
Rate for December 31, 19X4 inventory	1.32
Retained earnings 12/31/X3 (current rate method)	$11,560
Dividend rate 6/30/X4	1.42
Assumes that taxes were paid evenly throughout the year	
Retained earnings 12/31/X3 (temporal method)	$12,360

Table 5.7 Local Currency Balance Sheet (in thousands) for Grover Mfg. PLC

	December 31	
	19X4	19X3
Assets		
Current assets		
Cash and receivables	4,000	3,000
Inventory	4,500	3,000
Total	8,500	6,000
Fixed assets		
Land	3,000	3,000
Building (cost 10,000)	7,000	8,000
Equipment (cost 10,000)	4,000	6,000
Total	14,000	17,000
Total assets	22,500	23,000
Liabilities and stockholders' equity		
Current liabilities	5,500	6,000
Long-term liabilities		
Notes payable	3,000	5,000
Deferred income taxes	2,500	2,000
	5,500	7,000
Stockholders' equity		
Capital stock	5,000	5,000
Retained earnings	6,500	5,000
	11,500	10,000
Total liabilities and stockholders' equity	22,500	23,000

Exhibit 5.3 Local Currency Statement of Income and
Retained Earnings

Grover Mfg. PLC
Statement of Income and Retained Earnings
for the Year Ended December 31, 19X4
(FC in thousands)

Sales		18,000
Expenses:		
Cost of sales	9,000	
Depreciation	3,000	
Other expenses	2,100	14,100
Income before taxes		3,900
Income taxes		1,900
Net income		2,000
Retained earnings, December 31, 19X3		5,000
		7,000
Dividends		500
Retained earnings, December 31, 19X4		6,500

---

rency. Assume that Grover Mfg. PLC is the British subsidiary of a U.S. firm and that the functional currency is defined as the U.S. dollar rather than the British pound. The use of the temporal method requires that we do the following:

1. Translate cash, receivables, and liabilities at the current balance sheet rate.

2. Translate inventory (which is carried at historical cost in this case), fixed assets, and capital stock at the appropriate historical exchange rates.

3. Translate most revenues and expenses at the average rate for the year; cost of sales and depreciation expense are translated at the appropriate historical exchange rates.

4. Take all translation gains or losses directly to the income statement.

To accomplish these translation purposes, it is easier to translate the balance sheet before translating the income statement. Notice in Exhibit 5.4 that there is no exchange rate beside retained earnings. That is because the December 31, 19X4, retained earnings amount is the difference between total assets and liabilities plus the other stockholders' equity accounts (in this case just capital stock). Thus, the retained earnings balance must be $13,940 at the end of the year.

The translated statement of income and retained earnings is found in Exhibit 5.5. Notice in the income statement that cost of sales and deprecia-tion expense are not translated at the same exchange rate as other revenues

Exhibit 5.4 Translated Balance Sheet—Temporal Method

Grover Mfg. PLC
Translated Balance Sheet
(Temporal Method)
December 31, 19X4
(in thousands)

	LC	Exchange Rate	Dollars
Assets			
Cash and receivables	4,000	1.30	$ 5,200
Inventory	4,500	1.32	5,940
Land	3,000	1.90	5,700
Building—net	7,000	1.90	13,300
Equipment—net	4,000	1.90	7,600
	22,500		$37,740
Liabilities and stockholders' equity			
Current liabilities	5,500	1.30	$ 7,150
Notes payable	3,000	1.30	3,900
Deferred taxes	2,500	1.30	3,250
Capital stock	5,000	1.90	9,500
Retained earnings	6,500		13,940
	22,500		$37,740

and expenses. In the case of cost of sales, different rates are used for beginning inventory, purchases, and ending inventory.

In the case of ending inventory, it would be good at this point to briefly explain more specifically how the translation process works. U.S. GAAP adheres to the lower of cost or market concept, so those two amounts must be calculated before determining which is the correct inventory figure. Cost is determined by multiplying the historical cost in local currency by the exchange rate in effect when the inventory was acquired. Market is determined by multiplying the market in local currency by the current exchange rate (actually the exchange rate in effect when the market was determined). The lower of cost or market test is then conducted in dollars. It is important to note that the test is not performed in the local currency but in dollars.

Notice in the income statement that there is a translation gain of $1710. This figure is derived by working backwards. We know from the balance sheet in Exhibit 5.4 that the ending retained earnings balance must be $13,940. Since we translate the dividend amount and were provided the beginning retained earnings balance, we can derive the net income figure for the year. All of the other accounts were translated, so the translation gain is the amount that must be plugged in to arrive at the net income

Exhibit 5.5 Translated Statement of Income and Retained Earnings—
Temporal Method

Grover Mfg. PLC
Translated Statement of Income and Retained Earnings
(Temporal Method)
For the Year Ended December 31, 19X4
(in thousands)

	LC	Exchange Rate	Dollars
Sales	18,000	$1.40	$25,200
Expenses			
Cost of sales	9,000	*	13,320
Depreciation	3,000	1.90	5,700
Other expenses	2,100	1.40	2,940
Translation loss (gain)			(1,710)
	14,100		20,250
Income before taxes	3,900		$ 4,950
Income taxes	1,900	1.40	2,660
Net income	2,000		$ 2,290
Retained earnings (12/31/X3)	5,000		12,360
	7,000		$14,650
Dividends	500	1.42	710
Retained earnings (12/31/X4)	6,500		$13,940
*Beginning inventory	3,000	1.52	$ 4,560
Purchases	10,500	1.40	14,700
Goods available for sale	13,500		$19,260
Ending inventory	4,500	1.32	5,940
Cost of sales	9,000		$13,320

figure. It is possible to derive the translation gain or loss without treating it as a plug figure, and that process is illustrated in Exhibit 5.9 (which will be discussed later) for the current rate method. The important thing to note here is that the translation gain is taken directly to the income statement rather than to the balance sheet.

Current Rate Method.　The current rate method is far easier to negotiate. It is used when the functional currency is defined as the local currency. In order to accomplish the translation process, the following things need to be done:

1. Total assets and liabilities are translated at the current exchange rate.
2. Stockholders' equity accounts are translated at the appropriate historical exchange rates.
3. All revenue and expense items are translated at the average exchange rate for the period.

Exhibit 5.6 Translated Statement of Income and Retained Earnings—
Current Rate Method

Grover Mfg. PLC
Translated Statement Income and Retained Earnings
(Current Rate Method)
For the Year Ended December 31, 19X4
(in thousands)

	LC	Exchange Rate	Dollars
Sales	18,000	$1.40	$25,200
Expenses			
Cost of sales	9,000	1.40	12,600
Depreciation	3,000	1.40	4,200
Other expenses	2,100	1.40	2,940
	14,100		19,740
Income before taxes	3,900		$ 5,460
Income taxes	1,900	1.40	2,660
Net income	2,000		$ 2,800
Retained earnings (12/31/X3)	5,000		11,560
	7,000		$14,360
Dividends	500	1.42	710
Retained earnings (12/31/X4)	6,500		$13,650

---

4. Dividends are translated at the exchange rate in effect when they were issued.

5. Translation gains and losses are taken to a special accumulated translation adjustment account in stockholders' equity.

In the current rate method, it is better to translate the income statement before translating the balance sheet, because the translation gain or loss becomes a balance sheet plug figure rather than an income statement plug figure as was the case with the temporal method. Notice in Exhibit 5.6 that all income statement accounts are translated at the average exchange rate for the period. The beginning retained earnings balance was provided in Table 5.6, and dividends are translated at the exchange rate in effect when they were paid. Thus, the ending retained earnings balance is derived from the other figures rather than plugged in from the balance sheet.

In Exhibit 5.7, all the assets and liabilities are translated at the current exchange rate. Capital stock is translated at the exchange rate in effect when it was issued, and retained earnings is picked up from Exhibit 5.6. All that is left is the accumulated translation adjustment, which is an $8200 loss that makes the balance sheet balance. A more specific derivation of that amount will be explained later in Exhibit 5.9. Once again, it is important to note that the translation adjustment is taken to stockholders' equity

Exhibit 5.7 Translated Balance Sheet—Current Rate Method

Grover Mfg. PLC
Translated Balance Sheet
Current Rate Method
December 31, 19X4
(in thousands)

	LC	Exchange Rate	Dollars
Assets			
Cash and receivables	4,000	1.30	$ 5,200
Inventory	4,500	1.30	5,850
Land	3,000	1.30	3,900
Building—net	7,000	1.30	9,100
Equipment—net	4,000	1.30	5,200
Total	22,500		$29,250
Liabilities and stockholders' equity			
Current liabilities	5,500	1.30	$ 7,150
Notes payable	3,000	1.30	3,900
Deferred taxes	2,500	1.30	3,250
Capital stock	5,000	1.90	9,500
Retained earnings	6,500		13,650
Accumulated translation adjustment			(8,200)
Total	22,500		$29,250

rather than the income statement, as was the case under the temporal method.

Transition.   Statement 52 is effective for fiscal years beginning on or after December 15, 1982, although many firms decided to implement the statement earlier. For new firms that adopted Statement 52 on time, it was necessary to restate some of the financial statements in order to make a proper transition. The exact restatement process as outlined by the Board is as follows:

> Financial statements for fiscal years before the effective date, and financial summaries or other data derived therefrom, may be restated to conform to the provisions of paragraphs 5–29 of this Statement. In the year that this Statement is first applied, the financial statements shall disclose the nature of any restatement and its effect on income before extraordinary items, net income, and related per-share amounts for each fiscal year restated.[11]

In making the adjustment, it is necessary for a transition to occur in the first year of adoption. In the examples given earlier, assume that the firm is making the transition on January 1, 19X4. In reality, the transition

[11]Ibid., p. 13.

Exhibit 5.8 Accumulated Translation Adjustment—Transition Year

Temporal Method
Deferred taxes
  As reported 2,000 × 1.9 = $3,800
  As adjusted 2,000 × 1.5 =   3,000
  Increase to 12/31/X3 retained earnings $ 800

Current Rate Method
Net assets 12/31/X3   10,000
Exchange rate 12/31/X3   1.5 $15,000
Net worth 12/31/X3
  Capital stock $ 9,500
  Retained earnings   11,560   21,060
Accumulated translation adjustment 12/31/X3   (6,060)

would have taken place earlier, but it is more convenient for the purpose of this illustration to use the information already provided in Tables 5.6 and 5.7 and Exhibits 5.3 through 5.7. In the case of the temporal method, it is necessary to make any adjustments in the December 31, 19X3, balance sheet translated at the old temporal method so that the balance sheet will be consistent with the temporal method described in Statement 52. The major change occurs in deferred taxes. Under the temporal method in Statement 8, deferred taxes were translated at the historical rate if they originated from timing differences that related to assets carried at historical cost. Under the temporal method in Statement 52, deferred income taxes are translated at the current exchange rate. Assume that the deferred taxes account in Table 5.7 was translated at the historical rate of $1.90 when the fixed assets were acquired. Exhibit 5.8 illustrates the calculation of the transition amount. The deferred taxes account would have been translated as $3800 under the old temporal method but would be translated at the December 31, 19X3 balance sheet rate of $1.50 ($3000) under the new temporal method, for a difference of $800. The Board recommended that the difference be treated as an adjustment to the beginning retained earnings balance for the transition year when the temporal method is being used. The beginning retained earnings balance under the old temporal method would have been $11,560 (you can actually compute that amount from the information given in Tables 5.6 and 5.7 and Exhibit 5.3 if you want to), but it is adjusted to $12,360 under the new temporal method ($11,560 + $800).

In the case of the current rate method, the Board requires that firms set up an accumulated translation adjustment account rather than adjust the opening retained earnings amount for the transition difference. Exhibit 5.8 illustrates the computation of that amount. One must first realize that, under the current rate method, all assets and liabilities are translated at the current rate. In the accounting equation,

$$Assets = Liabilities + Stockholders'\ equity$$

or

$$Assets - Liabilities = Stockholders'\ equity\ (or\ net\ worth\ or\ net\ assets)$$

Thus, in the year of transition, it is important to translate the opening balance sheet at the current exchange rate. The easy way to do this is simply to translate the net asset balance at the current exchange rate at the opening date, as is shown in Exhibit 5.8. From that amount, you need to subtract the dollar capital stock and retained earnings balances at the opening date (the same as the net asset balance under the temporal method employed before the year of transition) to find the accumulated translation adjustment at the beginning of the year. That loss of $6060 is treated as a new balance in stockholders' equity rather than as an adjustment to the beginning retained earnings balance, as was the case under the transition to the new temporal method.

Calculation of Translation Adjustment. As was mentioned earlier, the translation adjustments under both the temporal and current rate methods are essentially plugged into the financial statements. However, it is possible to derive those amounts more specifically. Exhibit 5.9 illustrates how that process takes place using the current rate method. In the case of the current rate method, net assets are used because they are all translated at the current exchange rate. If you wanted to attempt the same thing for the temporal method, you would use only the net monetary assets because these are the only ones translated at the current rate.

As can be seen, the calculation approach yields a translation loss for 19X4 of $2140. That is added to the beginning balance of $6060, to yield a

Exhibit 5.9 Calculation of the Year-End Translation Adjustment

Net assets 12/31/X3		10,000	
Decrease in exchange rate during 19X4:			
Exchange rate, 19X4	1.30		
Exchange rate, 19X3	1.50 ×	.20	($2,000)
Addition to net assets for 19X4			
from operations		2,000	
Exchange rate 12/31/X4	1.30		
Average exchange rate	1.40 ×	.10	(200)
Less dividends			
Exchange rate 12/31/X4	1.30		
Dividend rate	1.42 ×	.12	60
			($2,140)

Accumulated Translation Adjustment Equity Account

Balance 12/31/X3	($6,060)
Add: aggregate adjustment for the year ended 12/31/X4	(2,140)
Balance 12/31/X4	($8,200)

negative translation adjustment balance of $8200 for the December 31, 19X4, balance sheet. The amount in any given year can also be found by subtracting the ending balance of the prior year from the ending balance of the current year. However, that assumes that there were no other movements in the accumulated translation adjustment account during the year.

SUMMARY

- The accounting standard under which the United States operates for the purposes of accounting for foreign currency is Statement 52, issued by the Financial Accounting Standards Board in 1981.
- The functional currency of an entity is the currency of the primary economic environment in which the entity operates. The foreign currency is any currency that a firm deals in other than the functional currency.
- Foreign currency transactions are transactions whose terms are denominated in a currency other than the entity's functional currency.
- The method required by the FASB in accounting for foreign currency transactions is the two-transactions perspective. This requires that the original transaction be translated into dollars at the exchange rate in effect on that date. Amounts receivable or payable in a foreign currency are translated at the current exchange rate at the subsequent balance sheet date. Foreign exchange gains and losses are taken to income immediately.
- Foreign exchange gains and losses and premiums and discounts on forward contracts used to hedge a foreign currency commitment are deferred until the transaction date and used to adjust the value of the transaction.
- When the forward contract is used to hedge the monetary obligation on a transaction, the premium or discount is written off over the life of the contract and the foreign exchange gains and losses are taken to income in the period in which they occur.
- The foreign exchange gains and losses on a forward contract to hedge an exposed balance sheet position are usually taken to stockholders' equity.
- Forward contracts entered into for speculative purposes are treated as investments and are updated each balance sheet date to reflect their new market value. Foreign exchange gains and losses are taken directly to income.
- The following four methods have been used to translate financial statements into the reporting currency of the parent company: the current–noncurrent method, the monetary–nonmonetary method, the temporal method, and the current rate method.
- Until recently, U.S. companies had operated under the influence of Statement 8, which required the use of the temporal method. Now U.S.

firms must follow Statement 52, which permits the use of the temporal and the current rate methods, depending on certain circumstances.

- If the books and records of the foreign entity are kept in the local currency and the functional currency of that entity is the local currency, the financial statements must be translated into dollars using the current rate method. If the entity is in a highly inflationary country, the functional currency is considered to be the dollar, and the financial statements are translated into dollars using the temporal method.

- If the books and records are kept in the local currency and the functional currency is considered to be the U.S. dollar, the statements are restated into dollars using the temporal method.

- Under the current rate method, assets and liabilities are translated at the current exchange rate, stockholders' equity is translated at the historical rate, net income is translated at the average rate, and translation gains and losses are taken to a special account in stockholders' equity.

- Under the temporal method, cash and amounts receivable and payable in cash are translated at the current rate. Assets carried at past exchange prices are translated at the historical rates. Assets carried at current exchange prices are translated at the current rate. Revenue and expense items are translated at the average rate except for cost of sales and depreciation expense, which are translated at their relevant historical rates. Translation gains and losses are taken to the income statement.

Study Questions

5.1. Define the following terms: functional currency, local currency, foreign currency, and reporting currency.

5.2. Define "foreign currency transaction." Give some examples of foreign currency transactions.

5.3. What is the rationale behind using the two-transactions perspective as opposed to the one-transaction perspective in accounting for foreign currency transactions?

5.4. Why do you think that the Board allowed firms to defer the premium or discount and gains and losses on forward contracts used to hedge a foreign currency commitment? Why do you think that they allowed a different procedure when the contract is used to hedge foreign currency transaction?

5.5. Describe the differences between the current–noncurrent and the monetary–nonmonetary methods of translating foreign currency financial statements.

5.6. Trace the evolution of the standards for translating foreign currency financial statements in the United States.

5.7. If the books and records of a foreign entity are kept in the local currency, how do you know whether or not to translate the financial statements into U.S. dollars using the current rate method or the temporal method?

5.8. What are some major ways that you could use to decide whether or not the local currency or the reporting currency of the parent company is the functional currency of a foreign entity?

5.9. Assume the following exchange rates for Parts 1 and 2. The rates quoted are the number of units of U.S. dollars for one unit of the foreign currency.

Spot	January 1	$1.50
Spot	January 31	$1.45
Spot	February 28	$1.48

1. On January 1, a U.S. exporter sells merchandise abroad for FC100,000. The sale is denominated in the currency of the importer, and the exporter will receive payment in the importer's currency on February 28. The exporter's accountant closes the books at the end of each month.
   a. What entries would be made by the exporter at each of the above dates under the one-transaction perspective?
   b. what entries would be made by the exporter at each of the above dates under the two-transactions perspective in which gains and losses are recognized in each accounting period?
   c. What entries would be made by the exporter at each of the above dates under the method required by Statement 52?
2. On January 1, a U.S. importer imports FC100,000 of equipment with payment to be made in the exporter's currency on February 28. The books are closed at the end of each month.
   a. What entries would be made by the importer at each of the above dates under the one-transaction perspective?
   b. What entries would be made by the importer at each of the above dates under the two-transactions perspective in which gains and losses are deferred?
   c. What entries would be made by the importer at each of the above dates under the method required by Statement 52?

5.10. Assume the following exchange rates for Parts 1 and 2.

Spot	December 1	$0.55
Spot	December 31	$0.60
Spot	January 31	$0.57

1. On December 1, a U.S. exporter sells merchandise to a foreign importer for FC500,000. The sale is denominated in the foreign currency and payment will be received in the foreign currency on January 31. The books are closed at the end of each month.
   a. What entries should be made by the exporter at each of the above dates under the one-transaction perspective?
   b. What entries should be made by the exporter at each of the above dates under the two-transactions perspective in which gains and losses are deferred?
   c. What entries should be made by the exporter at each of the above dates under the method required by Statement 52?
2. On December 1, a U.S. importer imports merchandise from a foreign exporter for FC500,000 with payment to be made on January 31. The books are closed at the end of each month.
   a. What entries should be made by the importer at each of the above dates under the one-transaction perspective?

b. What entries should be made by the importer at each of the above dates under the two-transactions perspective in which gains and losses are deferred?

c. What entries should be made by the importer at each of the above dates under the method required by Statement 52?

3. On March 1, Loa Laminating Inc. considered buying a piece of laminating equipment from a German supplier. The exchange rate on that date was $0.3000, and the equipment was worth DM500,000. On April 15, Loa bought the equipment with payment to be made on May 12. On April 15, the exchange rate had moved to $0.3200. By May 12, when the payment was due, the rate had moved to $0.3150.

a. For how much should Loa carry the equipment on its books?

b. How much cash did it have to pay for the equipment?

c. How much gain or loss, if any, did Loa incur on the transaction, and where was it recognized in the financial statements?

d. Explain how Loa might have been able to protect itself at any of the above dates and what impact that protection would have had on the carrying value of the asset and the cash paid out for it.

5.11. Assume the following exchange rates for Parts 1 and 2.

Spot	June 1	$0.6000
60-day forward	June 1	$0.6400
Spot	June 30	$0.6300
Spot	July 30	$0.6500

1. On June 1 a U.S. manufacturer enters into a commitment to manufacture goods for a foreign importer for FC1,000,000, with delivery to be made on July 30 and payment to be received on that day. The exporter closes the books at the end of each month.

a. If the manufacturer decides not to hedge the commitment, what journal entries would be made at the above dates?

b. If the manufacturer decides to hedge the commitment with a forward contract on June 1, what journal entries would be made at the above dates?

2. On June 1, a U.S. importer enters into a commitment to purchase equipment from a foreign exporter for FC1,000,000 with delivery to be made on July 30 and payment to be received on that day. The importer closes the books at the end of each month.

a. If the importer decides not to hedge the commitment, what journal entries would be made at the above dates?

b. If the importer decides to hedge the commitment with a forward contract, what journal entries would be made at the above dates?

5.12. Assume the following exchange rates for Parts 1 and 2.

Spot	November 1	$1.30
60-day forward	November 1	$1.20
Spot	November 31	$1.26
Spot	December 28	$1.22

1. On November 1, a U.S. exporter sells equipment it has manufactured to a foreign importer for FC500,000 with payment to be made on December 28. The exporter's books are closed at the end of each month.
   a. If the exporter decides to hedge the transaction with a forward contract, what would the journal entries be for each of the above dates?
   b. If the exporter decides not to hedge the transaction, how much would the sale be worth, and how much cash would be received from the importer?

2. On November 1, a U.S. importer buys equipment from a foreign exporter for FC500,000 with payment to be made on December 28. The importer's books are closed at the end of each month.
   a. If the importer decides to hedge the transaction with a forward contract, what would the journal entries be for each of the above dates?
   b. If the exporter decides not to hedge the transaction, how much would equipment be carried for on the books and how much cash would the importer have to pay?

5.13. The British subsidiary of a U.S. firm has inventory that is carried on the books at historical cost of £4000. The current market value of the inventory is £5000. The exchange rate in effect when the inventory was purchased was $2.00 and the current rate is $1.50. What would be the translated dollar value of the inventory if the functional currency was the
   a. British pound?
   b. U.S. dollar?

5.14. The German subsidiary of a U.S. firm has fixed assets on the books at original cost of DM500,000. Half of the assets were bought on January 1, 1980, when the exchange rate was $0.5000. There is no salvage value projected, and the useful life for straight-line depreciation is five years. The other half of the assets were bought on July 1, 1982, when the exchange rate was $0.4500. No salvage value is projected on those assets either, and the useful life for straight-line depreciation is ten years. Compute the dollar book value of the depreciation expense on December 31, 1984, when the exchange rate was $0.3500:
   a. If the functional currency is the deutsche mark.
   b. If the functional currency is the dollar.

5.15. Bullfrog Enterprises bought merchandise from a foreign supplier on December 1, 1984, for FC10,000 when the exchange rate was $0.95. At the end of the year, the dollar value of the liability had changed to $11,000. At the same time, Bullfrog had a subsidiary in Upper Volta that had a translation gain of $15,000 for 1984. What should be the amount of the foreign exchange gain or loss, if any, that should be included in Bullfrog's income statement if it translates foreign currency financial statements according to the
   a. Temporal method?
   b. Current rate method?

5.16. At the start of 1983, Mt. Nittany Mfg. Company's only foreign subsidiary had local currency assets of LC500,000 and local currency liabilities of LC200,000. Its capital stock at the start of the year was $100,000 and retained earnings was $5000. Assume the following information:

$0.4000 = the exchange rate on 1/1/83.
$0.4500 = the exchange rate on 12/31/84.

$0.3500 = the exchange rate when the subsidiary was first organized.
  a. What was the cumulative translation adjustment at the start of 1983, assuming that the firm was beginning the transition from temporal method to current rate method at that time?
  b. Where would that adjustment appear in the financial statements?
5.17. Beehive, Inc., has a foreign subsidiary that needs to be translated into U.S. dollars. The financial statements are as follows:

Balance Sheet
December 31, 1985

	Local Currency
Cash	50,000
Receivables	125,000
Inventory	100,000
Net fixed assets	400,000
	675,000
Current liabilities	170,000
Long-term debt	200,000
Common stock	250,000
Retained earnings	55,000
	675,000

Statement of Income and Retained Earnings
for the Year Ended December 31, 1985

	Local Currency
Sales	400,000
Cost of sales	160,000
Gross profit	240,000
Depreciation expense	10,000
Other expense	95,000
	105,000
Net income before tax	135,000
Income tax	60,000
Net income	75,000
Retained earnings 1/1/85	20,000
	95,000
Dividends	40,000
Retained earnings	55,000

The following additional information is also necessary:

Exchange rates:
$1.50   12/31/85
$1.75   historical rate when fixed assets were acquired, long-term debt was incurred, and capital stock was issued

$1.60   average rate, 1985
$1.65   5/31/85
$1.55   9/30/85
$1.70   rate for 1/1/85 beginning inventory
$1.52   rate for 12/31/85 ending inventory

Revenues and expenses were incurred evenly throughout the year. This also includes inventory purchases and taxes.

Dividends were paid in equal amounts on 5/31 and 9/30.

Retained earnings on 12/31/84 was $10,000

Beginning inventory was LC50,000, and ending inventory was LC60,000 for 1985.

    a. Translate the financial statements under the current rate method.
    b. Translate the financial statements under the temporal method.

CHAPTER 6

Additional Translation and Reporting Issues

In Chapter 5, we discussed how to translate financial statements, but we left a number of issues unanswered. The purpose of this chapter is to fill in some of the more technical details, look at how financial statements are translated in other countries, and examine in more depth some of the issues surrounding the consolidation of financial statements that were introduced in Chapter 2.

STATEMENT 52 ISSUES

Highly Inflationary Economies

In some respects, it is inaccurate to limit the accounting for inflation to Statement 52 because that statement essentially deals with translation of foreign currency financial statements. However, the process of translation introduced in Statement 52 required that the Board take a look at firms operating in highly inflationary economies. In addition, it resulted in the issuance of Statement 70, "Financial Reporting and Changing Prices: Foreign Currency Translation," in order to bridge the gap between accounting for changing prices (Statement 33) and accounting for foreign currency (Statement 52).

In Chapter 5, we learned that the translation methodology used to translate financial statements from a foreign currency to the reporting currency (assumed in our examples to be the U.S. dollar) depended on the definition of the functional currency. If the functional currency is the local currency, then local currency financial statements are translated into the reporting currency using the current rate method; if the functional currency is the reporting currency, the local currency is restated into the reporting currency using the temporal method. The functional currency designation was to depend on operating characteristics of the foreign operation.

However, a problem developed in the first exposure draft issued by the Board in 1980. A number of companies with operations in highly inflationary economies correctly pointed out that the use of the current rate method to translate financial statements into dollars could result in distort-ing relationships among accounts. For example, fixed assets carried at historical cost in the local currency of a highly inflationary country would quickly lose value. As pointed out in Chapter 3, the assets would be under-valued compared with their current cost or with their historical cost ad-justed for the general price index. In addition, the dollar value of the assets would erode in an inflationary environment. As explained in Chapter 4, this results from the purchasing power parity theory. As inflation rises in one country in relation to another, its exchange rate deteriorates at approx-imately the same rate. For example, a 100% rise in inflation in Mexico in relation to the U.S. dollar should lead to approximately a 100% fall in the value of the peso compared to the dollar. Because the peso assets are carried on their books at historical cost, the dollar equivalent would drop by the amount of the deterioration of the peso against the dollar.

As a result of this reported phenomenon, the Board decided in its revised exposure draft to allow firms to adjust the foreign currency finan-cial statements of operations in highly inflationary economies for the ef-fects of changing prices using a general consumer price index. However, that suggestion met strong resistance for the following reasons:

a. Information restated to reflect changes in the general price level should not be required in the primary financial statements until and unless the usefulness of that information has been adequately demonstrated in the Statement 33 experiment.

b. The primary financial statements should not mix information presented in constant measuring units that reflect changes in the general price level with information presented in nominal monetary units.

c. The lack of reliable and timely price-level indexes in some highly inflation-ary economies constitutes a significant obstacle to practical application of the proposal.[1]

As a result of these objections, the Board reconsidered its proposal and recommended a pragmatic solution. The solution, as pointed out in Chap-ter 5, was to require that financial statements of firms in highly inflationary economies be restated into dollars using the temporal method, even if its functional currency is the local currency from an operating standpoint.

In order to accomplish this objective, it is important to know how to identify a highly inflationary economy. The Board decided to allow max-imum flexibility to management to make this decision on an individual basis. The basic rule is that a country with a cumulative rate of inflation of approximately 100% or more over a three-year period is considered highly inflationary. However, the firm needs to look at the trend in inflation rather than just the absolute amounts. For example, a country whose infla-tion rate is steadily falling and who is gaining control of its economy might

---

[1]Financial Accounting Standards Board, *Statement of Financial Accounting Standards No. 52*, "Foreign Currency Translation," (Stamford, Conn.: FASB, December 1981), p. 56.

still have a cumulative rate of inflation in excess of 100%, but management might choose not to consider it highly inflationary because of the trend. On the other hand, a country might have lost control over its economy, with inflation skyrocketing but still not exceeding 100% during the latest three-year period. In such a case, management may decide that the signals are clearly bad and restate the financial statements using the temporal method.

Changing Prices and Foreign Currency Translation

As pointed out in Chapter 3, Statement 33 is the standard in the United States that deals with accounting for changing prices. It was explained in that chapter that firms must provide supplementary information on specific and general price level changes. However, we did not deal with the issue of inflation in foreign operations. For example, how does a U.S. firm with a subsidiary in Brazil take into consideration Brazilian inflation when providing information to shareholders on a consolidated basis?

Up to the issuance of Statement 70, "Financial Reporting and Changing Prices: Foreign Currency Translation," two major methods of accounting for inflation in a foreign country were discussed in the United States: the translate/restate method and the restate/translate method. The first method recommended translating foreign currency financial statements into dollars and then adjusting them for inflation in the United States. This method adopted a general price level philosophy and reflected the feeling that U.S. investors were concerned about the change in purchasing power in dollars of their investments, irrespective of where that money may have been invested around the world. The second method recommended that one restate the foreign currency financial statements for inflation in the foreign country and then translate the adjusted statements into dollars.

As a result of the adoption of Statement 52, it was necessary to amend Statement 33 so that the procedures for adjusting for changing prices in foreign operations would be consistent with the new translation standard. In Statement 70, a distinction was made between foreign operations whose functional currency is the reporting currency (the dollar for most U.S.-based firms) and those whose functional currency is something else. If the functional currency is the reporting currency, the procedures worked out in Statement 33 still hold. If the functional currency is something else, the amendments in Statement 70 supersede the procedures followed in Statement 33.

Functional Currency Is the Reporting Currency

Remember in the discussion of Statement 33 in Chapter 3 that information must be presented in historical cost/constant dollars (also referred to as General Purchasing Power or GPP adjustments), current cost, and the increase in current costs net of inflation. The translation procedure required depends on the type of information being disclosed on changing prices.

Historical Cost/Constant Dollars. Statement 33 requires that historical cost/constant dollar information be provided for income from continuing operations (essentially cost of goods sold and depreciation, depletion, and amortization expenses) and the purchasing power gain or loss on net monetary items. When dealing with foreign currency financial statements, the standard requires the use of the translate/restate method. This means that the financial information must first be translated into dollars according to the temporal method of translation, and the dollar amounts are then adjusted for inflation by using the U.S. consumer price index. This procedure essentially ignores foreign inflation.

Current Cost. The current cost adjustment can be accomplished in one of two ways. The easiest way is to use the current cost of assets as measured in dollars. This would be the case particularly for assets that were actually bought in the United States and transferred to the foreign location. The current cost in dollars could also be used when the U.S. assets are essentially the same as the foreign assets. An alternative method of computing current cost would be to determine the current cost of the asset in the local currency and then translate that amount into dollars using the exchange rate in effect when the current value is determined (essentially the current exchange rate). That procedure is consistent with the restate/translate method mentioned previously.

Increases in Current Cost Net of Inflation. The current cost/constant dollar adjustment must be made for inventory and property, plant, and equipment amounts, and it is reflected in terms of the increase in those accounts over the year. The Board requires that the current cost amounts be translated into dollars and adjusted for changes in the U.S. consumer price index. As mentioned, the current cost values can be determined on the basis of U.S. assets or assets in the foreign country. The key is that the constant dollar adjustment be in terms of U.S. rather than foreign inflation.

Functional Currency Is Not the Reporting Currency

It is possible that a subsidiary in France, for example, could have a functional currency other than the reporting currency of the parent company. In fact, it is possible that the functional currency could be something other than the French franc. However, we will assume that in most situations in which the reporting currency is not the functional currency, the functional currency will be the currency of the country in which the subsidiary is located. Using the situation of the French subsidiary of a U.S. company, the functional currency would be the French franc rather than the U.S. dollar (the reporting currency of the parent company) or another functional currency, such as the German mark. When the functional currency is not the reporting currency, the provisions of Statement 70 must be adhered to.

Historical Cost/Constant Dollar. The first major departure to Statement 33 is in this category. Statement 70 does *not* require firms to provide historical cost/constant dollar information as long as they provide current cost information about their foreign operations. The Board basically used a cost/benefit justification for eliminating the disclosure of historical cost/constant dollar information. There were strong objections to the preparation of this information because of its cost and limited usefulness, so the Board decided to stick with the current cost data for operations in which the functional currency is not the reporting currency of the parent.

Current Cost. The current cost measurements are the same here as when the functional currency is the reporting currency. This means that the restate/translate method would be used: income from continuing operations, inventory, and property, plant, and equipment would be restated to current costs in the local currency and translated into the reporting currency at the current exchange rate.

Increases in Current Cost Net of Inflation. Statement 70 provides another area of significant departure from Statement 33 in the preparation of this information. There are two ways that current cost/constant functional currency information can be prepared: by translating the increases or decreases in current cost into dollars and adjusting for the U.S. consumer price index (the restate/translate method) or by adjusting the assets at current cost for the functional currency consumer price index and then translating the amounts into dollars according to the current rate method in Statement 52.

It is in this area that the terminology becomes especially confusing. Previously, we had always used *constant dollars,* since all adjustments had been made in terms of U.S. dollars, the reporting currency of U.S.-based firms. However, Statement 52 injected the notion of functional currency. Thus, we need to begin to think of constant functional currency rather than constant dollars when computing the increase or decrease in current costs net of inflation. The translate/restate option stated earlier actually uses the "constant dollar" concept, since the adjustments are made for the U.S. consumer price index. However, the second option—the restate/translate option—uses a "constant functional currency" concept because it is the consumer price index of the functional currency rather than the reporting currency that is being used. Using the example of the French subsidiary of a U.S. firm in which the functional currency is the French franc, the second option would involve adjusting assets to current cost and then determining the impact of general inflation in France by using the French consumer price index.

An Example

Statement 70 has an excellent appendix that goes through all of the adjustments described here. The purpose of the discussion in this chapter is to describe the adjustments conceptually rather than get heavily involved in detailed computations. However, a numerical example would help to explain the concepts better. Rather than go through examples for all possible accounts, we will show the adjustments for equipment. The following represents the balance in the equipment account in local currency at historical cost and current cost:

	19X5	19X4
Historical cost	100,000	100,000
Accumulated depreciation	30,000	20,000
Net equipment	70,000	80,000
Current cost	145,000	130,000
Accumulated depreciation	43,500	26,000
Net equipment	101,500	104,000

The following assumptions also need to be made:

1. The equipment was acquired on January 1, 19X3. It is depreciated on a straight-line basis over ten years and is expected to have no salvage value. There were no acquisitions or disposals of assets during the year.

2. The exchange rates between the functional currency and dollars are as follows:

January 1, 19X3   FC 1 = $3.00

December 31, 19X4   FC 1 = $2.00

Average 19X5   FC 1 = $1.75

December 31, 19X5   FC 1 = $1.50

3. The U.S. and local consumer price indices are as follows:

	Local	U.S.
January 1, 19X3	85.0	96.0
December 31, 19X4	100.0	100.0
Average 19X5	110.0	102.5
December 31, 19X5	120.0	105.0

The Functional Currency Is the Reporting Currency. As explained above, this first situation is governed by Statement 33. At that time, it was correct to say that the functional currency was the dollar because the concept of reporting currency was not introduced until Statement 52. In this case, we will assume that the reporting currency is the dollar. Three types of adjustments need to be made: historical cost/constant dollar, current cost, and increases in current cost net of inflation.

The first adjustment is historical cost/constant dollar. Since Statement 33 requires that the translate/restate method be used for this adjustment, the equipment and accumulated depreciation must be translated into dollars using the historical exchange rate as shown below:

$$
\begin{array}{lll}
LC\ 100,000 \times \$3.00 = \$300,000 \\
\underline{LC\ \ \ 30,000} \times \$3.00 = \ \ \ \underline{90,000} \\
LC\ \ \ 70,000 \qquad\quad = \$210,000
\end{array}
$$

Then the translated amounts must be restated for U.S. inflation by multiplying the asset and depreciation by the average consumer price index for 19X5 and dividing by the index in effect on the date the asset was acquired:

Historical Cost Nominal Dollars	Conversion Factor	Historical Cost/ Constant Dollars
$300,000	× 102.5/96	$320,313
90,000	× 102.5/96	96,094
$210,000		$224,219

The next adjustment is current cost in nominal dollars. This is determined by translating the current cost in local currency by the exchange rate in effect on the date that the current cost determination is made. That is usually at the balance sheet date and is illustrated as follows:

	Local Currency	Exchange Rate	Dollars
Current cost	LC145,000	$1.50	$217,500
less accumulated depreciation	43,500	$1.50	65,250
Net equipment	LC101,500		$152,250

The last major adjustment is the increase in current cost net of inflation. This adjustment is considerably more complex than the others and no good examples are given in Statement 33 on how it should be made. However, Statement 70 provides an example we can use. It is pointed out in Statement 70 that it is necessary to exclude foreign exchange gains and losses in making the adjustment. In order to do that, the Board suggests translating the beginning and ending net current cost balances at the average exchange rate for the year. Then the dollar equivalents can be restated to average constant dollar equivalents for the year as follows:

	Current Cost (FC)	Exchange Rate	Current Cost ($)	Conversion Factor	Current Cost Constants
Current cost, net 12/31/X4	104,000	$1.75	$182,000	102.5/100	$186,550
Depreciation[a]	(13,750)	$1.75	(24,063)	[b]	(24,063)
Current cost, net 12/31/X5	(101,500)	$1.75	(177,625)	102.5/105	(173,396)
Increase in current cost	11,250		$19,688		$10,909

[a]Depreciation is figured as follows:
　Current cost, beginning of year　　　　LC130,000
　Current cost, end of year　　　　　　　145,000
　Average　　　　　　　LC275,000/2 = LC137,500
　Depreciation expense = LC137,500 × 10% = LC13,750
[b]Assume to be in average 1982 dollars.

Increase in current cost　$19,688
Increase net of inflation　 10,909
Inflation component　　　 $ 8,779

The Functional Currency Is Not the Reporting Currency.   As explained above, this situation is governed by the requirements in Statement 70. As before, there are three potential situations for making adjustments. In the first case, historical cost/constant dollars, no adjustments need to be made according to Statement 70. In the second case, current cost/nominal dollars, the adjustments and translation are done exactly as explained earlier when the functional currency is the reporting currency.

The third situation is the most difficult, because it involves two options. The first option, described above, is that in which the translate/restate method is used. In that case, the adjustments are made just as illustrated when the functional currency is the reporting currency. The second option is that in which the restate/translate method is used. In this situation, the current cost in the local currency is adjusted for changes in the price level in the local country before it is translated into dollars. The

	Current Cost (FC)	Conversion Factor	Current Cost/ Constant FC
Current cost, net 12/31/X4	104,000	110/100	114,400
Depreciation	(13,750)	[a]	(13,750)
Current cost, net 12/31/X5	(101,500)	110/120	(93,042)
Increase in current cost	11,250		(7,608)

[a]Assumed to be in average constant functional currency units.

	Current Cost/ Constant FC	Exchange Rate	Dollars
Increase in current cost	11,250	$1.75	$19,688
Increase net of inflation	(7,608)	$1.75	(13,314)
Inflation component	18,858		$33,002)

current cost/constant functional currency amounts are then translated into dollars at the average exchange rate in order to eliminate any possible exchange rate gains or losses. The implication in this example is that inflation far outstripped any increases in current costs.

Exhibit 6.1 summarizes conceptually how the adjustments are made for equipment in the preceding illustrations.

Consolidation of Foreign Operations

Chapter 5 presented the method of translation that must be followed when preparing financial statements for consolidation purposes. Once the statements have been translated into the parent currency, it is a relatively simple process to add the dollar balances together to get the consolidated financial statements. However, there are a few problems that must be considered: the elimination of intercompany profits, intercompany loans

Exhibit 6.1 Summary of Changing Prices and Foreign Currency Translation

	Historical Cost/Constant Dollars	Current Cost	Increases in Current Cost Net of Inflation
Functional currency is reporting currency	1. Translate using temporal method 2. Adjust for U.S. CPI	1. Adjust to local current cost 2. Translate using current rate method	1. Translate current cost into dollars using average rate 2. Adjust for U.S. CPI

Functional currency is not reporting currency	Not required	Same as above	1. Translate/restate option—same as above
			2. Restate/translate
			  a. Adjust to local current cost
			  b. Adjust for local CPI
			  c. Translate at average rate

treated as a long-term investment that will never be paid back, and inter-company loans that are intended to be paid back.

Elimination of Intercompany Profits

Assume that a parent company sells inventory to its German subsidiary for $300,000 when the exchange rate was DM1 = $0.35. The inventory cost $150,000, so the profit on the intercompany transaction was $150,000. The German subsidiary would record the inventory and liability at DM857,143 ($300,000 ÷ $0.35). Assuming that the functional currency is the German mark in this case, the inventory would have to be translated into dollars at the current exchange rate at the next balance sheet date. Assuming a rate of $0.40, the inventory would be valued at $342,857 for consolidation pur-poses before any adjustments (DM857,143 × $0.40). However, Statement 52 requires that firms eliminate any inventory profits and recognize any translation gains or losses in the separate component of stockholders' equity.

> $342,857 value of inventory at new balance sheet date
> 150,000 intercompany profit on original transaction
> $192,857 value of inventory for consolidation purposes

> $192,857 value of inventory for consolidation purposes
> 150,000 value of inventory when sold to German subsidiary
> $ 42,857 increase in value of inventory

The inventory is carried on the consolidated books at $192,857, so the translation gain of $42,857 is recognized in the inventory balance. Howev-er, the offset to that amount goes to the separate component of stock-holders' equity rather than to income.

Intercompany Loans

Assume that a parent company loans its German subsidiary $10,000,000 to finance expansion when the exchange rate is $0.35/DM. At the subsequent balance sheet date, the exchange rate has changed to $0.40.

> $10,000,000/$0.35 = DM28,571,429
> $10,000,000/$0.40 =   25,000,000
> Translation gain = DM3,571,429

How the exchange rate change is dealt with depends on the intent of management in regard to the intercompany debt. If the intent is to never have the debt repaid, then the translation gain is taken to the separate component of stockholders' equity. If the debt is expected to be repaid, then the translation gain is taken to income in that period.

Equity Investees

Although most of the discussion thus far has focused on the situation in which the investor owns a majority interest in the investee, a great deal of foreign investment is undertaken on a minority basis. Thus, the investor company needs to determine its equity interest in the investee at the end of the period and record that interest in its books. It should be noted that the financial statements of the investee need to be translated into dollars according to the requirements of Statement 52. Then the equity adjustments can be made.

Assume that a U.S. company owns 40% of a foreign company and that its beginning and end-of-year balances in the equity section of the foreign company are as follows:

	Beginning of Year	End of Year
Common stock	$500,000	$500,000
Retained earnings	700,000	1,100,000
Equity adjustment from translation	300,000	400,000
Stockholders' equity	$1,500,000	$2,000,000

The adjustment that the investor would make at the end of the period to reflect the change in the equity interest of its investment would be as follows:

Investment in foreign entity	200,000	
Equity interest in income		160,000
Equity adjustment, translation		40,000

The investment in foreign entity balance is found by multiplying the increase in the total change in stockholders' equity ($500,000) by 40%. It is assumed that the change in retained earnings is due only to income during the period. Thus, the equity interest in income is found by multiplying the income amount ($400,000) by 40%. Finally, the investor must also recognize its equity interest in the translation adjustment by multiplying the change in the adjustment during the period ($100,000) by 40%.

The foregoing illustration implies that the current rate method is used for translation purposes, because there is an "equity adjustment from translation" section in stockholders' equity. One of the problems with the temporal method used previously in Statement 8 was that translation gains and losses were taken directly to income rather than to the balance sheet as is the case with the current rate method. That meant that an investor would pick up translation gains and losses in its equity interest in income along with operating income. In cases where there was a large translation loss, the equity interest in income could be very low or possibly a loss.

One way around that dilemma is to use the cost method to recognize foreign source income. Under the cost method, the only income recognized is the dividend declared by the foreign corporation to the investor. That means that translation gains and losses would be ignored, since they relate to the translated value of income, not to the dividend. However, the cost method can be used by U.S. firms only when the equity interest in the foreign corporation is less than 20%.

Statement 52 uses both the current rate and temporal methods of translation, depending on the circumstances of the foreign corporation. Thus the problem of the temporal method does not disappear entirely. However, the earnings effect that exists with the temporal method would not be a factor for financial statements translated by the current rate method.

Disclosure of the Impact of Statement 52

Statement 52 is very specific about what must be disclosed:

1. The aggregate transaction gain or loss included in income.
2. An analysis of the change during the period of the separate component of stockholders' equity, including at least the following:

    a. Beginning and ending amount of cumulative translation adjustments
    b. The aggregate adjustment for the period resulting from translation adjustments and gains and losses from certain hedges and intercompany balances
    c. The amount of income taxes for the period allocated to the translation adjustments
    d. The amounts transferred from cumulative translation adjustments and included in determining net income for the period as a result of the sale or complete or substantially complete liquidation of an investment in a foreign entity.[2]

That information can be provided "in a separate financial statement, in notes to the financial statements, or as a part of a statement of changes in equity." There does not seem to be any uniform or suggested way on where the information is to be displayed or in which format.

One of the difficulties of this process is that the focus is on the measurable transactions and translation gains and losses. It is important for management to also spend some time in the annual report explaining the rest of the impact of the translation of financial statements on the operations of the firm. During the early 1980s, when the dollar was rising rapidly against most foreign currencies and those economies were experiencing relatively

[2]Ibid., pp. 12–13.

slow growth, many U.S. firms found that they were experiencing a translated dollar profit squeeze. This can be illustrated with the following example:

	Income LC	Exchange Rate	Dollars
First quarter 19X4	LC 100,000	$1.00	$100,000
First quarter 19X5	LC 110,000	$0.25	$ 27,500

Income rose in local currency from 100,000 to 110,000 over the year, an increase of only 10% due primarily to a weak economy. However, the dollar equivalent fell from $100,000 to $27,500, a drop of 72.5%. Thus, one can see how a local currency gain can be turned into a dollar loss if the local economy is growing slower than the local currency is weakening in relation to the dollar. This type of situation would be important to report to shareholders so that they could better understand the reported results.[3]

As noted in Chapter 5, one of the major differences between the temporal method and the current rate method is that the latter exclude translation gains and losses from income. This has made it much easier for companies to forecast earnings because the translation gyrations need no longer be dealt with.

Foreign Exchange Risk Management

In reality, foreign exchange risk management is a subject that fits more in an international finance discussion than in an international accounting discussion. However, it helps for the accountant to be familiar with some of the basic issues that the Treasury people deal with so that he or she can provide more relevant information.

The Objective of Foreign Exchange Risk Management

The main objective of foreign exchange risk management is to minimize risk *and* cost, subject to governmental and organizational constraints. Three costs must be considered: (1) the direct costs of the financing and hedging operations; (2) the cost, expressed as a loss, caused by a change in a currency's value (net exposure times the change in currency value); and (3) the cost, expressed as opportunity cost (lost business), of changing the company's normal operating activities in order to reduce exposure. There are also three risks involved: guessing wrong on the direction, magnitude, or timing of the currency change.

[3]For a more complete discussion of this issue, see Lee H. Radebaugh, "The Impact of a Strengthening Dollar, Weak World Economy, and New Accounting Standard on Performance Evaluation of Foreign Operations," *Managerial Accounting: An Analysis of Current International Applications* (Champaign: University of Illinois, 1984).

One of the most interesting aspects of foreign exchange risk management is that there is no single optimal solution to this dual minimization problem. Instead, the optimal solutions are virtually infinite. An *optimal solution* is defined as one in which no other combination of policies has the same expected cost with a lower associated risk. Stated another way, no other combination of policies has the same level of risk with lower expected cost. What results is a *spectrum* of optimal solutions, ranging from the lowest risk/highest cost solution to the highest risk/lowest cost solution, with variations in between. Once this array of optimal solutions has been generated, the decision maker must choose the solution that is consistent with corporate desires and capabilities and is acceptable in terms of government policies. For example, if a company is very risk-averse or not in a position to take much risk, the lowest risk strategy would be selected. Alternatively, the company may not have sufficient funds to pursue the higher cost/lower risk strategies, and may therefore need to select a lower-cost/higher risk strategy. If all this sounds rather vague, it generally is less so in practice. Most companies have definite policies with regard to managing foreign exchange risk, ranging from aggressive to defensive. And within a company's guidelines, the corporate treasurer is usually constrained as to the acceptable level of risk and cost. In addition, government policies in the countries where the company has operations may preclude the use of certain otherwise optimal strategies. For example, the government may prohibit swap arrangements.

The Process of Foreign Exchange Risk Management

Foreign exchange risk management involves 10 steps:

1. Determine a relevant planning period.
2. Forecast the change in relevant currencies during the planning period.
3. Prepare a company funds flow for the period, together with its expected effects on the company's financial position.
4. Determine the net accounting exposure and estimate the possible exchange rate gain or loss for the period.
5. If necessary or desired, rearrange the accounting exposure to minimize expected losses, bearing in mind the potential impact of this action on the firm's economic exposure.
6. Determine all the operational constraints that cannot be violated by hedging solutions.
7. Identify all the acceptable hedging and financial solutions and estimate their costs.
8. Plug all this information into a computer and generate the optimal solution spectrum.

9. Choose the solution most acceptable to the company.

10. Check to see that you have done everything correctly and accurately.

Choosing the Planning Period. Choosing the planning period is largely a function of the reliability of the exchange rate forecast data, the corporate planning horizon, and the maturity period of the decisions and transactions. Because exchange rate forecasting becomes increasingly difficult and speculative as the time period under consideration increases, time is the major constraint. Planning periods of over a year are rare and probably ill-advised. Because most companies operate from yearly plans and quarterly reporting periods, a yearly plan divided into quarterly segments makes sense for most companies. Shorter segments are often necessary or desirable if the exchange rate is particularly volatile and large sums are involved.

Predicting the Change in Exchange Rates. Knowing that exchange rates will change, the next step in the foreign exchange risk management process is predicting exchange rate movements. This prediction in itself involves three predictions of the movement: the direction, the magnitude, and the timing. The prediction of *direction* is obviously important, for the results are drastically different if the currency appreciates in value rather than depreciates. The *magnitude* of the change is also important not because the results are different from a gain versus loss standpoint but because the magnitude of the gain or loss is affected. The *timing* of the change is important because it affects the timing of the gains or losses and hence their realization and recognition. Finally, the direction, magnitude, and timing of the movement are important taken as a group because they jointly determine the direction, magnitude, and timing of the actions taken to manage the foreign exchange risk. For example, if a foreign currency is expected to move upward only slightly and only at the very end of the fiscal year, and if the company has no transactions in that currency, the company's strategy might be to do little or nothing and then only as the end of the year approaches because there is not much at stake in terms of gains or losses during most of the year. On the other hand, if the currency's rise in value is expected to be continuous and large, and the company has a great deal of payables in that currency, the foreign exchange risk management would be quite different and certainly more important, calling for exposure minimization and considerable hedging activities throughout the period. In Chapter 4, we discussed the major variables that one must consider in predicting exchange rate changes.

Preparing the Funds Flow Budget. The next step in foreign exchange risk management is specifying all the financing requirements and funds flows in each currency that cannot (or should not) be altered. Examples are changes in working capital and debt repayments. In other words, this process determines the funds flows that will be necessary to keep operations operational in the normal business context. Pro forma income statements and balance sheets should also be prepared for the planning period, or at least for those accounts that will be exposed to changes in the foreign currency values.

Determining the Accounting Exposure. Being reasonably certain that a major change in exchange rates is forthcoming, a wise company will seek to ascertain what would be the effect of the expected change on its financial position—that is, will it cause a gain or loss. To ascertain this, the company must first calculate its accounting exposure, of which there are two kinds. As described in Chapter 5, the first is transaction exposure and the second is translation exposure. An exposed account is one whose value changes as the exchange rate changes. According to Statement 52, amounts receivable or payable in a foreign currency resulting from a transaction are exposed to exchange rate changes because their values must be adjusted at each balance sheet date.

Translation exposure is more complex. If the functional currency is the local currency, then essentially all assets and liabilities are exposed; if the functional currency is the reporting currency, then only those accounts translated at the current exchange rate (essentially monetary assets and liabilities) are exposed.

One of the interesting results of Statement 52 is that the use of the current rate method can provide a significantly different size and mix of exposed accounts. It also changes the urgency of exposure because translation gains and losses are taken to stockholders' equity rather than directly to income. Thus, many firms appear to be paying very little attention to accounting exposure when they use the current rate method of translation.

Acting on the Accounting Exposure.   Once a firm has calculated the potential financial impact from an exchange rate change, it is then faced with several options:

1. It can choose to do nothing.

2. It can choose to alter its net accounting exposure.

3. It can cover its existing accounting exposure.

4. It can do some combination of these three alternatives.

Doing nothing is a strategy most often selected when conditions are expected to result in a *gain*. These conditions would prevail when (a) the net exposure is positive in a currency that is expected to rise in value, (b) the net exposure is negative in a currency whose value is expected to decline, (c) the sum of the expected gains from exposed positions in some currencies is greater than the sum of the expected losses from exposed positions in other currencies, or (d) the overall net exposure is zero. As mentioned before, the "do nothing" strategy might also be relevant when the current rate method of translation is used.

Rearranging the Accounting Exposure. Rearranging the accounting exposure is an appropriate strategy when the conditions listed above do not exist and the firm expects a foreign exchange loss. If accounting exposure is the difference between assets and liabilities whose values are subject to change when exchange rates change, it follows that the exposure itself can be changed. This can be done by adjusting the amounts of assets and liabilities included in the exposure. For example, local currency held by the U.S. company's Mexican subsidiary is subject to a decline in its translated value if the Mexican peso declines in relation to the U.S. dollar. So too would the subsidiary's peso-denominated accounts receivable and peso-denominated debts. To minimize the negative effects of a peso depreciation on these exposed accounts, the subsidiary could speed up collection of its peso-denominated accounts receivables and get rid of its pesos on hand—perhaps investing them in land or some other asset whose value would not be affected by a shift in the exchange rate. Since the U.S. dollar value of its peso debts would decline with the depreciation of the Mexican peso, the company could keep its present level of peso debt or increase the debt to help offset any peso monetary assets it could not decrease.

On the other hand, the Mexican subsidiary's dollar-denominated payables and loans would increase in amount if the peso declined. To avoid these potential losses, the subsidiary could speed up its repayment of dollar-denominated payables and loans. At the same time, any dollar receivables or dollars on hand in the Mexican subsidiary would be worth more *after* the peso declined, resulting in a translation gain. The Mexican subsidiary could increase its dollar-denominated accounts receivable or delay the collection of existing ones, and try to increase its holdings of dollars or other currencies that are expected to rise in value against the peso. By carefully juggling the composition and amounts of its peso-denominated and foreign-currency-denominated assets and liabilities that comprise its accounting exposure, the firm can reduce, eliminate (balance), or even reverse its net accounting exposure.

However, before getting too excited about rearranging the exposure as a cheap and riskless way of protecting against exchange losses or avoiding the use of covering or hedging techniques, a few sobering words of caution are in order. Rearranging the *accounting* exposure can also affect the firm's *economic* exposure. More important, changing the firm's *economic* exposure may be far more risky and costly than losses from changes in exchange rates.

Of the several possible definitions of economic exposure, the one suitable here is "the loss of future business, or opportunity cost." *Opportunity cost* in this sense means the cost of the profitable business opportunities a firm passes up when it takes certain actions that prevent it from taking advantage of other alternatives. To be more specific, the opportunity cost of doing business on a cash-only, no-credit basis is the loss of additional sales that might be made if the company were willing to provide credit to buyers. Similarly, the opportunity cost of having all a company's investable funds tied up in long-term nonliquid assets is the loss from having to forgo potentially more profitable short-term investments.

As an example, suppose a company has a net asset exposure in a currency whose value is expected to decline. Ignoring temporarily the concept of economic exposure, the firm could rearrange its exposed assets and liabilities to bring the accounting exposure to zero: reduce the appropriate assets and increase the appropriate liabilities until the sums of the two are equal. To accomplish this, it could discontinue local currency sales on credit, speed up collection of local currency receivables, and delay payment of its own local currency by investing in land. However, these actions make the firm extremely illiquid, more heavily in debt, on worse terms with its customers and creditors, and in danger of losing customers who need to buy on credit. Any one of these results alone, and certainly several of them in combination, will increase the firm's economic exposure, which means the firm is not in as sound a business position as it was previously. Angering its existing customers by speeding up the collection of accounts receivable and angering its potential customers by not extending credit could affect the company's future revenue streams. Increasing its debt puts the firm under a future cash outflow squeeze to repay the debt when it comes due, whereas investing funds in long-term illiquid assets further decreases working capital and liquidity. In sum, by attempting to decrease its accounting exposure the company increases its economic exposure. Any gains from doing the former may be more than offset by losses from the latter. The real trick, as Aristotle pointed out centuries ago (although probably not with reference to foreign exchange risk management), is to find the golden mean.

Applied to foreign exchange risk management, the *golden mean approach* entails carefully analyzing the accounting exposure to make sure that nothing can be done to change it further without significantly increasing the firm's economic exposure. If some things still can be done in this regard, they should be done in by means of contractual devices.

Once this golden mean has been achieved, if an accounting exposure that is expected to result in a foreign exchange loss remains, the firm has two options. It can do nothing, or it can cover the accounting exposure by utilizing one or a number of techniques that are discussed below. Again, the choice largely hinges on the availability and cost of the covering techniques and the firm's policies toward risk.

Determining the Operational Constraints That Cannot Be Violated. This step involves examining corporate policies and government restrictions with respect to hedging strategies. Corporate policies may preclude swap arrangements because of bad experiences with them, or may preclude costly hedging policies owing to a shortage of corporate funds. Government restrictions may preclude or limit forward foreign exchange contracts or local bank loans in periods of tight money. Clearly there is little point in considering hedging methods that would be unacceptable to the company or the country.

Identifying the Acceptable Alternatives. After all of the operational options have been exhausted, it is possible to use contractual approaches to protection, such as the use of forward contracts and loans as described in Chapters 4 and 5. As can be learned in courses in international finance, the contractual options are plentiful and creative.

NON-U.S. TRANSLATION PRACTICES

Up to this point, we have tried to focus essentially on practices in the United States. However, the general rules of translation described in the temporal and current rate methods are essentially the same worldwide. In spite of this, there are some interesting differences in practice. As mentioned in Chapter 5, the United Kingdom, Canada, and the International Accounting Standards Committee were involved in the deliberations at the FASB that led to the issue of Statement 52. Thus, it is not surprising that elements of Statement 52 would be found in the standards of the other three. The purpose of this section is to describe the practices of the United Kingdom, Canada, and the IASC.

The United Kingdom

In April 1983, the Accounting Standards Committee of the United Kingdom issued Statement of Standard Accounting Practice No. 20 (SSAP 20), *Foreign Currency Translation*. Prior to that time, the method of translation most widely used in the United Kingdom was the current rate method (known in the United Kingdom as the closing rate method). However, SSAP 20 allows the use of the closing rate method or the temporal method, depending on the operating relationship that exists between the investor and investee. This is similar to the concept of the functional currency described in Statement 52.

In spite of the similarities between the standards of the United States and the United Kingdom, some important differences also exist.

1. SSAP 20 does not deal with foreign currency transactions. It comments in the foreword to the standard that foreign currency transactions must be translated into the reporting currency, but it does not deal with many of the issues covered in Statement 52.
2. Statement 52 requires that the average exchange rate be used to translate the income statement when using the current rate method, but SSAP 20 allows a choice between the current rate and the average rate.
3. Statement 52 requires the use of the temporal method to translate

the financial statements of operations in highly inflationary economies. SSAP 20 recommends that companies, where possible, adjust
financial statements to current price levels before translating them
into pounds. Since the British permit adjustments for changing
prices in their primary financial statements, the procedure recommended in SSAP 20 is not inconsistent with best practice.

4. SSAP 20 does not require the level of disclosure on translation gains
   and losses that is required in Statement 52. In addition, British
   firms do not have to set up a separate section in stockholders'
   equity to hold translation adjustments, since they already use a
   reserve account for a variety of adjustments. SSAP 20 requires disclosure of the movement on reserves during the year, but it does
   not require that the reserve account be broken down into different
   categories.[4]

A reading of SSAP 20 reveals a couple of interesting points. The first is
that the vast majority of firms affected by the standard will not have to
change their practices materially because it has been estimated that over
90% of the British multinationals were using the closing rate method when
the standard was adopted. The experience in the United States was just the
opposite when Statement 52 was issued: essentially all firms were using
the temporal method. The other point is that the British standard seems to
have more flexibility built in than the U.S. standard.

Canada

The Canadian standard on Foreign Currency Translation became effective
in July 1983. That standard, which dealt with both transactions and translation, has elements that are similar to and others that are different from the
U.S. and British standards.

In the area of transactions, the Canadian standard requires the same
basic concepts as Statement 52. However, there are some interesting differences. A firm that buys assets originally denominated in a foreign currency may make a cost or market test in that foreign currency at subsequent balance sheet dates. If the market test is selected, the value is
translated into Canadian dollars at the balance sheet exchange rate. Also,
gains and losses on long-term debt can be deferred and amortized over the
life of the debt.

In terms of translating foreign currency financial statements, the temporal and current rate methods can be used, depending on the operating
characteristics of the foreign operations. If the reporting enterprise is an
integrated foreign operation, the temporal method of translation must be
used. This is similar to defining the functional currency as the reporting
currency in Statement 52. Translation gains and losses are taken to income

---

[4]"SSAP 20: Foreign Currency Translation," *Accountancy*, May 1983, pp. 120–128.

unless they relate to long-term debt. As previously noted, those gains and losses can be deferred and amortized.

If the reporting enterprise is a self-sustaining foreign operation, the current rate method must be used. This is similar to defining the functional currency as something other than the reporting currency in Statement 52. Translation gains and losses are taken to a separate section in stockholders' equity rather than to income, which is consistent with Statement 52.

If the foreign operation is in a highly inflationary country, its financial statements should be translated into the reporting currency using the temporal method. This is consistent with Statement 52 but inconsistent with SSAP 20, which prefers the adjustment for price level changes before translation using the closing rate method.[5]

The International Accounting Standards Committee

International Accounting Standard 21, *Accounting for the Effects of Changes in Foreign Exchange Rates* (IAS 21), was approved in March 1983 for publication in July 1983. As you can tell from the dates, the British, Canadian, and international standards were all completed about the same time and within a few years of the issuance of Statement 52. IAS 21 is a fascinating standard, because it was obviously written to accommodate the British and Americans, and it also contained a few ideas relevant to some of the developing countries. As pointed out in Chapter 10, the value of the international standard is to narrow the options in practice and focus on a few best ways to account for different transactions.

IAS 21 contains provisions for both transactions and translation of financial statements. The provisions for accounting for foreign currency transactions are essentially the same as those contained in Statement 52, except for the following key points:

1. A receivable or payable covered by a forward contract may be recorded at the contract rate rather than the spot rate at each balance sheet date.

2. Exchange losses that result from a maxidevaluation can be included in the cost of the related asset as long as it is less than or equal to the lower of replacement cost or net realizable value. This was included to assist companies in developing countries that buy lots of capital equipment from abroad and prefer to spread out potential losses over a long period of time rather than recognize them immediately.

3. Exchange losses on long-term debt can be amortized over the life of the debt.

[5]Canadian Institute of Chartered Accountants, *CICA Handbook*, Vol. 1 (Toronto: CICA, December 1983), Section 1650.

In the case of translating foreign currency financial statements, the closing rate and temporal methods are used, depending on the operating characteristics of the foreign operations. This is consistent with all three countries. When using the closing rate method and translating the income statement, the current rate or the average rate can be used. This is consistent with the flexibility allowed in the British standard. Operations in highly inflationary countries can be adjusted for local inflation before translation into the reporting currency, or the temporal method can be used. This neatly allows the standards of all three countries to comply with the international standard. Translation gains and losses are taken to stockholders' equity.

The temporal method in IAS 21 has a lot of interesting departures from Statement 52. However, IAS 21 is broad enough that Statement 52 fits within its guidelines. Although monetary items are normally carried at cost, those covered by forward contracts can be carried on the books at the closing rate, the initial spot rate, and the forward rate. Most translation gains and losses are taken to income. However, gains and losses on long-term monetary items can be taken to income or deferred to future periods and systematically realized in the income statement.[6]

The international standard is an interesting one, because it is the product of compromise. It is flexible enough to include what was considered to be best accounting practice when it was issued. Therefore, it does not threaten any of the established standards, but it does eliminate those considered less theoretically correct.

CONSOLIDATED FINANCIAL STATEMENTS

General Concepts and Practices

One of the major differences in financial reporting worldwide concerns the presentation of group accounts. A group is defined as a parent company and all its subsidiaries. To qualify as a subsidiary, a company must be controlled by another company (the parent). In addition, a parent may have an interest in an associated company, defined by the International Accounting Standards Committee as a company that is not a subsidiary but whose parent holds at least a 20% voting interest.

There are three options in presenting the accounts of the group to outsiders: (1) present parent company financial statements only, (2) present parent company and consolidated financial statements, or (3) present consolidated financial statements only. The consolidated statements normally include domestic and foreign operations, but separate domestic and foreign consolidated statements could be presented. Exhibit 6.2 compares

---

[6]International Accounting Standards Committee, *International Accounting Standard 21*, "Accounting for the Effects of Changes in Foreign Exchange Rates" (London: IASC, July 1983).

Exhibit 6.2 Practices Followed by a Majority of the Companies in Presenting Group Accounts

Parent Company Statements Only	Parent Company Statements Supplemented by Consolidated Statements		Consolidated Statements Only
Brazil	Australia	Malaysia[a]	Bahamas
Costa Rica	Botswana[a]	Mexico[a]	Bermuda
El Salvador	Denmark[a]	Netherlands[a]	Canada
Guatemala	Dominican Republic	New Zealand[a]	Panama
Honduras	Fiji[a]	Nigeria[a]	Philippines
Ivory Coast	France[a]	Norway[a]	United States
Island of Jersey	Germany[a]	Singapore[a]	
Nicaragua	Hong Kong[a]	South Africa[a]	
Senegal	Ireland[a]	Sweden[a]	
Spain	Jamaica[a]	Trinidad	
	Japan[a]	United Kingdom[a]	
	Kenya[a]	Venezuela[a]	
	Korea[a]	Zambia	
	Malawi[a]	Zimbabwe Rhodesia[a]	

[a]Required practice.
Source: Price Waterhouse, *International Survey of Accounting Principles and Reporting Practices* (Canada: PWI, 1979).

the policies of several countries in presenting group accounts. Note that the approach of the United States differs from that of the other industrialized countries in which parent as well as consolidated reports are presented.

Consolidated financial statements are statements in which like items of assets, liabilities, revenues, and expenses are combined on a line-by-line basis to present the parent and its subsidiaries as one single entity or enterprise. When consolidation takes place, transactions between the parent and its subsidiaries or among related subsidiaries are eliminated from the statements. Thus, the consolidated statements reflect transactions of the group with outsiders. When only parent company statements are presented, there are many ways to distort the financial statements. Prior to 1977, when it became mandatory to publish consolidated financial statements in Japan, the following practices were common:

> During periods of slack turnover, some parent companies have been known to ship merchandise to their subsidiaries and list the goods as sold, even though the subsidiaries didn't have any customers on hand. Workers also could be transferred from a parent to a subsidiary to lower unit costs. And managers skipped over for promotions in the head office could be transferred to subsidiaries, where their performances couldn't be as easily seen.[7]

[7]*Wall Street Journal*, 6 February 1977, p. 6.

As an example of the difference between consolidated and unconsolidated earnings, Toshiba, a large Japanese multinational, showed an unconsolidated net income of $30 million in 1976 which would have been a $13 million net loss on a consolidated basis.[8] Consolidated financial statements help eliminate or at least minimize some of these problems so that users can get a pretty good idea of the results of operations and the financial position of the entire group.

There are situations in which consolidation of certain subsidiaries may not take place. According to International Accounting Standard 3 (IAS 3) of the IASC, the three major reasons for avoiding consolidation are that (1) control is likely to be temporary, (2) the ability of the parent to control assets is impaired, or (3) business activities are dissimilar.[9]

According to the rules of consolidation, an associated company (one that the parent does not control) is not consolidated with parent statements. In some cases, companies have tried to avoid consolidation by divesting ownership in a subsidiary. For example, in Japan, where since 1977 consolidation has been required for subsidiaries 50% or more owned by the parent.

> Mitsubishi Chemical Industries Ltd., Japan's largest chemical concern, reduced its equity interest in deficit-plagued Asia Oil Company to 48.7% from 74.7%, apparently to avoid wrapping the petroleum venture into consolidated results. Showa Denko K.K., another chemical concern, sold half its money-losing aluminum subsidiary late last year to just squeak under the definition of a unit that needn't be consolidated.[10]

Minority Interests

It is appropriate and desirable for a company with minority interests in several companies to report the results of those operations. There are two ways to do this: the cost and equity methods. According to the more conservative cost method—which is favored in much of continental Europe—the income of a minority interest is not reflected in parent or consolidated income until a dividend is declared to the parent. In some countries the dividend is not even recorded until the treasurer has the money stashed away in the corporate vault. Alternatively, the equity method is less conservative and reflects the investor orientation of the United States, focusing on earning potential. Under the equity method, income is recognized on parent and consolidated financial statements as soon as it is earned—whether or not a dividend is declared.

[8]"Japan's Accounting Shake-up," *Business Week*, 25 April 1977, p. 114.
[9]"International Accounting Standard No. 3: 'Consolidated Financial Statements,'" *Accountancy*, September 1976, p. 102.
[10]"Japan's Accounting Shake-up," ibid.

International Standards

The International Accounting Standards Committee

In June 1976, the IASC published IAS 3, "Consolidated Financial Statements." IAS 3 recommended that firms issue consolidated financial statements including all of its branches and subsidiaries, both domestic and foreign. It also recommended that the equity method be used to account for investees when the parent held less than a majority interest but at least a 20% voting interest. This standard was significant in terms of its definition of control (a majority interest in the voting stock) as well as its recommendation of the equity method. This latter requirement has had a strong impact on many countries around the world, including Japan, as mentioned.

The European Economic Community (EEC or EC)

As will be pointed out in more detail in Chapter 10, the EC is also involved in the process of accounting harmonization, and it has issued a series of directives that must be incorporated into law in each of the member countries. The Seventh Directive, which was adopted on June 13, 1983, deals with consolidated financial statements. The directive must be enacted into legislation in each member country by January 1, 1988, and consolidated financial statements must be prepared for fiscal years beginning on or after January 1, 1990. The reason for such a long lead time is that very few countries in the EC currently require consolidated financial statements.

The Seventh Directive is very much in line with generally accepted international standards in that it follows the practices of IAS 3 and of the United States and the United Kingdom. In essence, it requires consolidation of all subsidiaries in which the parent has legal power of control determined by a majority of voting rights, the right to appoint a majority of the board of directors, the right to exercise dominant influence pursuant to control contract, or control over majority of voting rights pursuant to agreement with other shareholders.[11]

When the Seventh Directive was issued, the only countries with consolidation standards were the United Kingdom, Ireland, Sweden, Germany, the Netherlands, France, and Denmark. However, the practices among the countries were not necessarily uniform. The German standard provides some interesting differences from the approaches of the United States and United Kingdom. For one thing, only domestic German subsidiaries need to be included in the consolidated financial statements. For another, control is determined by management control rather than legal ownership of stock. The difference in this latter characteristic is interesting.

[11]Price Waterhouse, *Special Supplement on the EEC Seventh Directive* (Brussels: Price Waterhouse, July 1983), p. 6.

In the U.S./UK view, "the objective is to give the investor a proper measure of the performance and capital employed of the company in which he holds his investment and the subsidiaries under its power of control." From the German perspective, "the objective is to obtain proper information on the resources exploited by a single or central seat of management: in other words, to obtain information about the resources and results of concentrations of economic power."[12]

In spite of these basic differences in existing legislation concerning consolidation, the Seventh Directive could be very effective in harmonizing consolidation standards. At the very least, it will provide a base on which the individual countries can develop more extensive standards.

DISCLOSURE OF SEGMENTS

Consolidated financial statements usually tell a shareholder or creditor little about a firm's business by product group and geographical area. Without segmented data, the outside user would have to rely on the unaudited narrative for information.

The U.S. Perspective

In 1977, FASB issued Statement 14, "Financial Reporting for Segments of a Business Enterprise." The statement focused on disclosure of information on four segments: industry, foreign operations, export sales, and major customers. For industry segments, firms are called on to group products or services worldwide and then select for reporting purposes segments whose revenue, profits or losses, or assets are 10% of the combined revenue, profits or losses, or assets of the identifiable segments of the firm. Industry segments are normally determined by the nature of the product so that similar products are grouped together. Once the industry segments are identified, the following information is to be disclosed: revenue, operating profit or loss, and identifiable assets. This information is to be provided as a supplement to the main financial statements in interim as well as annual statements.

Statement 14 also requires that sales be disclosed to major customers. If 10% or more of total corporate revenue is derived from sales to a single customer, that amount of sales must be disclosed. The classes of major customers specifically identified are any single customer, domestic government agencies in the aggregate, and foreign governments in the aggregate.

The international aspect of Statement 14 deals with foreign operations and export sales. Firms are to disclose information about domestic and foreign operations. Foreign segments can be disclosed in the aggregate, by

---

[12]Ibid., p. 4.

groups of countries or by individual country. Most disclosure involves one form of aggregation or another; few firms disclose information by separate country. In order to qualify, a segment must meet one of two conditions: either its revenue from sales must be at least 10% of consolidated revenues or its identifiable assets must be at least 10% of consolidated assets. Once this test has been met and the segments identified, each segment's revenue from sales to unaffiliated customers, revenue from intracompany sales, operating profit (or loss), and identifiable assets must be disclosed.

The determination of international segments varies considerably from firm to firm, as does the volume of information per segment. IBM uses three geographical segments—United States, Europe/Middle East/Africa, and Americas/Far East—which corresponds with its organizational structure. Many companies, in trying to disclose as little foreign information as possible, simply aggregate the data into "total foreign."

From a theoretical and practical standpoint, geographical segments should be determined to help the investor make some kind of risk analysis. However, typical groupings currently do not provide that for most companies. Although Mexico and the United States are geographically proximate, they are not very similar from an economic or political-risk standpoint. It would be more sensible to the investor for the firm to aggregate countries according to characteristics, such as political stability, rate of economic growth, currency stability, and convertibility. The problem with this approach is that conditions change almost yearly, and it would be impossible to generate data that would be comparable from year to year.

The British Perspective

In the United Kingdom, regulations are relatively general and flexible in comparison with those in the United States. Although the disclosure of international segment information has been required by the London Stock Exchange since 1965, it has been incorporated in the Companies Act only since 1981 when the provisions of the Fourth Directive of the EC were adopted.

It is interesting to note the similarities and differences between the standards of the Fourth Directive and the London Stock Exchange. Under the Fourth Directive, only sales revenues by geographic area need to be disclosed. Under the Stock Exchange regulations, both sales and profits need to be disclosed. More specifically, a broad geographic analysis, using percentages, not necessarily by individual country is acceptable. A segment analysis of sales consistent with the United States is required only if foreign operations as a whole are greater than 10% of consolidated revenues, in which case the segments should be analyzed by continent unless 50% of total foreign operations relates to one continent, in which case a further analysis is required. In the case of trading profit, no analysis is required unless profit in a specific area is significantly different from the normal ratio of profit to sales for the company as a whole.[13]

The OECD Perspective

The Organization for Economic Cooperation and Development (OECD) issued a Code of Conduct, which, among other things, called for improved disclosure of information about operations. In terms of segmented information, the OECD recommended the disclosure of the geographical areas and principal activities in each area; operating results and sales by geographical and industry segments; capital investment by geographical and, where practicable, industry segments; and the average number of employees by geographical segment. The only guidelines given for geographical segments are the following:

> While no single method of grouping is appropriate for all enterprises, or for all purposes, the factors to be considered by an enterprise would include the significance of operations carried out in individual countries or areas as well as the effects on its competitiveness, geographic proximity, economic affinity, similarities in business environments and the nature, scale and degree of interrelationship of the enterprise's operations in the various countries.[14]

The Code of Conduct is a guide, but the OECD has no power to force companies to adhere to its disclosure principles. However, it is a pattern for national accounting bodies to follow in setting up their requirements.

The IASC Perspective

In August 1981, the International Accounting Standards Committee issued IAS 14, "Reporting Financial Information by Segment." The standard is slightly different from FASB Statement 14 in that it requires only data on industry and geographic segments. In terms of data for each segment, IAS 14 requires the same information as is required in Statement 14 and also requires that the firm describe the activities of each industrial segment and the composition of each geographic segment. In addition, it permits firms that provide information for both parent and consolidated operations to disclose segment information for consolidated operations only. Thus, the international standard is as comprehensive as Statement 14 in terms of the information required per segment, but it does not require information about export revenues or revenues from significant customers. Also, it requires the information to be disclosed for "significant" segments, but it

---

[13]S. J. Gray and Lee H. Radebaugh, "International Segment Disclosures by U.S. and U.K. Multinational Enterprises: A Descriptive Study," *Journal of Accounting Research*, Vol. 22, No. 1, Spring 1984, pp. 353–354.

[14]*The OECD Observer*, No. 82, July/August 1976, p. 14.

does not attempt to define significance as Statement 14 does. It leaves more leeway to management to make that decision.

Examples of Disclosures

It is interesting to note some different ways to disclose segment data. In Exhibit 6.3 is the segment information from the 1983 Annual Report of General Electric Company. This information is contained in the annual report after the financial statements and is in conformity with the guidelines in Statement 14. There are only two segments in the report that refer to operations in countries outside of the United States, which is consistent with the concept that will be discussed later on the propensity of U.S. multinationals to have few geographic segments in their disclosures. Because General Electric is one of the largest exporters in the United States, it provides information on export revenues in the narrative following the table of disclosures.

Exhibit 6.4 contains two pieces of information on geographic segments contained in the business narrative of the Philips 1982 annual report. Note the more extensive breakdown of segments than is found in Exhibit 6.3. Philips also provides other geographic segment data in discussions of special issues, such as employees. The information is all placed in the annual report before the financial statements and footnotes.

In Exhibit 6.5 is the segment data of the Swedish Match Company. Note that the data are for sales and export sales only rather than profits. In spite of the lack of different kinds of information, Swedish Match provides more details on sales and export sales than would be typical with a U.S. firm. Many of its categories are significantly smaller than the 10% test made by U.S. firms, but the information is still provided for the shareholder.

Comparisons of Disclosures

Before the Fourth Directive was issued, there was no common standard for segmented disclosure in Europe, and wide differences existed from country to country. A survey was conducted on the segment-reporting practices of the hundred largest industrial multinational companies based in the EC and listed on stock exchanges in 1973. Of the firms surveyed, 92% provided sales data by segment, 49% provided profits, 28% production, 26% assets, and 7% capital expenditure.[15] Differences in disclosure between the British and Continental firms are summarized in Table 6.1. In general, the level of disclosure was higher for the British firms. Sales data are more

[15]S. J. Gray, "Segment Reporting and the EEC Multinationals," *Journal of Accounting Research,* Autumn 1978, p. 244.

Exhibit 6.3 Geographic Segment Data, General Electric Company, 1983 Annual Report

Revenues for the Years Ended December 31

(in millions)	Total Revenues			Intersegment Sales			External Sales and Other Income		
	1983	1982	1981	1983	1982	1981	1983	1982	1981
United States	$23,513	$22,311	$22,697	$ 590	$ 609	$ 667	$22,923	$21,702	$22,030
Far East including Australia	1,603	1,453	1,624	430	316	397	1,173	1,137	1,227
Other areas of the world	3,826	4,568	4,798	241	215	201	3,585	4,353	4,597
Elimination of intracompany transactions	(1,261)	(1,140)	(1,265)	(1,261)	(1,140)	(1,265)	—	—	—
Total	$27,681	$27,192	$27,854	$ —	$ —	$ —	$27,681	$27,192	$27,854

(in millions)	Net Earnings for the Years Ended December 31			Assets at December 31		
	1983	1982	1981	1983	1982	1981
United States	$ 1,667	$ 1,415	$ 1,373	$18,105	$16,379	$16,004
Far East including Australia	278	240	228	1,458	1,337	1,187
Other areas of the world	80	155	68	3,864	4,036	3,902
Elimination of intracompany transactions	(1)	7	(17)	(139)	(137)	(151)
Total	$ 2,024	$ 1,817	$ 1,652	$23,288	$21,615	$20,942

Geographic segment information (including allocation of income taxes and minority interest in earnings of consolidated affiliates) is based on the location of the operation furnishing goods or services. Business restructuring activities in 1983 pertained to operations in the United States but had virtually no effect on net earnings as gains and losses offset each other after taxes. Included in United States revenues were export sales to unaffiliated customers of $3639 million in 1983, $3312 million in 1982 and $3681 million in 1981. Of such sales, $1873 million in 1983 ($1829 million in 1982 and $2024 million in 1981) was to customers in Europe, Africa, and the Middle East; and $1086 million in 1983 ($866 million in 1982 and $776 million in 1981) was to customers in the Far East including Australia. U.S. revenues also include royalty and licensing income from unaffiliated foreign sources. Revenues, net earnings, and assets associated with foreign operations are shown in the tables above. At December 31, 1983, foreign operation liabilities, minority interest in equity, and GE interest in equity were $2818 million, $168 million, and $2336 million, respectively. On a comparable basis, the amounts were $2877 million, $163 million, and $2333 million, respectively, at December 31, 1982; and $2789 million, $154 million, and $2146 million, respectively, at December 31, 1981.

Exhibit 6.4 Geographical Segment Data, Philips Annual Report, 1982

Development of Sales by Geographical Area

		1982			1981
Geographical Area	Sales[a]	As Percentage of Total	Growth Amount	Growth Percent	Growth Percent
Netherlands	2,842	7	11	0	−6
EEC excluding Netherlands	16,728	39	32	0	4
Europe excluding EEC	4,492	10	85	2	8
United States and Canada	9,803	23	386	4	53
Latin America	3,452	8	53	2	25
Africa	1,274	3	−37	−3	14
Asia	2,874	7	61	2	22
Australia and New Zealand	1,526	3	−11	−1	39
Total	42,991	100	580	1	16

Amounts in millions of guilders.
[a]The sales figure is the total proceeds from goods and services supplied to third parties in the geographical area concerned.

Trading Profit[a]

	1982		1981	
	Amount	As Percentage of Deliveries[b]	Amount	As Percentage of Deliveries[b]
Netherlands	−52	−0.4	79	0.6
EEC excluding Netherlands	967	4.6	532	2.6
Europe excluding EEC	345	5.9	255	4.7
United States and Canada	221	2.2	356	3.7
Latin America	400	12.6	440	13.7
Africa	87	10.8	141	16.9
Asia	184	7.7	272	11.3
Australia and New Zealand	3	0.2	94	6.3
Results not attributed to geographical areas	−25		24	
Total	2,130		2,193	
Trading profit as percentage of sales		5.0		5.2

Amount in millions of guilders.
[a]Trading profit is defined as the proceeds from deliveries less costs. The costs of deliveries do not include financing costs. Trading profit is also exclusive of miscellaneous income and charges, and before tax.
[b]Deliveries are defined as the sum of the sales of companies established within a geographical area to third parties both inside and outside that area, and the deliveries to consolidated companies outside that area (interregional deliveries).
The prices for deliveries between the consolidated companies in international trade are fixed in the same way as if they were deliveries to third parties, that is, taking into account the conditions of sales and payment, the total volume and the continuity of all goods deliveries as well as the norms applicable in the different countries. This implies that, wherever possible, these deliveries are invoiced at market prices. Insofar as the same or similar goods are not freely available from independent firms in the same markets, the prices for these deliveries are fixed on the basis of production costs with a surcharge for profit and general costs of the supplying company.

Exhibit 6.5 Swedish Match Sales and Exports, 1982 (Amounts in millions of Swedish Krona)

Sales per Market	Tarkett	Match	Åkerlund & Rausing	Doors	Kitchens	Other Activities	Total	Total Exports from Respective Country
Sweden	474	47	493	313	448	242	2 017	1 417
Denmark	15	39	92	51	11	4	212	8
Finland	98	6	12	77	5	7	205	27
France	43	306	24		2	222	597	114
Netherlands	18	63	30			24	135	34
Norway	159	28	78	172	101	115	653	39
Great Britain	55	81	81	28	7	108	360	17
West Germany	64	137	210	43		376	830	201
Rest of Europe	70	234	43	3	2	144	496	154
Total Europe	996	941	1 063	687	576	1 242	5 505	2 011
Africa	1	88	11			5	105	
Asia	13	222	55	2	9	23	324	31
North America	779	237	2			14	1 032	73
Central America	4	59	110			2	175	
South America	6	386				89	481	11
Australia, Oceania	16	6	4			1	27	

Total other countries	819	998	182	2	9	134	2 144	115
Total	1 815	1 939	1 245	689	585	1 376	7 649[a]	2 126[b]
Less: internal sales	9		14	29	1	69	122	804
Total	1 806	1 939	1 231	660	584	1 307	7 527	1 322

[a]Includes sales between but not within groups.
[b]Includes exports of products manufactured in the respective countries, including total internal export sales.

Exports from Sweden	Tarkett	Match	Åkerlund & Rausing	Doors	Kitchens	Other Activities	Total
Nordic countries	146	47	169	129	112	9	612
Rest of Europe	112	147	154	19	4	86	522
Africa		56	11			4	71
Asia	5	76	9	2	8	10	110
North America	19	2	2			4	27
Central America		27				2	29
South America		13				16	29
Australia, Oceania	10	2	4			1	17
Total	292	370	349	150	124	132	1 417

Swedish Match exports from Sweden represent approximately 1% of total Swedish exports.

Table 6.1 Segmented Disclosures

	Percentage of UK Companies	Percentage of Continental Companies	Percentage of Total Companies
Sales—industry segment	86.7	76.4	81
Sales—geographical segment	93.3	70.9	81
Profits—industry	77.8	12.7	42
Profits—geographical	75.6	3.6	36
Production (by volume)	6.7	45.5	28
Assets	24.4	27.3	26

Source: Adapted from S. J. Gray, "Segment Reporting and the EEC Multinationals," *Journal of Accounting Research*, Autumn 1978, p. 246.

frequently disclosed for both sets of companies, but the British were stronger on disclosure in all areas except production by volume and assets analyses. The study concluded that the major reason for the differences in disclosure was differential stimulus to disclosure provided by the regulatory environment of legal, professional, and stock market requirements.

In a more recent survey of 58 U.S.-based and 35 UK-based multinational enterprises, the following information was found:

1. U.S. firms exhibited a greater extent of disclosure for all classes of geographic segment data except for employees. The categories of information investigated were sales to customers, intraenterprise sales, profits, assets, investment, and employees.
2. The average number of geographic segments disclosed by U.S. firms tends to be less than UK firms, with an average of four and six segments being disclosed respectively.
3. Firms tend to identify segments by continent rather than by individual country. In the case of U.S. firms, the aggregation is often by hemisphere, supporting the contention that UK firms tend to disclose more segments than U.S. firms.[16]

SUMMARY
- Financial statements of firms in highly inflationary economies (those whose cumulative rate of inflation over a three-year period is approximately 100%) should be restated into dollars using the temporal method.
- FASB Statement No. 70 explains how to adjust foreign currency financial statements for inflation so that they can be combined with other supplementary information on changing prices.
- If the functional currency is the reporting currency, historical cost/constant dollar data are prepared by translating foreign currency accounts

[16]Gray and Radebaugh, op. cit., 351–360.

into dollars according to the temporal method and adjusting the dollar balances for inflation in the United States. Current cost amounts are determined in the local currency and then translated into dollars at the current exchange rate. Increases in current cost for the year are then adjusted for U.S. inflation.

- If the functional currency is not the reporting currency, historical cost/constant dollar information does not need to be prepared. Current cost information is prepared in the same way as described above. Increases in local currency current cost can be adjusted for local inflation before being translated into dollars, or the current costs can be translated into dollars and then adjusted for U.S. inflation.

- When consolidating financial statements of a subsidiary with its parent in a situation in which inventory is bought and sold between the two units, the inventory profits must be eliminated, and translation gains and losses need to be recognized in the separate component of stockholders' equity.

- If intercompany debt is never intended to be repaid, the translation gain or loss on that debt is taken to stockholders' equity; if it is intended to be repaid, the gain or loss is taken directly to income.

- Statement 52 requires that firms disclose the balance in accumulated translation adjustment account, any changes in that balance during the year, and the amount of the translation adjustment taken to income during the year.

- The objective of foreign exchange risk management is to minimize the potential loss on transaction, translation, and economic exposure subject to the cost of protection.

- The United Kingdom and Canada use the same procedures that the United States requires for translating financial statements. However, there are a few differences in each case that make their procedures unique. The translation standard adopted by the International Accounting Standards Committee is broad enough to encompass all of the options mentioned in conjunction with the United States, the United Kingdom, and Canada, but it eliminates other translation procedures that were used several years ago.

- When presenting group financial statements to outsiders, firms can present parent company financial statements only, both parent company and consolidated financial statements, or consolidated financial statements only. Minority interests in a foreign corporation can be recognized by the cost method (income is not recognized until a dividend is declared by the investee to the investor) or by the equity method (the investor recognizes its equity interest in the income of the investee when earned).

- The IASC recommends that firms consolidate financial statements of all branches and subsidiaries, both foreign and domestic. It also recommends the use of the equity method for minority investees when at least a 20% interest is held.

- The European Economic Community recently passed the Seventh Directive, which essentially follows the international standard mentioned above. The standard is consistent with practice in the United Kingdom and the United States. Many European countries are going to have to change their consolidation practices in order to comply with the Seventh Directive.

- FASB Statement 14 requires that firms disclose information about their business and geographic segments, as well as their major customers and export sales, assuming those segments and categories are at least 10% of consolidated revenues or profits. Information must be provided on revenues, profits, and identifiable assets.

- The British require revenue data for geographic segments, but profit data are required only if profit margins in individual segments differ significantly from that of the company as a whole.

Study Questions

6-1. Trace the evolution in the thinking of the FASB that led to the procedure adopted to translate financial statements of branches and subsidiaries in highly inflationary countries. What is your opinion of that procedure in light of the concept of the functional currency?

6-2. Explain how you prepare historical cost/constant dollar information for operations whose functional currency is the reporting currency.

6-3. Why is the method used to prepare current cost/nominal dollar information the same when the functional currency is the reporting currency and when it is another currency?

6-4. Why do firms not have to provide historical cost/constant dollar information for operations whose functional currency is not the reporting currency?

6-5. Compare the methods used in the preparation of information on the increase in current cost net of inflation for operations whose functional currency is the reporting currency with those whose functional currency is not the reporting currency.

6-6. Some have felt that the placement of the translation adjustment in a separate component of stockholders' equity is a violation of the all-inclusive principle of the income statement. What is your opinion of that?

6-7. Compare the disclosure of translation adjustment information in Statement 52 with SSAP 20 of the British.

6-8. What is the difference between accounting exposure and economic exposure?

6-9. What are the risks of rearranging account balances or entering into contractual obligations to minimize accounting and economic exposure?

6-10. Identify the differences between Statement 52 and SSAP 20 in foreign currency translation. How substantive do you feel these differences are?

6-11. What are the major differences between Statement 52 and the Canadian standard on foreign currency translation? How substantive do you feel these differences are?

6-12. How does IAS 21 of the International Accounting Standards Committee compare with the British, U.S., and Canadian standards described earlier? What is your opinion of the value of that standard for U.S. firms? for firms in countries without an existing translation standard?

6-13. Why do you feel that it is important to have an internationally recognized standard on consolidating financial statements?

6-14. Compare IAS 3 with the Seventh Directive of the EEC in terms of consolidation principles.

6-15. What do you think the impact of the Seventh Directive will be on the EEC?

6-16. Compare the U.S., British, OECD, EEC, and IASC standards on accounting for geographic segments.

6-17. Rouse Co., a developer of major shopping centers, built two shopping centers in Canada and financed more than 90% of the cost with a loan from Canadian lenders. The loan would be paid off with rental income from the shopping centers and no recourse to Rouse Co.

    a. Assume that Rouse treated the U.S. dollar as the functional currency for translation purposes and that the Canadian dollar was weakening against the U.S. dollar. What do you think would have been the impact of that situation on the income statement?

    b. Rouse argued to the FASB that its operations in Canada constituted a natural hedge and that it should not have to reflect any translation gains or losses in income. What do you think they meant by a "natural hedge," and what is your opinion about their contention?

    c. How would your answer in Part a differ if Rouse treated the Canadian dollar rather than the U.S. dollar as the functional currency?

6-18. The following is an adaptation of a hypothetical example (with actual exchange rates) from the First Quarter Report 1976 for Scholl, Inc.

	First Quarter 1975			First Quarter 1976		
	Pound Sterling	U.S. Dollar Equivalent per Pound	U.S. Dollars	Pound Sterling	U.S. Dollar Equivalent per Pound	U.S. Dollars
Net sales	£5,020	2.40	12,050	£5,390	1.99	$10,730
Cost of sales	3,320	2.35	7,800	3,465	2.15	7,450
Gross profit	1,700		4,250	1,925		3,280
Operating expenses	1,170	2.40	2,800	1,315	1.99	2,620
Pretax results	530		1,450	610		660
Income taxes	310	2.40	750	315	1.99	630
Net earnings	£ 220		$ 700	£ 295		$ 30

    a. Was the U.S. dollar strengthening or weakening against the pound from the fourth quarter of 1974 to the first quarter of 1975? from the first quarter of 1975 to the first quarter of 1976?

    b. Was the temporal method or the current rate method used to translate this income statement?

    c. Analyze the effect of translation on reported sales and earnings from one year to the next and compare the dollar and pound changes.

    d. Assume that the average exchange rate for the first quarter of 1975 was $2.40 and that the average exchange rate for the first quarter of 1976 was $1.99. If the income statements were translated at the average exchange rate, what would the impact on your answer for Part c have been?

6-19. Assume the following information:
   1. An asset is acquired on January 1, 19X4, for LC400,000 in a foreign country where a U.S. firm has a subsidiary. The asset has a useful life of five years and is depreciated on a straight-line basis.
   2. Current cost/nominal dollars was LC800,000 on 12/31/X4 and LC1,600,000 on 12/31/X5.
   3. The relevant exchange rates and inflation rates are as follows:

Date	Exchange Rate	U.S. CPI	Local CPI
1/1/X4	LC2/$	110	650
12/31/X4	LC3/$	121	900
12/31/X5	LC4.5/$	130	1500
Average, 19X5	LC3.8/$	125	1200

   Required:
   a. Assuming that the functional currency is the dollar, provide the following information in dollars:
      i. Historical cost/constant dollars.
      ii. Current cost/nominal dollars.
      iii. Increase in current cost net of inflation.
   b. Assuming that the functional currency is the local currency, provide the following information in dollars:
      i. Historical cost/constant dollars.
      ii. Current cost/nominal dollars.
      iii. Increase in current cost net of inflation.

6-20. Assume the following information:
   1. An asset is acquired for LC400,000 on January 1, 19X4, in a foreign country where a U.S. firm has a local subsidiary. The asset has a useful life of five years and is depreciated on a straight-line basis.
   2. The current cost of the asset is LC420,000 on 12/31/X4 and LC450,000 on 12/31/X5.
   3. The relevant exchange rates and inflation rates are as follows:

Date	Exchange Rate	U.S. CPI	Local CPI
1/1/X4	LC2/$	110	90
12/31/X4	LC1/$	112	93.6
12/31/X5	LC0.5/$	125	97.3
Average, 19X5	LC0.75/$	119	95.5

   Required:
   a. Assuming that the functional currency is the dollar, provide the following information in dollars:
      i. Historical cost/constant dollars.
      ii. Current cost/nominal dollars.
      iii. Increase in current cost net of inflation.

b. Assuming that the functional currency is the local currency, provide the following information in dollars:
   i. Historical cost/constant dollars.
   ii. Current cost/nominal dollars.
   iii. Increase in current cost net of inflation.

6-21. Assume that a U.S. parent company sells inventory to its Mexican subsidiary for $1,000,000 when the exchange rate was Mex$150 per U.S. dollar (pesos per dollar). Assume that the functional currency is the Mexican peso and that the exchange rate at the subsequent balance sheet data was Mex$195. Compute the value of the inventory on the subsidiary's books at the initial and subsequent balance sheet dates, the intercompany profit on the original transaction, and the value of the inventory for consolidation purposes. What is the amount of inventory profits due to the exchange rate change, and where do these profits, if any, show up in the financial statements?

6-22. Assume that a parent company loans its Japanese subsidiary $25,000,000 to finance expansion when the exchange rate is Yen 124 per dollar. At the subsequent balance sheet date, the exchange rate is Yen 130 per dollar. Provide the following information:
   a. The value of the loan on the parent and subsidiary books at the initial and subsequent balance sheet dates.
   b. The amount of the translation gain or loss and where that amount should show up in the financial statements.

6-23. Assume that a U.S. company owns 25% of a foreign company and that its beginning and end-of-year balances in the translated dollar equity section of the Japanese company are as follows:

	Beginning of Year	End of Year
Common stock	$850,000	$850,000
Retained earnings	900,000	1,500,000
Equity adjustment from translation	600,000	350,000
Stockholders' equity	$2,350,000	$2,700,000

The increase in retained earnings is due to income earned during the year.
a. What adjustment would the investor have to make at the end of the period to reflect the change in the equity interest of the investment?
b. Would your answer to Part a be the same if the investor owned 18% of the investee?
c. What if the investor owned 52% of the investee?

Case

KAMIKAZE ENTERPRISES

Ray Addis, 63-year-old chairman of the board of Ace Inc., a medium-size airplane manufacturing company, had called Frank Anderson into his office to talk about an investment made by Ace in Japan five years ago. Ray was really upset, because its Japanese affiliate, Kamikaze Enterprises, owned 40% by Ace and 60% by Mitsoo-hoo, was not doing well. He expected Frank, the CEO of Ace, to explain what was going on. Ray had been involved in marketing all his life, unlike Frank, who came up through the finance route.

"How are you doing, Frank?"

"Pretty good, I guess, Ray. I gather from your note that you're not too pleased with Kamikaze Enterprises."

"That's an understatement. In our last set of statements, I noticed that we picked up a dollar loss from Kamikaze for the fifth year in a row. I wouldn't mind it so much but that loss reduced our earnings by nearly 40%. Why can't we get that blasted operation in the black? I thought those Japanese were supposed to be cost-efficient. I feel like we're tapping money down a rathole."

"I can understand your concern, Ray, but we've gotten a healthy yen dividend from Kamikaze every year since we've been in operation. Because the yen keeps revaluing, the dollar equivalent of that dividend goes up every year."

"I realize that, Frank, but we report in dollars to our shareholders, and I have to explain those foreign exchange losses at the next annual meeting. What am I going to do? I understand that the book value of our investment has been written down to practically nothing because of those losses. Either that operation becomes profitable or we cut bait. Let me know in three weeks what our plan of action should be."

"OK, Ray. I'll see what I can do."

"What a circus," thought Frank as he walked back to his office. "There's no way I can explain this situation so that he understands."

Ace Inc. had entered into the minority joint venture with Mitsoo-hoo to produce small corporate aircraft in Japan. Ace provided the technical expertise and some equity financing. However, Mitsoo-hoo provided most of the funds through debt financing with its bank. The investment was almost 90% debt financed.

Kamikaze Enterprises had actually been quite profitable, increasing yen profits by nearly 25% a year. Sales were growing at about the same rate. This growth and high profitability allowed Kamikaze to declare sizable dividends each year. When translated into dollars, however, the yen profits turned into losses, which reduced Ace's equity investment in Kamikaze. Frank had spoken to the managers of Kamikaze, who did not appear to understand the problem or want to do anything about it. Ace had been offered $50 million for its investment in Kamikaze, which seemed ironic since the book value on Ace's books was close to zero.

Questions

1. According to the situation described here, what was the functional currency of the Japanese firm?
2. Describe how this situation would differ when the functional currency is the yen from when it is the dollar.
3. Discuss some alternatives that Frank could consider to resolve this problem.

Bibliography

Alleman, Raymond H. "Why ITT Likes FAS 52." *Management Accounting* July 1982, pp. 23–29.

Analysis of Statement 52 by any of the major public accounting firms. The exact titles will depend on the firm.

Beaver, W. H., and M. A. Wolfson. "Foreign Currency Translation and Changing Prices." *Journal of Accounting Research,* Autumn 1982, pp. 528–550.

Bender, D. E. "Foreign Currency Translation-FAS 52—Part I." *The CPA Journal,* June 1982, pp. 9–14.

Bender, D. E. "Foreign Currency Translation-FAS 52—Part II." *The CPA Journal,* July 1982, pp. 20–26.

Bender, D. E. "Foreign Currency Translation-FAS 52—Part III." *The CPA Journal,* August 1982, pp. 40–43.

Donaldson, H. "Implementing FAS No. 52: The Critical Issues." *Financial Executive,* June 1982, pp. 40–50.

Evans, Thomas G. and William Folks, Jr. "Analysis of the Impact of Statement 52 on Disclosures of the Effects of Changing Prices." University of South Carolina Working Paper Series.

Financial Accounting Standards Board. "Accounting for the Translation of Foreign Currency Transactions and Foreign Currency Financial Statements." *Statement of Financial Accounting Standards No. 8* (Stamford: FASB, October 1975).

Financial Accounting Standards Board. "Foreign Currency Translation." *Statement of Financial Accounting Standards No. 52* (Stamford: FASB, December 1981).

Heckman, Christine R. "Measuring Foreign Exchange Exposure: A Practical Theory and its Application." *Financial Analysts Journal,* September–October 1983, pp. 59–65.

Hepworth, Samuel R. *Reporting Foreign Operations* (Ann Arbor: University of Michigan, 1956).

Lorensen, Leonard. "Reporting Foreign Operations of U.S. Companies in U.S. Dollars." *Accounting Research Study No. 12* (New York: AICPA, 1972).

McKinnon, Sharon M. *Consolidated Accounts.* Alan D. H. Newham, Ed. (The Netherlands: Amsa in Europe and Arthur Young International, 1983).

Methven, Paul and Chris Willows. "How RT2 Handles Multi-Currency Consolidation by Computer." *Accountancy,* Vol. 90, June 1979, pp. 101–106.

Norton, C. L. and G. A. Porter. "The Comprehensive Income Approach and FASB Statement No. 52: Are They Compatible?" *Journal of Accountancy,* December 1982, pp. 94–96.

Revsine, Lawrence. "The Rationale Underlying the Functional Currency Choice." *The Accounting Review,* July 1984, pp. 505–514.

Seidler, L. J. and P. A. McConnell. "FASB Statement No. 52 on Foreign Currency Translation: A First Look." *Financial Analysts Journal,* January–February 1982, pp. 18–20.

Strauss, Norman N. and Lawrence C. Best. "Accounting for Foreign Currency Translation." *Corporate Controller's Manual.* Paul J. Wendell, Ed. (Boston: Warren Gorham & Lamont, Inc., 1982 update prepared by Robert L. Shultis and Alfred M. King).

Taussig, R. A. "Impact of SFAS No. 52 on the Translation of Foreign Financial

Statements of Companies in Highly Inflationary Economies." *Journal of Accounting, Auditing and Finance*, Winter 1983, pp. 142–156.

Walker, R. G. "International Accounting Compromises: The Case of Consolidation Accounting." *Abacus*, Vol. 14, December 1978, pp. 97–111.

Wojciechowski, Stanley R. "DuPont Evaluates FAS 52." *Management Accounting*, July 1982, pp. 31–35.

CHAPTER 7

Taxation

The game between tax authority and corporation or individual is an ancient one that is played with all the gusto of any natural rivalry. As the tax authority sets up a new defense to plug the gaps, the corporation adjusts its strategy and tries to open up a new hole or take advantage of existing ones. For the multinational corporation, every taxing authority around the world has its own set of defenses that must be adjusted to.

The challenge is exhilarating and worthy of far more resources than the corporate tax director can be expected to have personally. Specialists in parent country tax law must be combined with specialists in tax law from each country where the firm operates as well as with technical advisers in exchange controls and cash flow possibilities. This chapter considers the philosophy of taxation, especially as it relates to foreign source income, and taxes related to revenues and earnings from international operations. The major focus is on U.S.-based corporations.

TAX SYSTEM PHILOSOPHY

Although tax systems vary around the world, it is commonly accepted that each country has the right to tax income earned inside its borders. That is where the similarity stops. Opinions diverge as to the classes of revenue considered taxable, how expenses are determined, and what kinds of taxes should be used (such as direct or indirect). In addition, there are differences in adherence to tax laws, as those who pay taxes—and those who do not—in countries such as Spain and Italy can attest.

Sources of Income

Source of income is a complex issue that has domestic as well as international dimensions. The domestic side involves deciding when income has really been earned and is therefore subject to tax. In addition, business practices and tax laws differ from country to country.

Our major concern here is with domestic versus foreign source income. Foreign source income is derived from the sale of goods and services abroad by a domestic company as well as from a foreign branch and from a foreign corporation in which the domestic company has an equity interest. Foreign source income from the export of goods and services is taxable when earned; that concept is applied worldwide. Tax incentives may be used to encourage exports, however, and these incentivies have the effect of placing the foreign source income in a category different from other sources of income. Examples of using taxes as incentives to export are the Foreign Sales Corporation (FSC) and Domestic International Sales Corporation (DISC) in the United States and the refund of the value added tax on exports in many European countries.

Taxing the earnings from foreign branches and foreign corporations is more complex. The territorial approach as used by Hong Kong, for example, asserts that foreign source income should be taxed where earned and not mixed with domestic source income. The opposite worldwide philosophy treats all income as taxable to the parent. This leads to double taxation since that income is usually also taxed where it is earned. The two major ways to minimize double taxation where the worldwide philosophy exists is through the tax credit (allowing the firm a direct credit against domestic taxes for the foreign income taxes already paid) and tax treaties. In addition, some countries that use the worldwide approach do not tax earnings of foreign subsidiaries until the parent receives a dividend. This approach, known as the deferral concept, is widespread except in the United States and a few other countries, where the deferral principle is applied to most but not all classes of foreign source income.

Within a given country, the tax authorities normally tax income on earnings of all corporations, even when they are owned by foreign investors. For example, the German subsidiary of General Motors is taxed like all corporations in the Federal Republic of Germany. The domestic branch of a foreign corporation is normally taxed at the same rate as domestic corporations. In the United Kingdom, for example, that rate is 52% for corporate and branch income.

The Unitary Tax Debate

A special problem related to the determination of income is the unitary method of taxation used by the state of California and several others. This method was developed by California in the 1930s to keep the movie studios from transferring assets out of state to escape California taxes. The basic concept is to tax a portion of a corporation's worldwide earnings. Taxable income is determined by applying to worldwide earnings a percentage based on the average proportion of the firm's in-state sales, property, and payroll to the firm's total sales, assets, and payroll. Thus, the taxable income may have no relation to the actual activity or profitability within the state.

If the relationship between the variables identified above and earnings are the same in the unitary tax state as they are for the corporate entity, then the unitary tax method has no impact on taxes paid. If the firm is more profitable in the state than it is worldwide, the unitary tax method results in a lower taxable income figure and, therefore, lower state tax. However, if the operations in the state are relatively unprofitable, the unitary method results in higher state taxes.

The unitary tax method works for U.S. companies with operations worldwide as well as for foreign firms with operations in the unitary state. In a case brought before the U.S. Supreme Court, Container Corporation tried to get out of paying taxes on its foreign source income. However, the Supreme Court ruled that California had a right to pursue its tax concepts. In that particular case, Container Corporation computed its taxes owed in 1965 at $174,000, whereas California computed the taxes at $197,000.[1]

Shell Petroleum, N.V., the Dutch parent of Shell Oil Company, tried to argue through the Supreme Court that the unitary tax concept did not apply to foreign corporations with branches or subsidiaries in California, but the Supreme Court again ruled in favor of California.[2]

A major problem that unitary tax states face in enforcing the concept on firms with foreign operations is that the foreign financial statements need to be translated from the foreign currency to U.S. dollars. The method of translation and the exchange rate used can have a big impact on reported earnings. There is an attempt by foreign companies and their governments to get Congress to rule that the unitary tax concept needs to stop at "water's edge," but that problem has not yet been resolved.

As can be imagined, some interesting cases, such as those described here, have occurred in California. The Shell Oil Company case alluded to involved a California corporation owned by Shell Petroleum, N.V., that lost $390 million during the period 1973–1976. After taking into consideration the Shell Group's 900 companies worldwide, California asserted that the California subsidiary actually earned $46 million. In another sticky situation, California had a hard time trying to figure out the taxable earnings of a Lever Brothers subsidiary. The problem that occurred was in determining the proper exchange rate to use in 1976. Lever Brothers is jointly owned by a British firm and a Dutch firm. At that time, the Dutch guilder was strong in relation to the dollar, but the British pound was weak. The choice of currency and exchange rate were very influential in determining unitary taxable income.[3]

[1]Linda Greenhouse, "Court Lets States Tax Companies on Portion of Worldwide Income," *New York Times*, 28 June 1983, p. 1.
[2]Deloitte Haskins & Sells, "Foreign Parent Denied Standing to Challenge California Unitary Tax," *The Week in Review*, 9 December 1983, p. 6.
[3]Philip T. Kaplan, "The Unitary Tax Debate, the United States Supreme Court, and Some Plain English," *Journal of Corporate Taxation*, Winter 1984, pp. 286–287.

Determination of Expenses

Another factor that causes differences in the amount of taxes paid is the way countries treat certain expenses for tax purposes. Expenses are usually a matter of timing. If research and development expenses are capitalized, for example, their impact on taxable income will be spread over the period in which they are written off. If they are treated as expenses in the period in which they are incurred, the impact will be immediate.

Opinions also differ from country to country as to the useful life of an asset. If one government allows a firm to write off an asset in five years whereas in another country the same asset has a taxable useful life of ten years, the tax burdens in the two countries will be quite different. In the United Kingdom, for example, a 100% write-off, known as a "first-year allowance" is normally given on plants in the year of acquisition.[4] Also, the government allows a range of useful lives for assets, and companies have the discretion to pick what they consider to be the best useful life for tax purposes.

In the United States, the Investment Tax Credit (equal to 6 or 10% of the acquisition price of real property, depending on the classification of the property) is allowed in the year of acquisition. The Accelerated Cost Recovery System issued by the IRS allows companies to write off an asset over a faster period of time than would be the case under the concept of useful life. In addition, the amount of depreciation allowed each year is computed without taking into consideration salvage value, which tends to result in a larger depreciation charge. Also in the United States, a firm is allowed to value inventory in cost of goods sold at last-in first-out (LIFO), which tends to increase the cost of goods sold and decrease taxable income. This practice is prohibited in a number of other industrial countries. In Sweden, companies are allowed to write down inventories for tax purposes, which tends to reduce taxable income and therefore the tax liability.

What is noteworthy here is that there may be a big difference between the statutory and effective tax rate in a country. A high statutory tax rate with a liberal determination of expenses may result in a relatively low effective tax rate, and this is the rate that is of concern to the investor.

Another dimension of determining taxable income and deductible expenses involves the status of perquisites, or perks, a type of fringe benefits. Opinions differ worldwide on how perks should be treated for tax purposes. In Britain, perks are a national institution. Because of the high marginal personal income tax rate, corporations have found other ways to compensate employees—they provide automobiles, free parking, stereos, antiques, and even pay for spouses' expenses on business trips. The key, of course, is that the perks are not treated as income to the recipients.

[4]Coopers & Lybrand International Tax Network, Alexander Berger, Ed. *1983 International Tax Summaries: A Guide for Planning and Decisions* (New York: John Wiley & Sons, 1983), p. U-14.

Types of Taxes

The impact of taxation on a multinational company depends largely on whether the tax is considered an income tax. The reason for this will be clearer as we discuss the tax credit. The major taxes that we will focus on in this chapter are the corporate income tax and various indirect taxes, such as the value added tax. A special dimension of the corporate income tax is withholding taxes paid on dividends declared to foreign investors.

Corporate Income Tax

The two approaches to taxing corporate income are the classic and the integrated systems. The classic system, used in the United States, taxes income when it is received by each taxable entity. Thus, the earnings of a corporation could be taxed twice—when they are earned by the corporation and when they are received as dividends by shareholders. The integrated system tries to take into consideration the corporation and the shareholder in order to eliminate double taxation. One way to do this is through a split rate system such as Germany's, in which the normal tax rate for most companies is 56%; the rate is reduced, however, to 36% for profits that are distributed.[5] In Japan, the income tax rate of 42% is reduced to 32% for earnings earmarked as dividends.[6] Another approach to the integrated system is to tax earnings at the same rate whether remitted as a dividend or not but to allow a partial or full tax credit for the shareholders. This is the approach followed in France.

Withholding Tax. The income earned by the foreign subsidiary or affiliate of a U.S.-based multinational is taxable in the foreign country, and the tax is levied against the foreign corporation, not against the U.S. parent. However, the actual cash returns to the parent in the form of dividends, royalties (payments made by the foreign corporation to the parent for the use of patents, trademarks, processes, and so on), and interest on intracompany debt are taxable to the parent.

Normally a country levies a withholding tax on payments to the nonresident investor. This tax varies in size from country to country and depends on whether the country has a tax treaty with other countries. In France, for example, profits of French corporations owned by non-French shareholders (such as the French subsidiary of a U.S. multinational) are considered to be distributed to the non-French shareholders whether or not that is the case. The after-tax profits of the company are subject to a 25% withholding tax when the profits are realized. However, full or partial refund of the tax is permitted if the firm does not distribute a dividend

[5]Ibid., p. G-2.
[6]Ibid., p. J-7.

Table 7.1 Withholding Tax Rates Applicable to Foreign
Investors

	Dividends (%)	Interest (%)	Royalties (%)
Australia	30	10	46[a]
Brazil	25	25[a]	25
Canada	25	25	25
France	25	45[a]	33⅓
West Germany	25	0[a]	25
Italy	32.40[a]	15	30[a]
Japan	20	20	20
Mexico	21	42[a]	42[a]
Netherlands	25	0	0
Switzerland	35	35[a]	0[a]
United Kingdom	0	30	30
United States	30	30[b]	30

[a]Special rates apply for different situations. Most of the rates in
this table vary with tax treaties.
[b]In 1984, the U.S. government eliminated the withholding tax on
interest from new securities.
Source: Ernst & Whinney, "Foreign and U.S. Corporate Income
and Withholding Tax Rates," 1984.

within 12 months after the end of the year or if the dividend is obviously
smaller than the earnings on which the withholding tax was based.[7]

Table 7.1 compares the withholding rates in several countries. As can
be seen from the table, the rates are often dependent on the situation at
hand. In Mexico, for example, there are four classes of withholding rates
on interest, and the rates vary from as low as 15% to as high as 42%. The
withholding tax for copyright royalties for the use of artistic, literary, and
scientific works, and for movies and television films and radio recordings is
only 10%, whereas the withholding tax on royalties for the use of patents,
trade names, trademarks, and publicity is 42%.[8]

Brazil provides a different situation with respect to withholding taxes.
A 25% withholding tax is applied on dividends paid to a foreign investor.
However, the tax can also be affected by a three-year moving average of
the registered capital base of the Brazilian firm. For dividends up to 12% of
the registered capital base, the foreign investor is subject to the 25% tax.
However, for dividends from 12 to 15%, a supplementary tax of 40% is
assessed. The supplementary tax rises to 50% for dividends from 15 to 25%
of invested capital and to 60% for dividends over 25% of invested capital.[9]

[7]Ibid., p. F-20.
[8]Ibid., pp. M-49, M-50.
[9]Ibid., p. B-69.

In addition to the variation of withholding rates for different classes of transactions, tax treaties can affect rates, as we shall see later in this chapter.

Indirect Taxes

In countries such as the United States, the direct income tax is the most important source of revenue for the federal government. In other countries, indirect taxes are very important. In Europe, the value added tax (VAT), sometimes referred to as the tax on value added, is a source of considerable national income and is also the major source of revenue to fund the operations of the European Economic Community. The basic concept behind the VAT is that a tax is applied at each stage of the production process for the value added by the firm to goods purchased from the outside. The two major methods for computing the VAT are the additive method and the subtractive method. In the following illustrations in Exhibit 7.1, assume that the VAT is 7%, the rate used in France for some food products, listed pharmaceutical products, books, water, and a few other listed products.

The EC member countries are required to use the subtractive form of the VAT illustrated in the exhibit. This means that firms subtract from the selling price of their products the invoiced purchases from firms that include the VAT in their selling price and apply the VAT against the difference. This method is simple and easy to document. Although the method is uniform throughout the EC, the VAT rates are not. As mentioned, France applies a 7% VAT rate against some transactions. For others, the rate could be 5.5% (for some food products), 33⅓% (for some listed luxury

Exhibit 7.1 Vat Illustrations

The Additive Method	
Value added in production:	
Wages	$400,000
Rent	20,000
Interest	40,000
Profit	20,000
Total	$480,000
VAT payable: $480,000 × 7% = $33,600	

The Subtractive Method	
Sales revenues	$1,000,000
Less purchases of goods and services on which VAT has been paid	520,000
Total value added	$ 480,000
VAT payable: $480,000 × 7% = $33,600	

items), or 18.6% (for all other transactions). In Germany, the rate is 13% for most transactions. In Italy, the basic rate is 18%, but other transactions are taxed at 2 to 10% (some food products) and 20 to 38% (certain luxury items).[10]

Since the EC derives most of its operating revenues from the VAT collected from member countries, there is a strong interest in harmonizing the tax. Although the methods of computation and collection have been harmonized, the member states still determine their own tax rate for certain transactions. The EC is trying to make more uniform the situations under which the VAT should be applied to exports and imports. Over 11 VAT directives have been issued or proposed, and some important issues still need to be resolved.

HOW TO AVOID DOUBLE TAXATION

The foreign branches and subsidiaries of U.S. corporations are subject to a variety of taxes, both direct and indirect, in the countries where they operate. The problem is that the income earned in the foreign country may be subject to income taxes twice: when the earnings are realized in the foreign location and in the United States. In the latter case, income from foreign corporations is usually taxed in the United States when a dividend is remitted to the U.S. investor, such as the parent company. In general, a company may avoid double taxation by deducting foreign taxes paid from worldwide earnings in order to reduce taxable income and, therefore, the tax liability to the U.S. Internal Revenue Service. It may choose to treat the taxes paid as a credit that can be applied against their U.S. tax liability. The simple illustration in Table 7.2 demonstrates the difference in U.S. tax liability that arises from double taxation, a tax deduction, and a tax credit.

The U.S. government has also attempted to help firms escape double taxation by entering into a number of tax treaties with different countries.

Deductions

The IRS permits firms to deduct from revenues the expenses that relate to their trade or business. Taxes paid to foreign governments fall in that category. Although most firms would find it more advantageous to take the tax credit as Table 7.2 illustrates, there are some benefits to taking taxes as a deduction to determine taxable income. For one thing, the tax credit is limited to income taxes, whereas all taxes may be treated as a deduction. In addition, the tax credit applies only when the firm has earned income, whereas there is no limit to the amount of expenses that can be deducted from income since the firm can carry back or carry forward a loss recognized in a particular year.

[10]Ibid., pp. F-28, G-6, and I-52.

Table 7.2 Treatment of Foreign Corporate Income Tax

	Double Taxation	Deduction	Credit
Income earned by the foreign corporation	$100.00	$100.00	$100.00
Foreign tax at 40% on $100	40.00	40.00	40.00
Net income	$ 60.00	$ 60.00	$ 60.00
U.S. tax at 48% on $100	48.00		
U.S. tax at 48% on $60		28.80	
U.S. tax at 48% on $100 less foreign tax at 40% on $100			8.00
Net income after taxes	$ 12.00	$ 31.20	$ 52.00

Tax Credits

The idea of the tax credit, as briefly illustrated here, is that a U.S. firm can reduce its tax liability on a dollar-for-dollar basis. If a U.S. corporation has a wholly owned subsidiary in Canada, the Canadian corporation must pay corporate income tax of 46% of taxable income and withhold another 15% on dividends paid to the U.S. parent. If the parent is taxed again on the income in the U.S. at 48%, there would not be very much left over. That is why the tax credit was adopted in 1918. It allows a U.S. corporation to reduce its U.S. tax liability by the amount of income taxes paid to the foreign government.

A key point to realize is that a tax must be considered an income tax to be creditable; the VAT described above would be eligible for deduction but not for the credit. The predominant nature of the foreign tax must be that of an income tax as defined in the United States. Thus, a tax might be considered an income tax abroad but still not be eligible for the credit if that tax is deemed something else from the perspective of the IRS in the United States.

The IRS allows three tests to determine if the tax is an income tax: the realization test, the gross receipts test, and the net income test. The realization test is met if the tax is imposed at or just after the time income is earned as defined by the Code. The gross receipts test is met if the tax is based on the gross receipts of the firm. The net income test is met if the tax is imposed on gross receipts reduced by expenses incurred to generate the receipts.[11] Although the credit was originally allowed only for income, war profits, or excess profits taxes, the IRS does allow taxes that are assessed on the foreign corporation in lieu of income taxes, as long as those taxes meet specific tests set by the IRS.

[11]*CCH—Standard Federal Tax Reports* (Chicago: Commerce Clearing House, Inc., 1983), paragraph 4303.03.

Exhibit 7.2 Computing the Tax Credit

Earnings before foreign tax (EBFT)	$500,000
Foreign income tax paid	200,000
Earnings after foreign tax (EAFT)	$300,000
Dividend paid to U.S. corporation	$150,000
Foreign withholding tax at 15%	22,500
Net dividend received by parent	$127,500
Computation of tax credit:	
Direct credit for withholding tax	$ 22,500
Deemed direct credit	
$\dfrac{\text{Dividend}}{\text{EAFT}} \times \text{Foreign tax}$	
$\dfrac{150}{300} \times 200,000$	100,000
Total credit	$122,500

It should be noted that the credit is available only for taxes on income paid directly by the U.S. corporation (e.g., the withholding tax on dividends) or deemed to have been paid by it. The deemed direct tax is the corporate income tax actually paid by the foreign corporation to the foreign government and deemed to have been paid by the U.S. parent.

The tax credit applies to all income that must be recognized by the parent. The only exception to this is for income that arises from activities related to boycotts, such as the Arab boycott of Israel. Foreign income taxes paid on that income are not eligible for the credit. The credit is available for income of foreign branches of U.S. corporations as well as for income of foreign corporations in which the U.S. parent has an equity interest. The example in Exhibit 7.2 illustrates how the tax credit can be computed. Even though the total credit as computed is $122,500, the parent may not be able to apply all the credit against the current year's tax liability because of the overall limitation set by the IRS.

In order to illustrate how the limitation works, assume that a U.S. firm's worldwide income is $1 million, that its U.S. tax liability before credits is $480,000, and that its only foreign source income is what is computed in Exhibit 7.2. The amount of income from the foreign operation included in the total worldwide income is figured as follows:

Dividend	$150,000
Deemed direct credit	100,000
Included in income	$250,000

The addition of the deemed direct credit to the dividend is known as *grossing up the dividend*. The overall limitation is computed as follows:

$$\text{Overall limitation} = \frac{\text{Foreign source income}}{\text{Total worldwide income}} \times \text{U.S. tax liability}$$

$$= \frac{250,000}{1,000,000} \times 480,000$$

$$= \$120,000$$

This means that the parent can take no more than $120,000 in credits. Since the credit as computed was $122,500, the total credit allowed is $120,000 and the final tax liability is $360,000 ($480,000 − $120,000). The excess credit of $2500 ($122,500 − $120,000) can be carried back two years and forward five years and applied against income taxes of those years. If the computed credit had been $115,000 instead of $122,500, the parent would have been allowed to take the whole amount, since it was less than the overall limitation.

In the example it was assumed that there was only one source of foreign income. If several sources had existed, the income would have been added together to get the foreign source income in the formula. Losses of foreign corporations or income retained by a foreign corporation rather than declared as a dividend would not be included. The credits from each of the foreign sources would have been added together, then compared with the upper limit, to determine the actual credit that could be applied against the U.S. tax liability.

The tax credit in the previous examples assumed a foreign corporation, but credits are allowed on any foreign source income. For example, a movie company may pay withholding taxes on royalties received from showing movies abroad, and the withholding tax would qualify for the tax credit. The same concept applies for an oil company that pays a withholding tax on royalties it receives for oil production abroad.

The firms could end up with large excess credits that can never be applied against the U.S. tax—even if they are carried back and forward. This is because many countries have higher tax rates than the United States. As pointed out in one article on high corporate tax rates abroad, "Britain . . . has a general corporate income tax rate of 52% and taxes North Sea oil production at about 70%. Norway's regular corporate rate is 33%, but its oil rate is 67%. . . . Nigeria's oil rate is 85% and Oman's is 70%."[12] This is why some multinationals could pay an effective tax rate for worldwide operations that exceeds the U.S. rate.

Tax Treaties

As noted, with the spread of business worldwide, income earned in one country may be subject to taxation in other countries. Differences in philos-

---

[12]*Business Week,* 28 January 1980, p. 122.

ophy on how income should be taxed have given rise to treaties between countries to minimize the effect of double taxation on the taxpayer, protect each country's right to collect taxes, and provide ways to resolve jurisdictional issues. In the area of double taxation, treaties can specify that certain classes of income would not be subject to tax, can reduce the rate on income and/or withholding taxes, and can specifically deal with the issue of tax credits. Although the latter point could be considered a duplication of the Internal Revenue Code, its specification in a tax treaty would simply strengthen the tax credit concept. It could also deal with specific types of taxes that could be considered creditable, and so on.

A pattern for tax treaties was developed by the Organization for Economic Cooperation and Development (OECD) in 1963 and later amended and reissued in 1977. That pattern, initially resisted by the United States, was accepted in principle in the model tax treaty approved by the United States in 1977. The treaty contains 29 articles dealing with such issues as the taxes covered, the persons and organizations covered, relief from double taxation, the exchange of information between competent authorities of contracting nations, and the conditions under which a treaty may be terminated. The model treaty also deals with issues such as who is allowed to tax income, how income is to be characterized, how expenses are to be allocated, what rights exist to certain types of deductions, and how rates of tax on foreign investors can be reduced.[13]

The United States has 26 tax treaties with 38 countries, which is low compared with other developed countries. Britian has treaties with 72 countries and restricted agreements with several others. Among other things, tax treaties have an impact on dividend, interest, and royalty payments. In West Germany, for example, the withholding rate not only on dividends and royalties but on the interest on certain loans is 25%, whereas the interest on loans secured by real property and interest from a permanent establishment such as an operating subsidiary in Germany are subject to a 50% rate. In the tax treaty with the United States, however, the withholding rate on dividends is reduced to 15%, and interest and royalty payments are totally exempt from withholding tax. Canadian dividends, interest, and royalties are normally subject to a 25% withholding tax rate but to only 15% for U.S. firms as a result of the tax treaty. Under a new treaty awaiting confirmation in both countries, the withholding rate would drop to 10%.[14]

Although tax treaties are formal agreements between countries over certain tax principles, other forms of cooperation on tax issues exist. In 1979, for example, the tax authorities of Canada, France, Germany, the United Kingdom, and the United States entered into an agreement to

---

[13]Robert J. Patrick, Jr., "Leading Treaty Issues," *Tax Executive*, July 1977, p. 367.
[14]See Ernst & Whinney, *Foreign and U.S. Corporate Income with Withholding Tax Rates*, for other examples.

coordinate the examination of the tax returns of multinational enterprises. The explicit objectives of the agreement are as follows:

- Determination of correct tax liabilities and avoidance of double taxation where costs are shared or profits are allocated between taxpayers.
- Study of transfer pricing practices.
- Improvement of information exchange.
- Sharing of intelligence on tax avoidance techniques.
- Efficient use of government and company personnel[15]

U.S. TAXATION OF FOREIGN SOURCE INCOME

There are profits to be made from international business, but what are the relevant tax effects? First, it is important to separate earnings into two groups: (1) those generated in the parent country from the import and export of goods and services and (2) those generated in a foreign country through a branch of the parent or a foreign corporation in which the parent has ownership. Our focus here is on U.S. tax law unless explicitly stated otherwise, so the United States will serve as the parent country in the examples.

There are a few key principles that relate to taxation of foreign source income. The deferral principle implies that income is not taxed until received by the U.S. shareholder. Thus, if the shareholder is entitled to income from a foreign source but has not yet received it, the recognition of income may be deferred until it is received. Another key principle already discussed is the tax credit.

The equity and neutrality principles are sources of endless conflict in the taxation of foreign source income. The equity principle says that, under similar circumstances, taxpayers should pay the same tax. One side feels that foreign as well as domestic source income should be taxed at the same U.S. rate. The other side says that income earned in a foreign country should be taxed at the same rate as all income in that country and not at that rate plus the U.S. rate. The neutrality principle states that the tax effect should not have an impact on business decisions. One side feels that the foreign tax credit encourages firms to invest abroad because firms do not get a credit for income taxes paid to state governments in the United States. The other side feels that when firms are taxed on foreign source income, they must forgo some investment opportunities because their competitors in foreign countries are not taxed twice on income.

In this section of this chapter, we will discuss earnings generated from a foreign branch or subsidiary. Later, we will discuss various tax incentives provided by the government to encourage exports.

[15]Deloitte, Haskins, and Sells, *The Week in Review,* 26 October 1979, pp. 6–7; and Ernst & Whinney, *Tax Notes,* April 1979, p. 1.

The Tax Haven Concept

A phenomenon that has emerged from the philosophy that foreign source income should not be taxed at all or should be taxed only when declared a dividend is the tax haven. A tax haven is defined as "a place where foreigners may receive income or own assets without paying high rates of tax upon them."[16] Tax havens offer a variety of benefits, including low taxes or no taxes on certain classes of income. Because of these benefits, thousands of so-called mailbox companies have sprung up in such exotic places as Liechtenstein, Vanuatu (formerly New Hebrides), and the Netherlands Antilles.

The following characteristics seem to best describe the attributes of a tax haven country:

a. either impose no tax or impose a low tax when compared with the United States;

b. have a high level of bank or commercial secrecy, which the country refuses to break even under an international agreement;

c. relative importance of banking and similar financial activities to its economy;

d. the availability of modern communication facilities;

e. lack of currency controls on foreign deposits of foreign currency; and

f. self-promotion as an offshore financial center.[17]

As pointed out, the major advantage of tax havens is tax reduction. There are four broad categories of tax havens:

1. Countries with no income taxes, such as the Bahamas, Bermuda, and the Cayman Islands.

2. Countries with taxes at low rates, such as the British Virgin Islands.

3. Countries that tax income from domestic sources but exempt income from foreign sources, such as Hong Kong, Liberia, and Panama.

4. Countries that allow special privileges; generally their suitability as tax havens is limited.[18]

It is possible that companies could operate in tax haven countries as legitimate operations and reap the tax benefits without the stigma of being called a tax haven or fictitious business. To take advantage of a tax haven, a corporation would ordinarily set up a subsidiary in the tax haven country

[16]Milka Casanegra de Jantscher, "Tax Havens Explained," *Finance and Development*, March 1976.

[17]*Standard Federal Tax Reporter* (Chicago: Commerce Clearing House, Inc., 1983), paragraph 305.

[18]Jean Doucet and Kenneth J. Good, "What Makes a Good Tax Haven?" *Banker*, May 1973, p. 493.

through which different forms of income would pass. The goal is to shift income from high-tax to tax haven countries. This is normally accomplished by using the tax haven subsidiary as an intermediary. For example, a U.S. manufacturer could sell goods directly to a dealer in West Germany and concentrate the profits in the United States, or it could sell the goods to a tax haven subsidiary at cost and then sell the goods to the German dealer, thus concentrating the profits in the tax haven corporation.

Government Responses to Tax Havens

When John F. Kennedy became president of the United States in 1961, he was determined to examine more closely the taxation of foreign-source income and its effect on the foreign investment policy of U.S. corporations and on the generation of revenues by the government from corporation income tax. In his 1961 message to Congress, President Kennedy indicated that among other things more and more U.S. firms were maximizing the accumulation of profits in tax havens by artificial arrangements of intercompany pricing and other intercompany transactions. He directed the Secretary of the Treasury to undertake the research and preparation of a comprehensive international tax reform program that would include proposed legislation, as well as administrative action to improve compliance with existing statutes.

As noted earlier, a U.S. corporation may choose to produce and sell in the foreign country through a branch of the parent or through a foreign corporation in which the parent has an equity interest. The tax implications of these situations are interesting. The income or loss of a foreign branch must be combined with parent income for tax as well as book purposes. In most cases, however, a U.S. corporation does not declare income for tax purposes from a foreign corporation until it actually receives a dividend. This is the principle of deferral—the income is deferred from U.S. taxation until it is received as a dividend. As mentioned earlier in the chapter, the deferral principle is a basic tenet of the taxation of foreign source income.

The Controlled Foreign Corporation

The deferral principle works most of the time, but an exception is made for a certain class of income (Subpart F income) of a certain type of corporation (a controlled foreign corporation). That income is not deferred but must be declared by the U.S. corporation as soon as it is earned by the foreign corporation. However, the place to start is to define a controlled foreign corporation (CFC). A CFC is a foreign corporation in which "U.S. shareholders" hold more than 50% of the voting stock. A "U.S. shareholder," for tax purposes, is a person or enterprise that holds at least 10% of the voting stock of the foreign corporation. Table 7.3 illustrates how to determine whether or not a foreign corporation is a CFC. The first corporation is

Table 7.3 Determination of Controlled Foreign Corporations

Shareholders	Percentages of the Voting Stock		
	Foreign Corporation 1	Foreign Corporation 2	Foreign Corporation 3
U.S. shareholder A	100%	35%	35%
U.S. shareholder B		10	10
U.S. shareholder C		10	5
U.S. shareholder D			5
Foreign shareholder E		45	45
	100%	100%	100%

a CFC because shareholder A qualifies as a U.S. shareholder and holds more than 50% of the voting. The second corporation is also a CFC because shareholders A, B, and C all qualify as U.S. shareholders, and the total voting stock they control exceeds 50%. The third corporation is not a CFC because only shareholders A and B qualify as U.S. shareholders, and their combined total of the voting stock is only 45%.

Subpart F Income

Why does it make a difference for tax purposes whether a foreign corporation is a CFC? If it is not a CFC, its income is automatically deferred until remitted as a dividend to the shareholders. If a foreign corporation *is* a CFC, the deferral principle may not apply to certain kinds of income. In order to understand that, it is necessary to go back in history a few years. As was said earlier, sometimes U.S. corporations do business in tax haven countries and therefore benefit from low or nonexistent income taxes. If a tax haven corporation was actively involved in the production and sale of goods and services, there was no problem. However, the U.S. government noticed that many firms were setting up tax haven corporations just to avoid paying U.S. tax. Therefore, the Revenue Act of 1962 minimized the tax avoidance practices of multinationals. The act allowed a U.S. corporation to apply the deferral principle to its portion of income from the active conduct of a trade or business of a CFC, but it could not defer its portion of passive income, referred to as Subpart F income in the Internal Revenue Code.

Subpart F income is divided into seven groups: (1) insurance of U.S. risks, (2) foreign base company personal holding company income, (3) foreign base company sales income, (4) foreign base company services income, (5) foreign base company shipping income, (6) boycott-related income, and (7) foreign bribes.

The first category of Subpart F income, *insurance of U.S. risks,* arose because many U.S. corporations were setting up a foreign insurance subsidiary in a tax haven country and paying insurance premiums to the subsidiary on U.S. and foreign risks. The parent could deduct the premiums as expenses, and the subsidiary was paying little or no tax on the premium income. Now the income from the premiums is taxable to the parent when earned by the CFC.

Foreign base company personal holding company income includes dividends, interest, royalties, and similar income that arises from holding rights rather than actually producing or selling goods and services. However, the income must be derived from sources outside the country where the CFC is organized. For example, if Multicorp established a holding company in Switzerland that owned Multicorp's subsidiaries in France and Spain, the dividends received by the holding company would be considered Subpart F income to Multicorp.

Foreign base company sales income arises from the sale or purchase of goods produced and consumed outside the country where the CFC is incorporated. For example, a U.S. firm could sell merchandise to an unaffiliated buyer in France but have the paperwork go through a tax haven CFC in Switzerland. On paper, the U.S. firm would sell to the Swiss firm (probably a wholly owned subsidiary), which would sell to the French firm. Prices would be set to concentrate profits in the Swiss firm. However, that income would be considered Subpart F income in the new law and would have to be declared by the U.S. firm. It should also be noted that the income is considered Subpart F income as long as the CFC in Switzerland is not actively involved in selling and servicing the product with its own staff. If that were to happen, the income would be active rather than passive.

Foreign base company services income arises from contracts utilizing technical, managerial, engineering, or other skills. For example, a U.S. hotel management firm could enter into a contract to manage a hotel for a sheikdom in the Middle East and have the management fee billed to a tax haven subsidiary in Switzerland. That fee would be considered Subpart F income to the U.S. firm.

Foreign base company shipping income arises from using aircraft or ships for transportation outside the country where the CFC is incorporated.

The inclusion of *bribes* and *boycotts* as Subpart F income is a phenomenon that came with the compliments of the Tax Reform Act of 1976. In order to penalize companies that supported the Arab boycott of Israel, Congress decided to classify income from these boycott operations as Subpart F income. Also, bribes paid to foreign government officials as explained in the Foreign Corrupt Practices Act of 1976 are considered a new class of Subpart F income, even though the bribes are not really a form of income to the parent. These two twists of the law have nothing to do with tax avoidance, like the other dimensions of Subpart F income; they were included simply to punish offenders of other laws.

Now that we have divided foreign corporations into groups and income into types, let's summarize the tax implications. For foreign corporations that are not controlled foreign corporations, income is not taxable to the U.S. shareholder (the parent corporation) until a dividend is declared. For controlled foreign corporations, active income is also deferred, but passive or Subpart F income must be recognized by the parent when earned, regardless of when a dividend is declared. The only major exception to the rule is that if foreign base company income of a CFC is less than 10% of gross income, none of it is treated as Subpart F income. If the foreign base company income exceeds 70% of gross income, all the company's income is treated as Subpart F income.

TRANSFER PRICING

The basic concept behind responsibility accounting is that managers need to be able to control their destiny. This is difficult for vertically integrated companies in which divisions are buying and selling from each other, and the international market complicates the process dramatically. The price established on goods and services bought and sold between related entities, such as a parent and its subsidiary, is known as a transfer price. Although the managerial considerations of transfer pricing are discussed in Chapter 8, it is important to discuss the tax aspects of transfer pricing in this chapter.

Section 482—The U.S. Government Response

Governments are not all alike, nor are they all equally concerned about transfer prices and their effects. The Japanese, French, and Italian governments appear to rank among the least concerned, the United States, Canada, and a majority of developing countries rank among the most concerned.[19] The government attitude is important to a multinational in terms of its business-government relations. In the current world atmosphere of nationalistic fever and fervor, the position of multinationals is increasingly perilous. As a consequence, they are increasingly on the defensive in terms of justifying their presence and demonstrating their benefits to the countries concerned. Because most governments rightly or wrongly view market-based transfer prices as less manipulative, less suspicious, fairer, and hence more desirable than cost-based transfer prices, companies utilizing arm's-length prices have one less area of contention and possible conflict with governments.

In an increasing number of countries, national governments are stressing and even requiring market-price equivalents for international intracor-

[19]Jeffrey S. Arpan, *International Intracorporate Pricing: Non-American Systems and Views* (New York: Praeger, 1972).

porate transfers. In some cases, government officials have the authority to recompute nonmarket-based transfer prices to determine the proper tariff to be assessed. In others, they have the power to reallocate income in order to determine the income to be taxed.

Section 482 of the Internal Revenue Code permits the IRS to "distribute, apportion, or allocate gross income, deductions, credits, or allowances" between related enterprises if it feels that tax evasion is taking place. The IRS prefers that all transfers among related enterprises take place at "arm's-length" prices, defined as the price that would take place between unrelated entities. As a result, the IRS is concerned about monitoring transfers in the following five areas: loans and advances, performance of services, use of tangible property, use of intangible property, and sale of tangible property.

Table 7.4 illustrates the impact on tax burdens that can take place when the IRS allocates income among related entities in order to achieve what it feels is an arm's-length transaction. Assume that the selling division in a low-tax country (tax rate is 20%) sells products to the buying division in the United States (tax rate is 50%) for $2000. The total tax liability is $1600 and the combined net income after tax is $1900. However, if the IRS decides to allocate income to the parent company under the assumption that the subsidiary is charging too high a transfer price in order

Table 7.4 Allocation of Income Under Section 482

	Selling Division	Buying Division	Consolidated Results
Before IRS Allocation			
Sales	$2,000	$10,000	$12,000
Cost of goods sold	1,000	4,000	5,000
Gross profit	$1,000	$ 6,000	$ 7,000
Other expenses	500	3,000	3,500
Taxable income	$ 500	$ 3,000	$ 3,500
Income tax[a]	100	$ 1,500	1,600
Net income	$ 400	$ 1,500	$ 1,900
After IRS Allocation			
Sales	$1,500	$10,000	$11,500
Cost of goods sold	1,000	3,500	4,500
Gross profit	$ 500	$ 6,500	$ 7,000
Other expenses	500	3,000	3,500
Taxable income	$ 0	$ 3,500	$ 3,500
Income tax	0	1,750	1,750
Net income	$ 0	$ 1,750	$ 1,750

[a]20% for the selling division and 50% for the buying division.

to capture profits in the low-tax area, it could do so by determining the sale to be $1500 instead of $2000. This results in the total tax liability being $1750 and combined net income being $1750. Thus, taxes go up and profits go down under the reallocation.

The key for the IRS in making the allocations is that it tries to establish what an arm's-length price should be. For the sale of tangible property, that price can be determined in one of three ways: the comparable uncontrollable price method, the resale price method, and the cost-plus method. The first method is preferable from the standpoint of the IRS, and it uses the concept of a market price to determine the transfer price. Of course, an external market for the same or very similar product must exist for this method to be used. The IRS also allows for differences resulting from reductions in variable expenses (such as selling expenses).

If it is impossible to use the comparable uncontrollable price method, the firm must then use the resale price method. Assume that the manufacturer in the United States sells a product to its wholly owned distributor in Hong Kong, which sells the product to final consumers in the Orient, and that the manufacturer does not sell the product directly to any other firm. The IRS would take the price established by the distributor to outside customers and back out any costs to completion plus a normal profit margin in order to determine the transfer price from the manufacturer to the distributor.

If all else fails, the IRS permits the cost-plus method. That method involves the costs of manufacturing the product plus a normal profit margin from the sales of similar products. Obviously, it is difficult to justify costs and normal profit margins.

Although there are a number of good cases that illustrate the problems that firms can run into through improper transfer pricing policies, the Eli Lilly and Company case is one of the best known. In the early 1940s, Eli Lilly decided to set up two wholly owned domestic subsidiaries to promote export sales: Eli Lilly International Company (International) to service business in the Eastern Hemisphere, and Eli Lilly Pan-American Corporation (Pan-American) to service the Western Hemisphere.

In order to encourage sales, management decided to sell goods to International and Pan-American at a substantial discount that increased with volume. This incentive contributed to strong growth in export sales over the next few years.

In 1946, Eli Lilly instituted another organizational change by making International the sole distributor of Lilly products worldwide. International sold to unrelated wholesalers in the Eastern Hemisphere and to Pan-American in the Western Hemisphere. Pan-American qualified as a Western Hemisphere Trade Corporation, which was allowed a special deduction in computing taxable income. The deduction was determined by multiplying taxable income by a fraction, the numerator of which was 14 and the denominator the tax rate for the year. Assuming a 48% tax rate, a Western

Hemisphere Trade Corporation would have an effective tax rate of 34 rather than 48%. This provided a distinct advantage for Lilly to sell products to wholesale distributors in the Western Hemisphere through Pan-American instead of directly from International. The same advantage did not exist for sales to wholesale distributors in the Eastern Hemisphere.

Initially, sales to International from Eli Lilly were made at a discount of 60% from domestic prices on finished and packaged merchandise, and at Lilly's cost plus 15% on bulk merchandise. In 1952, however, this policy was changed. Because International and Pan-American were having trouble making a profit, Eli Lilly decided to forgo its own profit by selling to International at a price that recovered manufacturing cost of goods sold, plus royalties payable by Eli Lilly to third parties, plus all operating expenses incurred by Eli Lilly incident to the servicing of the export business. International sold the products to Eastern Hemisphere distributors at suggested domestic retail price less 15%. International sales to Pan-American, however, were at its cost of goods sold plus administrative and selling expenses allocated to International's business with Pan-American. There was no provision for specific profit to International on its sales to Pan-American.

As would be expected, the IRS allocated income back to Eli Lilly. As pointed out by the Court,

> Eli Lilly has adopted a pricing policy on its products destined for international markets which results in its selling organizations receiving the bulk of the overall profits from sales abroad. That policy disturbs the Government only insofar as it involves Eli Lilly's products sold in the Western Hemisphere. Because one of Eli Lilly's selling subsidiaries qualifies as a Western Hemisphere Trade Corporation and therefore enjoys a reduced rate of tax on its income, the Government asserts that Eli Lilly's pricing policy results in tax avoidance and does not clearly reflect the incomes of the related organizations.[20]

The IRS determined the correct transfer price by computing a profit margin on Eli Lilly's domestic sales to uncontrolled wholesale distributors. Given that International was receiving bulk shipments that could be construed as available for a substantial discount, the IRS added half of the normal profit margin to the direct expenses of International to determine what the transfer price should be.

Section 861—The Allocation of Expenses

In 1977, Regulation 1.861–8 became a new thorn in the side of the multinational and a new IRS tool for reducing tax credits. This section of the Code allocates and apportions all of a firm's expenses, losses, and other deductions to specific sources of income (sales, royalties, dividends) and then

---

[20]*U.S. Tax Cases* 67-1, (Chicago: Commerce Clearing House, Inc., 1967), pp. 83, 536.

apportions the expenses between domestic and foreign source income. Although all expenses must be allocated and apportioned, there are three major groupings of expenses: interest expenses, research and development expenses, and general and administrative expenses. The regulations give specific guidelines on the allocations, in some cases stating what classes of income certain expenses are to be allocated to. The guidelines range from very specific for some types of expenses (such as R&D) to very general for others.

If the income to which the expenses have been allocated is strictly foreign source, then the expenses are charged solely to foreign source income. If the expenses are attached to composite sources of income, then the firm must allocate the expenses between domestic and foreign source income based on guidelines set by the regulations.

The following example illustrates the impact these allocations could have on the tax credit. In the example, the U.S. company's only foreign source income is royalty income from country Z.[21]

	Worldwide	U.S.	Foreign
Gross profit and royalties	$3100	$2100	$1000
U.S. expenses (before allocation)	1600	1600	
Taxable income by sources	$1500	$ 500	$1000
Tax liabilities:			
U.S. tax—48% of $1500	$720		
Foreign income tax—30% of $1000	300		

Tax credit limitation—$\dfrac{1000}{1500} \times 720 = \$480$

Since the upper limit ($480) exceeds the actual foreign tax ($300), the U.S. company can take the full $300 credit. The U.S. tax liability would be $420 ($720 − $300), and the total taxes paid worldwide would be $720 ($420 in the United States and $300 in country Z).

If a portion of the expenses were to be allocated to the foreign source income, the tax situation might appear as follows:

	Worldwide	U.S.	Foreign
Gross profits and royalties	$3100	$2100	$1000
Expenses after allocation	1600	975	625
Worldwide gross income	$1500	$1125	$ 375

[21]The example is taken from James W. Schenold, "A Tool for Maximizing Foreign Tax Credits," *Price Waterhouse Review*, Vol. 2, 1978, pp. 38–51.

The U.S. and foreign tax liabilities would stay the same ($720 and $300), but the tax credit would change as follows:

$$\frac{375}{1500} \times 720 = \$180, \text{ the upper limit.}$$

Because the upper limit is less than the taxes paid ($300), the U.S. company is constrained by the upper limit and the worldwide tax liability would be as follows:

$720	U.S. tax on $1500
180	tax credit
$540	U.S. tax liability
300	foreign tax liability
$840	total taxes paid worldwide

TAX EFFECTS OF FOREIGN EXCHANGE GAINS AND LOSSES

In Chapter 5, we discussed the accounting requirements in FASB Statement No. 52 for translating foreign currency transactions and foreign currency financial statements into the parent currency (hereafter referred to in this section as dollars). At that time, we noted that the Board prefers to recognize the impact of an exchange rate change when the event takes place rather than defer that impact into the future. Therefore, foreign currency transaction gains and losses are recognized in income when the rate changes, not when the transaction is finally settled. In the case of financial statements, gains and losses that arise under the current rate method are taken directly to a separate component of stockholders' equity, whereas gains and losses that arise under the temporal method are taken directly to income. For listed companies, these adjustments take place at least quarterly when financial statements are released to the public.

The treatment of these gains and losses for tax purposes is not consistent with the requirements of Statement No. 52, and specific rulings on the tax effects have been confusing, especially since they tend to rely on accounting standards that have been changed in recent years. The key tax concept that underlies what is discussed here is that foreign currency is considered by the IRS to be a capital asset. This means that a realizable event must take place in order for a gain or loss to be recognized for tax purposes; gains or losses cannot be recognized while foreign currency balances are being held.

Foreign Currency Transactions

The IRS treats foreign currency transactions from the two-transactions perspective just as Statement No. 52 does. However, it does not recognize gains and losses until the financial obligation has actually been settled. Assume that a U.S. importer purchases a piece of equipment on credit from a German supplier for DM1,000,000 on December 1 when the rate is $0.40/DM. On December 31, the rate moves to $0.38, and on January 31 when the supplier is paid by the importer, the rate is $0.39. For financial reporting and tax purposes, the original transaction would be recorded at $400,000. On December 31, the firm would recognize a gain of $20,000 [1,000,000 × (0.40 − 0.38)] for financial statement purposes to reflect the lower value of the liability, and on January 31 it would recognize a loss of $10,000 [1,000,000 × (0.38 − 0.39)] to reflect the increase in value of the liability.

For tax purposes, however, the firm would wait until January 31 when it settles the financial obligation to determine the gain or loss. In this case, it would recognize a gain of $10,000 [1,000,000 × (0.40 − 0.39)] to reflect the difference between the amount at which the liability is initially recorded and the amount at which it is settled.

The situation involving long-term debt is not as clear-cut. Statement No. 52 requires a two-transactions perspective for long-term debt, with foreign exchange gains and losses being taken to income in the period in which they occur. The tax law, however, is not consistent with Statement No. 52. In certain cases the IRS may allow a firm to treat the gain or loss arising from loans payable as an adjustment to the base of the asset that was purchased by it. Alternatively, the IRS may allow the firm to treat the gain or loss as a short-term capital adjustment, which has little tax effect. This contrasts with the situation described previously, in which foreign exchange gains and losses are treated as ordinary gains and losses.

In Chapter 5, we discussed several ways to account for forward contracts. According to the Code, the tax treatment of a forward contract depends on whether or not the contract is entered into as a hedge. If it is, then gains and losses on the contract are not recognized until the contract is closed. This could lead to timing differences between tax and financial accounting treatments of the contract. If the contract is not used as a hedge, then the gain or loss is determined by the market-to-market approach. That approach determines the market value of the contract at the end of the year and compares that with the market value of the contract at the beginning of the year or inception of the contract (whichever is more recent) to determine the gain or loss on the contract.[22]

Branch Earnings

For tax purposes, branch earnings can be divided into two parts: earnings that have been distributed back to the home office, and earnings that are

[22]Kathy Bindon, "Forward Contracts: A Comparison of the Accounting and Tax Implications," a paper delivered at the American Accounting Association annual meeting in Toronto in August 1984.

Exhibit 7.3 Determination of Taxable Income on a Foreign Branch Using the Profit and Loss Method (in DM)

Sales	1,000,000
Cost of goods sold	600,000
Gross profit	400,000
Other expenses	300,000
Branch profits	100,000

DM100,000	branch profits
20,000	distribution on 6/30
DM80,000	balance on 12/31

DM20,000 × $.36 = $ 7,200
DM80,000 × $.40 = 32,000
Taxable income $39,200

retained in the foreign location. Both types are taxable to the home office. The amount of earnings distributed to the home office is translated at the exchange rate in effect on the date of the transfer. However, computing the dollar value of earnings not distributed is not quite as simple. The IRS allows firms to use one of two methods to determine taxable income: the profit and loss method or the net worth or balance sheet method. Exhibit 7.3 illustrates the profit and loss method. In the example, note that the relevant exchange rates are $0.36 on June 30 when the branch makes a distribution of DM20,000 to the home office and $0.40 on December 31 at the end of the fiscal year of the branch. It is interesting to note that under this method, branch profits are translated at the year-end rate rather than the average exchange rate required under Statement No. 52.

The other method allowed is the net worth or balance sheet method. The basic idea of this approach is to determine the change in net worth during the year. In order to accomplish this, the following steps need to be followed:

1. Net current assets in dollars are determined by subtracting current liabilities from current assets at year end and multiplying the difference by the current exchange rate.

2. Net long-term assets in dollars are determined by subtracting year-end, long-term liabilities translated at their relative historical exchange rates from long-term assets translated at their relative historical exchange rates.

3. The sum of steps 1 and 2 equals net worth in dollars at the end of the year.

4. The increase in the value of the branch during the year is derived by subtracting the value of net worth at the beginning of the year from

the value of net worth at the end of the year. The value of net worth at the beginning of the year can be determined by following steps 1 through 3 if the net worth figure is not available.

5. The amount of taxable income is determined by adding to the amount derived in step 4 any distributions and subtracting any contributions made by the home office.

As can be seen from this description, the translation procedure required under tax law is the current–noncurrent method that has been rendered obsolete for financial reporting purposes for years.

Taxable Earnings from Foreign Corporations

As noted earlier in the chapter, the recognition of earnings of a foreign corporation depends on whether or not the corporation is a controlled foreign corporation.

Noncontrolled Foreign Corporation

When the foreign corporation is not a CFC, income is not recognized by the U.S. parent until a dividend is distributed. In such a case, the tax credit formula, as discussed, is as follows:

$$\frac{\text{Dividends}}{\text{Profits}} \times \text{Foreign taxes paid} = \text{Tax credit}$$

Assume that a British corporation earns £500,000, pays corporate income tax of £250,000, and declares two dividends to the U.S. investor of £10,000 each (on June 30 when the exchange rate was $1.50 and on December 31, when it was $1.45). In this case, the tax credit for each dividend would be computed as follows:

$$\frac{10,000}{250,000} \times 250,000 = £10,000$$

$$
\begin{array}{ll}
£10,000 \times \$1.50 = & \$15,000 \\
£10,000 \times \$1.45 = & \underline{14,500} \\
\text{Tax credit} & \$29,000
\end{array}
$$

As can be seen, the IRS has determined that the appropriate exchange rate to use for translating every element in the tax credit formula is the exchange rate in effect when the dividend is declared. Thus, taxes are not translated at the rate in effect when the taxes are paid, and income is not translated at the average rate for the period as required for Statement No. 52.

Controlled Foreign Corporation

As discussed earlier, a CFC has two types of income: non-Subpart F income and Subpart F income. The non-Subpart F income is not taxed to the parent company until a dividend has been distributed, so the same rules apply as described above for the non-CFC situation. In the case of Subpart F income, the IRS assumes that a constructive dividend has been declared at the end of the year, so it is necessary to translate the financial statements of the firm into dollars. The profit and loss statement is translated in essentially the same manner as is required under the temporal method. To the translated income figure is added or subtracted a translation gain or loss. This item is computed by translating the balance sheet under the temporal method with the exception that long-term debt is translated at the historical rather than current rate.[23]

TAX INCENTIVES

Tax incentives for the purposes of this discussion are of two major types: incentives by countries to attract foreign investors and incentives by countries to encourage exports of goods and services.

Tax incentives to invest usually involve tax holidays of one form or another. A good example involves an advertisement in the *Wall Street Journal* by South Korea to tout its investment climate. Foreign investors that are deemed by the government to greatly contribute to the South Korean economy are permitted a five-year tax holiday, which can be taken during any period within ten years after the investment is registered with the government. In addition, the government will exempt and reduce customs duties on certain capital assets. These moves will substantially improve the cash flow position of any new investment in South Korea.[24]

Another popular form of incentive involves exports. In the EC, many export products are exempted from the value added tax, which allows firms to offer their products at a lower price than they otherwise could.

Foreign Sales Corporation

The Foreign Sales Corporation Act of 1984 was signed into law on July 18, 1984, as a part of the Tax Reform Act of 1984, and that new law was designed to replace the Domestic International Sales Corporation (DISC) legislation that had been in existence in the United States since 1972.

The DISC

The DISC was established in the early 1970s to encourage exports by U.S. firms. The DISC itself was not subject to corporate income tax, but a portion of the income was taxable to its shareholders.

The DISC was a U.S. corporation, usually organized as a wholly owned corporation by a manufacturer, that bought merchandise from its

[23]The interpretation of the tax law is from Rufus von Thulen Rhoades and Marshall J. Langer, *Income Taxation of Foreign Related Transactions* (New York: Matthew Bender, 1984), Chapter 6.
[24]"Conditions for Foreign Investment Eased," *Wall Street Journal*, 29 June 1984, p. 10.

parent company and sold that merchandise outside of the U.S. The IRS provided deferral benefits of 50% of the adjusted taxable income of the DISC that exceeded income attributed to a base period.

The problem with the DISC was that it violated subsidy rules laid down by the General Agreement on Tariffs and Trade (GATT), an organization formed after World War II to facilitate trade worldwide. Since the Reagan administration had been attempting to increase the free flow of trade, it felt that it needed to come up with an alternative to the DISC in order to press for some of its more important trading points. The result of that process was the development of the Foreign Sales Corporation (FSC).

Organization of the FSC

GATT rules insist that countries not use taxes as a form of subsidy. At the same time, they feel that countries should be allowed to tax earnings as they see fit. The GATT allows countries to use the territorial approach discussed above, in which offshore profits from exports do not need to be taxed, as long as transfer pricing rules are not violated. Thus, a qualified Foreign Sales Corporation must satisfy the following requirements:

1. It must be incorporated in and have its main offices in a foreign country or U.S. possession (except Puerto Rico).
2. It must have economic substance rather than just be a paper corporation.
3. The export services that it performs for its parent company or companies must be performed outside of the United States.
4. Up to 25 shareholders may own an FSC, which permits export trading companies to set up FSCs if they so desire.

Tax Benefits of the FSC

If the foreign corporation qualifies as a FSC, a portion of its income is exempt from U.S. corporate income tax. Also, the law provides for a 100% dividends-received deduction for dividends distributed by the FSC out of earnings from foreign trade income.

The difficult part of the bill is the determination of income of the FSC. Because the FSC will usually be owned by the parent company that sells it merchandise, the price set on the merchandise is a transfer price that is subject to artificial manipulation. Thus, the legislation requires that the price be either an actual arm's-length transfer price or a formula price that is designed to fit the GATT's definition of a transfer price.

If the transfer price set on the merchandise is an arm's-length price, then 34% of the income from the transaction is considered exempt from U.S. taxation, similar to the deferral principle discussed in connection with foreign source income. If the transfer price is set according to the special administered pricing rules, then the exempt foreign source income is 17/23 of the income from the transaction.

The major foreign trading gross receipts on which foreign trade income is computed are the sale of export property, the lease or rental of export property, services related and subsidiary to the sale or lease of export property, engineering and architectural services, and export management services. In order for these transactions to count as foreign trading gross receipts, the management of the transactions must take place outside of the United States, and economic processes must take place outside of the United States. The major economic processes that qualify for the conditions are (1) advertising and sales promotion, (2) processing customer orders and arranging for delivery, (3) transportation, (4) determination and transmittal of a final invoice or statement of account and the receipt of payment, and (5) the assumption of credit risk.[25]

In order for a transaction to qualify as a foreign trading gross receipt under the economic processes concept, 50% of the total direct costs of the transaction must take place in a foreign location. Alternatively, the transaction qualifies if 85% of the total costs in any two of the preceding five economic processes categories take place outside of the United States.

Exhibit 7.4 illustrates how the transfer price and therefore taxable income would be computed under two variations of the administrative pricing method and under the Section 482 method.

In this example, which was included in the Senate explanation of the law as included in the Congressional Committee Report, a number of assumptions need to be made. The FSC purchases export property from a related supplier and sells it for $1000. The sale qualifies as foreign trading gross receipts according to the characteristics discussed above. The FSC incurs expenses of $225 that relate to the sale, and the supplier's cost of goods sold totals $550. In selling the export property to the FSC, the supplier incurs a cost of $125. According to Section 482, assume that the correct transfer price in this situation is determined to be $720, allowing the FSC to realize a profit of $55 on the sale.

Under the administrative pricing guidelines, there are two methods that can be used: the combined taxable income method and the gross receipts method. Under the combined taxable income method, the transfer price to the FSC is the sales price less the FSC expense and FSC profit, which is 23% of the combined taxable income of the FSC and the related supplier. Part a in Exhibit 7.4 shows how the combined taxable income is computed. Part b shows how the profit and transfer price are computed.

Under the gross receipts method, FSC taxable income is the lesser of 1.83% of foreign trading gross receipts or twice the FSC taxable income under the combined taxable income method. Part c shows how taxable

[25]*A Complete Guide to the Tax Reform Act of 1984* (Englewood Cliffs, N.J.: Prentice-Hall, 1984), pp. 1791–1805.

Exhibit 7.4 FSC Transfer Price and Profit Computations

(a)	*Combined taxable income:*	
	FSC's foreign trading gross receipts	$1,000.00
	Cost of goods sold of related supplier	(550.00)
	Combined gross income	$450.00
	Less expenses:	
	Direct expenses of related supplier	$125.00
	Direct expenses of FSC	225.00
	Total expenses	$(350.00)
	Combined taxable income	$100.00
(b)	*FSC's taxable income and transfer price under combined taxable income method:*	
	Transfer price to FSC	23.00
	Sales price	1,000.00
	Less:	
	FSC expense	$(225.00)
	FSC profit	(23.00)
	Total	$(248.00)
	Transfer price	$752.00
(c)	*FSC's taxable income and transfer price under gross receipts method:*	
	FSC taxable income—lesser of 1.83% of foreign trading gross receipts ($18.30) or two times amount in (b) above ($46.00)	$18.30
	Transfer price to FSC:	
	Sales price	1,000.00
	Less:	
	FSC expenses	$(225.00)
	FSC profit	(18.30)
	Total	$(243.30)
	Transfer price	$756.70
(d)	*FSC's taxable income under Section 482:*	
	FSC profit:	
	Sales price	$1,000.00
	Less:	
	FSC cost of goods sold	$720.00
	FSC expenses	225.00
	Total	$(945.00)
	FSC profit	$55.00

Source: A Complete Guide to the Tax Reform Act of 1984 (Englewood Cliffs, N.J.: Prentice-Hall, 1984), p. 1798.

income and the transfer price are computed under the gross receipts method. Part d shows what FSC profit would be under the assumption of an arm's-length transfer price of $720.

If Section 482 pricing is used, 34% of the foreign trade income is exempt from U.S. taxes. If the administrative pricing rules are used, the exempt income is 17/23 of the foreign trade income. Exhibit 7.5 illustrates how to compute the taxable income of the FSC not subject to U.S. taxes under the three transfer pricing methods (combined taxable income method, gross receipts method, and Section 482 method). As noted in Exhibit 7.4, the transfer price used to compute the cost of goods sold in each of the three cases is $752, $756.70, and $720. The expenses of the FSC are $225. If all the income of the FSC were taxable in the illustration in Part a of Exhibit 7.5, the FSC would have to declare income of $23 (foreign trade income of $248 − $225). However, 17/23 of the foreign trade income is exempt, as is that proportion of the FSC expenses. Therefore, the income exempt from taxation is $17, and only $6 is taxable. The same computations for the other two transfer pricing methods are given in Exhibit 7.5.

Exhibit 7.5 Computation of Taxable Income of FSC Not Subject to Tax

(a) If the transfer price to the FSC was determined under the combined taxable income method:	
Foreign trading gross receits	$1,000.00
Cost of goods sold	(752.00)
Foreign trade income	$248.00
Exempt foreign trade income (17/23 × $248)	$183.30
Expenses allocable to exempt foreign trade income	
(183.30/248 × $225)	(166.30)
Taxable income of FSC not subject to U.S. tax	
($183.30 − $166.30)	$17.00
(b) If the transfer price to the FSC was determined under the gross receipts method:	
Foreign trading gross receipts	$1,000.00
Less cost of good sold	(756.70)
Foreign trade income	$243.30
Exempt foreign trade income (17/23 × $243.30)	$179.83
Expenses allocable to exempt foreign trade income	
(179.83/243.30 × $225)	(166.30)
Taxable income of FSC not subject to U.S. tax	
($179.83 − $166.30)	$13.53
(c) If the transfer price to the FSC was determined under Section 482:	
Foreign trading gross receipts	$1,000.00
Less cost of goods sold	(720.00)
Foreign trade income	$280.00
Exempt foreign trade income (34% × $280)	$95.20
Expenses allocable to exempt foreign trade income	
(95.20/280 × $225)	(76.50)
Taxable income of FSC not subject to U.S. tax	
($95.20 − $76.50)	$18.70

Source: A Complete Guide to the Tax Reform Act of 1984 (Englewood Cliffs, N.J.: Prentice-Hall, 1984), p. 1798.

Smaller Companies

A number of smaller companies may find it difficult to set up an FSC as detailed in the legislation. As a result, these companies may set up an interest charge DISC or a small FSC. The interest charge DISC is a DISC as set up under the old legislation, but now companies must pay interest at the Treasury Bill rate on accumulated tax deferrals. Also, the DISC benefits are available for no more than $10 million of export sales. There have also been other modifications in that income tax on 94% of DISC income can be deferred, and there are no incremental rules. The deferral principle applies as long as the income is retained by the DISC in qualified export assets.

The small FSC is available for income generated by $5 million or less in gross revenues on exports. The FSC must still be organized offshore, and its books of account must be kept in that offshore office. However, most of its economic activities can be done in the United States.[26]

Transition

The FSC legislation is effective as of January 1, 1985. One nice thing about the legislation is that deferred DISC income from previous DISCs is not taxable now. That effectively shelters literally billions of dollars from taxation.

TAX DIMENSIONS OF EXPATRIATES

It is the right of every country to tax the earnings of its citizens. However, the United States goes further than most industrial countries by taxing the worldwide income if its residents. A survey by Business International revealed that of eight major Western countries, the United States is the only one that taxes its expatriates on worldwide income.[27] This forces U.S. companies abroad to equalize the tax burden by paying their expatriates more or to replace their expatriates with locals.

The Economic Recovery Tax Act of 1981 changed the tax law to provide a series of benefits of U.S. expatriates that are much better in most situations than they had been under the previous law. The major benefits under the new law are the foreign earned income exclusion, the foreign housing-cost exclusion and/or deduction, and the foreign tax credit.

In order to qualify for the provisions of the law, the taxpayer must have been a resident outside of the United States for an uninterrupted period that includes an entire taxable year or during any 12 consecutive months must have been outside of the United States for at least 330 full days.

---

[26]John C. Wagner, "Foreign Sales Corporation Act Replaces DISC Tax Incentive," *Business America*, 6 August 1984, pp. 17–19.
[27]*Wall Street Journal*, 8 February 1979, p. 2.

The foreign earned income exclusion allows the expatriate to exclude from income a certain amount depending on the year involved as shown below:

Year	Exclusion
1982	$75,000
1983	80,000
1984	85,000
1985	90,000
1986+	95,000

For expatriates that are given a housing allowance by their employers, a housing-cost exclusion is allowed for the amount of total expenses in excess of a base amount. In 1983, that base amount was $6604. For expatriates that are not given a housing allowance by their employer, a deduction is permitted for excess housing costs.

The tax credit is permitted on foreign income taxes paid. However, the expatriate is not allowed a credit for income taxes paid on income that is included in the earned income exclusion.

TAX PLANNING IN THE INTERNATIONAL ENVIRONMENT

As can be seen from the different subjects discussed thus far in this chapter, tax dimensions of international operations are very complex. The tax environment is unique in each national setting, which requires a competent local staff that understands the tax situation. In spite of the individual nature of each country, we can use some general concepts as tax planning guides.

Choice of Method of Servicing Foreign Markets

There are a variety of ways in which a firm can choose to service its foreign markets: exports of goods and services and technology, branch operations, and foreign subsidiaries.

Exports

When exporting goods and services, a firm must decide whether to service the products from the United States or a foreign location. If the sales and servicing come from the United States, then the firm needs to take advantage of the DISC provisions if it qualifies for DISC benefits. Otherwise, the firm needs to consider the benefits of operating through a sales office abroad. The Foreign Sales Corporation provides such an opportunity and can provide substantial tax benefits if the operations are legitimate ones that result in active rather than passive income. If the income is active, it makes sense to set up the sales office in a tax haven country where income can be sheltered.

When the firm decides to license technology abroad, it must be aware of the withholding taxes that it might be forced to pay on royalties. Being aware of the withholding taxes and relevant tax treaties is very important.

Branches

Operating abroad through a branch has several distinct benefits. Because branch profits and losses are not subject to deferral, it is often beneficial to open a branch when first operating abroad since the initial years are normally loss years. The home office could use branch losses to offset home office income for tax purposes. Branch remittances are usually not subject to withholding taxes as dividends are from subsidiaries. In one country, Belgium, there is a withholding tax on branch remittances, but a tax treaty between the United States and Belgium eliminates that tax. Natural resource companies like to operate through branches abroad because the branches are allowed to use the depletion allowance and other tax benefits relating to natural resources. These benefits come back directly to the parent company.

One problem with a branch is that its profits are immediately taxed to the home office because the deferral principle does not apply. This is why many firms prefer to operate during their early loss years through branches.

Subsidiaries

The major benefit of operating abroad through a subsidiary is that its income is sheltered from U.S. taxes until a dividend is remitted. That is true for all subsidiary income except passive income of a CFC. This underscores the importance of making sure that the operations of a CFC in a tax haven country are legitimate so that the firm does not have to worry about the Subpart F provisions. The major problem of operating through a subsidiary is that any losses sustained cannot be recognized by the parent company. Thus, the subsidiary form of organization is much more valuable after the start-up years, when the operations become profitable.

Location of Foreign Operations

The location of foreign operations depends on three major factors: tax incentives, tax rates, and tax treaties. The importance of tax incentives was emphasized in the South Korean illustration. The existence of tax incentives can materially reduce the cash outflow required for an investment project, which will increase the net present value of the project. That tax effect could change the timing of an investment decision.

Because the determination of revenues and expenses for tax purposes is a function of tax law in most countries, it is important to be intimately familiar with local tax laws. This is almost impossible for someone in corporate headquarters, so it is necessary to have competent tax and legal help in each local country.

Tax treaties are critical in terms of how they impact on the cash flows related to withholding taxes on dividends, interest, and royalties. Strict attention to tax treaties can help investors to choose wisely the location of their legal operations (which may or may not be the same as the location of their managerial operations). For example, the withholding tax between the United States and the United Kingdom is 15% according to a bilateral treaty, whereas each country has a 5% withholding agreement with The Netherlands. A U.S. company would be better off establishing a holding company in The Netherlands to receive dividends from its British operations, subject to a 5% withholding tax. The Dutch holding company could then remit a dividend to the U.S. parent subject to a 5% withholding tax, which would be better than the 15% tax for dealing between the United States and the United Kingdom directly. This is just one example of how tax treaties can be used to improve cash flows of foreign investors.

SUMMARY

- The territorial approach to taxing income asserts that foreign source income should be taxed where earned and not mixed with domestic source income. The worldwide philosophy treats all income as taxable to the parent. This leads to double taxation, which can be minimized by the tax credit and tax treaties.

- Under the deferral concept, earnings of foreign subsidiaries are not taxed until remitted as a dividend. Under the unitary tax used by some states in the United States, taxable income is a function of a company's worldwide income rather than its income in that state.

- Tax laws in different countries often allow an accelerated recovery of the cost of assets in order to encourage economic growth.

- The classical system of corporate income taxation taxes income when it is received by each taxable entity, which leads to double taxation. The integrated system of taxation tries to eliminate double taxation through a combination of a split-rate system and tax credits.

- Countries often collect a withholding tax on dividends, interest, and royalties paid to foreign investors. These levies can be reduced through tax treaties.

- The value added tax is an indirect tax that is an important source of revenue in many countries, especially in European countries. It is applied at each stage of the production process for the value added by the firm to goods purchased from the outside.

- The IRS allows U.S. firms a credit against their U.S. tax liability for income taxes paid to a foreign government. A firm can choose to treat those taxes, along with all other direct and indirect taxes that they might incur, as a deduction to arrive at taxable income.

- Tax treaties can specify that certain classes of income would not be subject to tax, reduce the rate on income and/or withholding taxes, and specifically deal with the issue of tax credits.

- A tax haven is a country that has no income tax, taxes income at low rates, or exempts from taxation income from foreign sources.

- A controlled foreign corporation (CFC) is any foreign corporation that is majority-owned by U.S. shareholders.

- Income from a non-CFC is not taxed until a dividend is sent to the U.S. investor. Active income from a CFC also qualifies for the deferral privilege and is not taxed until remitted as a dividend.

- Passive income (Subpart F income) is income not derived from the active conduct of a trade or business. It is taxable to the parent when earned and the deferral principle does not apply.

- A transfer price is a price on products sold between businesses that are part of the same corporate organization. Because of different tax laws, exchange controls, and so on, transfer pricing between firms in two different countries can lead to substantial manipulation of income and taxes. Section 482 of the Internal Revenue Code requires that firms set transfer prices at arm's length. Section 861 of the Code requires U.S. firms to allocate some of their expenses to foreign source income.

- For tax purposes, foreign exchange gains and losses on foreign currency transactions are not permitted until the financial obligation has been settled.

- Branch remittances are translated at the rate in effect on the date of the remittance. Remaining branch earnings are translated using the profit and loss method or the balance sheet method.

- Dividends from subsidiaries are translated into dollars at the exchange rate in effect on the date that the dividend is paid. The different elements in the tax credit are also translated at that same exchange rate.

- The Foreign Sales Corporation provides tax advantages to exporters, but it requires the exporters to set up a sales office abroad.

- Some countries provide tax holidays, such as the forgiveness of income taxes for a period, to attract foreign investors.

- U.S. expatriates are allowed a foreign earned income exclusion, a foreign housing-cost exclusion and/or deduction, and a foreign tax credit in determining their U.S. tax liability.

- International tax planning requires that a firm take into consideration taxes for the determination of the type of operation to be used in servicing international markets (exporting, licensing, branches, or subsidiaries) and the location of the operation (by considering tax incentives, tax rates, and tax treaties).

Study Questions

7-1. A company has subsidiaries in host countries A and B. Country A has a statutory corporate tax rate of 48%, whereas Country B's is 52%. What are some specific reasons that country B's effective tax rate might actually be more favorable to the firm?

7-2. Assume a VAT of 10%. What would be the selling price and taxes at each stage if the following were the values added?

Seller	Value Added by Seller
Extractor	$300
Processor	500
Wholesaler	75
Retailer	75

What would be the difference in the effect of the VAT on a U.S. wholesaling subsidiary in the VAT country if (1) it exported the good to the U.S. market or (2) it sold the good to local retailers?

7-3. Export Inc. organized an FSC in 1985 to sell many of its products. During the year, the FSC sold $800,000 of merchandise it bought from Export Inc. for $440,000. The FSC incurred expenses of $180,000 to generate the sales, and Export Inc. incurred expenses of $100,000 to make the sale to the FSC. The transfer price on the sales to the FSC as determined by Section 482 was $576,000. What was the amount of the transfer price, FSC profit, and taxable income of FSC not subject to U.S. tax under the Section 482 method, the combined taxable income method, and the gross receipts method of transfer price determination?

7-4. Which of the following are CFCs and which are not? Why?

Shareholders	Percentage of the Voting Stock		
	Foreign Corporation 1	Foreign Corporation 2	Foreign Corporation 3
U.S. shareholder A	10%	20%	5%
Foreign shareholder B	30	20	20
U.S. shareholder C	10	20	5
U.S. shareholder D	5	10	5
Foreign shareholder E	15	20	15
U.S. shareholder F	30	10	50
	100%	100%	100%

Why is this distinction important?

7-5. ABC Company has income from the following countries:

Country	Type of Operation	EBFT	Income Tax Rate
United States	Parent	$200,000	46%
X	Branch	(4,000)	42
Y	CFC	60,000	5
Z	100% owned	200,000	60

The subsidiary in Z declares a 50% dividend; Z's withholding tax on dividends is 10%. Both the branch and the CFC retain all earnings. The CFC earnings are considered to be foreign base company sales income. What is ABC Company's overall U.S. limitation and what is the tax liability in each country? If the foreign taxes paid exceed the overall limitation, how would the excess be treated?

7-6. Multicorp has a production division in Singapore that produces components used by another division in Cleveland, which sells a final product to the outside. In 1984, the Singapore division's total sales to the Cleveland division were $850,000 with production costs totaling $500,000 and other expenses totaling $150,000. The Cleveland division sold its final product for $1,500,000 with production costs in excess of its purchases from the Singapore division of $200,000 and other expenses of $250,000. Assume that Multicorp's only two divisions are the Singapore and Cleveland divisions.

a. If the tax rates in both countries were 48%, what would be the amount of tax paid and net income after taxes of each division and the company as a whole?

b. What would be the answer to Part a if the tax rate in Singapore was 20% instead of 48%?

c. As the IRS began to look at the transfer pricing policies of Multicorp, it decided that the internal sales should have been priced at $700,000. What would be the amount of taxes and net income for each subsidiary and the company as a whole with Singapore taxes at 48%? At 20%?

d. Given the data in Part c, what do you think the IRS would do and why?

e. What do you think the response of the tax authorities in Singapore would be to the actions of the IRS?

f. How do you think Multicorp could justify its transfer price?

7-7. Intercorp's new cost accountant, Ms. I. Allocate, decided to make a thorough review of corporate common expenses to see if any of them could be charged to foreign source income. In her investigations, she noticed that U.S. source income for 1984 was $5,000,000 and foreign source income was $4,000,000. Included in U.S. source income were corporate expenses incurred in the U.S. of $1,000,000, which she felt could be allocated between U.S. and foreign source income at a rate of 60%/40%. However, the tax rate on the foreign source income was only 20%, compared with the U.S. rate of 48%.

a. What would be the impact on taxes, net income, and the tax credit of keeping expenses the way they are? of allocating common expenses?

b. What do you think the IRS would do and why?

7-8. On July 1, Multicorp, a U.S. firm, sells DM500,000 worth of merchandise on account to an importer in Germany with payment due on September 30. During that time, the exchange rates were:

July 1	$0.3600
July 31	$0.3800
August 31	$0.3400
September 30	$0.4000

Assume that the tax year ends on August 31.

a. How would gains and losses be recognized on the receivable according to FASB Statement No. 52?

b. How would the gains and losses be recognized for U.S. tax purposes?

7-9. Ace Manufacturing has a branch in Britain that sells products manufactured at Ace's plant in Boalsburg, Pennsylvania. In 1984, Ace UK's balance sheet and income statement were as follows:

Balance Sheet
(in pounds)

Cash and receivables	100,000
Inventory	100,000
Fixed assets	300,000
Total assets	500,000
Current liabilities	150,000
Long-term debt	200,000
Net worth	150,000
Total liabilities and net worth	500,000

Profit and Loss

Sales	500,000
Cost of sales	250,000
Gross profit	250,000
Expenses	100,000
Net income	150,000

On June 30, Ace UK sent a remittance to the parent company of £70,000 when the exchange rate was $1.40. The exchange rate at the end of the year was $1.50, the average rate during the year was $1.45, and the rate in effect when fixed assets were acquired and long-term debt incurred was $1.60. The inventory at the end of the year was accumulated at the average rate for the year, as were cost of sales. Net worth at the beginning of the year was $10,000.

      a. What would be the dollar profit or loss of Ace UK for U.S. tax purposes under the profit and loss method?

      b. What would be the dollar profit or loss of Ace UK for U.S. tax purposes under the net worth method?

7-10. Two separate court cases in the 1960s that dealt with Section 482 of the Internal Revenue Code involved Eli Lilly and PPG Industries. The courts ruled in favor of PPG Industries and against Eli Lilly. Refer to the cases to determine the basis for these decisions.

7-11. Assume that the Netherlands Antilles is used by a U.S. company to shelter its foreign source income from U.S. taxes. Using a review of the literature outside of the text, answer the following questions.

      a. Why is the Netherlands Antilles such a good tax haven country?

      b. What problems does the Netherlands Antilles face as a tax haven country? What impact could the repeal in the U.S. of the 30% withholding tax on interest from securities have on the use of the Netherlands Antilles as a tax haven country?

7-12. How does the existence of classic and integrated corporate tax systems affect the financing decisions of multinational corporations?

Case

COMPAGNIE FISCHBEIN, S.A.*

David Fischbein, who migrated from Russia at the turn of the century, operated a partnership with his son during the 1930s and early 1940s specializing in repairing industrial sewing machines and selling rebuilt industrial sewing machines. David and his son Harold were fairly successful, but David was not content to repair and sell someone else's products for the rest of his life. In the early 1940s David decided to try his hand at inventing, and he came up with an idea for making a small bag-closing machine. After four years of design changes and modifications, the Fischbein machine was ready for the market, which enthusiastically received it. The machine was the first as well as the only one of its kind.

    Business was so good that David decided to set up two separate companies: David Fischbein Manufacturing Company (DFMC) and the David Fischbein Company (DFC). The DFMC handled the manufacturing of the machine, which was sold exclusively to DFC, the sole shareholder of DFMC. DFC was a closely held family corporation involving David's immediate family.

    In the early 1950s DFC decided to expand sales into Latin America through David Fischbein Western Sales Corporation (DFWSC) a wholly owned subsidiary of DFC. DFWSC did not manufacture any of its own bag-closing machines but purchased them from DFMC and sold them abroad. In spite of DFWSC's early success, it was obvious that the market in Europe had considerably greater potential than that of Latin America. Therefore, in 1956 DFC organized a wholly owned subsidiary in Belgium by the name of Compagnie Fischbein, S.A. (CFSA). CFSA became the international selling arm of DFC.

    At the time CFSA was organized, DFC had to decide whether to manufacture the machines in the United States and ship them to CFSA or allow CFSA to assem-

---

*The background for this case and the quotes contained in the case are found in *United States Tax Court Reports*, Vol. 59, 1973, pp. 338–361.

ble as well as sell the products. DFC soon found the following advantages to assembly in Belgium: (1) local assembly qualified the machines for a Belgian certificate of origin, which gave CFSA access to the European Economic Community countries without tariff and quota restrictions; (2) it was cheaper to assemble products in Belgium because of lower labor and overhead expenses; (3) many components could be purchased more cheaply from suppliers in Belgium than from DFMC; and (4) it was easier to comply with European standards (such as the types of plugs and voltage of motors) by producing in Europe.

CFSA assembled the bag-closing machines from parts supplied largely by DFMC, although some of the 283 parts were purchased locally, as mentioned above. The assembly took six hours and involved 58 different steps, ranging from tailoring some of the more sophisticated parts to assembly and final testing. The mechanics were highly trained and most had worked for CFSA for many years. In spite of this, CFSA's operations accounted for less than 20% of the cost of the machines sold.

CFSA's selling efforts were fairly minimal. It maintained no sales force as such, preferring to operate through exclusive distributors around the world. Only 5% of its sales came in other ways. CFSA provided support for its distributorships via trade fairs and advertising, but it was not heavily involved in direct sales to consumers. In 1966, CFSA's total sales of $737,853 came from 47 different countries. Sales in Belgium were less than 10% of the total. Europe was the largest market, with over 80% of the total sales. The top four countries in sales were Germany, France, England, and Spain.

Prior to the Revenue Act of 1962, DFC would not have had to declare CFSA's income in DFC's U.S. taxable income until a dividend was declared. The Revenue Act of 1962, however, changed that by requiring certain "U.S. shareholders" to report their portion of income earned by controlled foreign corporations if that income were considered Subpart F income. In looking at CFSA's operations, the Internal Revenue Service decided that DFC owed back taxes on CFSA's foreign source income for 1964–1967. The IRS maintained that "the components purchased by CFSA were so perfect that they only had to be simply put together in short periods of time by not too highly skilled mechanics, whose tasks in this operation were nothing more than ministerial functions." It contended that CFSA's income was foreign base company sales income because it qualified under the following two tests: "(1) the property which is purchased [from a related person] is manufactured . . . outside the country under the laws of which the controlled foreign corporation is created or organized, and (2) the property is sold for use, consumption, or disposition outside such foreign country."

CFSA maintained that its income was not foreign base company sales income because it manufactured the end product, thereby qualifying for a major assembly operation. The Code specifies that packaging, repackaging, labeling, or minor assembly would not be enough to exclude a firm from foreign base company sales income provisions. However, operations are substantial if the product sold by the controlled foreign corporation is, in effect, not the product purchased from the related party.

Questions

1. Explain whether or not CFSA qualifies as a controlled foreign corporation and DFC qualifies as a "U.S. shareholder."

2. Why did the IRS think that CFSA was earning Subpart F income? Why did the rules for Subpart F income come into being?
3. According to the information given in the case and the chapter, do you think that CFSA's income was foreign base company sales income? Substantiate your answer.

Bibliography

Arpan, Jeffrey S. *International Intracorporate Pricing: Non-American Systems and Views* (New York: Praeger, 1972).

Burns, Jane O. "DISC Accounting: An Empirical Investigation." *International Tax Journal*, Vol. 4, April 1978, pp. 882–891.

Burns, Jane O. "How IRS Applies the Intercompany Pricing Rules of Section 482: A Corporate Survey." *Journal of Taxation*, Vol. 52, May 1980, pp. 308–314.

Commerce Clearing House, Inc. *Standard Federal Tax Reporter.* (Chicago: Commerce Clearing House, Inc., current year). Various volumes that relate to specific sections of the Code that deal with international taxation.

Coopers & Lybrand International Tax Network, Alexander Berger, Ed. *International Tax Summaries 1983.* (New York: John Wiley & Sons, 1983).

Dilley, Steven. "Allocation and Apportionment Under Reg. 1.861.8." *CPA Journal*, Vol. 50, December 1980, pp. 33–38.

Falk, C. E. and A. R. Soberman. "Section 482 After Keller and Foglesong." *CPA Journal*, September 1982, pp. 30–38.

Green, William H. "Analysis of the New ITT Case." *International Tax Journal*, Vol. 7, August 1981, pp. 466–473.

Heinz, Peter Danser. "Mathematical Strategies for the Foreign Tax Credit Limitation." *International Tax Journal*, Vol. 7, August 1981, pp. 454–460.

Moore, Michael L. *U.S. Tax Aspects of Doing Business Abroad,* 2nd ed. (New York: American Institute of Certified Public Accountants, 1983).

Rhoades, Rufus von Thulen and Marshall J. Langer. *Income Taxation of Foreign Related Transactions* (New York: Matthew Bender, 1984).

Sale, J. Timothy and Karen B. Carroll. "Tax Planning Tools for the Multinational Corporation." *Management Accounting*, Vol. 60, June 1979, pp. 37–41.

Tillinghast, David R. *Tax Aspects of International Transactions* (New York: Matthew Bender, 1978).

Yunker, Penelope J. *Transfer Pricing and Performance Evaluation in Multinational Corporations: A Survey Study* (New York: Praeger, 1982).

CHAPTER 8

Management Accounting Issues and Practices

The complexity and risks of international business operations provide many opportunities for things to go wrong or to vary from what was expected. Unexpected changes in currency values, in government policies, and in business conditions can all materially affect the success of any international operation. Multinational enterprises (MNEs) therefore have to plan and monitor operations with particular care.

In order to minimize surprises, and especially unfavorable results, a firm doing business internationally must first thoroughly investigate the decision to be made before making it. This process is more difficult than the similar process for a domestic operation because the variables, alternatives, and unknowns are more numerous. In addition, the available information on which to make decisions is not as complete or as reliable as that for domestic decisions. Examples of such types of decisions include deciding where the best markets in which to sell are, where the best location to produce the product is, and estimating the costs and ultimate prices of the products and the expected profitability of operations.

In addition, the dynamics of international business make control more difficult and more critical than for purely domestic operations. Operating at great geographic distances in many diverse environments and with people of different nationalities impedes the ability of an MNE to exercise control over its operations and its employees. These difficulties, when combined with frequent turbulences in the international environment, make control especially important for MNEs.

In order to make better decisions and be able to exercise appropriate control, it is necessary for a firm to carefully design its organizational structure and to change it when necessary. These changes become especially important as a firm expands its international operations to include new products and countries in an attempt to better exploit new opportunities. Organizational changes are also required to respond and adapt to new threats and/or to correct adverse performance. With these changes in organizational structure come related changes in the firm's information and reporting systems—both internal and external. If suitable changes are not implemented, the appropriate information may not be collected and disseminated to the proper people on a timely basis, if at all. This can result in poor decision making, poor performance, and even legal problems.

Finally, it is essential for an MNE to design a suitable management information system (MIS). An MIS provides the firm with the critical information it needs to make proper decisions, and becomes, in essence, the central nervous system of the firm.

Thus, for international operations to be successful, and particularly those of MNEs, greater attention must be devoted to planning, control, organization, costing/pricing, and information systems. Each area must be carefully considered and designed and also be compatible with and supportive of the other areas. And although many people in different functional areas are involved in these considerations, a key role is played by the firm's accounting staff.

PLANNING

Some people believe in the old refrain *que sera, sera*—whatever will be, will be. That is, future events are beyond any mortal's knowledge or control, and, therefore, there is no point in planning for the future. After all, planning is based on the assumption that by taking certain actions, the future can be determined and influenced, at least partially. In effect, planning is the direct application of the scientific method to business operations and is in direct conflict with a fatalistic (*que sera, sera*) mentality.

So what does all of this have to do with MNEs and their international operations? Often a great deal. As pointed out in Chapter 2, different cultures are more fatalistic than others, as are certain people in any particular culture. Because MNEs operate with employees from many cultures, there is an increased likelihood that they will encounter and employ people with fatalistic beliefs. If so, these people will not be as interested or willing to participate in the planning process, thereby reducing its effectiveness. This phenomenon can be a major problem in implementing an adequate planning system. However, it is by no means the only planning-related problem for MNEs.

Investment Decisions

Even without problems related to fatalism, planning for an MNE encounters many difficulties. The main reason for this is the vast array of factors that must be included in the plan and the greater difficulties in predicting changes that are likely to occur in the complex, dynamic international setting. Consider, for example, the decisions and planning related to building a new production facility.[1] Unlike a purely domestic firm, an MNE can

[1]For a good summary of the factors entering into a plant location decision, see Robert Stobaugh, "Where in the World Should We Put that Plant," *Harvard Business Review*, January–February 1969, pp. 129–136.

locate a plant in one of more than 150 different countries. Like a domestic firm, the MNE must evaluate the cost and availability of land, materials, energy, and labor, as well as the suitability of the available infrastructure. However, each factor varies considerably from one country to another, making comparative analysis much more difficult for an MNE. There are also different governments and governmental policies to consider and assess for an MNE. Some governments may offer investment or other financial incentives to the MNE, whereas others may present substantial constraints. Some governments are also more stable than others, and the same is true for economic conditions in general.

So how does an MNE decide where to build a plant? Very carefully, to be sure, and never without considerable anxiety and sleepless nights. It generally begins with an application of existing economic/financial decision-making models, such as payback, present value, or internal rate of return. In whatever model it selects, the MNE attempts to estimate the costs and revenues of potential sites in order to ascertain some comparative estimate of expected profitability. In this process, the firm's accountants play an important role by preparing and analyzing in a systematic manner the information obtained and putting the information into pro forma income statements, balance sheets, and so on. The greater number of variables to be considered by an MNE, however, requires greater worker-hours and greater sophistication than for a purely domestic firm. Most important, perhaps, is the need for greater sensitivity analysis. Because the required information is often less available, less reliable, and almost always less comparable, resulting estimates are less certain. Therefore, greater allowances must be made for errors in estimation, and a greater number of possible scenarios must be forecasted and analyzed.

To cite but one example of how wrong estimates can be, consider the case of Cummins Engine Company's venture into India in the 1950s.[2] It appeared that the economic development plans of the Indian government would result in a large demand for diesel engines, Cummins's main product. Labor costs in India were often one fifteenth to one hundredth of those for comparable jobs in Cummins's production facilities in the United States. With these and hundreds of other factors in mind, Cummins decided to build the plant in India, only to find out subsequently that the errors in their estimates were enormous. The market did not grow as rapidly as expected, decreasing significantly the company's revenue projections. The Indian engine ended up costing three times as much as one produced in the United States because, among other things, Indian labor productivity was so much lower than estimated. Many components expected to be available locally were not available at all or were not available at prices or quality comparable to those in the United States. Greater production prob-

---

[2]For more information about the Cummins Engine Venture in India, see Charles Kindleberger, *American Business Abroad—Six Lectures on Direct Investment* (New Haven, Conn.: Yale University Press, 1969), p. 22.

lems arose than were estimated, and so on. After more than two decades of operation, the venture was still not profitable.

Still another planning complication for MNEs evolves from the interrelationships of its operations in different countries. One distinct competitive advantage of an MNE can be its ability to produce products and each product's components in countries with the lowest cost and sell the final products in the most profitable countries—a process called international production rationalization. To accomplish this successfully, however, requires a number of intercountry shipments. For example, components made in countries A, B, and C are assembled in country D and shipped to countries E, F, and G for final sale. Such intercountry shipments require estimates of production costs, freight, insurance, import tariffs, export taxes or export tax credits, exchange rates, and possible changes in any of these. Also to be considered in such transactions are exchange controls, quotas, and a host of other international trade-related restrictions. Thus, international trade factors must also be taken into account in the planning process, also with proper sensitivity analysis.

Finally, the planning process encompasses far more than the preinvestment stage. Planning for subsequent operation of the investment must also be done: yearly plans, five-year plans, and even longer-term plans must also be continually prepared and adjusted as necessary. Such operating plans rely heavily on accountants and, for MNEs, on accountants sensitized to and trained for international complexities. This is particularly true in the financial budgeting area.

Budgeting

Ethereal projections are important but not sufficient for planning purposes. Proper planning and decision making requires appropriate numbers to be generated and suitably organized and analyzed. This transformation into numbers is largely the responsibility of accountants, particularly in terms of preparing budgets. The budgets perform multiple functions. They formulate the plans into specific measurable units of value; they communicate priorities of the firm by specific resource allocations; they constrain activities of individual units and managements; and they provide one measure against which subsequent performance can be judged.

Because budgeting is an integral part of the planning process, it suffers from most, if not all, of the problems of planning discussed above. But from an MNE-wide budgeting standpoint, the budget must be made in a single currency (e.g., dollars if it is a U.S.-based MNE, francs if it is a French-based MNE) and also be made in the local countries' currencies. This phenomenon once again brings currency exchange rates into the picture. For example, if the French subsidiary of a U.S. firm needs 8 million francs in the coming year, the dollar value of 8 million frances depends on the dollar franc exchange rate. If $1 = 8 francs, this is $1 million; if $1 = 10 francs, this is only $800,000; if $1 = 6 francs, this is $1.33 million. So if, when the budget is prepared the exchange rate is expected to be $1 = 8 francs, $1 million is budgeted (allocated) by the U.S. parent, and the French operation ultimately will receive the 8 million francs it needs and was expecting, *as long as the actual rate is $1 = 8 francs.* But if the rate becomes $1 = 6 francs when the money is transferred, the French subsidiary receives only 6 million francs, 2 million francs less than it needed. At the same time, however, the estimated dividends from the French subsidiary in dollars (based on an exchange rate of $1 = 8 francs) could rise if the exchange rate goes to $1 = 6 francs. Therefore, such exchange rate fluctuations and their impact on budgets must be taken into account in the budgeting process. And, if the plan for the French subsidiary dictates borrowing in dollars, purchasing some components in pesos, and others in yen, and selling in Germany (where it receives deutsche marks), possible fluctuations in each of these currencies vis à vis the franc must also be incorporated into the budgeting process for the French subsidiary, and ultimately for the MNE as a whole.

If all of this sounds complicated and tedious, it proves to be even more so in reality. In fact, currency fluctuations are only one type of budgeting problem for an MNE. Each budget must also consider possible changes in inflation rates, productivity levels, international currency conversion problems (you may not be able to get money in or out of a country), changes in borrowing and lending rates and capital availability, just to mention a few. Small wonder that accountants in the budgeting area of an MNE often lose their hair at an early age!

Yet the importance of proper planning and budgeting for an MNE should be clear by now. Without it, bad decisions can and probably will be made.

OTHER CONTROL DEVICES

The planning and budgeting processes described above constitute an important and integral part of a firm's control system. However, they do not constitute the entire control system. This firm's organizational structure, methods of decision making, employee training and development, and its method(s) of performance evaluation are other key components. Although accountants play fairly minor roles in all but the last area, some understanding of the other areas is nonetheless important for accountants. Therefore, we first turn to a brief discussion of these other areas before getting to a more detailed look at performance evaluation.

Organizational Structure

As a domestic firm evolves into a multinational firm, numerous pressures internal and external to the firm put strains on the firm's existing organizational structure.[3] Some responsibilities are shifted, new ones are created, and occasionally some existing ones are eliminated. As responsibilities change, so do the reporting and communication flows. Furthermore, the degree of control, both exercised and exercisable, change over time as the firm grows in size, geographic spread, and product lines, and as changes occur in countries' sociopolitical–economic environments. New opportunities arise, as do new threats. Thus, a firm's organization is constantly evolving. Failure to properly adjust the organizational structure to the changing environments may result in internal conflict and poor performance—strains that themselves cause pressure for organizational change.

Initial Structure

Consider the typical evolution of a multinational firm from its beginning as a purely domestic firm. The first evolutionary stage concerns export activities, as occasional, unsolicited orders come in from foreign buyers. The effect on product pricing must be analyzed in terms of international shipping and insurance rates, customs duties, and all the related paperwork. In addition, if the foreign purchasers desire to pay in their local currencies, the impact of possible changes in exchange rates must be considered. Typically, no one in the purely domestic company has much, if any, knowledge about these matters. If the firm tries to handle the request on its own, it may receive less profit and more headaches than it expected, or it may decide it is not worth the extra work and forgo the export opportunity. One alternative is the services of outside international business experts—customs brokerage firms, export management companies, or international departments of banks.

As exports grow in volume, the use of external experts can become increasingly expensive, and the firm may, and typically does, decide to internalize the export activities by hiring some new personnel for what becomes an export department, thereby also gaining greater control over its export activities. This export group at first is typically a subgroup of the firm's marketing division, with only advisory or clerical capacity but no authority to commit resources (see Figure 8.1). As foreign market opportunities and sales increase, this export group grows commensurately in size and sophistication. Foreign sales representatives may be added, leading ultimately to the establishment of foreign sales offices to better identify new customers and better serve all customers. By this stage, several internal strains have occurred. The first concerns responsibility for exports. Does the export group only advise domestic divisions, or is it empowered to make commitments (see Figures 8.2 and 8.3). In the advisory situations, the export group feels constrained and seeks greater authority. In the

[3]For a classic discussion of such pressures, see Howard Perlmutter, "The Tortuous Evolution of the Multinational Corporation," *Columbia Journal of World Business*, January–February 1969, pp. 2–18

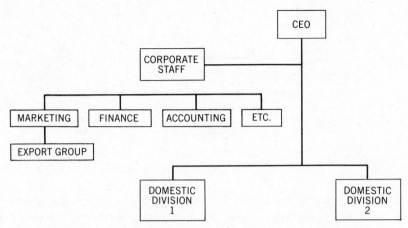

FIGURE 8.1 Domestic organization with initial export group.

commitment situation, domestic divisions feel a loss of power. In addition, there are strains related to internal pricing and profit allocations. The export group wants low transfer prices from the domestic division so it can obtain larger profits on its export sales, whereas the domestic divisions seek higher transfer prices on goods they sell to the export group so they can capture more of the profit. Furthermore, the export group may need to rely on the product and technical expertise of the larger domestic divisions, which if obtained, puts strain on the domestic staff and also leads them to request greater compensation.

International Division Structure

At a later stage, it often becomes advisable to establish foreign production facilities. For example, it may become cheaper to produce abroad, or foreign governments may restrict imports or raise tariffs. Once foreign production is established, be it by a licensing agreement, a joint venture, or a wholly owned subsidiary, some existing organizational pressures abate

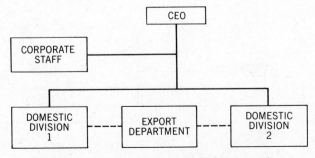

FIGURE 8.2. Export department: advisory capacity.

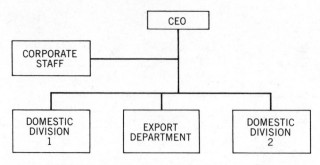

FIGURE 8.3. Export department: line authority.

while others arise. What abates are many of the previous disputes over production allocation, scheduling, product adaptations, and transfer pricing because previous export markets are now served by foreign rather than domestic production. What arises are new problems of responsibility and control. Someone or some group must take responsibility for the growing foreign operations, and control becomes more difficult as a result of changes occurring in at least two operating environments (domestic and foreign). Typically, because of the growing diversity of international operations, an international division replaces the old export division (see Figure 8.4). And because foreign activities are still a rather insignificant percentage of total corporate sales, substantial autonomy is given the new division. As foreign operations expand further, however, the international division itself must exercise tighter control over its numerous operations and activities. To do so, it adds staff and often internally reorganizes into product or geographic areas (see Figure 8.5). It also begins to fight harder for more corporate resources, which puts it into conflict with domestic divisions that also want greater resources. In essence, the firm can become split into two rival factions, and suboptimization can result.

Global Structure

To minimize conflicts and potential suboptimization, a major reorganization typically occurs, with the firm adopting a global product structure or a

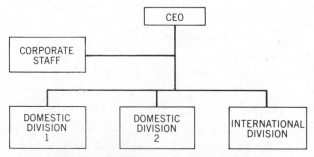

FIGURE 8.4. Simple international division.

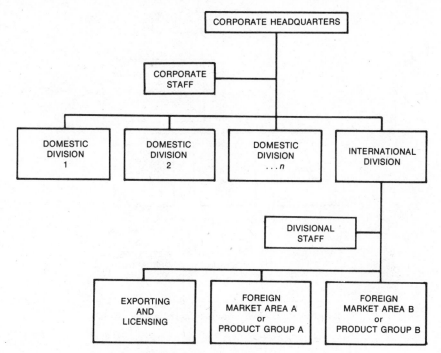

FIGURE 8.5. Complex international division organization.

global geographic structure (see Figures 8.6 and 8.7). In the former, previous distinctions between domestic and international divisions are eliminated, and product division managers are given responsibility and control over worldwide production and sale of their products. In the global geographic structure, existing domestic and international operations become part of one of several geographic divisions.

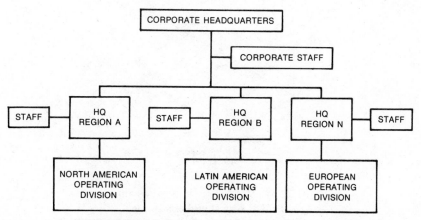

FIGURE 8.6. Global geographically oriented organization.

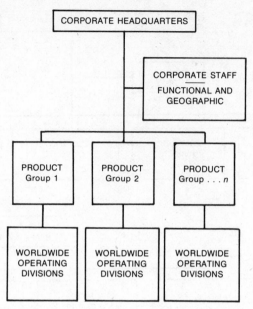

FIGURE 8.7. Global product-oriented organization.

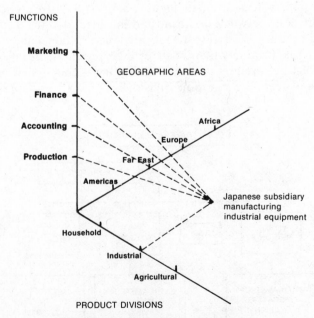

FIGURE 8.8. Global grid organization.

Firms typically select one of these structures based on a number of criteria related to their products and markets. For example, companies with narrow, relatively simple and stable product lines often choose the global geographic structure, and particularly when their products require many local adaptations or expert knowledge of local consumption practices, government policies, and so on. In short, a geographic structure works best when country or regional expertise is more important than product knowledge and expertise. Conversely, when the product line is wide, or when the products are complex and subject to rapid technological change, (i.e., product knowledge and expertise is more important) the global product structure is often chosen. Global product structures are also more likely to emerge when there is a greater need for production and logistical coordination, as in vertically integrated firms or firms pursuing international production rationalization.

Yet as was the case with preceding organizational changes, some old problems and pressures abate while others arise. In the global product structure, old battles between domestic and foreign divisions are reduced, but battles between product divisions are accentuated. In the geographic structure, new battles emerge between geographic divisions.

To better coordinate and control global operations, still another organizational structure may emerge—a global grid/matrix structure (see Figure 8.8). In this three-dimensional structure, product divisions, geographic areas, and functional areas share power and responsibilities.[4] For example, a proposed expansion of sales of industrial equipment in the Far East would involve the MNE's industrial equipment group, its Far East regional group, and the headquarter's finance and marketing groups. In this manner, better coordination of global activities can be obtained by taking a more wholistic perspective, and suboptimization possibilities are decreased. Note, however, that internal conflicts remain even in this grid structure, particularly concerning who has the ultimate authority and responsibility when disagreements occur, as well as conflicts over individual loyalties. Accounting and accountability problems are also more significant. It is to one of these problems of accounting accountability we now turn—specifically that of performance valuation.

Performance Evaluation

Properly measuring the performance of an individual, a division, or even a company as a whole is never simple or easy. One main reason for this is that different bases of measurement result in different measures of

---

[4]For an example of the use of a grid structure, see William C. Goggin, "How the Multidimensional Structure Works at Dow Corning," *Harvard Business Review*, January–February 1974, pp. 54–55.

performance; that is, how you choose to keep score affects the final score.[5] In addition, many events affecting performance are not controllable by the individual or unit being evaluated. Both problems are exacerbated when attempting to evaluate an MNE and any of its parts.

First, let us consider the basis of measurement. As can be seen in Table 8.1, there are many possible criteria against which to judge performance. Furthermore no single basis is equally appropriate for all units of an MNE. For example, a production unit is more appropriately evaluated on cost reduction, quality control, meeting shipment targets (dates and quantities) and other measures of efficiency. For a sales subsidiary, however, these measures are less appropriate (if appropriate at all) than such measures as market share, number of new customers, or other measures of effectiveness. Similarly, profitability may be appropriate for a subsidiary that is a true profit center but inappropriate for a subsidiary in a high-tax-rate country that, for global tax minimization purposes, is instructed to minimize profits or even maximize losses. These situations suggest the desirability and advisability of using multiple bases for performance measurement— different ones for different kinds of operations in different countries. Yet even multiple measures have their problems. First, is it more difficult to compare the performance of different units measured under different criteria. Second, it is more expensive to set up and operate a multiple-criteria system. Thus, the decision must be based on a cost-benefit analysis.

Problems Related to Foreign Currencies

One measurement problem unique to MNEs is the choice of currency in which to evaluate performance. For a French MNE, for example, is it better to evaluate all of its foreign operations in terms of the local currency results or the results translated into francs? This choice can be highly significant if major changes occur in the exchange rates. As was explained in Chapter 5, it is possible for a profit in local currency to become a loss in the parent company's currency, and vice versa. If a French firm's Chilean subsidiary earned a profit in pesos but a loss when translated in francs, should the subsidiary's performance be evaluated favorably or negatively? Most firms resolve this dilemma by considering the main purpose of the foreign operations. If it is to provide a return to parent company shareholders that maximizes their domestic purchasing power, then typically an "after-translation" basis is used. A "before-translation" basis is more likely to be used by a firm that truly considers itself a multinational firm seeking global optimization, or one that leaves considerable automony to each foreign operation.

The foreign currency issue also raises the issue of controllability. Whether a currency rises or falls in value is clearly beyond the control of a

[5]See, for example, S. M. Robbins and Robert Stobaugh, "The Bent Measuring Stick for Foreign Subsidiaries," *Harvard Business Review*, September–October 1973.

single MNE or any one of its parts. Therefore, because proper performance evaluation should exclude the impact on results of events over which the unit or person had no control, one can argue that the before-translation basis is better than the after-translation basis. In the case of the French–Chilean situation, if the peso profits become translated into franc losses, the Chilean manager should not be penalized for a result out of his or her control. On the other hand, if the Chilean manager is given the authority and responsibility to hedge against potential foreign exchange losses, then he or she could be evaluated in terms of translated profitability.

Other Problems

Foreign currency fluctuations are but one of a host of events outside the control of foreign subsidiaries. Wars, insurrections, natural disasters, changes in government policies (e.g., price controls, higher minimum wages, changes in tariffs, or export duties or subsidies) can all affect the performance of a subsidiary, no matter which currency is used. Of course, some of these events can also effect a domestic firm, and hence their impact should also be excluded, but for an MNE the frequency and variety of such events is much greater.

Making matters even more complicated are the interdependencies of an MNE's operations. For example, a multinational automobile company may produce its steel in Japan, have it stamped in the United States, have its tires made in Canada, its axles in Mexico, its transmissions in France, its engines in Germany, and its radios in Taiwan, all for final assembly in the United States. If any one part of its far-flung operations experiences performance problems, that operation's problems will spread to the other operations. Thus, a dock strike in Germany could affect the performance of the German affiliate and the U.S. assembly plant and all sales affiliates worldwide. Proper performance evaluation would need to eliminate these uncontrollable impacts for the interdependent affiliates as well as for the German subsidiary. Furthermore, if other than arm's-length transfer prices were used on any of the intercorporate sales, the reported results were not within the control of either the selling or buying affiliate (unless they both agreed to the transfer price), and in any case, do not reflect real performance.

Separating Managerial and Subsidiary Performance

It is also difficult but important to separate managerial performance from subsidiary performance. It is possible to have good management performance despite poor subsidiary performance, and vice-versa, again largely due to noncontrollables. In other words, a manager may have done a superb job in the face of real adversities largely beyond his or her control, and although the subsidiary's performance did not measure up to expectations, it would have fared even worse without the manager's herculean

Table 8.1 Evaluating Foreign Subsidiary Performance

Profitability Evaluation

1. Determine what shall constitute the investment figure; for example, total funds invested, net assets, or net fixed assets.
2. Determine the basis for computing profit. This may be actual dollar remittances or total book profits.
3. Adjust for distortions due to the position of a sub in an international profit plan; tax factors may have pegged profits through artificial pricing, royalty, management, and interest arrangements.
4. Apply the standard financial ratios used in domestic evaluation: rate of return on investment, liquidity, sales and inventory turnover, return on sales, and sales margin analysis.
5. Check the disposition of funds available for acquisition and investment where the local manager is independent.
6. Watch the distribution of assets, especially in an inflationary economy. Has the local manager hedged properly?
7. Analyze performance against budgeted goals and determine why variances, if any, occurred.
8. Temper these considerations with the outlook for actual long-term dollar profits; be sure that immediate profitability does not hamper future performance.

Market Penetration and Product Performance Evaluation

1. Check percentage of market in toto and by product.
2. Gauge the degree of competition, local and foreign.
3. Consider the impact of substitute products in the market.
4. Judge the treatment of export sales by the sub, both of its own products and of those of related companies.
5. Weight the reliance of the sub on captive sales to related companies, to U.S. parent, and to dependent local buyers.
6. Review the level of the sales effort (wholesale, retail, ultimate consumer). Do not penalize the sub for an erroneous selection of distribution channels by the parent.
7. Analyze the sub's advertising and promotion program.
8. Note the frequency of suggestions for new-product development and improvements of existing items.
9. Check the quality of after-sales servicing.
10. Appraise the performance and attitudes of distributors under the sub's control.

Productivity Evaluation

1. Determine production per hour, without regard to cost.
2. Relate output costs, using either value added or sales billed.
3. Adjust for such variables as wage scales, volume of production, degree of automation, efficiency of equipment.
4. Express productivity in physical units when inflation and currency deterioration might distort a monetary figure.

Table 8.1 *Continued*

Labor Relations Evaluation

1. Assess employee morale and attitudes.
2. Examine the general administration of personnel policies.
3. Consider the effectiveness of training programs.
4. Calculate work time lost through absenteeism, turnover.
5. Review union relations, especially for time lost owing to walkouts and strikes.

Personnel Development Evaluation

1. Count the number of promotions within departments.
2. Note the transfers to higher posts in other units of the company group.
3. Determine the number of promotable personnel available.
4. Assess the worth of the sub's medium- and long-range personnel-need forecasts.

Public and Government Relations Evaluation

1. Appraise degree of identification and national goals.
2. Assess the tenor of community relations.
3. Check relations with local and national business leaders.
4. Review relationships with government officials.

Planning Evaluation

1. Search for clear statements on future targets.
2. Weigh the balance between long-range goals and short-term requirements.
3. Examine the coordination of functional and staff planning at all levels in the foreign sub.

Finally, temper these quantitative and qualitative factors with the judgment of an experienced international executive and the priority a particular company may place on one or more of these evaluation categories.

Source: Business International. 28 February 1984.

efforts. Simlarly, a subsidiary's good performance may have been due to considerable luck or occurred despite poor managerial performance. Thus, in order to properly reward and keep good managers and not inadvertently reward poor managers, the evaluation system must be able to separate subsidiary and managerial performance.

Choosing the right system is therefore no easy task. Nonetheless, a system must be designed and implemented. Many of the larger U.S. multinationals have developed multiple measurement systems and computer models to assist in the separation of controllable and uncontrollable impacts. These models, for example, can estimate what the translated financial results of a foreign subsidiary *would* have been *if* the foreign currency had not moved in the direction or magnitude that it actually did. Earlier budgets can be recast using the actual exchange rates that were in effect as the year progressed, and these recast budgets can then be compared with actual results. Or actual results can be recast in terms of the exchange rates that had been predicted earlier when the budget was prepared and then compared with the original budget and plan.

In sum, if plans and budgets were properly prepared, including expected ranges to allow for major contingencies, comparisons of performance to the original plan and related budgets present viable and equitable methods of evaluating performance. To some degree, it can also permit performance comparisons among units or managers, or both. For example, one subsidiary that achieved 95% of its planned activities and goals by utilizing 10% less funds than it had been allocated can be compared favorably to one that achieved only 90% of its goals and went 5% over budget (all other factors being equal, of course!).

Yet despite evidence that some MNEs are doing a fairly sophisticated job of performance evaluation, a preponderance of the evidence suggests that most do not.

Recent Studies of MNE Performance Evaluation System

Three noteworthy studies of performance evaluation systems of multinationals are those by Robbins and Stobaugh,[6] McInnes,[7] and Morsicato.[8]

Robbins and Stobaugh studied nearly 200 U.S.-based MNEs, representing almost all major U.S. industries with investments abroad, and ranging in size of total foreign sales from $20 million upward. With regard to measures of financial performance, the main conclusions from their research were as follows:

1. The many tangible and intangible items that entered into the original investment calculations were rarely taken into account in evaluating the foreign subsidiaries' performance—for example, the value or cost of a parent company's loan guarantee for a subsidiary, cost of safety stocks of inventory for foreign and U.S. operations, or the potential cost of being excluded from a market by a competitor who moves first.

2. Foreign subsidiaries were judged on the same basis as domestic subsidiaries.

[6]S. Robbins and R. Stobaugh, *Money in the Multinational Enterprise: A Study in Financial Policy* (New York: Basic Books, 1973).
[7]J. M. McInnes, "Financial Control Systems for Multinational Operations: An Empirical Investigation," *Journal of International Business Studies*, Fall 1971, pp. 11–28.
[8]Helen Morsicato, "An Investigation of the Interaction of Financial Statement Translation and Multinational Enterprise Performance Evaluation," Ph.D. dissertation, Pennsylvania State University, 1978, and *Currency Translation and Performance Evaluation in Multinationals* (Ann Arbor, Mich.: UMI Research Press, 1980).

3. The most utilized measure of performance for all subsidiaries was return on investment (ROI).

4. Because of the inherent limitation and problems of calculating ROI equitably for all subsidiaries, nearly all the multinationals used some supplementary device to gauge foreign subsidiaries' performance.

5. The most widely used supplementary measure was comparison to budget.

6. The budgets used were a yearly capital budget (including a list of individual projects with an indication of their profitability) and an operating budget containing pro forma income statements, balance sheets, and cash flow projections (prepared monthly or quarterly for the forthcoming year).

7. Even the firms that used budgets as supplementary measures selected ROI as the key item in the budgets.

8. Fewer than half (44%) judged subsidiary performance in terms of translated dollar amounts, and only 12% used both standards.

McInnes later studied 30 U.S. multinational manufacturing companies and also focused on financial control and performance. The companies in his sample were of moderate size ($100 million to $300 million in sales), had at least 20% of their assets and sales abroad, and had operating entities in six or more foreign countries. His major findings were quite similar to those of Robbins and Stobaugh:

1. Of the 30 firms, 19 used identical techniques for evaluating the performance of foreign and domestic subsidiaries.

2. In virtually all cases in which there were differences in technique, more techniques were used for domestic subsidiaries.

3. ROI was cited by a majority of the firms as the most important evaluation criterion.

4. When differences occurred, firms tended to put more emphasis on purely financial techniques of analysis for foreign subsidiaries and more emphasis on operating control techniques for domestic subsidiaries.

The more recent study by Morsicato focused on the use of dollar and local currency information in evaluating subsidiary performance—that is, translated and not translated methods. Her study of 70 U.S. multinationals in the chemical industry revealed that profit, return on investment, budget compared to actual profit, and budget compared to sales were, in order of frequency, the measures most commonly employed *after translation into dollars*. Budget compared to actual profit, budget compared to actual sales, and profit were the most frequently utilized measures in local currency *before* translation. Also, how often these measures were used depended on whether the measures were translated into dollars or remained in local country currency. This was particularly true for ROI and cash flow measurements, as shown in Table 8.2. One of the major contributions of the Morsicato study is its excellent discussion and analysis of the differences in the budgeting and performance evaluation process resulting from using local versus parent country currency.

Taken as a group, these studies show that there is little significant difference between the performance evaluation systems used for domestic and for foreign operations.

One of the more curious aspects of these empirical studies was their finding that multinationals rely on ROI as the major or even the only measure of performance. Where intercorporate transfers are significant and are not at arm's-length prices, the ROI income numerator is highly arbitrary and, in one sense, fictitious. Also, a subsidiary manager whose evaluation is based on ROI may choose to borrow heavily in the local currency, affecting the borrowing capacity of the entire firm and potentially the price of its stock, possibly subjecting the parent's consolidated financial statements to significant foreign currency losses if the borrowings are in hard currencies. Perhaps most important, ROI is not appropriate for some foreign operations, such as subsidiaries producing only for other

Table 8.2 Financial Measures Used as Indicators of Internal Performance Evaluation

After Translation in U.S. Dollars (%)	Before Translation in Local Currency (%)	Financial Measures
80.0	52.9	Return-on-investment (assets)
48.6	31.4	Return-on-equity
21.4	18.6	Residual income
81.4	70.0	Profit
65.7	35.7	Cash flow potential from foreign subsidiary to U.S. operations
45.7	38.6	Budget compared to actual return on investment
78.6	72.9	Budget compared to actual profits
72.9	72.9	Budget compared to actual sales
34.3	30.0	Ratios
12.9	11.4	Others

Note: These figures represent the percentage of the total 70 firms that report using each particular measure.

Source: Helen Morsicato, *Currency Translation and Performance Evaluation in Multinationals* (Ann Arbor, Mich.: UMI Research Press, 1980).

subsidiaries, marketing subsidiaries buying all their products from other affiliates, or subsidiaries striving to break into highly competitive markets.

Properly Relating Evaluation to Performance

The problems related to using ROI as a standard measure of performance apply to other measures as well. Virtually any financial ratio analysis or payback method suffers from similar limitations if it is uniformly applied to all subsidiaries. The main reason for this is that a multinational's objectives for its affiliates are based on the reasons for their creation and their particular operating environment. Some subsidiaries serve as sources of products, funds, or services for others. Some try to maintain market share; others try to increase it. Some face strict profit remittance controls by foreign governments; others do not. These differences in objectives and operating environments call for different performance measures. This need is recognized by most multinationals, even if only slightly, as evidenced by their reported use of multiple measures of performance. At the same time, there is a need to have some uniformity in performance evaluation so as to simplify the procedure and enable intersubsidiary comparisons.

The need for standardization brings us back to the one method of performance evaluation that can meet most criteria without undue limitations: the comparison of performance with plan. This method is probably the only globally applicable evaluation method. It permits each affiliate to be judged on its own, according to the plan it was given, and can be used to compare subsidiary performances. However, it is reasonable basis of performance measurement only if the original plans were logical and reasonable. Therein lies one danger of the comparison to plan technique. The other danger is that subsidiary managers' input to the plan may be tempered by their desire to surpass the plan's expectations. For example, they might deliberately project a bleak picture, such as stating that they will need a larger budget to achieve a 5% growth in sales when, in fact, they could achieve a 10% growth with a smaller budget. If given the larger budget, they can show a greater than 5% growth in sales and appear to have done a great job even though they could have achieved the same results with less money. However, if the planning and budgeting process is sufficiently deliberative, participative, iterative, and honest, both of these dangers can be minimized.

Several other performance evaluation issues deserve mention. First, it is neither realistic nor advisable for most firms to treat all subsidiaries as independent, autonomous operations, such as profit centers. Foreign affiliates are an integral and strategic part of the worldwide family. Their true value evolves from their contribution to this larger whole, rather than from their individual performance. It is precisely this characteristic that gives the multinational its strength and competitive advantages. Therefore, individual subsidiaries' performance in their respective countries should remain largely a secondary criterion for evaluation, regardless of the performance measures used.

Second, the method of performance evaluation should be clearly understood by the managers and actually utilized by the company. If the managers do not understand the system, its intended results will not be achieved. And if the method ultimately used for performance evaluation is not the one that was originally planned to be used, the firm will have a hard time keeping its managers.

All of the preceding discussion suggests that there is still much fertile ground to be plowed by the international accountants of MNEs in terms of designing and implementing better performance evaluation systems.

COSTING AND PRICING

Costing and pricing considerations in international business are more numerous, more complicated, and more risky than in strictly domestic business. A firm must consider at least two sets of laws, two competitive markets, the reactions of two sets of competitors, and two governments. In turn, each of these considerations varies in importance and interaction over time. Thus, the firm selling internationally is confronted with two different and constantly changing market collages. It should not be surprising that determining costs and prices for international sales is difficult, even for the occasional exporter. Yet despite the problems, costing and pricing are critical to the profitability of any business operation, domestic or international. As a result, these policies and procedures are highly secretive areas for virtually all firms. The cloud of secrecy enshrouding pricing also covers quasi-illegal or even outright illegal practices, making it even more difficult for outsiders to obtain information.

Product Costing

Product costing typically involves the estimation and subsequent accumulation of direct costs such as material and labor, plus allocations of certain fixed costs. For products produced in a single foreign country from components and labor supplied locally, the costing procedure is similar to that for a domestic company. The only differences are when certain costs (e.g., fixed costs or R&D) incurred in one country are allocated to operations in other countries. In such cases, an acceptable method of allocation must be used, and the appropriate foreign exchange rate must be selected for booking/costing purposes.

Acceptability refers to both internal and external parties. Internally, headquarters and field operations should agree on the method. Externally, the governments of both countries should agree on the allocation itself, and the method of allocation. For example, the United States and many other countries require a systematic, nondiscriminatory method of allocation. Thus, the costs of a headquarter's $5 million R&D project might be allocated to all foreign subsidiaries based on the percentage of total MNE sales accounted for by each subsidiary rather than allocating expenses only to subsidiaries in high-tax-rate countries. In addition, some governments such as Brazil's may not permit such allocations to subsidiaries in Brazil for expenses incurred by parent companies located outside Brazil (reasons for this stance are explained in the next section).

A more complicated costing process involves products that are made from raw materials or components purchased from other countries. First, the cost of the purchased item must be established in the foreign country. Second, transportation costs, insurance, export taxes or credits, and tariffs must be taken into account. Third, changes in the foreign exchange rate must be considered, and any costs related to protecting the transaction from changes in exchange rate (e.g., costs of using forward contracts to hedge transactions). If only a small percentage (in total value) of a final product is sourced from other countries, errors in cost estimation may not be important. However, if a major percentage is foreign-sourced, errors of estimation in any or all of these factors may significantly affect the final cost of the product. For example, for some subcompact cars assembled and sold by U.S. automotive companies, more than 60% of the final product's cost are incurred outside of the United States, and some are imported directly in final form after being assembled abroad from components manufactured in a dozen countries.

The accurate estimation of future product costs is clearly important for competitive strategy formulation, for product cost will influence final pricing, the future marketing of the product, and ultimately the profitability of the firm. However, the true cost of the product may have less influence on the internal pricing of the product, a subject to which we now turn.

Internal (Transfer) Pricing

As was discussed in the chapter on taxation, internal pricing refers to the pricing of goods and services that are transferred (bought and sold) between members of a corporate family, for example, parent to subsidiaries, between subsidiaries, from subsidiaries to parent, and so on.[9] As such, internal transfers include raw material, semifinished and finished goods,

---

[9]When referring to prices of internal transfers, one can make a fine distinction between intracorporate prices and intercorporate prices by using the former to refer to sales among divisions of a single incorporated entity and the latter to refer to sales among different corporate entities of one large company. However, in this chapter intercorporate refers to any transfer made within the global corporate family. It is also used synonymously with internal transfers and transfer pricing. See James Shulman, "Transfer Pricing in Multinational Business," Ph.D. dissertation, Harvard University, 1966; *Solving International Pricing Problems* (New York: Business International Corp., 1965); and Jeffrey S. Arpan, *International Intracorporate Pricing: Non-American Systems and Views* (New York: Praeger, 1972).

allocation of fixed costs, loans, fees, royalties for use of trademarks, copyrights, and other factors. In theory, such prices should be based on costs, but in reality, they often are not.[10] Chapter 7 included a discussion of one reason for this—specifically, that transfer prices may be set to maximize global after-tax income or otherwise maneuver profits to lower-tax-rate countries. Thus, a product costing $100 made in a high-tax-rate country may be sold for $100 to an affiliate in a low-tax-rate country, which then sells the product for $200, resulting in the entire profit ending up in the lower-tax-rate country.

Yet taxation is only one of a number of reasons why internal transfers may be priced with little consideration to actual costs. Companies can underprice goods sold to foreign affiliates, and the affiliates can then sell them at prices that their local competitors cannot match. And if tough antidumping laws exist on final products, a company could underprice components and semifinished products to its affiliates. The affiliates could then assemble or finish the final product at prices that would have been classified as dumping prices had they been imported directly into the country rather than produced inside.

Transfer prices can be used in a similar manner to reduce the impact of tariffs. Tariffs increase import prices and apply to intercorporate transfers as well as to sales to unaffiliated buyers. Although no company can do much to change a tariff, the effect of tariffs can be lessened if the selling company underprices the goods it exports to the buying company. For example, a product that normally sells for $100 has an import price of $120 because of a 20% tariff. If the invoice price were listed as $80 rather than $100, however, if could be imported for $96. Underpricing intercorporate transfers can also be used to get more products into a country that is rationing its currency or otherwise limiting the value of goods that can be imported. A subsidiary can import twice as many products if they can be bought at half price.

Advantages of High Transfer Prices

In other situations, artificially high transfer prices can be used to circumvent or significantly lessen the impact of national controls. A government probibition on dividend remittances can restrict the ability of a firm to maneuver income out of a country. However, overpricing the goods shipped to a subsidiary in such a country makes it possible for funds to be taken out. High transfer prices can also be of considerable value to a firm when it is paid a subsidy or earns a tax credit on the value of goods it exports. The higher the transfer prices on exported goods, the greater the subsidy earned or tax credit received.

High transfer prices on goods shipped to subsidiaries can be desirable

---

[10]See Jeffrey Arpan, "Multinational Firm Pricing in International Markets," *Sloan Management Review*, Winter 1972–1973, Vol. 14, No. 2, pp. 1–9.

when a parent wishes to lower the apparent profitability of its subsidiary. This may be desirable because of the demands of the subsidiary's workers for higher wages or greater participation in company profits, because of political pressures to expropriate high-profit foreign-owned operations, or because of the possibility that new competitors will be lured into the industry by high profits. There are also inducements for having high-priced transfers go to the subsidiary when a local partner is involved, the inducement being that the increase in the parent company profits will not have to be split with the local partner. High transfer prices may also be desired when increases from existing price controls in the subsidiary's country are based on production costs (including high transfer prices for purchases).

Transfer pricing can also be used to minimize losses from foreign currency fluctuations or shift the losses to particular affiliates. By dictating the specific currency used for payment, the parent determines whether the buying or selling firm has the exchange risk. Altering the terms and timing of payments and the volume of shipments causes transfer pricing to affect the net exposure of the firm.

Matching Price to Market Conditions

Table 8.3 summarizes the particular conditions that make it advantageous for firms to utilize a particular level of transfer price. The maximum advantage can be gained when all these conditions line up on a country basis. For example, the parent operates from a country with the characteristics calling for high transfer prices coming in and low transfer prices going out, whereas the conditions of the subsidiary's country call for the opposite.

Consider the left side of Table 8.3. If the parent sells at low prices to the subsidiary and buys from it at high prices, income is shifted to the subsidiary, lessening the overall tax burden. At the same time, the impact of the high ad valorem tariffs in the other country is lessened and the financial appearance of the subsidiary is enhanced for local borrowing purposes. In addition, the impact of foreign exchange rationing on imports from the parent and dividend payments to the parent are lessened, the subsidiary's ability to penetrate its local market is enhanced, the parent is less affected by its government's restrictions on capital outflows, and so on.

Under this set of conditions, the subsidiary's country gains somewhat more than the parent's: more funds, more taxable income, greater economic growth of the subsidiary, and more export revenues. It loses somewhat in other areas, however: local competitors may suffer adversely, have lower profits, pay less taxes, and lay off workers if the foreign subsidiary actively pursues a market penetration strategy. The government pays greater subsidies or gives more tax credits because of the subsidiary's artificially high value of exports and, like the government of the other country, has its national control lessened.

Table 8.3 Conditions in Subsidiary's Country Inducing High and Low Transfer Prices on Flows Between Affiliates and Parent

Conditions in Subsidiary's Country Inducing *Low Transfer Prices* on Flows from Parent and *High Transfer Prices* on Flows to Parent	Conditions in Subsidiary's Country Inducing *High Transfer Prices* on Flows from Parent and *Low Transfer Prices* on Flows to Parent
High ad valorem tariffs	Local partners
Corporate income tax rate lower than in parent's country	Pressure from workers to obtain greater share of company profit
Significant competition	Political pressure to nationalize or expropriate high-profit foreign firms
Local loans based on financial appearance of subsidiary	Restrictions on profit or dividend remittances
Export subsidy or tax credit on value of exports	Political instability
Lower inflation rate than in parent's country	Substantial tie-in sales agreements
Restrictions (ceilings) in subsidiary's country on the *value* of products that can be imported	Price of final product controlled by government but based on production cost
	Desire to mask profitability of subsidiary operations to keep competitors out

Source: Jeffrey S. Arpan, *Intracorporate Pricing: Non-American Systems and Views* (New York: Praeger, 1972).

Unfortunately for firms, conditions seldom line up as nicely from their standpoint as is depicted on either side of Table 8.3. It is far more likely that a country will simultaneously have conditions appearing on both sides of the table. For example, a country experiencing balance of payments difficulties typically would be restricting dividend outflows and the amount or value of imports. A company using high transfer prices on sales to its subsidiary in such a country would gain in terms of taking out more money than it might otherwise have been able to get out but would lose by having to decrease the quantity of imported materials its affiliate needs in order to compete. Alternatively, a country may have high ad valorem tariffs and high income tax rates. Underpricing goods shipped to an affiliate in such a country lessens the tariffs duties and increases subsidiary profits because of lower input costs, resulting in higher taxes for the subsidiary. Therefore, in situations in which conditions in a country are taken from both sides of Table 8.3 the company must weigh the gains and losses from utilizing a particular level of transfer prices.

So far we have discussed the problems related to a two-country model. As additional countries are added arithmetically, the problems and headaches of transfer pricing grow geometrically. Theoretically and realistically, the multinational's management should weigh the overall gains and losses from each shipment and transfer price for each member. When we recognize that the specific combination of environmental conditions changes in each country over time, we begin to understand why the effort of constantly reevaluating and changing intercorporate pricing strategies becomes truly gargantuan. That is, considerable complexity is added to record keeping by having different transfer pricing schemes for transfers to and from a large number of subsidiaries, each of which may need to be changed as conditions or objectives change. Furthermore, the United States and most other countries' government do not look favorably on transfer price manipulation. Also, remember that intercorporate transfers at any prices other than arm's length, fair market values cause additional complications in evaluating the performance of subsidiaries and can have a deleterious effect on management morale, as was discussed earlier in this chapter.

National Differences in Transfer Pricing Systems

There is some evidence that the nationality of the parent company affects the transfer pricing system utilized by multinationals and the relative importance given to the various factors considered in setting transfer prices. An early study of the intracorporate pricing systems of 60 foreign-based multinationals drew these conclusions:[11]

1. American, French, British, and Japanese managements seemed to prefer cost-oriented transfer prices, whereas Canadians, Italians, and Scandinavians prefer market prices. No particular orientation or preference along either line was discernible from German, Belgian, Swiss, or Dutch multinationals. Overall, however, the transfer pricing systems of foreign-based multinationals were generally less complex and more market-oriented than American Systems.

2. Although foreign-based companies generally considered the same environmental variables when formulating guidelines for transfer prices, especially among the larger companies, there were distinguishable national differences in the relative importance attached to each of these considerations. These differences are summarized in Table 8.4.

   As can be seen from the table, American, Canadian, French, and Italian companies considered income taxes to be the most important variable affecting transfer pricing policy, whereas British companies considered the improvement of the financial appearance of their U.S. subsidiaries as most important. With the exception of

---

[11]See Jeffrey S. Arpan, *International Intracorporate Pricing, Non-American Systems and Views,* (New York: Praeger, 1972).

Table 8.4 National Differences in Relative Importance Given to Variables in Transfer Price Determination

Variables	Parent's Nationality						
	United States	Canada	France	Germany	Italy	Scandinavia	United Kingdom
Income tax	1	1	1	3	1	3	3
Customs duties	2	2	2	3	3	3	3
Inflation	1	2	2	2	2	3	2
Changes in currency exchange rates	3	3	2	2	3	3	2
Exchange controls	2	3	5	5	5	5	5
Improving financial appearance of subsidiary	3	3	3	4	4	4	1
Expropriation	3	3	5	5	5	5	5
Export subsidies and tax credits	4	2	2	4	2	4	2
Level of competition	4	2	2	3	2	3	3

Weighting scale: 1 = high importance, 2 = medium importance, 3 = low importance, 4 = not mentioned, 5 = mentioned only with respect to operations outside the United States.
Source: Jeffrey S. Arpan, *Intracorporate Pricing: Non-American Systems and Views* (New York: Praeger, 1972).

Scandinavian companies, inflation was also identified as an important variable in transfer pricing policy deliberations.

3. In contrast to the external influences just mentioned, foreign-based multinationals considered only about half as many internal parameters as their American counterparts did. With the exception of the British, most firms in the study viewed transfer pricing more as a means of controlling subsidiary operations than as a technique for motivating and evaluating subsidiary performance. This is largely explained by the fact that the use of the profit center concept was not widespread among foreign-based companies. Aside from control, one consideration deemed important by all firms was the acceptability of transfer prices to both host and parent country governments.

Final Pricing

There are many factors that influence the setting the prices of goods and services to the final, external customer. One is the real cost of the product;

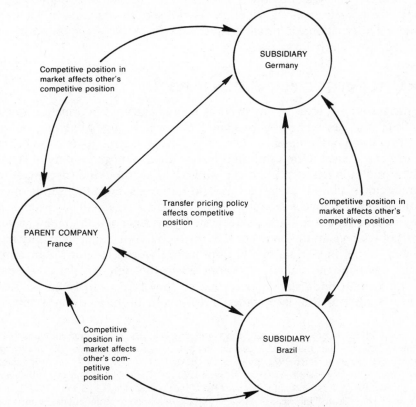

FIGURE 8.9. Transfer pricing and competitive position.

other factors include prices of competitors, purchasing power of buyers, price controls, foreign currency restrictions if the good is imported, and levels of inflation, just to mention a few. And although the real cost of the product is clearly important in the setting of final prices, transfer prices are often not an important influence in this process unless the MNE operates in a true profit center mode.

In the broadest sense, final prices reflect the firm's marketing strategy in a particular country or market and in many cases, its global market (see Figure 8.9). They are thus initially set by the firm's marketing staff, but are often subject to review by corporate headquarters staff to ensure their compatability with other nonmarketing goals and objectives. A similar pattern often emerges with the setting of transfer prices. Accountants provide the real cost information, but seldom determine the transfer prices—a pricing determination usually made neither by the accounting nor the marketing staff but by the chief financial officer.

In the final analysis, however, it is the MNE's accounting staff that develops cost estimates, sets up cost accumulation and allocation systems, provides needed cost information to others who set prices (internally and externally), analyze subsequent cost and revenue variances, and plays a key role in performance evaluation. To do all of this requires an elaborate internal international information system, which also provides information needed for external reporting.

MANAGEMENT INFORMATION SYSTEM

Crucial to the success of any MNE is its management information system (MIS)[12]—its central nervous system, if you will. A large MNE may operate in a hundred environments, each constantly changing in direction or rate, and have to deal with a hundred governments and thousands of regulations, multiple sets of stockholders and creditors, thousands of competitive predators, hundreds of currencies, and hundreds, even thousands of customers and employees. Simply trying to keep management abreast of *major* developments inside and outside of the firm is a major undertaking, a large part of which is in the hands of the firm's accounting staff. Not only must thousands of individual bits of information be collected and transmitted each day, but they must be channeled to the right people in a timely fashion in an understandable format so they can be analyzed properly. Once analyzed, this information must again be properly and speedily

[12]For additional information about MNEs and management information systems, see P. Bohos, "Management Information Systems for International Operations," *The International Accountant*, January–March 1972, pp. 6–8; P. Dickie and N. Arya, "MIS and International Business," *Journal of Systems Management*, June 1970, pp. 8–12; Alex J. Murray, "Intelligence Systems of the MNC's," *Columbia Journal of World Business*, September–October 1972, pp. 63–71; and George Scott, "Information Systems and Coordination in Multinational Enterprises," *International Journal of Accounting Education and Research*, February 1974, pp. 87+.

channeled to other individuals and units that need to be informed. Also, data must often be aggregated, disaggregated, and then reaggregated in different forms to serve different purposes or groups. The information system also has to be suited to the structure and philosophy of the firm. For example, if a firm operates through a highly decentralized structure, its information and control requirements will be different from those of a highly centralized firm. Put another way, largely autonomous subsidiaries do not require as much control from the parent and therefore need not transmit information as frequently to the parent. Thus, the adequacy, suitability, and timeliness of the information system are all key determinants of the success of decision making and control systems, particularly those of multinational enterprise. These are but a few of the considerations and complications of an MNE's MIS. We now turn to more detailed discussions of specific considerations.

Information Needs

In one sense, the information needs of a multinational are similar to those of a domestic corporation. Information has to be assembled and used in reports to the following individuals and groups:

1. Government and government agencies (e.g., details about taxes, prices, wages, pensions, and regulatory compliance).
2. Shareholders and creditors (e.g., consolidated financial reports, activity summaries, and future commitments).
3. Management (e.g., projections, budgets, expenditures, variances, and the effects of inflation).
4. Labor (e.g., wages and benefits, training and development expenditures).
5. Other publics (e.g., social responsibility activity and warranty information).

At the same time there are other information needs peculiar to a multinational firm:

1. Financial positions and operations in each country should be reported and analyzed separately, regionally, and ultimately globally, and often also by major product lines.
2. Information related to the economic risk of assets in each country should be collected and analyzed in terms not only of their potential local impact but also of their possible repercussions on global operations.
3. Separate yet integrated goals and strategies must be made for each operation. These must be based not only on global corporate objectives but also on the specific economic, legal, sociocultural, and

political environments in each country of operation. They are often based on highly variable and not always comparable data for each country.

Volume

The above needs suggest a considerable volume of reporting, both externally and internally. Several studies have shown an excess of two hundred

Table 8.5 Types of Reports to Headquarters

1.	Corporate controller	
	a. Management reports, such as	12
	Accounts receivable aging	
	Consolidated income and sales (a flash report)	
	b. Consolidations—not tabulated	
	c. Government reports, such as	
	Department of Treasury, such as	4
	Foreign Currency Forms FC-3/3a and FC-4	
	Foreign Exchange Form C-3	
	Department of Commerce	8
	Foreign units—data partly for Department of Commerce merchandise, Forms F-1 and F-2	
	Domestic units—data partly for Department of Commerce merchandise, Forms D-1, 2, & 3	
	Proxy questionnaire	2
2.	Corporate treasurer	
	a. Corporate finance, such as	12
	Cash forecast for month	
	Debt calendar	
	Calculation of cash excess (deficit) for month (ahead)	
	b. Tax	8
	c. Pensions	10
	d. Payroll	7
	e. Risk management	8
	f. Shareholders records	2
3.	Industrial relations, such as	13
	Pension plan history cards, for new entrants only	
	Employee stock purchase plan	
4.	Investor relations, such as	9
	Dividend reinvestment plan	
	Investor relations report	
5.	Legal	3
6.	Systems and data processing	3
	Total (excludes reports at the subsidiary level only)	106

Source: George C. Watt, Richard M. Hammer, and Marianne Burge, *Accounting for the Multinational Firm* (New York: Financial Executives Institute, 1977), p. 244.

Table 8.6 Frequency of Affiliate Reports to Headquarters

Monthly	Quarterly	Semiannually	Annually	Total
35	20	10	35	100
× 12	4	2	1	—
420	80	20	35	555
Number of reporting field locations, say				× 100
Total reports processed at headquarters				55,500

Source: George C. Watt, Richard M. Hammer, and Marianne Burge, *Accounting for the Multinational Corporation* (New York: Financial Executives Institute, 1977), p. 244.

types of regular financial reports required by headquarters, which over a year's time, based on a hundred reporting units, may require well over tens of thousands of reports to be processed at headquarters. Tables 8.5 and 8.6 provide some indications of what these report and volumes consist of. Without proper control, information overload can quickly result. Money is wasted on collecting and disseminating information that is not used properly, and storage costs themselves can be enormous. Thus, a key and related consideration is reporting frequency.

Frequency

Information overload is less likely when fewer reports are prepared and processed less frequently. The optimal solution is to have only truly necessary reports prepared and processed only when necessary—a nice ideal, but one difficult to achieve in reality. Furthermore, some operations are more important than others, and some are in more stable environments than others; some managers have more experience and need less supervision; some methods of transmittal take longer than others; some kinds of information are more important than other kinds. In designing a good system, these differences must be considered in deciding the frequency and methods of collection, transmittal, and analysis. Key types of information from key operations in highly unstable environments require greater frequency of preparation and communication than those under opposite conditions.

Timeliness

Information that arrives too late is virtually useless. Information that arrives prematurely may be misleading or may become outdated, lost, or forgotten. Hence the importance of the timeliness issue.

Several timing problems confront an MNE because of its geographic spread. Mail service may take weeks, or worse, may never arrive. Telephone calls are expensive, and differences in time zones pose problems. When it is 4 P.M. on Friday in New York City, it is 10 P.M. in Paris, and 3 A.M. on Saturday in Tokyo, which makes it difficult to arrange a conference call. Also, in some major cities of the world, it may take several months to get a telephone installed. Telexes can be sent or received around the clock but are also expensive, and the intended receiver may not be around to respond immediately. Face-to-face communication is even more expensive because of high travel costs. In all cases, the urgency of the information must be considered in light of the cost of transmittal. Only the most urgent information should be transmitted by the fastest and most costly method.

Access

From a control standpoint, access to information is another key consideration in the design and operation of an MNE's information system, both internally and externally. A properly designed system should prevent information from being received by persons who do not have a right or need to receive it. If they have no need for it, it is an unnecessary expense for them to receive it. If they have no right to receive it, it can be dangerous for the MNE for them to receive it. Internally, for example, problems can arise if employees in one country learn that their counterparts in another country earn higher salaries for wages or have better benefit packages. Externally, even greater problems can arise if sensitive information gets into the hands of competitors and, in some instances, government officials. Yet despite these dangers, it is important for information to be received by all persons who have a right and need to be informed. Determining who has a need or a right to information, however, can become a thorny issue, to be sure.

Information security is not only a major issue for an information system, it has become an industry in itself. Industrial espionage, investigative reporting by the media, investigation by governmental agencies, and corporate politics are all real-world phenomena that have heightened the need for information security. What makes security such a key issue for MNEs is that more groups want information about MNEs because they are such big actors on the world scene and in most countries in which they operate. They are also more closely watched because they have often been criticized for acting in unethical ways. Finally, legal protections against invasions of privacy customary, for example, in North America and many Western European countries, do not exist or are not enforced in many countries. Mail may be opened or censored by governments, telephones may be bugged, and other forms of communication (e.g., satellite) may be intercepted by various parties.

All of this suggests the need for, and generally results in, coded information transmittals within an MNE. Written communications are coded, transmitted, then decoded once received. Aural communications over the telephone must undergo similar precautions. If all of this sounds a bit cloak and dagger, it actually is. Consider, for example, transmitting political risk information, such as a pending *coup d'etat* in country X. The MNE's headquarters in country A needs to be apprised of the situation, as do other affiliates who buy from or sell to country X. The subsidiary manager in country X must transmit the relevant information to them, but in such a way that competitors and the government officials in country X do not intercept the information, or, if they do intercept it, cannot interpret it. Reporting actual financial results of operations to headquarters must be similarly safeguarded. In the latter case, what may appear to be a long list of random numbers is actually the subsidiary's closing income statement and balance sheet. Thus, a knowledge of crytography is useful for CPAs as well as CIA and KGB agents!

Uniformity

Still another major issue pertaining to information systems is uniformity— in how information is collected, prepared, and transmitted. If similar information is prepared in dissimilar ways, interpretation is more difficult and could be misleading, such as subsidiaries' income statements from 50 different countries, each prepared according to local accounting principles and procedures. Unless the analyzer is intimately familiar with all 50 countries' accounting systems, he or she cannot determine accurately or properly which subsidiaries are really profitable and which are not (in terms of some standard measure, such as the headquarters country's system). For MNEs headquartered in countries that require global consolidation for financial reporting and tax reporting, they must prepare consolidated reports in one currency, one language, one set of terminology, and most important, according to one set of accounting principles and procedures. Thus, somewhere within these MNEs, a transformation of accounting information must take place. The questions then become who does it, where is it done, by what method, and how often.

Who does it and where it is done is generally a single decision. For most MNEs, the transformation is done in the subsidiaries by the subsidiaries' accounting staff. For example, income statements of a U.S. MNE's French subsidiary are recast into U.S. GAAP for ultimate inclusion in the U.S. parent's consolidated financial statements. Therefore, the French subsidiary's accounting staff must be properly trained to make the transformation. The choice of method is generally determined by corporate headquarters, in conjunction with the headquarters country's accounting principles and procedures and laws. That is, for strictly internal management purposes, an MNE may select *any* method of preparation. However, for preparing a global tax return, a U.S.-based MNE must utilize a standardized system based on U.S. tax accounting laws and, for preparing its consolidated financial statements, use a U.S. GAAP-based system.

The frequency issue is similarly driven by corporate needs and headquarters-country laws or GAAP: once a year at year end (of course); quarterly for most large U.S. MNEs; and for certain critical kinds of information, perhaps monthly or even weekly. Naturally, the more frequent the process, the more expensive, so once again cost-benefit considerations arise.

To help mitigate the accounting transformation process, some MNEs keep several sets of books in each subsidiary. For a U.S. MNE's German subsidiary, for example, one set of books is maintained according to German accounting law, another according to U.S. GAAP (for consolidated financial reporting), and one according to U.S. tax laws and regulations (for ultimate consolidated tax returns). When an accounting entry is made on the books kept in accordance with German law, it is possible that no entry would be made on the books kept in accordance with U.S. tax law if, for example, the expense was legally deductible according to German law but not according to U.S. law. In this manner, one set of subsidiary books is always ready for consolidation at headquarters, the subsidiary's other set always conforms to local regulations, and the transformation process is virtually eliminated. However, the subsidiary's accounting staff must still be familiar with headquarters' system to know how the local transaction should be treated on the MNE-wide system.

Exceptions to these general procedures are found when foreign operations are a very small percentage of an MNE's total operation, when no one at the subsidiary level is capable of making the transformation, or when it is too costly to have it done in subsidiaries. In such cases, headquarters' accounting staff, or its regional office's staff, may do the conversion for the subsidiary. Or the services of an international accounting firm could be utilized to make the transformation, although such a firm is more likely to be used to assist in the training of the subsidiary's accountants.

But no matter what, the MNE needs internal accountants capable of dealing with differences in accounting systems. Without them, accounting reports will have only limited usefulness, and a great deal of needed information will not be generated or will be misinterpreted. Either situation can result in significant opportunity cost.

Relationship of the MIS to Corporate Philosophy and Structure

Another information system consideration pertains to the suitability of the system for the MNE's organizational structure and management philosophy, which should be consistent with each other. Although there are many ways to categorize management philosophies, Howard Perlmutler's typologies of ethnocentric, polycentric, and geocentric have become classics for international business.[13]

The ethnocentric philosophy essentially views international business operations as an extension of the firm's domestic business which are important as contributors to the wealth and well-being of the parent firm. Ethnocentric managers also tend to view parent company business practices as superior to foreign practices and therefore the ones to be used internationally.

The polycentric philosophy tends to view foreign operations as fairly autonomous units, whose major objectives are local rather than strongly connected to the parent company's country. The polycentric philosophy also tends to follow the adage of "when in Rome, do as the Romans do," believing that local business practices are more suitable for foreign operations than parent company practices.

Finally, the geocentric philosophy has a truly global perspective on operations and business practices. It is the total global performance that matters rather than either parent company or local subsidiaries. The geocentric philosophy recognizes that, in certain situations, some local practices may be better than parent company practices, whereas in other situations, the reverse may be true. If you will, it seeks to blend the best of what is available.

The general implications for compatibility of a firm's MIS with its organizational structure and management philosophy can be illustrated as follows. If the firm operates with a highly decentralized structure and a polycentric philosophy, the need for system uniformity is less, the frequency of communication among units is lower, as is the flow of communication to headquarters, and fewer transformations are necessary. Conversely, if the firm operates through a highly centralized structure under an ethnocentric philosophy, the reverse conditions exist. Thus, there should be a symbiotic relationship between structure, philosophy, and the internal information system. Furthermore, any changes occurring in the firm's structure and philosophy should result in commensurate changes in the firm's information system. If not, then much time, effort, and money will be wasted, and the right people will not get the right information in time to make the right decisions or prepare the necessary reports and analysis.

The Gathering Storm: MNEs and Transborder Data Flows

The free flow of information across national borders is vital for the successful operation of an MNE's management information system and, by extension, the operation of the MNE itself. Furthermore, as Arthur Bushin and others have suggested recently, the management of this information

---

[13]See Perlmutter, "Tortuous Evolution of the Multinational Corporation."

flow is as important as the management of company assets and production.[14] The ability of an MNE's computers to communicate with each other in a transnational network allows information to be stored, processed, retrieved, and used in decision making in a highly efficient manner, and facilitates communications, planning, strategy formulation, and control. During the 1970s, however, nearly a dozen countries enacted legislation that affects transborder (transnational) data flows, and more than twice as many countries have some related legislation under review.[15] For these and a number of other reasons, MNEs in the future will be confronted with increased risks related to transborder flows (TBF)—risks that constitute a veritable gathering storm.[16]

Underlying Concerns of Nation States

Foremost among many TBF concerns of nation states are those of privacy, economics, and national security. Privacy concerns generally deal with employee information such as religious and political affiliations, family background, race, sex, and employment history. To prevent misuse of such information, governments have striven to protect employees' (individuals') rights-to-know what records exist about them and to ensure that any records do not offend human dignity and rights or public liberties. Further, governments have sought to strengthen an individual's control over the content of such records and their distribution. Due to the diversity of national legislation concerning privacy and TBF, in 1980 the OECD established some guidelines recognizing the need for privacy without impeding TBF—the first multinational agreement dealing with TBF. However, the personal privacy concerns are small compared with those related to "nonpersonal" information, which comprise 80 to 90% of all data transmitted internationally.

Economic concerns center on a form of industrial espionage through corporate data piracy and the impact of TBF on local data processing industries and MNEs decision-making processes. By restricting TBF, some governments have sought to force MNEs to use local data processing industries and thereby increase their size and sophistication. (Otherwise, MNEs could have all their data processed in the headquarter's company, bypassing the local data processors). Others have hoped that by restricting TBF,

---

[14]See Arthur Bushin, "The Threat to International Data Flows," *Business Week*, 3 August 1981, p. 10.

[15]Countries enacting such legislation in the 1970s include Sweden (1973), Germany (1977), Australia, Austria, Brazil, Denmark, Finland, France, and Norway (1978), and Japan and Luxembourg (1979).

[16]For additional references and an excellent summary of growing TBF constraints, the issues and concerns underlying them, and their implications for MNEs, see Saeed Samiee, "Transnational Data Flow Constraints: A New Challenge for Multinational Corporations," *Journal of International Business Studies*, Spring–Summer 1984, pp. 141–150.

more autonomy in decision making would be given to subsidiaries because headquarters would have less information on which to make decisions for subsidiaries. (These governments believe that subsidiary managements are less likely to make decisions injurious to local economies.) The concern over data piracy has become increasingly important as international competition has increased, and countries seek to enhance or prolong the international competitiveness of their industries vis-à-vis those of foreign competitors.

These economic concerns are also related to national security concerns. Countries seek limitations on TBF to protect against political espionage and theft of industrial properties and designs and other economic data that could weaken their security. Satellite communication networks pose a major control problem in these respects. As international political tensions increase, so too will national security concerns related to TBF.

Implications for MNEs

Rising international concerns and regulatory limitations on TBF are certain to pose major operation problems for MNEs in the future. In the personnel area, it will be more difficult for MNEs to assess and compare performance of managers in different foreign locations as TBF of personnel records become more restricted. For example, Burroughs Corporation has already discovered that it cannot transfer its "Personnel Resource Inventory and Management Evaluation" system from its Germany subsidiary to locations outside Germany.[17]

In the planning area, certain "sensitive" information regarding political and economic conditions in foreign countries will likely be more difficult to transmit to headquarters or other locations. Data processing costs are also likely to increase as additional countries impose requirements for local processing and data storage, reducing the scale economies of a centralized system and, in some countries, forcing utilization of less efficient or sophisticated systems. Additional financial costs may also arise if countries legislate taxation of TBF transmissions, as several countries are currently considering. Formal authorization mechanisms and regulations are also likely to delay the timeliness of TBF, and, as was pointed out earlier in this chapter, time is not only money—it is often critical for proper decision making within an MNE. Last but not least, the entire control process of an MNE could be affected significantly if the communication links so vital for MNE control are hindered by increased restriction on TBF.

In short, TBF restrictions are almost certain to become another major area of controversy between MNEs and governments, and the accountants of MNEs will face new headaches, gray hairs, and challenges as a result.

---

[17]See Victor Block, "Barriers to the Free Flow of Information," *Infosystems*, September 1981, p. 108.

SUMMARY

- Because of the greater dynamics, complexities, uncertainties, and risks of international business, the planning and control functions of an MNE are more important and more difficult than for a domestic firm.

- Apart from economic and political complications, planning and control are further complicated by different cultural values, attitudes, and practices.

- The budgeting process is an integral part of the planning and control process, and hence suffers from most of the problems associated with them. It is particularly complicated by the fact that budgets must be made in multiple currencies as well as in the currency of the parent firm, and are therefore subject to changes in exchange rates.

- Other major aspects of an MNE control system are its organizational structure, methods of decision making, employee training and development system, and methods of performance evaluation.

- As a firm becomes more involved in international business, internal and external pressures cause organizational structure strains that ultimately result in new structures. Similarly, the degree of control exercised and exercisable over international business operations changes over time as international operations grow in size and complexity.

- No single method of performance evaluation is best. Because of differences in their objectives and operating environments, multiple measures of performance evaluation are advisable for MNEs. Yet although no one single method of performance evaluation is perfect, if the plans, objectives, and budgets for each affiliate are well designed and communicated, comparison of results to these plans and budgets is perhaps the most viable and feasible single method of performance evaluation.

- Regardless of the performance measure or measures used, it is critical to separate management performance from subsidiary performance, and to assess performance only on those results that were controllable.

- Determining product costs and prices for an MNE is also a highly complicated process, particularly when cross-country shipments occur and when exchange rates are unstable. Additional costs to be considered (not considered by a purely domestic firm) include international transportation, packaging and insurance costs, tariffs, export taxes or credits, and changes in foreign government regulations affecting costs and prices.

- Transfer pricing, a critical area of costing and pricing, refers to the internal pricing and allocation of costs of goods, services, and centralized expenses among various units of an MNE. Transfer pricing performs a legitimate function in an MNE, can be used to achieve a number of different corporate objectives, and can also be used to circumvent a number of government restrictions (legally and otherwise).

- Although there are many advantages to a nonuniform system of transfer pricing, simplicity, cost, and government policies put pressure on MNEs to utilize a standardized system.
- An MNE's management information system is its 'central nervous system. If it is not properly designed, implemented, and adjusted when necessary, the MNE cannot operate effectively or efficiently.
- The management information system of an MNE must handle a greater volume and diversity of information with more frequency than that of a domestic firm, and it suffers more from problems caused by greater geographic distance, different time zones, greater problems of security, and problems of cultural interpretation.

Study Questions

8-1. What are the basic objectives of management planning and control systems? Are they any different for a multinational enterprise than for a domestic enterprise?

8-2. What are the unique requirements and problems of a multinational firm's control system, particularly its system of performance evaluation?

8-3. Discuss the advantages and disadvantages of various evaluation measures used by multinationals to assess foreign subsidiary performance.

8-4. Discuss why a multinational enterprise must periodically alter its organizational structure, and what implications such changes may have for the firm's information and control systems.

8-5. Discuss why the importance of organizational structure and control systems may vary in terms of specific functions such as marketing, finance, and industrial relations.

8-6. In domestic accounting literature, there are a number of behavioral considerations related to the design and operation of a control system. What behavioral considerations might be unique to the control system of a multinational enterprise?

8-7. Could it be argued that a large multinational, operating a variety of businesses in more than a hundred countries, is never really able to control itself? Why or why not?

8-8. Why are pricing decisions more numerous, complex, and risky in international business than in strictly domestic business?

8-9. What are the realities of international business that make it possible and desirable for firms *not* to price uniformly?

8-10. What legitimate functions do intercorporate transfers and prices perform?

8-11. What illegitimate, unethical, or otherwise questionable functions do intercorporate transfers and prices perform?

8-12. Given that both cost-based and market-based transfer prices are arbitrary, what are the major advantages and disadvantages of each orientation?

8-13. What are the advantages to a multinational of having a uniform pricing policy regardless of whether it is cost based or market based?

8-14. It has been argued that the golden age of transfer pricing is over. That is, firms are no longer as able or willing to depart radically from the fair value of internal transfers. Why might this be the case?

8-15. What are the unique requirements and problems in terms of the design and operation of an information system for a multinational firm?

8-16. Discuss the relationships between a multinational firm's information system, organizational structure, and control system.

8-17. Explain why there might be different information system and control system problems for a multinational firm operating only in developing countries than for one operating only in developed countries.

8-18. What are the major concerns of governments regarding transborder information flows (TBF)?

8-19. What are the major implications for MNEs of increased TBF restrictions by governments?

Case 1

AUTOPARTS INC.

Autoparts Inc. is a large U.S.-based multinational with production operations in some 20 countries. In April the company acquired a small Italian firm that had been family owned and operated for more than 20 years. The Italian management had reacted strongly and negatively to the new parent company's plan to revamp the Italian firm's accounting system in order to bring it in line with that of the other Autoparts affiliates.

The Two Systems

Six years before the Italian acquisition, Autoparts implemented a complex, standardized internal reporting system for all its subsidiaries. A major objective of the system was to provide headquarters with directly comparable accounting information in a precise and timely fashion. Headquarters believed that such a system was necessary to facilitate the aggregation and disaggregation of financial data for reporting to its many constituencies and for internal management decision making.Headquarters also believed that the sophisticated system forced managers to plan better, think in terms of the United States impact of their operations, and maintain better control over their operations. All reports were to be prepared by the affiliates in English, in dollars, and according to U.S. generally accepted accounting principles (GAAP). Thirty basic items related to the income statement were due at headquarters by noon on the first Monday of each month, and 40 data items related to the balance sheet were due at headquarters on the following Wednesday. More extensive data were due quarterly, including trial balances with more than 1000 lines of data and narrative comments. Complete data were due at year end, along with extensive comments regarding performance in local currency, dollars, and comparisons to budgets and plans.

The Italian firm's existing accounting staff did not measure up to that of Autoparts, to put it mildly. The former owner had required only sporadic internal reports and had made even fewer external reports. The Italian accounting staff consisted of eight people, only two of whom had much formal accounting background, and none of whom spoke English or had any understanding of U.S. GAAP.

Resistance to the New System

The Italian staff believed that the proposed reporting requirements were burdensome, and neither necessary nor feasible. They had gotten along without them for years, and—more to the point—they were not capable of preparing the reports according to Autoparts' requirements. Furthermore, because they were not accustomed to such procedures, complying with the strict deadlines and rules would pose significant difficulties and hardships on them. They also argued that much of the data required by headquarters was of little value to the subsidiary and of no value to the accounting reports they were required to prepare by Italian law. They were also concerned that the Italian government, and particularly the tax authorities, might question them on why the reports submitted to Autoparts' headquarters would show significantly different results from those submitted in Italy.

Questions

1. Is the Autoparts' system of standardized reporting an intelligent one? What considerations support it and argue against it?
2. Is the Autoparts' policy of no exceptions, no excuses a logical one? What factors argue for this policy and against it?
3. Based on your answers to Questions 1 and 2, should the Italian subsidiary be forced to adopt the Autoparts system as is, with modifications, or not at all?

Case 2

NIESSEN APPAREL, INC.

Juan Valencia was upset. As general manager of the Niessen Apparel Peruvian assembly plant, he believed that his performance over the past two years was not being fairly evaluated. He had recently sent a memo to parent company headquarters itemizing his complaints and asking for an immediate response. Charles Niessen, the president of the company, asked his son Chuck to review the matter and report back to him immediately because he did not want to risk losing Valencia (who had threatened to quit).

Background

Niessen Apparel was a medium-size U.S. manufacturer of women's and children's clothing. Because of rising domestic production costs, Niessen had investigated the possibilities of sewing the garments outside the United States, after which they would be shipped back and sold in the United States. In this manner, they could lower overall production costs and be in a better position to compete with both domestic and imported products. This could be achieved by utilizing cheaper labor in a developing country for the most labor-intensive parts of the production process—assembly—and taking advantage of Section 807 of the U.S. Tariff Code. This section allowed U.S. companies to export components to a foreign operation, then import the finished products, paying duty only on the value added outside the United States rather than on the full value of the product. Thus, a product imported from a Peruvian Section 807 operation would have a smaller tariff than one imported from a strictly Peruvian company. This, of course, would give a U.S. company an advantage over a foreign company *not* owned by a U.S. corporation. For example, a product costing $100 imported from Peru might have a tariff of $20 levied against it (20% of its value). However, if the product had $50 worth of U.S. components in its value, then under Section 807 the U.S. tariff would be $10 (20% of the value added outside the United States). Thus the full Section 807 import price would be $110, compared with the $120 import price of the non-Section 807 import.

The Method of Performance Evaluation

In order to justify the Peruvian sewing plant, Niessen believed that it should be evaluated as a profit center. This would allow the operation's profitability to be compared to the next best alternative use of funds. Valencia was to be responsible for the profitability of the Peruvian operations and was to be evaluated and rewarded on that basis. In addition, Niessen believed that the subsidiary's performance should be evaluated in terms of U.S. dollars rather than local Peruvian currency, since its value to him and his company was its contribution to U.S. earning power.

Problems with the Operations and Systems

Initially, a transfer pricing system was established on an arm's-length basis for all intercompany shipments. This was consistent with the profit center concept in that any other method would result in artificial profits. However, over the past two years the transfer prices on components shipped to Peru had been increased and the transfer prices on finished goods shipped back to the United States had been decreased. These changes were made so as to take better advantage of Section 807 (pay less import duty) by increasing the U.S. content and decreasing the foreign value added of the finished product. This change in strategy was considered desirable by the U.S. marketing people, who wanted to sell more competitively in the United States, and by the treasurer, who wanted to save on import duties. In order to avoid problems with U.S. and Peruvian government agencies, the transfer prices had been adjusted gradually but steadily each month. Helping to conceal this procedure was the continued decline of the Peruvian currency relative to the U.S. dollar. This, in itself, increased Peruvian import (purchasing) costs while lowering U.S. import prices (costs).

Although the effects of the new transfer prices and currency values worked out very well for the U.S. marketing manager (whose profits increased significantly), just the opposite occurred for Sr. Valencia. The performance evaluation of its subsidiary's operations deteriorated to the point at which one member of the U.S. staff who was unaware of what had been going on suggested that Valencia be fired or the Peruvian operation be terminated. In addition, Valencia's annual salary bonus had virtually disappeared because it was based largely on his subsidiary's profit performance. To make matters worse, slower than anticipated U.S. sales growth had caused a cutback in shipments to and from Peru, idling much of the Peruvian capacity. And because the Peruvian subsidiary sold only to the U.S. parent, it could not use its surplus production capacity, causing its costs to rise further and its profits to decrease further.

Questions

1. What were the strengths and weaknesses of Niessen Apparel's original method of performance evaluation?
2. What factors should Niessen consider in deciding whether to change the company's method of performance evaluation?
3. Should the old evaluation method be changed for the Peruvian operation? If so, why and how?

Case 3

AT WHAT COST?

Uplift International, Ltd., which manufactures forklifts, is a multinational based in the United Kingdom. The forklift engines are designed and manufactured in its Manchester plant and then shipped to subsidiaries in Brazil and Canada where the forklift bodies are made. These subsidiaries, in turn, sell the finished forklifts worldwide. In 1980 Uplift introduced a line of forklifts featuring a new engine, on which it had spent several years and millions of dollars to develop.

In an attempt to spread out and recapture the research and development costs of the new engine, Uplift had increased the transfer price of the engines sold to its Brazilian and Canadian subsidiaries. In both cases, however, it had encountered problems with government agencies.

First of all, the Brazilian government had stated that the new transfer price included, in effect, a hidden royalty payment from the subsidiary to the parent. Such payments were illegal by Brazilian law and hence the new transfer price was unacceptable. The Canadian Inland Revenue department also was unhappy with the new transfer price because it would result in higher expenses and lower taxes for the Canadian affiliate. This effect had also not gone unnoticed by the Brazilian government. Both governments were also concerned about the headquarters overhead allocation component in the transfer price. In their eyes, the parent had little justification for charging the subsidiaries for overhead, which they did not really benefit from.

In 1981 Uplift lowered its transfer prices on engines shipped to Brazil (eliminating the R&D allocation) in order to comply with the Brazilian government's ruling. At that point, the Canadian, British, and Brazilian governments all became upset. The Canadians felt that if the Brazilian subsidiary was not going to be charged for research and development, then the Canadian subsidiary should not be charged either. The British government was upset because it felt that Uplift should have been collecting R&D fees from its subsidiaries (which were obviously benefiting from it). Furthermore, by not collecting R&D fees, Uplift was shifting taxable income out of the United Kingdom and into Brazil. Meanwhile, the Brazilian customs authority had become upset because, as a result of the lower transfer prices, it was receiving less duty (tariffs) than before.

In sum, Uplift seemed to be in a position in which it could not please anyone.

Questions

1. Was Uplift justified in attempting to allocate to its subsidiaries, through increased transfer prices, the development costs of the new engines? Would it be justified in allocating to its subsidiaries research and development costs of projects that ultimately did not result in any commercial application by the company?
2. If a company is justified in allocating overhead, R&D, and other similar expenses to its affiliates, what would be the most equitable method of doing so?
3. In situations in which some countries will not allow subsidiaries to pay the parents for such allocations, how should a parent handle these "debts"? How should it handle the complaints of the other governments, such as those of Canada in this specific case, which do allow the allocation but object to the nonuniform pricing policies?
4. In the case of Uplift International Ltd., what can it do to resolve the intra-Brazilian government conflict between the tax and customs authorities?

Case 4
ALTOGETHER INC.

Altogether Inc, is a U.S.-based MNE with production facilities in the United States, Germany, and France. Its chief cost accountant, Diane Vacaro, has been given the responsibility for estimating the cost of Altogether's product for the coming year. This product consists of three components, each capable of being produced in all three countries, but the final product is assembled by Altogether in the United States for sale in the U.S. market. Listed below are the components' current costs in each country, when the current exchange rates are $1 = 8 French francs (ff) and $1 = 2 deutsche marks (DM). Assume no transportation cost or other costs are involved.

	United States ($)	France (ff)	Germany (DM)
Part A	6.00	48	10
Part B	8.00	96	16
Part C	20.00	176	36

Questions

1. With no change in exchange rates, what is the lowest obtainable total cost, and which subcomponents should be obtained from which countries?
2. How would a potential 50% increase in the deutsche mark against the dollar affect your answer to Question 1?
3. How would a potential 50% decline in the French franc against the dollar affect your answer to Question 1?
4. If both the deutsche mark and French franc move in these directions, what is your answer?
5. What is the highest total cost possibility Diane should project for the final product if any, all, or none of the exchange rate changes listed above occur?

Bibliography

AlHashim, Dhia. "Internal Performance Evaluation in American Multinational Enterprises." *Management International Review*, Third Quarter 1980, pp. 33–39.

Arpan, Jeffrey S. *International Intracorporate Pricing: Non-American Systems and Views* (New York: Praeger, 1972).

Arpan, Jeffrey S. "Multinational Firm Pricing in International Markets." *Sloane Management Review*, Winter 1972–1973.

Barrett, M. Edgar. "Case of the Tangled Transfer Price," *Harvard Business Review*, May–June 1977, pp. 20–28, 32, 36, 176, 178.

Bursk, Edward C., et al., *Financial Control of Multinational Corporations* (New York: Financial Executives Research Foundation, 1971).

Choi, Frederick D. S. "Multinational Challenges for Managerial Accountants." *Journal of Contemporary Business*, Autumn 1975, pp. 51–68.

Choi, Frederick D. S. and Gerhard G. Mueller. *An Introduction to Multinational Accounting* (Englewood Cliffs, N.J.: Prentice-Hall, 1978), Chapter 8.

Davis, Gordon B. *Management Information Systems: Conceptual Foundations, Structure, and Development* (New York: McGraw-Hill, 1974), pp. 403–409.

Dickie, Paul M. and Niranjan S. Arya. "MIS and International Business." *Journal of Systems Management*, June 1970, pp. 8–12.

Duerr, Michael G. and John M. Roach. *Organization and Control of International Operations* (New York: Conference Board, 1973).

Fantl, Irvin L. "Control and the Internal Audit in the Multinational Firm." *International Journal of Accounting*, Fall 1975, pp. 57–65.

Farag, Shawki M. "The Problem of Performance Evaluation in International Accounting." *International Journal of Accounting*, Fall 1974, pp. 45–54.

Gorab, Robert S. "Effective Management Controls and Reporting Policies for the Multinational Company." *Selected Papers 1970*, Haskins & Sells, pp. 399–400.

Greene, James. "Intercompany Pricing Across National Frontiers." *Conference Board Record*, October 1969.

Greene, James and Michael G. Duerr. *Intercompany Transactions in the Multinational Firm* (New York: Conference Board, 1970).

Hawkins, David F. "Controlling Foreign Operations." *Financial Executive*, February 1965, pp. 25–56.

Keegan, W. J. "Multinational Pricing: How Far Is Arm's-Length?" *Columbia Journal of World Business*, May–June 1969, pp. 57–66.

Knortz, Herbert C. "Controllership in International Corporations." *Financial Executive*, June 1969, pp. 54–60.

Mauriel, John J. "Evaluation and Control of Overseas Operations." *Management Accounting* (U.S.), May 1969, pp. 35–38.

McInnes, J. M. "Financial Control Systems for Multinational Operations: An Empirical Investigation." *Journal of International Business Studies*, Fall 1971, pp. 11–28.

Milburn, Alex J. "International Transfer Transactions: What Price?" *CA Magazine* (Canada), December 1976, pp. 22–27.

Moore, Russell M. and George M. Scott, Eds. *Introduction to Financial Control and Reporting in Multinational Enterprises* (Austin: Bureau of Business Research, University of Texas Press 1973), pp. 52–57.

Morsicato, Helen. *Currency Translation and Performance Evaluation in Multinationals* (Ann Arbor, Mich.: UMI Research Press, 1980).

Murray, J. Alex. "Intelligence Systems of the MNCs." *Columbia Journal of World Business*, September–October 1972, pp. 63–71.

National Association of Accountants *Management Accounting for Multinational Corporations*, Vols. I and II (New York: NAA, 1974). A collection of selected readings, several of which address the subject of Chapter 8.

Obersteiner, Erich. "The Management of Liquid Fund Flow Across National Boundaries." *International Journal of Accounting*, Spring 1976, pp. 91–101.

"Report of the Committee on International Accounting." *Accounting Review*, Supplements to Vols. 48 and 49, 1973 and 1974, pp. 120–167 and 250–269.

Ricks, David A, *International Dimensions of Corporate Finance* (Englewood Cliffs, N.J.: Prentice-Hall, 1978), pp. 57–70.

Robbins, Sidney M. and Robert B. Stobaugh. "The Bent Measuring Stick of Foreign Subsidiaries." *Harvard Business Review*, September–October 1973.

Rutenberg, D. "Maneuvering Liquid Assets in a Multinational Company: Formulation and Deterministic Solution Procedures." *Management Science*, June 1970, pp. 671–685.

Scott, George M. "Financial Control in Multinational Enterprise—The New Challenge to Accountants." *International Journal of Accounting*, Spring 1972, pp. 55–68.

Scott, George M. "Information Systems and Coordination in Multinational Enterprises." *International Journal of Accounting Education and Research*, February 1974, p. 87.

Shulman, J. S. "Transfer Pricing in the Multinational Firm." *European Business*, January 1969, pp. 46–54.

Solving International Pricing Problems. (New York: Business International, 1965).

Watt, George C., Richard M. Hammer, and Marianne Burge. *Accounting for the Multinational Corporation* (New York: Financial Executives Research Foundation, 1977).

White, John D. "Multinationals in Latin America: An Accent on Control." *Management Accounting* (U.S.), February 1977, pp. 49–51.

Woo, John C. H. "Management Control Systems for International Operations." *Tempo* (Touche Ross), Summer–Fall 1970, p. 39.

Zenoff, David B. "Profitable, Fast Growing, but Still the Stepchild." *Columbia Journal of World Business*, July–August 1967, pp. 51–56.

Zenoff, David B. and Jack Zwick. *International Financial Management* (Englewood Cliffs, N.J.: Prentice-Hall, 1969), Chapter 12.

CHAPTER 9

Internal and External Audits Worldwide

Published financial statements serve a variety of purposes for investors, creditors, regulators, and planners. How do we know whether these statements accurately reflect what is going on in the business? Remember that financial statements are prepared by managers, and managers have a vested interest in the statements. Could managers massage the figures a little to make them look better than they are (or worse, if the reader is a tax authority)?

And what of the accountability for assets? Top managers want to be sure that the firm's assets are safeguarded at all levels and used properly in the generation of profits. At the same time, investors want to be sure that top managers practice what they preach by using assets properly as well. In the aftermath of Watergate, thousands of stories told how managers at all levels laundered cash and falsified books and records in order to bribe foreign government officials.

How do we solve these twin problems of internal controls and external reliability? The answer lies in an adequate system of internal controls, including internal auditors and independent, highly qualified external auditors. This chapter looks at internal control systems of multinational enterprises, compares and contrasts external auditing worldwide, and shows how the large public accounting firms are organized to perform the external audit of a multinational enterprise.

THE INTERNAL AUDIT

All large corporations are concerned that employees operate in a way that is consistent with corporate policy. Corporate policy and procedures in all areas of the business—personnel, marketing, and production as well as accounting—are normally communicated to personnel through codes of conduct and procedures manuals. A good control system starts with these codes of conduct and standard operating procedures, but the firm needs to determine whether these codes and procedures are being followed. The internal audit function is one of the cornerstones in determining compliance.

To demonstrate how the internal audit function works, let's look at IBM. The director of internal audit reports to the treasurer of IBM, and he is responsible for a team of auditors that operates worldwide. In addition to an audit team responsible for IBM in the United States, two other audit teams are responsible for IBM World Trade Americas/Far East (A/FE) and IBM World Trade Europe/Middle East/Africa (A/ME/A). The team responsible for auditing E/ME/A operations must cover 85 countries, which represented 28% of IBM's gross revenues in 1983. A/FE's team covers 46 countries, including Australia, Brazil, Canada, and Japan, and its countries generated 14% of IBM's gross revenues in 1983.

There are six major responsibilities assigned to IBM's internal audit team:

> . . . provide all management levels with an objective review of operations; review compliance with company policies and procedures; evaluate adequacy of the system of internal control and protection of assets; determine if the reporting system provides management with reliable and timely information; be alert to possibilities of fraud, bribes, political contributions, and other illegal transactions; and report findings to management and recommend corrective action.[1]

Problems of the Internal Auditor in a Foreign Operating Environment

Although the responsibilities are the same for international and domestic operations, there are some unique problems in the foreign environment that must be dealt with as described in the following sections.

Among the environmental considerations are local accounting practices, foreign currency, local legal and business practices, language and customs, and distance. Although most large companies attempt to standardize their accounting practice worldwide, it does not happen everywhere. Local records may be kept according to local accounting procedures, which makes it difficult to use a standardized audit package. Also, the infrequency of audits (because of distance) may mean that there are insufficient accounting data to provide a clear audit trail.[2]

Adapting to Local Business Practices and Customs

The local business practices and customs can also create problems. For example, expenses may be paid by cash rather than check, making cash control difficult. This is especially true in developing countries where checks are not widely used. The following example illustrates the problems of conducting a test of accounts receivable in a foreign location:

[1] "Corporate Auditing in IBM," a pamphlet published by IBM in Armonk, New York.
[2] Marikay Lee, "The International Auditor," *Internal Auditor*, December 1978, p. 45.

Accounts receivable confirmations are one example of how an international auditor must adjust or revamp auditing procedures. In most cases, the confirmation letter itself must be translated into another language. Relying on the customer to return the confirmation is another problem because foreign customers lack experience with confirmations. It may not be the custom for local auditors to send confirmations for accounts receivable or even to confirm year-end bank balances. The mail service may also be inefficient and unreliable, and it may take weeks before the confirmation letter is received by the customer— if the customer receives it at all.

If the international auditor doesn't plan to be in a country long enough for the confirmations to be sent and returned, alternate auditing procedures must be implemented or alternate means of receiving the confirmations must be applied. For example, the international auditor may arrange to have the confirmations mailed to a local public accounting firm or other independent source which will forward them to the international auditor. However, if the international auditor continually travels to other international audit locations, this procedure is unsatisfactory.[3]

Japan provides a good example of some of the problems that arise in cash management. It is very common for the Japanese to use cash instead of checks for some transactions. To send cash in the mail, they use money envelopes carried in special pouches by the mail carrier. Larger businesses use checks, but banks will often provide only computerized lists of transactions rather than canceled checks. This makes it difficult to check the signature and authorization of actual checks during the audit.

Because of the interlocking nature of banks, many payments are made by bank transfers directly from one bank account to another. The only verification of the transfers is a computer printout. Some firms will use a variety of transfers to keep the government from verifying earnings for a tax base.

Foreign Currency

Foreign currency restrictions and transfers requirements should be known for each country in which the auditor works. In addition, the auditor needs to be aware of corporate procedure for translating financial statements and recording foreign currency transactions so that reports sent to the parent in dollars are prepared properly.

Language

Ignorance of the language can be a fatal handicap when the auditor deals with bilingual personnel. Having to rely on a translator may mean that the auditor is not getting the full story. In many countries, the financial statements must be kept in the local language and currency, so knowledge of the local language would be essential. Sometimes, knowing the language

[3]Ibid.

Table 9.1 Decision Variables for Selecting Internal Auditors

	Home-Based Auditor Visiting Other Countries	Local National Resident Auditor	Expatriate Resident Auditor
Initial investment	Language training	Six months' investment in training	Language training
	Air travel per nonpeak season trip	Salary Travel	Moving expense
Single, small audit location	Generally, not economically sound in any case; it would be better to request a management letter from the outside auditors		
Several small audit locations within same country	Generally sound, provided return engagements are anticipated	Generally not sound unless growth expectations in the short run indicate that the investment is warranted	
Several small audit locations scattered over several countries	Generally not sound; too much investment in languages	Generally sound if growth expectations in medium-range future warrant it	Generally not sound; too much investment in languages
Single, medium-size audit location	Generally sound for one man on an extended trip, provided return engagements are planned	Generally not sound unless growth expectations in the short run indicate that the investment is warranted	
Several medium-size audit locations within same country	Generally not sound; too much travel between countries with attendant weariness from travel through time zones or excessive investment in languages	Generally ideally suited to this type of set-up	Generally ideally suited to this type of set-up
Several medium-size audit locations scattered over several countries	ditto	ditto	Could be sound if not too many languages are involved; could also work well jointly with a foreign national

Table 9.1 *Continued*

	Home-Based Auditor Visiting Other Countries	Local National Resident Auditor	Expatriate Resident Auditor
Several large audit locations within same country or scattered over several countries	ditto	Ideal, provided not too many languages are involved	Ideal, provided not too many languages are involved

Source: Lee D. Tooman, "Starting the Internal Audit of Foreign Operations," *Internal Auditor,* November–December, 1975, p. 60. Copyright 1978 by the Institute of Internal Auditors, Inc. Reprinted by permission.

can be useful in getting information in touchy situations. In one situation, two internal auditors for the developing country subsidiary of a large multinational manufacturing company noticed that a purchasing agent was driving a relatively expensive car. Because the two auditors spoke the local language, they were able to go to the man's home and interview his father. They found out from the proud father that his son was so important to the company, he received a 5% commission on everything he bought for the firm. Needless to say, the purchasing agent did not last long in his position.

Distance

A final problem is distance. Far-flung operations are not audited as frequently or as thoroughly as the domestic operations, which makes the foreign audit even tougher. It is often impossible to conduct preaudit and postaudit visits, so most communication has to be by telephone, Telex, or mail. The previous example of confirming accounts receivables illustrates the difficulty of distance. When postaudit problems arise, it may be impossible to get an answer quickly or to communicate adequately. If too many people are sent to conduct an audit far from headquarters, a great deal of money could be wasted. If too few people are sent, the scope of the audit may be too narrow because of time constraints. Furthermore, distances often hinder flexibility in personnel.[4]

Alternatives to the Traveling Auditor

These comments refer primarily to a traveling auditor. However, there are other possibilities: a resident auditor who is a local national; a resident

[4]Ibid.

auditor who is an expatriàte from the headquarters country or is a third-country national (TCN)—that is, someone from a country other than the headquarters or local operation; or a traveling team of auditors. Local nationals obviously have an edge in knowledge of the language, culture, and business customs, but the expatriate is more familiar with headquarters procedures. The TCN can be a cross between the two but is still considered a foreigner in the host country. Table 9.1 summarizes the pros and cons of using traveling, local resident, and expatriate resident auditors.

Although it is possible to use domestic auditors on temporary assignment to perform internal audits, they tend to be more specialized than regular international internal auditors. The latter need to be generalists, with skills in operational as well as financial audits. Also, the need for language skills and cultural adaptability make it advisable to identify for language skills and cultural adaptability make it advisable to identify a cadre of international internal auditors where possible. The smaller multinationals tend to use home office auditors for foreign duties, but some larger firms are using regionally based auditors with greater frequency.

FOREIGN CORRUPT PRACTICES ACT

Whether influence is bought with baksheesh (Middle East), mordida (Mexico), dash (West Africa), or bustarella (Italy), it can be very costly indeed because of the Foreign Corrupt Practices Act (FCPA) of 1977. The SEC, in investigating Watergate and its aftermath, was astounded at the extent to which corporate executives and employees falsified books and records and circumvented internal control systems (where they existed) in order to make foreign bribes. The SEC response—the FCPA—is affecting the way companies operate abroad and account for and control those operations.

Bribery itself has been termed everything from extortion to just another part of the marketing mix in international business. The problem of the multinational is that it operates in a variety of countries with different business practices and laws and competes with companies from other countries that also have different sets of business laws and customs. Let's look at each one of these problems. The SEC investigations have highlighted a number of points. Bribes are usually paid because the receiver of the bribe (normally in the foreign country) has a strong market position or has control over an aspect of the environment that can have a strong impact on the firm's operations.

Reasons for Bribes

Bribes to Place or Receive an Order

If the recipients are purchasing agents, they are usually confronted with an array of salespersons competing for a substantial amount of business. The firms, one or all of them, may be so desperate for the contract that they offer the purchasing agent a fee for the sale. Conversely, the purchasing agent may sense an opportunity and base the choice from among equally good competitors on the highest fee that can be extracted. American Hospital Supply Corporation, for example, paid a 10% commission (totaling $4 million to $5 million from 1972 to 1975) to certain individuals before it could sell hospital equipment to the Royal Cabinet Office of Saudi Arabia for the new King Faisal Specialist Hospital.[5]

Bribes to Government Officials

Sometimes bribes are paid to government officials other than purchasing agents. In Mexico, for example, six tire companies paid $420,000 in bribes to an official so that they would be exempt from price controls.[6] Tax authorities are frequent recipients of bribes, especially in countries like Italy and Spain where taxes traditionally have been negotiable.

Political Contributions

There is a fine line between paying bribes to *influence* the political process and making contributions to *support* the political process. In the United States it is illegal for corporations to make political contributions, even though individuals can if they so desire. In many countries, it is not only legally permissible but expected that corporations will make contributions. Whose system should the multinational defer to?

Paving the Way

Another dimension of the political process involves what is euphemistically known as grease payments, those made to a government official to do something that should be done anyway. Some examples are to "expedite shipments through customs, or to speed processing of certain documents; secure required permits or licenses; or obtain adequate police protection."[7]

Extortion

A final dimension of making payments to the political system involves extortion. In 1970, Gulf Oil Company paid $3 million to the reelection campaign of former President Park of South Korea, and Gulf officials assert that they were told by a representative of President Park that Gulf's continued prosperity depended on their making the payment.[8]

---

[5]Lee H. Radebaugh, "International Corporate Bribery: A New Dimension in Accounting," *The Multinational Corporation: Accounting and Social Implications* (Urbana, Ill.: Center for International Accounting, 1977), p. 22.
[6]Ibid., p. 23.
[7]Ernst & Whinney, "Foreign Corrupt Practices Act of 1977," Retrieval No. 38748, February 1978, p. 5.
[8]Radebaugh, "Bribery," p. 23.

These illustrations show that payments are made to get an edge on competitors, to cause government officials to bend or ignore laws, to grease normal channels, to support the political process, and to try to ensure the ability to continue operating. Sometimes the payments are made in countries where such shenanigans are accepted business practice, and sometimes they are made in countries where the payments are illegal. Sometimes they are initiated by the company and sometimes by the recipient.

An added complication is that payments could be made without head-quarters approval. It is virtually impossible to do business in many Middle Eastern countries except through a local agent. If a fee is paid to the agent to expedite business, who is to say what the fee is used for? Similarly, a local subsidiary, staffed by local nationals attuned to their environment, may play the payments game like everyone else.

Impact of FCPA on U.S. Firms

In a poll conducted of 1200 large U.S. corporations by Louis Harris & Associates Inc. for *Business Week*, a number of interesting things were found. Although 78% of the executives felt that the FCPA makes it difficult to sell in countries where bribery is a way of life, 55% felt that unless the law was tough, small grease payments would turn into major bribes of government officials. Indeed, the law is tough, with penalties including a fine of up to $1 million for a company and up to $10,000 and five years in prison for an individual convicted of being in violation of the FCPA.

Most of the criticisms of the law involve its complexity and its interpretation. Sixty-eight percent of the respondents favor reducing the detailed record-keeping provisions of the law, which will be discussed in more detail below. Also, 64% favor making the law more specific as to who in the foreign country can legally receive payments designed to facilitate business transactions.[9]

Accounting Implications

Clearly, bribery is illegal and could have an impact on the way some firms market their goods and services in certain countries. But what does that have to do with accounting and internal auditing? Remember that a good control system is designed to safeguard corporate assets and that the internal auditor is responsible for testing compliance with the system. During its investigation of foreign bribes, the SEC found that firms were falsifying records in order to disguise improper transactions, were failing to disclose the true purpose of some transactions, and were simply not recording some transactions. In the first case, firms would either overstate revenues or expenses to hide bribes or report fictitious transactions. In the case of

[9]"The Antibribery Act Splits Executives," *Business Week*, 9 September 1983, p. 16.

American Hospital Supply, the sales price of the equipment was increased enough to cover the amount of the kickback to the Saudi government purchasing agent, and the agent was then paid a "consulting" fee.

The case of failing to disclose the purpose of transactions usually refers to payments made to agents and distributors for unspecified purposes. This is often referred to as the quality of the disclosure. The entry has been made, but what does it mean? The final point mentioned above is the total failure to report transactions. For example, Braniff Airways sold 3626 tickets in Latin America for $900,000, did not record the sales, and kept the cash proceeds in a bank account that was not part of the regular financial statements.

There are two accounting implications of these cases. First, books and records were not being kept properly, so financial statements did not accurately reflect underlying transactions. Second, firms were encouraging the corrupt practices or had such a poor control system that the practices were going on in spite of corporate policy to the contrary. As a result, the FCPA added two other provisions to the one on bribery: one dealing with record keeping and the other with internal controls. The record-keeping provisions are to "make and keep books, records, and accounts, which, in reasonable detail, accurately and fairly reflect the transactions and dispositions of the assets of the issuer." In other words, if you are going to bribe someone, be sure you record and disclose it accurately—debit bribery expense and credit cash. Of course, the Justice Department will throw you in jail for making the payoff in the first place, but, if it is any consolation, the SEC will give you high marks for disclosure.

The second accounting implication relates to internal accounting controls. According to this provision, each firm is to

> devise and maintain a system of internal accounting controls sufficient to provide reasonable assurances that (i) transactions are executed in accordance with management's general or specific authorization; (ii) transactions are recorded as necessary (1) to permit preparation of financial statements in conformity with generally accepted accounting principles or any other criteria applicable to such statements, and (2) to maintain accountability for assets; (iii) access to assets is permitted only in accordance with management's general or specific authorization; and (iv) the recorded accountability for assets is compared with the existing assets at reasonable intervals and appropriate action is taken with respect to any differences.[10]

It has always been assumed that management would require good records to be kept and would design and implement an adequate internal control system. However, this is the first time that violation of these principles could lead to civil liability and criminal prosecution. In addition, the accounting provisions of the FCPA may be violated even though no foreign bribes are paid. Most firms did not realize this when the law went into

[10]Public Law 95-213, Paragraph 102.

effect, but the government has legislated accounting procedures in an area into which they had never before ventured. As a result, firms are paying much closer attention to the design and implementation of their control systems.

Compliance with the FCPA

In order to comply with the FCPA, a firm needs strong support from four levels: management, the internal auditors, the external auditors, and the board of directors. Top management needs to set the proper atmosphere for compliance with the FCPA by agreeing to abide by its provisions, formulating a written policy, communicating that policy to employees, and making sure the policy is understood and adhered to.

The internal audit staff is concerned about much more than the FCPA, and a cost-benefit analysis would preclude adding enough auditors to eliminate all risk of noncompliance. However, a number of things can be done by the auditor. In a study on what internal auditors are doing to evaluate their company's internal control system, it was found that the following standard methods were used, in order of frequency: written audit programs, compliance testing, statistical sampling techniques, internal control questionnaires, and flowcharts. As a result of the FCPA, more firms are increasing their emphasis on flowcharts, which are useful in documenting procedures and providing an overview of the entire control system.[11]

The role of the external auditor is discussed in more detail later, but it is appropriate to look at this role in relation to the FCPA now. There is the feeling on the part of the general public that independent auditors should be able to detect fraud and noncompliance with the FCPA. However, generally accepted auditing standards as developed by the AICPA call for an examination of the books and records to determine problems that may have a material effect on the financial statements. Although the auditors are always keeping an eye out for questionable or illegal acts, they are concerned with those having a material effect, whereas the FCPA is concerned with those leading to any effect. This creates some obvious problems.

Given this background, what is an auditor to do? The steps outlined for the internal auditor earlier are similar to those followed by the external auditor. Greater attention must be paid to the types of transactions and geographical areas where there is a high probability of illegal acts. This is why a general and specific risk analysis is so critical. As pointed out by one auditor, "specific skepticism naturally focuses on companies that have large sales to foreign governments, significant operations or sales in countries with traditionally relaxed commercial standards, or companies that

---

[11]Corine T. Norgaard and Robert W. Granow, "Internal Auditing's Response to the Foreign Corrupt Practices Act," *Internal Auditor*, December 1979, p. 60.

are subject to capricious governmental regulation, which can create a strong temptation to lubricate the wheels with a bit of grease."[12]

The final group directly concerned and able to affect the internal control system as it relates to the FCPA is the board of directors. It is up to management to design and implement an action plan in relation to the FCPA, but it is up to the board to monitor the timeliness and execution of the plan.

THE EXTERNAL AUDIT

The growth of national and international capital markets has turned the spotlight on the auditor as an important credibility link between the corporation and the investor-creditor. Outsiders are interested in an objective, independent view on the financial statements of a firm. National corporations—especially in countries where the auditing profession has not achieved an international reputation—are turning increasingly to multinational public accounting firms to certify their financial statements in order to attract international investors. The use of international auditors emphasizes that auditing standards and practices, like accounting standards and practices, vary considerably from country to country. Let's consider some of the differences, especially in the requirements and standards for audits and qualifications of auditors, and look at the process of harmonization.

Guideline Sources and Requirements

The development of auditing standards is a complex interrelationship of cultural, legal-political, and economic variables in a given country, so one would not expect total uniformity. Auditing standards come from the public (government) sector, the private sector, or a combination of the two. The first source of influence is prevalent in developing countries where the accounting profession is not well organized or sufficiently strong. The government often takes the lead by incorporating audit requirements and, to a lesser extent, standards into law. This thrust is also evident in industrial countries such as Germany, which is legalistic and prescriptive and whose auditing profession has been established and regulated by law historically. The German situation is interesting because the profession makes recommendations on audit standards that are then incorporated into law by the government.

This approach can be contrasted with that of the United States, where the SEC requires that an audit be conducted but does not say how. This is left to the accounting profession through auditing standards developed by

---

[12]Walter E. Hanson, "A Blueprint for Ethical Conduct," *Journal of Accountancy*, June 1978, p. 82.

the AICPA. A similar approach is followed in the United Kingdom and Canada. The audit profession originated in Britain, yet in that country it is only now developing generally accepted auditing standards issued and approved by the profession.

There are wide differences in requirements for audits. In the United States, annual independent audits are required of firms listed on national securities exchanges and of firms with more than 500 shareholders and assets of more than $1 million whose securities are traded over the counter. However, most other large companies have audits, and many banks and regulatory agencies require them. Similarly, in Japan all of the companies traded on the Japanese stock exchanges are required by law to be audited by a Japanese CPA or audit corporation.[13]

In Germany, the requirement for an audit is more extensive than it would be in the United States. All stock corporations (known as AG) are required to be audited. In addition, other companies that meet two of the following three criteria for three consecutive years must also be audited: (1) total annual sales in excess of DM250 million, (2) total assets in excess of DM125 million, and (3) average number of employees more than 5000. The balance sheet and income statement are the only two financial statements subject to an audit.[14]

Differences in Audit Standards

Just because a large number of countries require an audit does not mean that all audits are done the same way.

Financial statements come from the books and records of the firms, which reflect the underlying transactions that the firm engages in. The term *audit* could mean that the financial statements accurately reflect the books and records of the firm. The audit would entail tracing the data from the books and records to the financial statements, a relatively simple process. The auditor would rely primarily on the honesty of management and would not be as concerned as his or her counterpart in the United States or Britain with confirming inventory taking or bank balances.

A more extensive audit would see whether the books and records accurately reflect the original transactions. This would involve a more extensive investigation of the internal control system to make sure that corporate procedures for recording transactions are clearly established, communicated, and followed. It would also involve more extensive tests of original transactions and how they eventually flow through the records to the financial statements. In Britain, for example, it is regarded as normal practice for the auditor to be present at inventory taking. Similarly, ac-

---

[13]Thomas S. Watson, "Accounting in Japan: Regulation and Practice," *Journal of Accountancy*, August 1982, p. 85.

[14]Arlene G. Wenig and Godehard H. Puckler, "Public Accounting in West Germany: An Overview," *Journal of Accountancy*, April 1982, p. 84.

counts receivable are normally confirmed as a test of internal controls over sales.[15] In many countries, the required standards for field work may be less than what is carried out in practice. In Sweden, for example, there are no provisions for confirming accounts receivable, but most auditors do so. The observation of inventory taking is common practice, even though it is not required.[16]

There are many reasons why audit standards vary from country to country. In the United States and United Kingdom there are broadly based capital markets and highly qualified, highly thought-of accounting professions. The capital markets require that financial statements be independently verified, and the profession has developed and refined audit standards over time. The air of skepticism has encouraged fairly rigid tests. Culture often plays a part as well. In Japan, it is said that bank deposits and loans payable are obtained from the company rather than by independent confirmation because independent confirmation would show too much distrust in company personnel, which could mean a loss in face.

In other cases, prevailing business practices also affect audit standards. Until recently, it was difficult for nonresident auditors to confirm bank balances in Germany. German bankers have said that the reason for the reluctance was that they provide information for customers daily, which makes year-end confirmations unnecessary. Also, until recently German audit practices did not require confirmations of bank balances, which gave weight to the banks' belief that such practice was unnecessary. In spite of this, German banks routinely provided bank confirmation to local auditors, even though they would not do so for foreign auditors.[17] Is the problem one of business practices or distrust of foreigners—a cultural problem?

Audit Opinions

As will be discussed in more detail later, the International Federation of Accountants (IFAC) was organized in Munich in October 1977 to address the issues of the accounting profession. The International Auditing Practices Committee of IFAC was established to propose international auditing guidelines for the profession worldwide. International Auditing Guideline No. 13, "The Auditor's Report on Financial Statements," identifies a number of key items that should be included in a good audit report. The basic elements of the auditor's report are as follows:

1. Title.
2. Addressee—for whom the report is issued.

---

[15]American Institute of Certified Public Accountants, *Professional Accounting in 30 Countries* (New York: AICPA, 1975), p. 608.
[16]Ibid., p. 553.
[17]Michael Harding, "Problems of Obtaining Bank Confirmations in Germany," *Accountancy*, August 1977, p. 88.

3. Identification of the financial statements audited.

4. A reference to the auditing standards or practices followed.

5. An expression or disclaimer of opinion on the financial statements.

6. Signature.

7. The auditor's address.

8. The date of the report.[18]

It is interesting to note how different the audit opinions are in annual reports from different countries. It is also important to note that audit opinions for financial statements prepared for international capital markets are very similar, whatever the country of origin of the company issuing the financial statements. These latter opinions are more in harmony with the suggestions of Guideline No. 13.

The following audit report by Deloitte Haskins & Sells concerning the General Motors 1983 Annual Report is fairly typical of what one would expect to find in a U.S. audit report. Notice that it contains all eight of the elements recommended in Guideline No. 13.

ACCOUNTANTS' REPORT

Deloitte   1114 Avenue of the Americas
Haskins+Sells   New York, New York 10036
CERTIFIED PUBLIC ACCOUNTANTS
                                                      February 6, 1984
General Motors Corporation, its Directors and Stockholders:

We have examined the Consolidated Balance Sheet of General Motors Corporation and consolidated subsidiaries as of December 31, 1983 and 1982 and the related Statements of Consolidated Income and Changes in Consolidated Financial Position for each of the three years in the period ended December 31, 1983. Our examinations were made in accordance with generally accepted auditing standards and, accordingly, included such tests of the accounting records and such other auditing procedures as we considered necessary in the circumstances.

In our opinion, these financial statements present fairly the financial position of the companies at December 31, 1983 and 1982 and the results of their operations and the changes in their financial position for each of the three years in the period ended December 31, 1983, in conformity with generally accepted accounting principles consistently applied during the period except for the change in 1983, with which we

---

[18]International Federation of Accountants, *International Auditing Guideline No. 13: The Auditor's Report on Financial Statements* (New York: IFAC, October 1983) paragraph 3.

concur, in the method of accounting for foreign currency translation as described in Note 1 to the Financial Statements.

Deloitte, Haskins & Sells

Contrast the report by Deloitte Haskins & Sells with the typical German short-form audit report. The report is for Steag A.G., a German energy company similar to a utility.

According to our audit, made in conformity with our professional standards, the consolidated financial statements and the related report of the Board of Management comply with German law.

Düsseldorf, April 22, 1977

Treuarbeit
Aktiengesellschaft
Wirtschaftsprüfungsgesellschaft
Steuerberatungsgesellschaft

Dr. Jordan   ppa. Baumeister
Wirtschaftsprüfer   Wirtschaftsprüfer

Notice the reference here to German law rather than generally accepted accounting principles. The German law that sets forth accounting principles is extremely detailed, which implies that the financial statements do adhere to principles and standards. However, there is no mention of whether or not the financial statements present fairly or present a true and fair view of the operations of the firm. German auditing standards are developed by the private-sector Institute of Auditors. They are only valid, however, if included in German law, thus ensuring the cooperation of public and private sector.

The next report is from a Swedish firm, the Swedish Match Company. The report includes most of the information recommended in Guideline No. 13. As is the case with the German short-form report, the Swedish report refers to law as the source of generally accepted accounting standards and does not refer to a true and fair view. It is interesting to note that the report makes reference to the appropriation of earnings and the fact that the board of directors and president of the company should be discharged from their responsibilities.

AUDITORS' REPORT

We have examined the Annual Report and the consolidated financial statements, the accounting records and the administration by the Board of Directors and the President for the year 1982, in accordance with generally accepted auditing standards.

Parent Company

The Annual Report has been prepared in accordance with the requirements of the Swedish Companies Act.
  We recommend
that the Company's Income Statement
    and Balance Sheet be adopted,
that the unappropriated earnings be
    dealt with in accordance with the
    proposal in the Directors' Report,
    and
that the Board of Directors and the President be discharged from responsibilitiy for their administration in respect of the year 1982.

Consolidated Financial Statements

The consolidated financial statements have been prepared in accordance with the requirements of the Swedish Companies Act.

We recommend that the Consolidated Income Statement and the Consolidated Balance Sheet be adopted.

Stockholm, March 11, 1983

JÖRGEN ESKILSON   BERTIL E. OLSSON
Authorized Public Accountant   Authorized Public Accountant
Price Waterhouse HB   Bertil Olssons Revisionsbyrå AB

The following report by Klynveld Kraayehof & Co. on the 1982 financia statements of N. V. Philips, the Dutch electronics giant, is interesting because it makes no mention of generally accepted accounting principles. The report simply states that the statements present a true and fair view of the state of affairs of Philips. In addition, it does not make any reference to auditing standards or their source but merely states that the financial statements were audited.

AUDITORS' REPORT

We have audited the financial statements for the year 1982 of N. V. Philips' Gloeilampenfabrieken and of N. V. Gemeenschappelijk Bezit van Aandeelen Philips' Gloeilampenfabrieken.

In our opinion, the accompanying financial statements of N. V. Phillips' Gloeilampenfabrieken and of N. V. Gemeenschappelijk Bezit van Aandeelen Philips' Gloeilampenfabrieken give a true and fair view of the state of these companies' affairs at 31 December 1982 and of their results for the year 1982.

We have also audited the Combined Statements of Financial Position and of Results, which combine the consolidated financial statements for the year 1982 of N. V. Philips' Gloeilampenfabrieken and of the United States Philips Trust. As regards the consolidated financial statements of the United States Philips Trust we have relied on the report, dated 22 February 1983, of Messrs. Main Hurdman, Certified Public Accountants, New York.

In our opinion, based on our examination and on the aforementioned report of Messrs. Main Hurdman, the accompanying Combined Statements give a true and fair view of the combined state of affairs at 31 December 1982 and of the combined results for the year 1982.

Eindhoven, 9 March 1983   KLYNVELD KRAAYENHOF & CO.

The following audit report of the Royal Dutch/Shell group of companies contains the opinion of three auditors—the Dutch firm that audited Philips, the British partnership of Ernst & Whinney, and the U.S. partnership of Price Waterhouse. The audit report contains the information recommended in Guideline No. 13. The annual report itself gives a lot of information concerning the accounting policies pursued by the company.

REPORT OF THE AUDITORS

To Royal Dutch Petroleum Company and the "Shell" Transport and Trading Company, p.l.c.

We have examined the financial statements of the Royal Dutch/Shell Group of Companies for the years 1982, 1981 and 1980. Our examinations were made in accordance with generally accepted auditing standards and accordingly included such tests of the accounting records and such other auditing procedures as we considered necessary in the circumstances.

In our opinion, the financial statements appearing on pages 32 to 47 present fairly the financial position of the Royal Dutch/Shell Group of Companies at December 31, 1982 and 1981, and the results of operations and the source and use of funds for each of the three years in the period ended December 31, 1982, in conformity with the accounting policies described on pages 32 and 33 applied on a consistent basis after restatement for the change in the method of accounting for currency translation described in Note 1 to the financial statements.

Klynveld Kraayenhof & Co., The Hague

Ernst & Whinney, London

Price Waterhouse, New York

March 10, 1983

The audit report in the annual report of Imperial Chemical Industries PLC for 1982 makes reference to auditing standards but not generally accepted accounting principles. It mentions that the statements were prepared according to the historical cost convention and, more important, refers to a true and fair view of the state of affairs of the company.

AUDITORS' REPORT

To the Members of Imperial Chemical Industries PLC

We have audited the financial statements on pages 25 to 38 in accordance with approved auditing standards.

In our opinion the financial statements on pages 25 to 35, which have been prepared under the historical cost convention, give under that convention a true and fair view of the state of affairs of the company and the group at 31 December 1982 and of the results and source and application of funds of the group for the year then ended and comply with the Companies Acts 1948 to 1981.

In our opinion the supplementary current cost accounts for the year ended 31 December 1982 on pages 36 to 38 have been properly prepared, in accordance with the policies and methods described in the notes, to give the information required by Statement of Standard Accounting Practice No 16.

PRICE WATERHOUSE
THOMSON McLINTOCK & CO
Chartered Accountants

London 3 March 1983

It is interesting to compare the audit reports of these various companies with each other as well as with the standard suggested by Guideline No. 13 issued by the International Auditing Practices Committee of IFAC.

The Auditors Themselves

High audit standards are worthless if there are no auditors to implement them. Certification varies from country to country, and there may be different levels of certification in the same country. In Peru, anyone who has graduated in accounting from an accredited university receives a government license to conduct an audit. There are no experience or other special certification requirements. The situation is the same in Indonesia, except that an accountant must work with the government for three years before being allowed to practice publicly.

As noted above, requirements for auditors vary considerably from country to country, and the following additional countries offer interesting points of contrast and comparison: the United States, West Germany, the United Kingdom, Switzerland, France, Canada, and Japan.

The United States

In the United States, each state has its own requirements for certification, which combine a mixture of education, experience, and a common examination administered by the state but prepared by the Board of Examiners of the American Institute of Certified Public Accountants. In Utah, for example, an applicant is required to have a bachelor's degree in accounting in order to sit for the CPA exam and can be certified after having completed all parts of the exam. However, the individual cannot be licensed until after completing the experience requirement, which is two years with a bachelor's degree or one year with a master's degree. The common examination contains questions on auditing (3½ hours), accounting theory (3½ hours), accounting practice (two exams, 4½ hours each), and business law (3½ hours). The CPA exam is administered twice a year, and over 100,000 candidates sit for it during two sessions.

West Germany

Although the requirements in the United States are more rigid than those of Peru and Indonesia, they are not as rigid as those of West Germany. A wirtschaftsprüfer (WP) in West Germany, like his or her counterpart in the United States, must fulfill education and experience requirements and pass an examination to become certified. Normally, a candidate will be a college graduate in commerce, engineering, law, or economics. There is an experience requirement of six years, during which examinations are taken in accounting, business administration, law, ethics, and auditing. During this time when the experience requirements are being filled and examinations are being taken, most WP candidates qualify as tax advisers. Upon completion of the examinations and experience requirements, the candidate must write a thesis and pass a written and oral examination. It is very common for most WPs to attain their status after turning 30 years of age.[19]

The United Kingdom

The British profession is one of the most influential worldwide because of its influence on the U.S. profession as well as the professions in other countries where it had substantial colonial influence. The spread of British investment worldwide was followed by its accountants and their influence. Stamp and Moonitz estimate that there are approximately 70,000 British Chartered Accountants worldwide, of whom about 30,000 are engaged in

[19]Edward Stamp and Maurice Moonitz, *International Auditing Standards* (Englewood Cliffs, N.J.: Prentice-Hall International, 1978, p. 100.

public practice. In order to become certified, a candidate must work for a Chartered Accountant and pass a series of exams. Normally, a candidate will sign a three-year training contract with a Chartered Accountant firm after completing university level studies. Those studies may be in any subject, not necessarily accounting or business. In fact, one need not have a university-level degree to sign the training contract.

Once the candidate begins the experience portion of the preparation for certification, he or she is allowed ten weeks a year of paid study time to prepare for a series of three exams. The first examination, which is the foundation exam, may be waived depending on the educational experience of the candidate. The next two professional level exams must be taken by all candidates. After completion of the training contract and the successful passing of the examinations (which must be completed within five years of each other), the candidate becomes an Associate Chartered Accountant of the Institute of Chartered Accountants of England and Wales, which is the largest of the four institutes in the United Kingdom. The individual becomes a Fellow Chartered Accountant after five years of experience in the profession or ten years outside of public practice.[20] It is interesting to note the differences in education and experience requirements between the U.S. and British accountants. The training contract is much more like an apprenticeship than the work experience of the typical accountant in the United States. The lack of a specific accounting education requirement in the United Kingdom makes the training contract that much more significant.

Switzerland

In Switzerland nearly anyone, regardless of professional qualifications, can act as an auditor. A statutory audit, which certifies that the financial statements accurately reflect the books and records according to legal specifications, does not have to be done by a specialist, such as a CPA. The auditor cannot be a director or employee but may be a shareholder or have other financial interests in the company. An independent audit is required for firms beyond a certain size, and stricter auditing standards apply. However, even though more specialized knowledge and training are required of the auditor, certification is not.

France

In France, a statutory examiner is required to examine the financial statements of corporations annually. The statutory examiner has to have a diploma, certifying that a fairly simple exam has been passed, and two years' experience. The audit itself is not as extensive as one would find in Britain or the United States. The more prestigious member of the profes-

[20]Ibid., p. 64, and an interview with a British Chartered Accountant.

sion is the expert comptable (EC). The EC must meet fairly rigorous educational requirements, pass a set of preliminary exams leading to a diploma of advanced accounting studies, work under the supervision of an EC for three years, be certified in a specialized area by written and oral exams during these three years, then sit for a higher auditing exam, and finally present and defend a thesis to the examining board. An EC serves more as a business and tax adviser to management than as an auditor, since the latter role is less specialized and less lucrative and the law prohibits the same person from performing both roles.

Canada

The Canadian profession is highly developed and demonstrates the influence of the United States and United Kingdom. Its largest accounting firms have been strongly affiliated with U.S. and UK partnerships. There are over 20,000 members in the Canadian Institute of Chartered Accountants, and they are well educated and highly trained. Membership in the profession is regulated by the provinces, similar to the role of the states in the United States. To become a Chartered Accountant, one is required to have a university degree, pass a series of examinations, and have some professional experience.[21]

Japan

Japan is well-known for its tendency to borrow good ideas from the rest of the world and modify them to fit into its own context. The accounting profession is no exception. As pointed out by Watson,

> In Japan, prospective CPAs must pass three milestones. First, they must have a university degree or pass a uniform examination consisting of mathematics and a thesis. They are then eligible for a second examination that is given once a year. This test measures expertise on such subjects as bookkeeping, financial statements, cost accounting, management, economics and the Japanese Commercial Code. There is no conditional credit given, such as some states in the U.S. provide. The candidate's entire performance is considered and graded accordingly. The Japanese Institute of CPAs (JICPA) estimates that 7 percent to 10 percent of the candidates are successful at each sitting.
>
> After passing the second examination, successful candidates are eligible to work as junior CPAs in public practice. Many audit corporations hire only junior CPAs as entry level staff. Therefore, completion of the examination is almost a prerequisite for entry into the profession. There is strong competition among the firms to hire these relatively few new entrants into the profession.
>
> After three years of apprenticeship—one year of training and two years' practice experience—junior CPAs must face the third milestone—a test of technical competence that encompasses four areas: auditing, financial analysis, other accounting practices (systems, taxes and bookkeeping) and a thesis.

[21]Ibid., p. 87.

It is conducted twice a year and is both written and oral. The passing rate, according to the JICPA, is about 18 percent for each sitting.

All CPAs must be members of the JICPA. As with chartered accountants in Great Britain, membership in the JICPA is the CPA license. Only those in public accounting are eligible for membership. Those who have passed the exams but are not members of the JICPA are considered qualified but not registered and cannot use the CPA designation.[22]

As we look at the experience of these countries, who determines certification? In the United States, the SEC requires that an audit be done by a CPA, but it allows the profession to determine certification. In the United Kingdom, government statute lists the professional organizations whose members can conduct audits, but the organizations themselves determine education, training, examination, and experience requirements. As was noted earlier, in Peru and Indonesia it is government legislation, not the profession, that determines qualifications for certification. This is also common in Continental Europe, where the profession tends to be established and regulated by law. A notable exception is The Netherlands, where the profession is fairly independent of the government.

Reciprocity

Since the accounting profession is rather heavily regulated and licensed in most countries, the issue of reciprocity—allowing a person certified in one country to practice in another—is a critical one. Many countries do not allow audits of local firms to be performed by someone who is not licensed locally, and they make it very difficult, if not impossible, for a foreigner to qualify.

In the United States, the general rule that prevailed from 1916 to the late 1970s was that State Boards of Accountancy could wave the examination portion of certification if they felt that a foreign professional was qualified in other ways. In 1977, however, a class-action suit was brought against the California State Board of Accountancy (referred to hereafter as the Board) charging that its policy of waving the examination requirement for reciprocal certification was "arbitrary and discriminatory." The reason for the suit was that the Board automatically granted exemption for applicants from seven "predominantly English-speaking, Caucasian countries," while not granting exemption for several hundred Philippino CPAs. The Board lost and has essentially stopped granting reciprocity.

The National Association of State Boards of Accountancy (NASB) eliminated the waiver of examination provision in 1980, and very few states are now granting automatic reciprocity for fear that if they grant reciprocity for one accountant, they will be required to grant it for all applicants. The NASB attempted to compare examinations worldwide in order to find a

[22]Thomas S. Watson, Jr., "Accounting in Japan: Regulation and Practice," *Journal of Accountancy*, August 1982, p. 83.

way to differentiate for purposes of granting reciprocity, but found that infeasible. They did, however, develop a methodology for comparison that they felt had some long-run benefits. In addition, they recommended the following:

> Moreover, while the Committee was charged only to study the comparability of examinations, it recognizes that other factors must be considered in comparing the qualifications of foreign accountants. The Committee, therefore, also recommends that interested national and international organizations intensify their efforts to develop and implement better methods for assessing the competence of professional accountants of different countries. The Committee believes that persons of good faith, sound judgment, and integrity can develop workable standards of comparison that will enable qualified accountants to move freely across international boundaries.[23]
>
> That statement leads very naturally into our next topic: harmonization of auditing standards and practices worldwide.

HARMONIZATION OF AUDITING STANDARDS AND PRACTICES

As we discuss in detail in Chapter 10,[24] the world is moving slowly and tortuously toward the development of generally accepted accounting principles, principally through the European Community, for the members of that bloc, and the International Accounting Standards Committee, for the world at large. At the same time, the integrity of financial statements needs to be maintained through the efforts of auditors. International auditing standards would serve the function of reinforcing international accounting standards and increasing the confidence of the users of financial statements worldwide.

A Guide for the Development of Standards and Practices

In trying to develop the argument for an international set of auditing standards, Stamp and Moonitz defined what they consider to be the "nature and purpose of an audit":

> An audit is an independent, objective and expert examination of a set of financial statements of an entity along with all necessary supporting evidence. It is conducted with a view to expressing an informed and credible opinion, in a written report, as to whether the financial statements portray the financial position and progress of the entity fairly, and in accordance with generally accepted accounting principles. The purpose of the independent expert opin-

---

[23]*Report of the Committee on the Comparability of Foreign Licensing Examinations* (New York: National Association of State Boards of Accountancy, May 1979), p. 14.
[24]The various methods and approaches to setting accounting standards, nationally and internationally, are the focus of Chapter 10. Therefore, the discussion here focuses only on auditing standards.

ion, which should be expressed in positive and not negative terms, is to lend credibility to the financial statements (the responsibility for whose preparation rests with management).[25]

Flowing from this definition are nine factors that Stamp and Moonitz feel must be considered when setting international auditing standards:

1. independence and objectivity of the auditor;
2. the nature of an audit examination, including the organization of teams of people and the problems of planning, supervision and control;
3. the role of evidence, its nature and evaluation, including the scope of the examination and the use of and reliance upon outside experts (and other auditors in some cases of consolidated groups);
4. the degree of assurance that evidence can provide; tolerable levels of risk and uncertainty and the use of judgment, and due care, in forming opinions; the use of statistical techniques and reliance upon internal control;
5. levels of accounting and auditing expertise required to form an expert opinion; educational and training standards necessary to achieve these levels of expertise and the validation thereof;
6. technical and general issues related to fairness and to compliance with accounting standards, upon which the audit opinion is based;
7. levels of knowledge and competence required in other areas such as law, economics, etc.;
8. communication of the auditor's opinion in a clear and unambiguous format to the parties to whom the auditor is responsible;
9. the monitoring and enforcement of auditing standards.[26]

There are three major organizations that deal with issues relating to auditors and auditing standards: the Union Europeenne des Expertes Comptables Economiques et Financiers (UEC) and the European Community (EC), which are both European regional organizations, and the International Federation of Accountants (IFAC), which is a broader, more international organization.

The UEC

The UEC was organized in 1951 and currently claims membership from 19 European countries, thus involving more nations than the EC. It is involved in a variety of accounting projects, one of which is the development of auditing and ethics statements. It has issued a series of statements that are very similar in scope and content to those issued by the broader-based IFAC. Among the Auditing Standards (AS) and Ethics Standards (ES) issued thus far are:

[25]Stamp and Moonitz, *International Auditing Standards*, p. 38.
[26]Ibid., p. 39.

AS No. 1:	Object and Scope of the Audit of Annual Financial Statements
AS No. 2:	The Use of Another Auditor's Work
AS No. 3:	The Auditor's Working Papers
AS No. 4:	Audit Considerations Regarding the Going Concern Basis
AS No. 5:	The Audit of Foreign Exchange Contracts of Credit Institutions
AS No. 6:	Quality Control—Ensuring and Improving the Quality of Audits
AS No. 7:	Effect of an Internal Audit Function on the Scope of the Independent Auditor's Examination
AS No. 8:	The Audit Report
AS No. 9:	Review of an Independent Accountant of the Interim Statements of an Enterprise
AS No. 10:	The Auditor's Attendance at Physical Stocktaking (Inventory)
AS No. 11:	Management Representations to the Auditor
AS No. 12.	The Detection of Fraud within the Scope of an Audit of Financial Statements
AS No. 13:	Audit Considerations in Respect of Post Balance Sheet Events
AS No. 14:	The Audit of Financial Statements of Small Enterprises
ES No. 1:	Independence
ES No. 2:	Advertising
ES No. 3:	Professional Work
ES No. 4:	Confidentiality
ES No. 5:	Relations with Colleagues

The EC

The EC has not concentrated on the setting of auditing standards up to this point, but it has issued two standards that affect the work of auditors: the Fourth Directive on Company Accounts and the Eighth Directive on the qualifications of statutory auditors.

The Fourth Directive

As explained in more detail in Chapter 10, the Directives issued by the EC are important sources of standards because they must be incorporated into national law within a certain period of time. The Fourth Directive is primarily concerned with the form and content of the financial statements, but it also contains an audit provision. According to the Fourth Directive, all companies in the EC except small companies "must have their annual accounts audited by one or more persons authorized by national law to audit accounts. The person or persons responsible for auditing the accounts must also verify that the annual report is consistent with the annual accounts for the same financial year."[27] Small companies are defined as companies that on their balance sheet dates do not exceed the limits of two of the three following criteria: balance sheet total (approximately $1.3 million), net sales (approximately $2.6 million), and an average of 50 employees during the financial year.[28] The impact of the Fourth Directive is to require the audit of far more companies than had been required previously. No distinction is made in the Fourth Directive between companies that are closely held and those that are listed and traded on stock exchanges.

The Eighth Directive

The Eighth Directive was adopted by the Council of Ministers of the EC in 1984, and it deals with the qualifications of statutory auditors. As noted, the Fourth Directive simply requires that an audit be conducted, but it leaves the determination of the auditor up to national law. The Eighth Directive focuses directly on the determination of the auditor. Three major areas are covered in the Directive that relate to issues already discussed in this chapter: qualifications of statutory auditors, reciprocity, and independence.[29]

Qualifications of Statutory Auditors. In order to become certified, an auditor needs to demonstrate education, examination, and experience qualifications. Candidates need to exhibit at least university entrance–level qualifications and then must complete a program of theoretical instruction. In terms of experience, the candidates need to complete at least three years of practical training, at least two thirds of which must be completed under the supervision of an approved person. This establishes a minimum level of training, and the member states are free to exceed this limit if so desired. As noted earlier in the chapter, West Germany and the United Kingdom exceed these standards already. In addition to the education and experience requirements, candidates are expected to pass an examination of professional competence at graduation level organized or recogized by the state. The subjects to be covered in the exam are basically accounting but

---

[27]Price Waterhouse, *Handbook on the EEC Fourth Directive* (Brussels: Price Waterhouse, 1979), p. 148.

[28]Ibid., p. 7.

[29]The material below describing the Eighth Directive comes from the newsletter *EEC Bulletin*, No. 66 (Brussels: Price Waterhouse, March 1984).

may also include legal and general business subjects as they relate to the auditing profession.

Reciprocity. For auditors in one country to be allowed to practice in an another member country, the following two conditions must be met: they must have obtained qualifications that are deemed to be equivalent to the reviewing authorities in the host country, and they must demonstrate that they understand the laws and requirements for conducting statutory audits in the host country. It will be interesting to see if the first requirement is used as a means to exclude auditors from other countries in order to protect the profession.

Independence. One of the areas of strong disagreement in the draft stage of the Directive was how to define independence. Some countries felt that statutory auditors should do nothing but audit financial statements, whereas others felt that tax and advisory services could also be performed by auditing firms without impairing independence. In its final form, the Eighth Directive decided to allow the individual member countries to determine the conditions for independence. In other words, the EEC opted for the status quo. Unfortunately, this means that the international public accounting firms will have to adjust their operations from country to country in order to comply with national law.

The International Federation of Accountants

The International Coordination Committee for the Accounting Profession was organized in 1972 at the International Congress of Accountants held in Sidney, Australia. The purpose of establishing ICCAP was to lay the groundwork for more formal organizations to help achieve the goals of accounting harmonization. This was accomplished with the establishment of the International Accounting Standards Committee in 1973 and the International Federation of Accountants (IFAC) in Munich at the 1977 International Congress. IFAC's membership is comprised of representatives of accountancy bodies from over 60 countries.

In order to accomplish its original objectives, IFAC organized six major committees: Education, Ethics, International Auditing Practices (IAPC), Management Accounting, Planning, and the Regional Organizations Consultative Group. The first three committees are those most directly involved in activities that relate to auditors and auditing.

The Education Committee has issued the following guidelines:

Guideline No. 1:	Prequalification Education and Training
Guideline No. 2:	Continuing Professional Education
Guideline No. 3:	Test of Professional Competence

The last guideline is relevant to other issues that we have already treated in the chapter. It covers very generally the matters that need to be considered when reviewing an educational program or method of assessing students as a test of professional competence. It points out that an accountant should have "the required sum of knowledge relevant to his profession, the ability to apply that knowledge to practical problems, and a professional approach to work."[30]

The Education Committee has issued an exposure draft entitled "Core of Knowledge—Professional Subjects," and is working on drafts of proposed Guidelines on "Practical Experience" and "Specialization."

The Ethics Committee has issued the following Guidelines and Statements of Guidance:

Guidelines

"Professional Ethics for the Accountancy Profession"

Statements of Guidance

1. Advertising Publicity and Solicitation
2. Professional Competence
3. Integrity, Objectivity and Independence
4. Confidentiality
5. Ethics Across International Borders
6. Conditions for Acceptance of an Appointment When Another Accountant in Public Practice Is Already Carrying Out Work for the Same Client
7. Conditions for Superseding Another Accountant in Public Practice

Drafts of other Statements of Guidance that are in various stages of progress concern "Charging of Professional Fees and Payment and Receipt of Commissions," "Compliance with Technical Standards," "Incompatible and Inconsistent Businesses," "Ethics in Tax Practice," and "Philosophy of Ethics."

The International Audit Practices Committee has been by far the most active of the committees in terms of generating guidelines and exposure drafts. The guidelines tend to be relatively basic and easily understood, so they should be of great value to countries that are attempting to adopt audit standards to enhance their profession. The 15 guidelines that have been adopted thus far and a brief description of each follows:

IAG 1:   "Objective and Scope of the Audit of Financial Statements." The overall objective and scope of the audit of financial statements of an entity by an independent auditor.

[30]International Federation of Accountants, *Newsletter* Vol. 6 No. 2 (New York: IFAC, September 1983), p. 2.

IAG 2:   "Audit Engagement Letters." An auditor's engagement letter to his or her client is designed to document and confirm acceptance of the appointment, the scope of the work, and the extent of his or her responsibilities and the form of any reports.

IAG 3:   "Basic Principles Governing an Audit." Describes the basic principles governing an auditor's professional responsibilities that should be exercised whenever an audit is carried out.

IAG 4:   "Planning." Applies to the planning process of the audit of both financial statements and other financial information. It is framed in the context of recurring audits, identifies key elements in the planning process, and provides practical examples of items that should be considered when planning an audit.

IAG 5:   "Using the Work of an Other Auditor." It applies when an independent auditor reporting on the financial statements of an entity uses the work of another independent auditor with respect to the financial statements of one or more divisions, branches, subsidiaries, or associated companies included in the financial statements of the entity, especially when the other auditor is located in another country.

IAG 6:   "Study and Evaluation of the Accounting System and Related Internal Controls in Connection with an Audit." Describes the components of internal control and the audit procedures necessary for the study and evaluation of internal control.

IAG 7:   "Control of the Quality of Audit Work." Deals not only with the controls on an individual audit that are an integral part of the basic auditing principles, but also provides practical assistance to an audit firm in controlling the general quality of their practice.

IAG 8:   "Audit Evidence." Describes the nature and sources of audit evidence, the sufficiency and appropriateness of evidence, and the methods by which it is obtained by the auditor in the performance of compliance and substantive procedures.

IAG 9:   "Documentation." Provides guidance on the general form and content of working papers as well as specific examples of working papers normally prepared or obtained by the auditor.

IAG 10:   "Using the Work of an Internal Auditor." Much of the work of the internal audit department may be useful to the independent auditor for the purpose of examination of the financial information. This guideline provides guidance as to the procedures that should be considered by the independent auditor in assessing the work of the internal auditor for the purpose of using that work.

IAG 11:   "Fraud and Error." Defines the auditor's responsibility for the detection of fraud and error, includes a section on "the inherent limitations of an audit" and a statement on management's responsibility, suggests procedures that should be considered when the auditor finds some indication that fraud or error may exist and includes an appendix that gives examples of conditions or events that increase the risk of fraud or error.

IAG 12:   "Analytical Review." Provides the auditor with an understanding of the nature of analytical review procedures as well as guidance on the objectives, timing, and extent of reliance to be placed on such procedures in performing an audit.

IAG 13:   "The Auditor's Report on Financial Statements." Provides guidance to auditors on the form and content of the auditor's report issued in connection with the independent audit of the financial statements of any entity.

IAG 14:   "Other information in Documents Containing Audited Financial Statements." Discusses the auditor's consideration of other information on which he or she has no obligation to report and the action he or she should take if a material inconsistency or material misstatement of fact exists.

IAG 15:   "Auditing in an EDP Environment." Identifies the areas in which additional guidance is necessary to comply with the basic principles governing an audit when conducting an audit in an EDP environment.[31]

Is Harmonization of Audit Standards of Value?

Some might question the value of participating in the effort to generate internationally acceptable auditing standards. However, it is probably easier to develop auditing standards than it is to develop acceptable accounting standards and practices because the former can be used as a tool to verify

---

[31]These summaries can be found in the following issues of the IFAC *Newsletter*: June 1983, September 1983, and December 1983.

the accuracy and reliability of the latter. In addition, Stamp and Moonitz point out what they perceive to be the seven major benefits of developing and enforcing internationally acceptable auditing standards:

1. The existence of a set of international auditing standards, which are known to be enforced, will give readers of audit reports produced in other countries justifiable confidence in the auditor's opinion. By thus lending credibility to the work of the foreign auditor they enable that auditor to lend credibility to the financial statements upon which he [or she] is reporting.

2. International auditing standards will reinforce the benefits that are already flowing from the existence of international accounting standards, by providing readers with greater assurance that the accounting standards are being adhered to.

3. International auditing standards, by adding strength to international accounting standards, will assist readers in making international financial comparisons.

4. International auditing standards will provide further incentives to improve and extend the set of international accounting standards.

5. The existence of international auditing standards will assist in the flow of investment capital, especially to underdeveloped areas.

6. The development of an international set of standards will make it easier for underdeveloped countries to produce domestic auditing standards, and this will be of benefit to them.

7. Effective and credible auditing is necessary in all instances where there is a separation between management (who produce financial reports) and outsiders (who use the reports). The need is all the greater in the case of multinational enterprises since management is separated from the outsiders by greater differences in culture, political and economic systems, geographical boundaries, etc. Thus international auditing standards are, in this respect, even more important than national ones.[32]

INTERNATIONAL AUDITING FIRMS

As the world's largest corporations have expanded beyond their national borders, it has been necessary for the firms that service them to match that movement. As far as the public accounting profession is concerned, that has resulted in a variety of ways to service clients, from sending auditors abroad to conduct an audit to more complex forms of arrangement with local auditors in order to provide the necessary service.

From the U.S. perspective, most of the discussions of the public accounting profession has centered on the "Big Eight" firms that have handled the audits of most of the largest companies. However, the growth of the profession in the rest of the world has given rise to the "Big Nine," as listed below according to fees generated in 1982:[33]

[32]Stamp and Moonitz, *International Auditing Standards*, pp. 146–147.
[33]*Public Accounting Report*, March 1983, p. 8.

	Fees (in thousands) 1982
Peat, Marwick, Mitchell	$1150
Arthur Andersen	1123
Coopers & Lybrand	1066
Klynveld Main Goerdeler	970
Arthur Young	955
Price Waterhouse	946
Ernst & Whinney	887
Deloitte Haskins & Sells	852
Touche Ross	800

Four other firms that are included among the largest 13 public accounting firms in the world are Binder Dijer Otte & Co., Fox Moore International, Grant Thornton International, and Horwath & Horwath International.

A major development in the accounting profession that took place in 1984 was the merger of Price Waterhouse and Deloitte Haskins & Sells, two of the Big 8 firms. Their merger essentially changed the Big 8 to the Big 7. The new firm, which is to be known as Price Waterhouse Deloitte, should end up being the largest firm in the United States and the largest firm in the world. Price Waterhouse is the larger of the two firms, and it has a bigger international practice. The merger should give each other strong clients and strong international practices on which to build future growth. The culmination of that merger could very well increase the odds of other mergers.

The revenues or fees of the major Anglo-Saxon public accounting firms have always been derived from three major service areas: accounting and auditing, tax, and management services. Although the exact percentage of each varies from firm to firm, the order of importance is usually the same as listed here.

Although the firms are organized in a variety of ways internationally, the real strength of the organization lies at the office level. Each office has several levels of professionals—partners, principals, managers, senior accountants, and staff accountants. One of the partners is designated the managing partner of the office and is therefore responsible for its profitability. Partners and principals (at the organizational level of a partner, but not accountants) are responsible for generating the fees in their areas of expertise. In some firms, regional partners supervise the work of managing partners of a variety of offices and in turn report to the managing partner of the firm—the equivalent of shareholders in a corporate setting. The partners of the firm share in the nationwide profits, much as the shareholders of a corporation.

Trends and Characteristics

In a study conducted by researchers at the University of Connecticut, a number of interesting trends and characteristics were noted in the large international auditing firms:

1. Leading U.S.-based auditing firms' operations outside the U.S. are continuing to grow far more rapidly than in the U.S.

2. Some leading U.S.-based firms are strengthening and reshaping their international organizations and foreign offices.

3. Other leading U.S.-based auditing firms are acquiring major non-U.S. auditing firms, especially in Europe, for a stronger foothold in those markets.

4. Leading national auditing firms are regrouping internationally to form larger international partnerships.

5. Accounting and auditing requirements of companies based in the EEC countries are being standardized, which may result in reducing the competitive advantage of leading Europe auditing firms vis-à-vis U.S.-based leading auditing firms.

6. The international auditing firms had the greatest number of their offices in North America and Europe. This follows the concept of servicing clients abroad.

7. Some firms chose to operate throughout the world with a few large offices rather than many small offices. Arthur Andersen & Co. is an example of the former, and Binder Dijker Otte & Co. is an example of the latter.

8. The majority of the foreign subsidiaries of large multinational corporations were audited by different auditors than the parent. [This is surprising since the major reason why international firms expand abroad is to prevent encroachment by foreign firms.][34]

Reasons for Expansion

Public accounting firms have traditionally expanded abroad to service their clients better and provide a line of defense against more international public accounting firms that might be tempted to encroach on their client base. In a survey of companies that had switched from small or medium-sized auditors to more international auditors, the following reasons were given for the switch: "The need to reflect the increasing size of our overseas business"; "We wanted to have one firm auditing all companies within the group"; "To reflect our recent expansion overseas"; "We needed the services of an international accounting firm."[35]

---

[34]From two newsletters from the University of Connecticut, *Who Audits the World: Trends in the Worldwide Accounting Profession* and *Who Audits the World: Major Research Findings*. The research report is by Vinod B. Bavishi and Harold E. Wyman, *Who Audits the World* (Storrs, Conn.: Center for Transnational Accounting and Financial Research, University of Connecticut, 1983).

[35]"International Accounting Firms Consolidate Worldwide: A Study of a Multinational Service Industry," *Multinational Business*, No. 3, 1980, p. 5.

A third reason for international expansion that has become more critical in recent years is to increase the client base outside of the home market and not necessarily through referrals from other offices. This has been especially true in Europe, where the implementation of the Fourth Directive will require far more firms to be audited than had been done previously. In addition, many markets are opening up to mergers and acquisitions whereas those strategies had been precluded in the past.

Servicing Multinational Clients

Given the need for expansion, in what ways have the firms serviced their multinational clients? The simplest way is for a partner or staff member to travel from the home office to service a client abroad. This would be sufficient as long as the foreign sector was a small part of the client's overall operations. However, this approach is unsatisfactory in the long run owing to the complexity of the international audit and tax environment and the increasing internationalization of most of the firm's larger clients.

Beyond the traveling auditor approach are two philosophically different approaches: the branch or affiliate and the correspondent.

Branch Offices

Some U.S. firms have set up *branches* abroad. These branches may be separate legal entities that use the parent firm's name. Home office personnel fill the important positions until domestic personnel can be trained to take over. In some cases local firms are acquired; in others, new firms are established. The branch concept, coupled with a strong central management, provides for tighter control over services.

Correspondents

The *correspondent* relationship is multifaceted; it can range from very weak to very strong. At one end of the scale, the local correspondent may be a representative that performs services for more than one accounting firm. A very loose operating relationship may exist. At the other end of the scale, a very strong correspondent relationship may exist in which the local firm performs services exclusively for one foreign public accounting firm.

In some cases the correspondent relationship may involve a joint partnership between the United States and local firms. In the early 1900s, Arthur Young & Company set up a joint partnership in London and Paris with the British firm of Broads, Patterson, and Co. It also set up a joint partnership in Canada with the Canadian firm of Clarkson, Gordon, and Co. In other cases, the U.S. and local firms simply have a close working relationship. For example, the British correspondent might audit the records of the British subsidiary of a U.S. corporation that is the client of the U.S. public accounting firm. Another strategy is to use a licensing agreement in which a local firm uses the name and technical advice of the large foreign firm in exchange for a royalty payment.

Whether the U.S. firm expands abroad through strong or weak correspondent relationships, the fact remains that the partners in other countries are separate, autonomous organizations. Unlike a corporation, which retains equity control over its far-flung operations, these partnerships are built on mutual benefit and service. There *are* situations in which the U.S. firm owns the foreign operations, but those are the exception rather than the rule. Arthur Andersen & Company is fairly centralized; its chairman and vice-chairman have worldwide responsibility, and there is profit sharing among its international partners; but it is the only public accounting firm so organized.

Many firms have organized a worldwide partnership to integrate operations. Each member partner (such as United States, Britain, Canada, Continental Europe) retains its separate identity, but a more cohesive cooperative effort exists among the firms through the international partnership. In 1979, for example, Ernst & Ernst announced the formation of a new international firm named Ernst & Whinney International with offices in 71 countries. The U.S. partner changed its name to Ernst & Whinney to be consistent with the international partnership. EWI now has partners in the United States, Canada, United Kingdom, Continental Europe, Middle East, Far East, Australia/New Zealand, Africa, and Central and South America. The partners range in size from 14 offices in Canada to 117 in the United States. The stated purpose of the move is "increased ability to maintain uniformly high quality standards around the world; better coordination of investment in research, communications, and professional development; and more effective management of human resources."[36] Part of the reason for its desire to strengthen the international organization is that foreign fees made up 25% of total fees in 1977 and are expected to reach 40% by 1985.

There are a number of other interesting examples of how firms from different countries got together to take advantage of each other's client base. For example, Binder Dijker Otte & Co. (BDO) was the first major European federation, formed in 1973 from a UK, German, and Dutch firm. Since then, BDO has added Seidman and Seidman from the United States, as well as firms from Germany, Switzerland, and France. Arthur Young formed a new association for its European operations called AMSA. The group includes Arthur Young McClelland Moores from the United Kingdom, the second largest auditing firm in the Netherlands, and two of the largest auditing firms in Germany and Switzerland.[37]

Coopers & Lybrand had its origins in Cooper Brothers of the United

---

[36]From a pamphlet distributed by Ernst & Whinney in January 1979 announcing the change.
[37]"International Accounting Firms Consolidate Worldwide: A Study of a Multinational Service Industry," *Multinational Business*, No. 3, 1980, p. 5.

Kingdom, Lybrand, Ross Bros., and Montgomery in the United States, and McDonald Currie in Canada. Their first cooperative organizational venture took place in 1964, but it was not until 1973 that the firm adopted the name Coopers and Lybrand. Initially the firms divided up the world accordingly: Continental Europe and the Commonwealth for the British partnership, Central and South America and Japan for the U.S. firm, and the Caribbean and Pacific for the Canadian firm. Eventually, Coopers and Lybrand established coordinating and steering committees from each of the national firms to integrate the operations on a more worldwide basis.[38]

Audit Coordination

The auditor of a large multinational corporation has a very difficult time trying to perform the firm's services properly. Let's assume that a large multinational corporation headquartered in New York City has operations in different regions all over the world. In all probability, the corporation's auditor also has an office in New York City. One of the partners in the New York office will be assigned as the partner in charge of the worldwide audit. That partner must decide on the scope of the audit, taking into consideration factors such as the countries where the corporation has subsidiaries, the materiality of each subsidiary vis-à-vis the corporation as a whole, the existence of a branch, subsidiary, or correspondent of the auditor in the country or city of each major subsidiary, and so on.

The ability of the auditor to perform a good audit depends on a lot of different factors. Some of them, such as language, culture, and business practices, were discussed in the section on internal auditing. Others are more specific to the external audit: restrictions on the use of the firm's name, restrictions on rights of establishment and association, restrictions on scope of practice, restrictions on repatriation of fees, royalties, and profit, tax discrimination, and quality control. The first five of these issues relate to legal restrictions that the U.S. government is trying to combat through negotiations with other countries in the General Agreement on Tariffs and Trade, a multilateral organization that is devoted to reducing trade barriers.

Restrictions on the Use of a Firm's Name.   Some countries will not allow foreign firms to use their international names when practicing locally because it is felt that this would give the firms a comparative advantage over local firms. This is hard on the international firm that struggles to develop a reputation worldwide.

Restrictions on Rights of Establishment and Association.   Firms are often forced to change the way they would conduct business in order to conform to local organizational restrictions. These restrictions refer to the number of foreign partners allowed to practice with the firm and whether or not the firm can operate independently of a local firm. Some countries require that

[38]Ibid., p. 7.

the foreign firm enter into a formal relationship with a local firm, whereas other countries prohibit such an association.

Restrictions on Scope of Practice. In some countries, firms are prohibited from doing anything other than a statutory audit, whereas in others a full range of services can be offered. Also, a firm may be restricted in the number of audits it is allowed to sign.

Restrictions on Repatriation of Fees. Most public accounting firms do not share fees in the same way that corporations share profits in the form of dividends. The notable exception to that might be Arthur Andersen & Co. However, there are fees for maintaining the international partnership, and most firms charge a "finder's fee" for work referred from one office to another. Sometimes governments restrict the free flow of funds or tie the amount eligible for repatriation to the firm's capital base, which is a real penalty for a service firm that operates on a very small capital base.

Tax Discrimination. This simply refers to the fact that foreign consulting firms are often taxed at rates that far exceed those of local firms, giving the locals a differential advantage.[39]

Quality Control. This is an area of real concern because the reputation of the auditing firm depends on the quality of the work it does. Since most international public accounting firms are different degrees of loose associations of national public accounting firms, the quality of work performed is bound to vary. The firms are constantly trying to figure out how to find and train partners that can operate internationally. As a result, they concentrate on training and internship or foreign residency programs. It is common to find accountants in various stages of their careers—usually from the manager level on up—working in foreign offices to learn the problems of audits in those countries and to train local accountants in the ways of the international firm. This transfer is often two-way, with non-U.S. partners, for example, coming to the United States to learn the requirements of performing an audit in the U.S. environment. When these accountants return to their home countries, they are much more effective in performing local subsidiary audits that comply with the requirements in the United States that are necessary for the auditor to express an opinion.

SUMMARY

- A good internal control system starts with codes of conduct and standard operating procedures. The internal audit function is the cornerstone in determining compliance.
- The internal auditor in the international environment needs to deal with local business practices and customs, foreign currency, language, and distance.

[39]*U.S. National Study on Trade in Services* (Washington, D.C.: Office of the U.S. Trade Representative, 1983), pp. 231–233.

- In addition to using traveling auditors for internal audit work, firms may use local resident and expatriate resident auditors.

- The Foreign Corrupt Practices Act was passed in the United States to make bribery illegal and to force companies to use good internal control procedures.

- In order to cover up bribes, firms falsify records, fail to disclose the true purpose of transactions, and simply do not record transactions.

- The government often takes the lead in developing auditing standards in countries that do not have a well-developed accounting and auditing profession, as well as in some industrial countries that are very legalistic and prescriptive.

- Other countries, such as the United States, mix government require-ments for audits with private-sector development of specific standards.

- Audit standards vary considerably from country to country. An audit may simply mean that the financial statements reflect the books and records of the firm, or it may involve a sophisticated investigation of whether or not the books and records accurately reflect the original transactions.

- Audit opinions worldwide differ as to form and content, but a good audit opinion should contain the title of the report, the addressee, the identifi-cation of the financial statements being audited, a reference to the audit-ing standards or practices followed, an expression or disclaimer of opin-ion on the financial statements, the signature of the auditor, the auditor's address, and the date of the report.

- Although there is no standard set of requirements for auditors world-wide, it is widely felt that auditors should demonstrate education, exam-ination, and experience qualifications.

- The Union Europeenne des Expertes Comptables Economiques et Finan-ciers (UEC) is an organization of 19 European countries that is involved, among other things, in the development of auditing and ethics state-ments.

- The Fourth Directive of the European Community (EC) requires that all companies in the EC except small companies must have their annual accounts audited by one or more persons authorized by national law to audit accounts.

- The Eighth Directive of the EC covers the qualifications of statutory auditors, reciprocity, and independence.

- The International Federation of Accountants (IFAC), an organization of accountancy bodies from 64 countries, has issued 3 guidelines on the education of accountants, 1 guideline and 7 statements of guidance con-cerning ethical issues of accountants and auditors, and 15 auditing guide-lines. Many of the guidelines are similar to those issued by the UEC.

- The world's largest public accounting firms have established cooperative relationships worldwide. They have expanded abroad to provide better service for their domestic clients that have international operations and to protect their business from competing public accounting firms that may have wider geographical spread.
- Many of the problems that auditors have in servicing their clients internationally are the same as those experienced by internal auditors. In addition, they need to worry about restrictions on the use of the firm's name, restrictions on rights of establishment and association, restrictions on scope of practice, restrictions on repatriation of fees, tax discrimination, and quality control.

Study Questions

9-1. Discuss the role of the internal auditor. Indicate similarities and differences between the internal auditor's role in domestic and in multinational operations.

9-2. If you were an internal auditor assigned to work in Brazil, what differences do you think you might find in that environment compared with a similar assignment in the United Kingdom?

9-3. Discuss the forms of organization and types of personnel that a firm can use when conducting an international internal audit. What are the advantages and disadvantages of each?

9-4. Discuss how foreign bribery might affect the internal control system of your firm.

9-5. What would you do as an auditor if you were conducting your work in a country where bribery is a way of life?

9-6. What are the strengths and weaknesses of having the government set auditing standards as opposed to the accounting profession? In what ways could you see the government and the profession cooperating with each other to set auditing standards?

9-7. Compare audit reports in the text or other foreign audit reports that you might have with the basic elements of the auditor's report recommended in International Auditing Guideline No. 13. For those reports that do not comply with the guideline, how do you think adherence to the guideline would improve the report?

9-8. After reading about the qualifications of auditors worldwide, design what you think would be the best approach to certification of an auditor. Be sure to take into consideration the needs of the profession as well as any constraints that might exist in a country (such as developing versus industrial countries). Be sure to justify your approach.

9-9. Discuss the pros and cons of granting automatic reciprocity in the United States to anyone certified in his or her own country. How do you feel about granting a U.S. CPA permission to practice anywhere outside of the United States?

9-10. What are the major benefits to the harmonization of auditing standards and practices? What are the major problems with harmonization?

9-11. Given the different forums discussed for the harmonization of auditing standards, what do you feel is the best way to harmonize standards? Be sure to justify your position.

9-12. Compare any of the ethical statements or international auditing guidelines of the International Auditing Practices Committee of IFAC with similar standards that exist in the United States.

9-13. Using periodicals or other publications of any of the public accounting firms, report on stories written about foreign office activities of the firms. Be sure to take note of how the firm is organized for its international operations and what problems it faces in the international environment.

9-14. If you had a client operating in a foreign country where you did not have your own office, how might you service that client? What problems do you think you might face with various alternative ways of servicing that client?

Case 1

STAR OIL COMPANY

"How did I ever get stuck in this rat's nest?" thought Herb Johnston as he sat in his office in Seoul, Korea.

It was just prior to a crucial national election, and Herb had come from a meeting with S. I. Kim, a high official in the Democratic Republican Independent Party (DRIP) of President Kwon. Kim had just demanded a $5 million political contribution from Star Oil for the reelection of President Kwon, who was facing a stiff challenge.

When Herb balked at paying such a large sum, Kim angrily replied, "Either put up the money I am asking for or you and Star Oil can pack up your bags. I'm here to get the money, not negotiate."

At that point, Herb walked out. What do I do now? he thought.

Star Oil had begun investing in oil refining facilities in Korea in the early 1960s because of a surplus of crude oil from its Middle East fields and the belief that Korea was going to be industrializing heavily and would therefore be a good place for investment. Herb had been transferred there recently as the general manager of the subsidiary, with instructions to do whatever was necessary to be successful. Marv Hansen, Herb's predecessor, was now Herb's boss.

As Herb reviewed the situation, he become more and more uneasy. In the previous election, Marv had paid $900,000 to Kwon's campaign. Although corporate political contributions are legal in Korea, Marv had recorded the contribution as a consulting expense, and he had not felt it necessary to inform the auditor or the board of directors about the contribution.

Herb was concerned about other aspects of the environment. Star Oil was required to make payments to different levels of government officials, ranging from low-level tipping to kickbacks. It was customary to give gifts to government clerks and officials during three holiday seasons: Chusok (similar to Thanksgiving), Christmas, and the New Year. Higher officials got more expensive gifts, which were recorded as entertainment or miscellaneous expenses.

Marv had said that the wheels of progress do not turn without lubrication, and Herb soon found out how true this was. In order to keep permits or licenses from being lost or delayed, Herb had to pay $50 to $200, depending on the level of approval needed. Herb was told that these payments were needed to supplement the low salaries of government employees. Customs officials had to be paid off to get goods into the country, railroad switchmen had to be paid off to see that cargo was handled properly, planning boards had to be paid off to ensure approval of refinery expansions.

Even the military got into the act. Last year, Herb landed a lucrative contract to supply oil to the Ministry of Defense. Then the purchasing agent informed Herb that he would have to pay a kickback so that the Ministry of Defense could bolster its forces on the border of a neighboring hostile country. Herb offered to lower his price by a few cents a barrel to cover the cost, but the purchasing agent informed Herb that his competitors were paying the kickback and so should he.

As Herb shuffled his papers trying to decide what to do about Kim's demand, he came across a memo that had just arrived from Marv. Apparently, the internal auditors were raising a fuss about Herb's high entertainment and miscellaneous expenses. Marv wanted to set up an off-the-books cash fund that Herb could use to pay off government clerks and officials and wanted to know what Herb thought about the idea.

Questions

1. Analyze the various situations described from the perspective of the Foreign Corrupt Practices Act.
2. Assess the various options open to Herb.
3. Assume that you are in charge of worldwide internal audit for Star Oil and had just picked one of your best internal auditors from U.S. operations to head up the Star Oil-Korea audit. What problems would you warn your auditor that might be encountered, and what instructions would you give?

Case 2

DELOITTE HASKINS & SELLS NEDERLAND

Deloitte Haskins & Sells (DH&S) is one of the world's largest public accounting firms, servicing clients worldwide in a variety of ways, including formal arrangments with strong local firms. One such arrangement is with the Dutch firm, Van Dien & Co.

The formal association between the Dutch and U.S. firms had its roots in the World's Fair held in St. Louis in 1904. At the fair, Emmanuel Van Dien, who had established his own accounting firm in 1893, met Elijah Watt Sells, cofounder of the U.S. firm of Haskins & Sells. Because each firm had clients investing in each other's countries, they felt they could profit by doing referral work. At that point, neither firm could afford to expand and open offices all over the world. Their original association provided that each firm would represent each other in specific countries

Most of the information for this case is from "Van Dien & Co.," *Plus*, Issue 2, 1980, pp. 1–13, and from the DH&S International 1983 Worldwide Directory.

so that they could take advantage of offices already set up, and specialization developed.

Prior to 1971, Dutch law precluded Dutch public accounting firms from entering into associations with foreign firms, so the cooperation was basically in the form of referral work. Because of Van Dien & Co.'s specialization in Continental Europe, it began servicing the U.S. firm's clients in The Netherlands, Belgium, and Germany. This referral work soon expanded to include Switzerland, Italy, and other European countries. Van Dien & Co. (known initially as Van Dien, Van Uden & Co.) grew steadily through acquisitions and mergers in The Netherlands until it became one of the largest public accounting firms in The Netherlands.

In 1971, The Netherlands institute changed its rules so that Dutch accountancy firms could form associations with foreign firms. This gave rise to the creation of Deloitte Haskins & Sells Nederland. This firm handles all of the referral work of DH&S International and is composed of professionals that can devote at least 50% of their time to referral work. Van Dien & Co., which generates 95% of its revenues from its own practice, continues to operate under its Dutch name for nonreferral work. However, as some of Van Dien & Co.'s Dutch clients increase their investment in the United States and other areas serviced by DH&S International, the firm is finding it a lot easier to provide good quality service to those clients.

DH&S, according to its 1983 Directory, employs more than 26,000 people in 424 offices in 69 countries. It also has correspondents in 8 other countries (Austria, Bangladesh, Cyprus, Greece, Nepal, Pakistan, Sri Lanka, and the Sudan). In 1976, the firm formed DH&S International. Each of the member firms in DH&S International is represented in the international partnership by an executive committee, which is essentially composed of the managing partners of the major national firms. The international firm is managed by an executive director who is assisted by a director of professional services, a practice development director, a publications director, and professionals in charge of administration and personnel. In addition, there are a number of standing committees and project committees.

In order to better coordinate activities in Europe, DH&S International created a European Policy Committee "to bring the European firms closer together, build a stronger and better organization, and develop a more uniform approach for serving international clients."

Van Dien & Co.'s organization symbolizes the differences faced in firms worldwide, even though those firms may all be involved in the same international partnership. Partners in the Dutch firm come from a formal university training leading to a graduate degree in economics or from eight or nine years of specialized training with the Dutch institute. After experience requirements and examinations are completed, the candidates can become certified—usually between the ages of 27 and 30 years.

Dutch law requires the firm to have a works council, a committee of elected workers that management is required to consult before making implementing decisions that affect the work environment and strategic direction of the firm. This gives the members of the firm a strong say in the affairs of the firm, even though they may not have reached the level of partner.

Once the members of the firm have achieved partnership status, they are eligible for the highest levels of leadership in the firm. The members of the board of directors and major operational committee members serve four-year terms and are not eligible for renomination until after another person has served a term of office.

The only exception to the rule involves the chairman of the firm who is elected for three years and can serve two consecutive terms.

Questions

1. What are the reasons that DH&S and Van Dien & Co. were able to work out a cooperative relationship with each other?
2. What are the major types of problems that you think they may have faced over the years?
3. As you consider the international partnership that was developed in 1976, what do you think its major objectives might have been? What do you think some of its major committees were?
4. DH&S Nederland includes only professionals that spend at least 50% of their time on referral work. Why do you think DH&S requires this? Would it be any different for the United Kingdom? for Brazil?
5. What are some things that DH&S International could do to strengthen its professionals in offices such as DH&S Nederland?
6. What do you think DH&S means when it says that it has more than 26,000 people in 424 offices in 69 countries?

Bibliography

Agami, Abdel M. and Felix P. Kollaritsch. *Annotated International Accounting Bibliography 1972–1981* (Sarasota, Fla.: American Accounting Association, 1983), several references on pp. 56–64.

AICPA International Practice Executive Committee. *Professional Accounting in 30 Countries* (New York: AICPA, 1975).

Bavishi, Vinod B. and Harold E. Wyman. *Who Audits the World* (Storrs, Conn.: Center for Transnational Accounting and Financial Research, University of Connecticut, 1983).

Court, Peter. "The Multinational Audit Team: Who Holds the Reins?" *Accountancy*, Vol. 91, October 1980, pp. 85–88.

Ernst & Whinney. *Worldwide Statutory Audit and Reporting Requirements* (New York: Ernst & Whinney, 1979).

Kullberg, Duane R. "Management of a Multinational Public Accounting Firm." *International Journal of Accounting Education and Research*, Vol. 17, Fall 1981, pp. 1–6.

May, Robert L. "The Harmonization of International Auditing Standards," in *The Internationalization of the Accountancy Profession*, W. John Brennan, Ed. (Toronto: Canadian Institute of Chartered Accountants, 1979), pp. 58–64.

Stamp, Edward and Maurice Moonitz. *International Auditing Standards* (Englewood Cliffs, N.J.: Prentice-Hall International, 1978).

Stamp, Edward and Maurice Moonitz. "International Auditing Standards—Part I." *CPA Journal*, June 1982, pp. 24–32.

Stamp, Edward and Maurice Moonitz. "International Auditing Standards—Part II." *CPA Journal*, July 1982, pp. 48–53.

Tipgos, Manuel A. "Potential Liabilities in International Accounting Practice." *Journal of Accountancy*, Vol. 151, April 1981, pp. 24–30.

Weinstein, Arnold K., Louis Corsini, and Ronald Pawliczek. "The Big Eight in Europe." *International Journal of Accounting Education and Research*, Spring 1978, pp. 57–71.

Wu, Frederick and Donald W. Hackett. "The Internationalization of U.S. Public Accounting Firms." *International Journal of Accounting*, Spring 1977, pp. 81–91.

CHAPTER 10

Accounting Standards and Standard-setting Process: Within and Among Nations

Whether Gertrude Stein was correct or not when she commented that "a rose is a rose is a rose . . .", as Chapters 2 and 9 have observed, it is not correct to say that an accountant in one country is always the same as an accountant in another country. There are significant differences in the duties accountants are allowed to perform, their certification process, their training and sophistication, and, in some cases, their ethical standards and behavior. It is equally incorrect to assume that accounting standards are set in identical ways in different countries. In many countries, accounting standards are set by legal entities, and in other countries they are set by the accounting profession. In still other countries, they are established jointly by these and other groups, and in a few countries, there does not appear to be any identifiable process! The reasons for such differences should be clear by now. Environmental differences are once again responsible. This chapter briefly describes the accounting standard-setting process and the role in this process played by the accounting profession in several different countries and ends with a discussion of various attempts, past and on-going, to eliminate or reduce many of the major differences in accounting standards through a process called harmonization.

CLASSIFICATION OF ACCOUNTING SYSTEMS

Before delving more deeply into specific countries, it is useful to first classify national accounting systems in terms of certain similarities and differences. Even though no two systems are identical, some systems are similar to others while significantly different from still others. Thus, an understanding of certain groupings can be useful in determining how different one country's system is likely to be from another's and, hence, what degree of caution and further study is advisable when analyzing accounting information generated in another country.

Early Efforts of Classification: Economic Characteristics, Morphologies, and Spheres of Influence

In the past, several attempts have been made to develop accounting classification systems. According to Hatfield, there was some evidence of a three-group classification system (U.S., UK, and Continental) being used as early as the beginning of the twentieth century.[1] Other pioneering work was done by Mueller in 1967 when he attempted to classify accounting systems into four patterns of development: those developed in a macroeconomic framework, a microeconomic approach, an independent discipline, and uniform systems. These four groups were considered "sufficient to embrace accounting as it is presently known and practiced in various parts of the globe."[2] However, Mueller's classification was not based on differences in practices but rather, indirectly, on differences in business, economic, and governmental factors. And, as pointed out by Nobes and Parker, there are other limitations to Mueller's classification:

> The fact that there are only four exclusive groups and no hierarchy reduces the usefulness of the classification. In effect, the Netherlands is the only country in one of the groups and the classification does not show whether Dutch accounting is closer to Anglo-Saxon accounting than it is to Swedish accounting. Similarly, the classification cannot include such facts as that West German accounting exhibits features which remind one of macro-economic accounting as well as uniform accounting. Lastly, Russian or communistic accounting is left out entirely. This may, of course, be sensible if the classification is dealing with published financial reporting.[3]

Yet despite these limitations, Mueller's pioneering efforts did identify some of the major environmental influences on accounting systems, and showed a relationship between patterns of economic development and accounting systems.

In 1968, Mueller continued his classification efforts by focusing on business environments, making the point that business environments need different accounting systems—again, an environmental approach to classification.[4] Building on Mueller's work, Abu-Jbarah used formal statistical analysis to cluster countries by dominant economic characteristics for purposes of recommending segmented reporting according to the resultant

[1]See A. R. Hatfield, "Some Variations in Accounting Practices in England, France, Germany, and U.S.," *Journal of Accounting Research*, Autumn 1966. A similar conclusion with respect to these three groupings was made by L. J. Seidler in his article "International Accounting: The Ultimate Theory Course," *Accounting Review*, October 1967.

[2]Gerhard Mueller, *International Accounting* (New York: Macmillan, 1967), Part I.

[3]C. W. Nobes and R. H. Parker, *Comparative International Accounting* (Homewood, Ill: R. D. Irwin, 1981), p. 207.

[4]Gerhard Mueller, "Accounting Principles Generally Accepted in the U.S. Versus Those Generally Accepted Elsewhere," *International Journal of Accounting*, Spring 1968. pp. 91–103.

clusters.[5] Eight different clusters of countries with significant degrees of economic homogeneity were identified, and although accounting practices were not used to form the clusters, the countries in each group do share some major commonalities in terms of accounting practices.

Others have attempted to develop accounting practice morphologies, such as Buckley[6] in 1974 and the American Accounting Association (AAA) in 1977.[7] Although such morphologies again identified the importance of environmental variables, none went the final step of combining them with empirical data related to accounting practices.

Still other's approaches have strived to identify "spheres of influence," the most comprehensive of which was that of the AAA in 1977, which resulted in five groups: British, Franco-Spanish-Portuguese, German-Dutch, U.S., and Communistic. Yet the rather subjective inductive approach used to develop these spheres of influence is less useful then approaches using accounting practices and environmental characteristics.

Classifications Based on Accounting Practices

One of the first large-scale categorization of countries according to specific accounting practices and standards was done in 1977 by Watt, Hammer, and Burge.[8] Clusters were developed by analyzing published materials for 45 countries for the type of business organizations most closely resembling the U.S. corporation. One classification used audit requirements, and generated four distinct clusters.

> *Group A.* The financial statements of all or most public companies are required to be examined by independent public accountants.
>
> *Group B.* All or most companies must appoint one or more statutory examiners, and some companies—because of size, type of business, or sale of securities to the public—must be examined by independent public accountants.
>
> *Group C.* All or most companies must appoint one or more statutory examiners who need not be independent accountants.
>
> *Group D.* There are no requirements, or only a limited number of companies—such as banks, insurance firms, or listed companies—are subject to audit requirement.

[5]H. M. Abu-Jbarah, "A Subentity Approach for Financial Reporting by Multinational Firms: A Cluster Analysis," Ph.D. dissertation, University of Wisconsin, Madison, Wisconsin, 1972.
[6]I. W. Buckley and M. H. Buckley, *The Accounting Profession* (Los Angeles: Melville, 1972).
[7]American Accounting Association, *Accounting Review*, Vol. 52 Suppl., 1977.
[8]G. Watt, R. Hammer, and M. Burge, *Accounting for the Multinational Corporation* (New York: Financial Executives Research Institute, 1977).

In the A group were 19 countries (20 if one includes the United States); it was dominated by British accounting tradition. The B group included 8 countries, the C and D groups 9 countries each. Table 10.1 lists the countries in each group. Bear in mind that no representation has been made as to the degree of comparison between the foreign auditing standards and the auditing standards generally accepted in the United States.

In a second part of the study, in which categorization was made of the "probability of fair presentation," based largely on the U.S.–UK definition of fair presentation (see Table 10.2) the resulting five clusters were as follows:[9]

1. Those countries with fair presentation broadly equivalent to U.S. standards, with some differences in principles to be dealt with, but with fewer differences of less serious dimensions (17 countries).

2. Fair presentation based on standards from Canada, the United Kingdom, or the United States, but greater differences in number and extent than those in Cluster 1 (5 countries).

3. Statutory requirements approaching U.S. standards in many aspects but some valuation principles being *not* acceptable in the United States (3 countries).

4. Fair presentation recognized in principle but not found consistently in practice (7 countries).

5. Statutory requirements do not approach U.S. standards (2 countries).

The authors of this project limited their analysis to 45 countries and largely to countries of some significance in terms of world economic activity and interest. A more exhaustive examination of the other 100 or so countries in the world would result in a much larger number of countries in Group D in the audit area and in Group 5 the presentation area. In fact, these two clusters would probably be greater in total number than all the other clusters *combined*.

Using information contained in Price Waterhouse's 1973 *Survey of Accounting Practices in 38 Countries*, in 1978 DaCosta, Bourgeois, and Lawson analyzed 100 accounting practices to develop clusters.[10] Curiously, despite looking at 38 countries and 100 accounting practices, only two clusters were generated. One group contained the United Kingdom and nine former members of the British Empire, and the other group included the United States, France, Germany, and all other countries except Canada and the Netherlands (said by the researchers to be unclassifiable). And as Nobes and Parker observed, "any accounting classification that has the U.S.

---

[9]Ibid.
[10]R. C. DaCosta, I. C. Bourgeois, and W. M. Lawson, "A Classification of International Financial Accounting Practices," *International Journal of Accounting*, Spring 1978.

Table 10.1 Categorization of Audit Requirements in 45 Foreign Countries

---

A. The financial statements of all or most public companies are required to be examined by independent public accountants.

Australia	Netherlands
Canada	New Zealand
Colombia	Pakistan
Denmark	Peru
Germany	Philippines
Hong Kong	Rhodesia
India	Singapore
Israel	South Africa
Jamaica	United Kingdom
Kenya	

B. All or most companies must appoint one or more statutory examiners and some companies, because of size, type of business, or sale of securities to the public, must be examined by independent public accountants.

Argentina	Mexico
Brazil	Norway
Greece	Sweden
Japan	Venezuela

C. All or most companies must appoint one or more statutory examiners who need not be independent public accountants.

Belgium	Italy
Chile	Lebanon
France	Spain
Guatemala	Switzerland
Honduras	

D. There are no requirements or only a limited number of companies, such as banks, insurance firms, and listed companies, are subject to audit requirements.

Bahamas	Nicaragua
Bolivia	Panama
Cayman Islands	Paraguay
Indonesia	Uraguay
Netherlands Antilles	

Note: The above, which is based on a review of published material in 1975, lists the general audit requirements in 45 foreign countries for the form of business organization most closely resembling a U.S. corporation. Other forms of business entities may be subject to the same or less stringent requirements. No representation is made as to the degree of comparison between local auditing standards and auditing standards generally accepted in the United States.

Source: G. Watt, R. Hammer, and M. Burge, *Accounting for the Multinational Corporation* (New York: Financial Executives Research Institute, 1977), pp. 214–215.

Table 10.2 Probability of Fair Presentation in 45 Foreign Countries

Fair presentation is broadly equivalent to U.S. standards;[a] differences in principles must still be dealt with, but there are fewer such differences with less serious dimensions.

Argentina[b]	Netherlands
Australia	New Zealand
Bermuda	Peru
Canada	Philippines
Denmark	Rhodesia
India	South Africa
Ireland	United Kingdom
Jamaica	Venezuela
Mexico	

Fair presentation is based on standards imported from Canada, the United Kingdom, or the United States.

Bahamas	Panama
Barbados	Trinidad and Tobago
Nigeria	

Statutory requirements approach U.S. standards in many respects, but some valuation principles would not be acceptable in the United States.

Chile	Japan
Germany	

Fair presentation is recognized in principle but not found consistently in practice.

Brazil	Malaysia
Colombia	Pakistan
Ethiopia	Singapore
Kenya	

Tax legislation is the predominant influence.

Austria	Luxembourg
Belgium	Paraguay
Bolivia	Portugal
France	Sweden
Greece	Uruguay
Italy	

Statutory requirements do not approach U.S. standards.

Spain	Switzerland

[a]For this schedule, failure to require consolidation or the equity method of accounting for investments was not considered a block to fair presentation.

[b]Because of the extreme rate of inflation, fair presentation is dependent on the submission, together with historical-cost-based financial statements, of supplemental financial data restated for price level changes. The same requirement applies in other countries where inflationary conditions are similar.

Source: G. Watt, R. Hammer, and M. Burge, *Accounting for the Multinational Corporation* (New York: Financial Executives Research Institute, 1977), p. 187.

Table 10.3 Classification Based on 1973 Measurement Practices

British Commonwealth Model	Latin American Model	Continental European Model	United States Model
Australia	Argentina	Belgium	Canada
Bahamas	Bolivia	France	Japan
Eire	Brazil	Germany	Mexico
Fiji	Chile	Italy	Panama
Jamaica	Colombia	Spain	Philippines
Kenya	Ethiopia	Sweden	United States
Netherlands	India	Switzerland	
New Zealand	Paraguay	Venezuela	
Pakistan	Peru		
Rhodesia	Uruguay		
Singapore			
South Africa			
Trinidad & Tobago			
United Kingdom			

Source: R. D. Nair and W. F. Frank, "The Impact of Disclosure and Measurement Practices on International Accounting Classifications," *Accounting Review*, July 1980, p. 429.

in the same group as France but not in the same group as the UK or even Canada, seems to fly in the face of the mass of facts and analysis—of the previous conclusions of all other investigators."[11]

In 1980 Nair and Frank used a more elaborate analysis of the 1973 and 1976 Price Waterhouse surveys, dividing the accounting practices into measurement- and disclosure-related groups.[12] In terms of measurement practices, four clusters evolved: the British Commonwealth model (14 countries), the Latin American model (10 countries), the Continental European model (8 countries), and the United States model (6 countries), as shown in Table 10.3.

The usefulness and appropriateness of their method is that the groupings of countries change depending on the classification criteria. West Germany for example, is in the Continental European group in terms of measurement practices but in the United States group in terms of disclosure (advanced disclosure group).

The most recent attempt at classification by accounting practices was done by Nobes and Parker in 1981,[13] the result of which is shown in Figure

[11]Nobes and Parker, *Comparative International Accounting*, p. 210.
[12]R. D. Nair and W. F. Frank, "The Impact of Disclosure and Measurement Practices on International Accounting Classifications," *Accounting Review*, July 1980.
[13]Nobes and Parker, *Comparative International Accounting*.

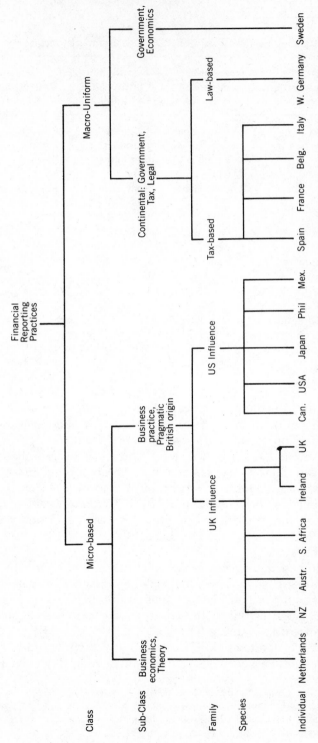

FIGURE 10.1 A suggested classification of accounting systems by practices. (*Source:* Christopher W. Nobes and Robert H. Parker, *Comparative International Accounting,* Homewood, Ill.: R. D. Irwin, 1981, p. 213.)

10.1. Their classification was based on the information contained in their book (contributed by several accounting researchers and practitioners), their own knowledge, and the comments by contributors and other "experts." Communist countries were excluded. Nobes and Parker used Mueller's four classifications to begin with, the DaCosta et al's "UK or U.S. influence" classification, and then four factors of their own selection (tax, conservatism, accounting aim, and base orientation) to develop their own categorizations. What was unique about the Nobes and Parker approach was its attempt to develop an accounting hierarchy and to show not only that two countries are in different groups but also how close or distant these groups are to each other. Thus, German accounting is different but not too different from French accounting, is even further away from U.S. accounting, and further still from Australian accounting. Unfortunately, only 17 countries were included in their classification, and Nobes and Parker admit that this was only a first attempt and needs to be tested against the facts. Nonetheless, their effort represents a new and significant step forward in the accounting system classification area, and is clearly worthy of further development and expansion.

With all these classification models in mind, we now turn to a more detailed description of the role in the standard-setting process in several specific countries, representing some of the different clusters. Our descriptions will focus primarily on standard setting for financial reporting purposes at the national level. This discussion will be followed by a description of standard setting on regional and international levels.

STANDARD-SETTING PROCESS AT THE NATIONAL LEVEL

United States

To serve as a basis for comparison, let us briefly review the standard-setting process and accounting profession in the United States. For financial reporting, the Financial Accounting Standards Board (FASB) and the American Institute of Certified Public Accountants (AICPA) constitute the dominant organizations involved in, and responsible for, establishing accounting and auditing standards. To develop standards, committees are formed, exposure drafts are prepared and circulated to the accounting, financial, and business communities, and if approved (generally accepted), these exposure drafts become standards. Unlike in most countries, though, these standards are not laws nor are they legally binding. However, standards issued are expected to be adhered to by members of the AICPA, and failure to comply with the standards for financial reporting is noted in the external auditor's opinion. Thus in the United States, the accounting profession plays the major role in establishing standards, a role it fiercely defends. This is not to say, however, that other groups and organizations are not important. The U.S. government plays an important role, to be sure. Principles and procedures for tax accounting are developed and established by Congress through various tax laws. In addition, the Securities and Exchange Commission (SEC) develops regulations and standards for financial reporting of publically held companies and firms selling bonds or other types of securities in the U.S. market.

Yet when all is said and done, the U.S. accounting profession maintains a very high level of influence on accounting standards in the United States and, on a comparative basis, perhaps the highest of any country. A large part of its influence stems from the high standards it has established for itself, and which it enforces on its membership.

The accounting profession in the United States enjoys a high status and level of remuneration and is generally considered to be one of the best in the world. Its high level of sophistication and self-policing nature are two of its most unique attributes and two of the major reasons why it has been given such autonomy and experienced relatively little government intervention in establishing accounting standards. There are approximately 200,000 CPAs in the United States, constituting the largest single national group in the world.

As for the accounting standards themselves, the single word that perhaps best characterizes the dominant U.S. approach and philosophy is "flexibility." A statement contained in an AICPA Special Committee report in 1932 concerning the variety of accounting practices in the U.S. succinctly summarizes this point:

> In considering ways of improving the existing situation two alternatives suggest themselves. The first is the selection by competent authority out of the body of acceptable methods in vogue today of detailed sets of rules which would become binding in all corporations of a given class. . . .The arguments against any attempt to apply this alternative to industrial corporations generally are, however, overwhelming.

> The more practicable alternative would be to leave every corporation free to choose its own methods of accounting within the very broad limits to which reference has been made, but require disclosure of the methods employed and consistency in their application from year to year.[14]

The tremendous diversity of the U.S. economy, business, and financial communities, along with the independent individualistic orientation of the U.S. society, are environmental conditions underlying the flexible approach of the U.S. accounting profession and standards and the opposition to uniform, legislated standards. In addition, the high levels of literacy and education in the United States permit the users of accounting information to handle the diversity of accounting practices permitted by this approach, at least in theory.

---

[14]*Audit of Corporate Accounts* (New York: American Institute of Accountants, 1934), p. 7.

As for the other countries listed in Figure 10.1 as following the U.S. approach, their significant commercial relationships—and in the case of Mexico and Canada, geographic proximity—with the United States are a major reason for the similarity in accounting standards and practices. And with the exception of Canada, the accounting professions in the other U.S.-patterned countries are not as developed as that of the United States, making it easier and more feasible for them to adopt the developed accounting system already in place in the United States.

United Kingdom

Accounting standards in the United Kingdom and particularly those related to financial reporting practices, are micro-based, pragmatic, and business-practice oriented, much as in the United States. This similarity is understandable for several reasons, the most obvious and influential being the many similarities existing in the economies, political and legal traditions, and societal characteristics of the United Kingdom and the United States. In addition, much of the U.S. heritage is of British origin, including U.S. accounting, and substantial commercial ties remain between the two nations. Furthermore, eight of the "Big Nine" international accounting firms are of either U.S. or UK origin. Finally, there are many similarities among the two countries' accounting professions and professional accounting bodies.

Yet despite these many similarities, there are some major differences, the most notable of which is the more legal nature of UK accounting. At the present, the Companies Acts of 1948 and Amending Acts of 1967, 1976, and 1980 contain specific accounting regulations for companies in terms of presentation, disclosure, and audit requirements, among others. In addition to these Companies Acts, accounting regulations can be found in professional pronouncements, called Statements of Standard Accounting Practice, issued by the major accounting professional bodies in the United Kingdom. These pronouncements supplement the regulations of the Companies Act, and compliance with them is mandatory for practicing accountants. As in the United States, any departure from them must be disclosed in the auditor's report. Furthermore, the Institute of Chartered Accountants in England and Wales issues specific accounting standards for its members, called "Recommendations on Accounting Principles," which are used to guide the practice of its members.

Unlike the United States, however, the United Kingdom has no unitary professional insitute equivalent to the AICPA. In fact, there are six accounting bodies: the Institute of Chartered Accountants in England and Wales, the Institute of Chartered Accountants in Scotland, the Institute of Chartered Accountants in Ireland, the Association of Certified Accountants, the Institute of Cost and Management Accountants, and the Chartered Institute of Public Finance and Accountancy. Although only the members of the first four are qualified as auditors by the UK government's Department of Trade, all six have formed joint committees to present the views of the accounting profession (Consultative Committee of Accountancy Bodies), to promote accountant standards (the Accounting Standards Committee), and to enhance auditing practices (the Auditing Practices Committee). The individual and collective efforts of these accounting bodies influence, to a great extent, the governmental legislation concerned with accounting, in what has typically been a cooperative manner. The Companies Acts' statutory disclosure requirements say nothing about accounting procedures or financial measurement, and the "true and fair view" the acts require is not defined. Thus, the accounting bodies have assumed the responsibility of developing and obtaining adoption of the specific accounting standards.

One other major difference between the U.S. and UK accounting systems is the influence on the United Kingdom of the EC Directives. Upon joining the EC in 1973, the United Kingdom became covered by various EC-wide laws and regulations, some of which concern accounting. These accounting Directives, described in greater detail later in this chapter, could have the effect of drawing the UK system closer to the Continental European system and further away from the U.S. system.

As for the other countries listed earlier in Figure 10.1, which follow the UK pattern (Ireland, South Africa, New Zealand, and Australia), the strong colonial influence of the old British Empire is the main reason for their similarities in accounting systems. However, if the United Kingdom does move more toward the Continental European system, the historic similarities may lessen in the future.

France

The accounting system in France, as in most Continental European nations, is essentially macro-based (whereas the U.S. and UK systems are micro-based), and is highly government inspired, oriented, and regulated. In the French case, the phenomenon results primarily from the desire and determination of the government to obtain data for economic planning purposes. And because the French planning system is only an indicative one (compliance is voluntary, not mandatory), French tax policy is designed to provide the financial incentives and/or penalties necessary to induce compliance. Therefore, the French accounting system is also highly tax oriented. For example, French law permits the deductability of expenses only if they are included in companies' financial statements.

Although numerous laws and decrees govern accounting practices in France, the single most dominant force is the General Accounting Plan (*Plan Comptable General*). This plan, initially established in 1947 by the National Council on Accountancy, was the first comprehensive effort in France to regulate accounting and has been revised periodically to respond to changing economic and societal needs. Perhaps best known for its uniform chart of accounts the Plan Comptable is in actuality a comprehensive, highly detailed accounting guide. It includes accounting definitions, model financial statements and statistical reports, and evaluation and measurement rules. It also contains sections on cost accounting, and accounting systems for small, medium, and large enterprises. Its reach encompasses businesses and national and local government agencies and is also used to produce national statistics.

One other fairly unique aspect of the French system is its recent emphasis on social accounting, as described previously in Chapter 2. The rising socialist trend in the French society and government was instrumental in the development and subsequent passage of a law requiring French enterprises to prepare and publish a "social balance sheet" (Bilan Social).

Despite the heavy government influence on the establishment of French accounting standards and practices, the French accounting profession has been actively involved in the preparation of legislation related to accounting. In addition, the professional institutes have issued numerous recommendations of their own concerning accounting guidelines: Order of Accounting Experts, (*Ordre des Experts Comptables et des Comptable Agrees*) and the National Council of Accountancy (*Companie Nationale de Comissaires aux Comptes*). The Order of Accounting Experts is the nearest equivalent to the AICPA but is far less independent and powerful. There are roughly 9000 *expert comptables*.

As was discussed earlier in the case of the United Kingdom, French accounting is also now being influenced by the European Community Directives. For the French, the main change will be to require financial statements to present a true and fair view (*une image fidele*)—something not done historically because of the macro, legal, and tax orientation. In addition, more disclosure will now be required.

West Germany

Similar to the French accounting system, West German (hereafter referred to as German) accounting is macro-oriented and heavily influenced by tax regulations and various commercial laws. Unlike the French approach, however, there is no general plan or uniform chart of accounts. Instead, there is reference in the laws to "principles of orderly bookkeeping."

Legal requirements for accounting date back to Germany's first commercial code (Handelsgesetz) in 1897, but presently the Corporations Act (Aktiengesetz) of 1965 and the Publicity Act of 1969 provide the legal bases for German accounting. These acts specify how books are to be maintained, accounting standards and procedures to be used in the preparation of financial statements, disclosure standards, when and what types of financial statements should be published, and many other details concerning classification and reporting requirements. And, in Germany as in

France, there is a requirement that financial statements must follow tax regulations. Furthermore, there is both a strong creditor and a highly conservative orientation in German accounting, because of the generally conservative nature of German society and the major role that German banks play in the economic sector. Not only are German banks the major source of loans, but they are also the major source of investment capital and comprise the largest single group of shareholders in Germany. Furthermore, German banks are permitted to own public accounting firms that can audit the financial statements of the companies owned by the banks. One result of this conservative and creditor-oriented approach is extreme conservatism in the valuation of assets and in the determination of income. Establishment and use of reserves (including some hidden reserves) is permitted and encouraged by law in order to protect creditors.

Compared to the United States, United Kingdom, and France, the German accounting profession is small—less than 4000 members. The Institute of German CPAs (*Institut der Wirtschaftsprüfer en Deutschland*) and the Chamber of Accountants (*Wirthschaftsprüferkammer*) are the two main professional bodies. Membership in the latter is mandatory whereas membership in the former is voluntary. Legally, the chamber's function is to observe professional standards and to educate accountants. In reality, however, the educational responsibility lies in the institute, which also periodically issues recommendations and releases to which compliance is not mandatory.

Switzerland

Switzerland is perhaps best known for three characteristics: its mountains, its political neutrality, and its penchant for, and practice of, secrecy in business and financial matters. Although the first two are of some interest, it is the third that is of direct interest to and has a direct influence on, the Swiss accounting system. Stated simply, Swiss accounting is the most secretive and conservative of any country, a characteristic that many consider an asset rather than a liability.

The Swiss accounting system is heavily influenced by the German and French systems, largely because roughly two thirds of the country is either German or French in language and heritage. As a result, the Swiss system is influenced by laws and tax regulations, with a good measure of secrecy, conservatism, and nondisclosure thrown in. Expenses cannot be deducted for tax purposes unless recorded in the accounting books, and uniform accounting systems have been developed for many industries.

Yet despite a generally legal orientation, the actual influence of legislation dealing with accounting and financial reporting, the Swiss Code of Obligations (*Obligationenrecht*) and its requirements are so broad that they invite and permit very broad interpretations. For example, accounting records must be kept in accordance with the "character and extent of the business." Minimum disclosure is required in financial statements, and requirements for the preparation of consolidated statements and statements of changes in financial position do not exist. Furthermore, the code does not require auditors to have any special expertise.

There is a Society of Swiss Certified Accountants (*Verband Schweizerischer Bucherexpaten,* or VSB), composed of independent professional accountants who normally perform Swiss audits. In fact, the VSB is a division of the Swiss Chamber of Fiduciary Auditors, a chamber that publishes recommendations and has a code of ethics and auditing standards that its members are expected to follow. And in the best Swiss manner, one of the binding rules of the chamber (subject to penalization and possible member disqualification) is that members must observe professional secrecy.

The Netherlands

No discussion of European accounting systems would be complete without mention of the Dutch system, for as portrayed earlier in Figure 10.1, the Dutch system is literally and figuratively in a class by itself. Tax regulations are relatively unimportant; there is no counterpart influence of the Securities and Exchange Commission or the German banking system; no general plan of accounting exists; and there is relatively little legislation concerning accounting, beginning only in 1970 with the passage of the Act on the Annual Accounts of Enterprises. In the absence of these influences, responsibility for accounting standards is in the hands of a unique organization, the Tri-Partite Committee, representing the Dutch Institute of Registered Accountants, also referred to as NIvRA (*Nederlands Institute van Registeraccountants*), the Dutch Employers Association, and the Deliberative Committee of the Central Trade Union Council. Established by the government after passage of the 1970 Action the Annual Accounts, the purpose of the committee is to provide "Observations on the Law on Annual Accounts." However, companies are not required to follow these "Observations," nor are they or their auditors required to state that they have not been followed nor, if not followed, why not. Thus, Dutch law and accounting standards are more permissive and less specific than their counterparts in other industrialized countries.

So what governs Dutch accounting? In three words, "sound business practice." In slightly more words, the Dutch Commercial Code (*Wetboeck van Koophandel*) requires that the books of accounts be maintained that provide information such that a sound judgment can be made on the financial position, profit and loss, and, to the extent possible, solvency and liquidity of the enterprise. The valuation and measurement bases for assets, liabilities, and income must comply with standards regarded as acceptable in economic and social life. Furthermore, the code requires that financial statements be prepared systematically and fairly.

With such a wide degree of freedom, accounting practices could be highly suspect—a situation found in many developing nations. In the case of the Netherlands, however, a sophisticated and well-respected accounting profession keeps things under control, as does a well-educated population and government. Within the Tri-Partite Committee, it is NIvRA that prepares most of the proposals for new pronouncements (observations), and the standards for entrance into the accounting profession and NIvRA are among the highest in the world. As a result, the financial statements of Dutch public companies (*Naamloze Veennootschap* or N.V.) are among the most disclosed, sophisticated, and reliable in the world.

Japan

The industrialization of Japan occurred more recently than in other industrialized nations, and as a result the current accounting system in Japan is relatively new. It is also heavily influenced by, and patterned after, both the German and U.S. accounting systems. Tax laws dominate most financial accounting standards and other accounting principles are contained in government regulations that were first introduced in 1949 by the Economic Stabilization Board. In addition, Japan's Commercial Code, as amended by the Ministry of Finance Regulations of 54 of September 1974, specifies that "fair and just accounting conventions shall be taken into consideration . . . in preparation of accounting books." These regulations require the maintenance of accounting books, the preparation of income statements, balance sheets, and various other supplementary schedules. The U.S. influence is evident in the 1977 regulation requiring consolidated financial statements and the use of the equity method for consolidation of majority-owned subsidiaries.

The Japanese government, and particularly the Ministry of Finance, remains the dominant force in the accounting standard-setting process for several reasons. Like the French government, the Japanese government uses an indicative planning system for economic development: targeting key economic sectors for expansion or contraction, and using significant tax incentives (in variety, scope, and magnitude), to "encourage" firms to follow government plans. A plethora of general and special reserves, tax credits, and tax deductions have been created and authorized toward this end. Unlike in France, however, no general accounting plan or uniform chart of accounts has been developed in Japan. In their place is a much more common and extensive system of interaction between the government and the commercial sectors. However, the Ministry of Finance sets the accounting standards to be followed through the publication of "Business Accounting Principles and Auditing Standards" and is empowered to set fee structures that are binding on all independent auditors.

The other main reason for the government's strong role in setting accounting standards is the relatively small size and newness of the Japanese accounting profession. The foundation for the Japanese Institute of Certified Public Accountants was established in 1948, and the qualification/licensing system is one of the strictest anywhere. Due to such stringent requirements, the number of CPAs in Japan grows by only 300 or so each year. Thus, though high in knowledge and training, the licensed profession in Japan remains small, lessening its potential impact. The Japanese Institute of CPAs primarily sets the CPA qualification standards and occasionally issues "notes" on rules of conduct for the profession and on auditing procedure. Virtually all other standards are promulgated by the Japanese government.

Brazil

As in most developing nations, Brazilian accounting practices are significantly influenced by legal statutes and regulations, established primarily by government agencies. In Brazil, the Commercial Code, the Corporation Law No. 6404 of 1976, tax laws, and various regulations of the Central Bank contain and specify Brazilian accounting standards and practices. As a group, they encompass rules for preparing financial statements (including consolidation and inflation adjustment procedures) for keeping "proper sets of books," and for auditing.

Compared with their counterparts in most developed nations, the Brazilian accounting profession plays a very minor role in establishing accounting standards and procedures. The Brazilian Institute of Independent Auditors simply lacks the size, status, and hence power to have any significant influence. In addition, the Brazilian government has not shown any great desire to relinquish its own power. To put it mildly, government Brazilian style is highly authoritarian, due in large measure to its desire for rapid economic growth and its need to control rapid growth's side effects, such as inflation.

Colombia

As in Brazil, the government determines virtually all accounting standards and practices in Colombia. The primary source of rules and regulations concerning accounting is the Colombia Superintendent of Companies, and no body of accounting principles generally accepted by the profession has been compiled in one publication. In addition, the group that approves, issues, and controls the licensing of public accountants, the Central Board of Accounting (*Junta Central de Contadores*), is a government agency. In contrast, Colombia's professional organization, the National Institute of Public Accountants (*Instituto Nacional de Contadores Publicos*) has as its members only about 10% of Colombia's total of over 5000 registered public accountants. Although its purpose is to secure regulatory legislation and aid in the development of the profession, its actual role is highly immasculated by the government. In addition, requirements for becoming the Colombian equivalent of a CPA (called a *contador publico titulado*), are comparatively minimal: a degree from a recognized Colombian or foreign university and one year's experience in accounting.

HARMONIZATION OF ACCOUNTING STANDARDS AND PRACTICES

The great diversity ard multiplicity of national accounting standards, procedures, and practices form a considerable stumbling block for international investors, creditors, financial analysts, and MNEs. As a result, international efforts to eliminate or significanily reduce the differences in accounting standards continue, through processes called standardization and harmonization. In a strict sense, standardization seeks to *eliminate* such differences by developing uniform standards, whereas harmonization seeks to *lessen* but not eliminate the differences, and to make differences more reconcilable with each other. Because of the obvious problems of achieving total uniformity, our discussion will focus primarily on harmonization efforts. In this final section of Chapter 10, the major forces for and against harmonization are discussed, and the efforts and successes of the various organizations pursuing harmonization are identified and assessed.

Underlying Pressures

The two major pressures behind harmonization efforts are the growth of international business and the increased need for capital. Virtually every nation has become more dependent on international trade and investment, and, therefore, more of their firms are involved in one or more types of international business activity. As interaction with foreign suppliers, customers, partners, creditors, investors, and governments increases, so does the awareness of differences in accounting systems and practices and the problems related to them. Paramount among these problems are analyses of financial statements prepared in different ways and trying to reconcile different national standards in preparing a globally consolidated financial report. For example, in 1980 Royal Dutch Petroleum received a qualified audit opinion from its independent auditor because U.S. and UK standards for income tax allocation were contradictory. Whichever standard it went with (U.S. or UK) one of the joint auditors (U.S., UK, or Dutch) would qualify their opinion.[15] Clearly, these and other analysis problems would be lessened if there were fewer differences in the preparation of the statements. Hence, one of the arguments for harmonization. Greater harmo-

---

[15]Royal Dutch Petroleum is based in the Netherlands but is partially owned by Shell Transport and Trading Company of the United Kingdom and has sizable investments in the United States, which it has to consolidate in preparing its financial report.

nization would also improve company efficiency by putting to more productive use the personnel, time, and money currently required to translate and interpret subsidiaries' financial statements and accounting records prepared under disparate principles and procedures. Pricing and resource allocation decisions would become easier and more accurate as well, and further economic and political integration (e.g., in the European Community) would be facilitated.

The increased need for companies to raise outside capital is another major force behind harmonization efforts. For decades, companies enjoyed higher levels of protection than they do now. In addition, formal oligopoly and cartel arrangements made the business environment less competitive than it is today, and there was less competition from developing countries. Over the past three decades, however, international competition has increased dramatically, and has made it necessary for firms to strengthen their competitiveness, a process that has required a level of funding beyond the level of many firms' retained earnings and local borrowing power. Increasingly, they have had to borrow or sell stock internationally in financial markets that are composed of highly sophisticated investors and creditors and markets in which the competition for funds has also increased.

The growing competition for domestic and international funds has forced a certain amount of accounting harmonization to take place because the suppliers of funds have required it. That is, lenders and investors have a wide variety of requests for their funds from companies of an equally wide variety of countries. In order to make the best investment or loan decision, these suppliers require greater standardization of financial reports. A company whose financial statements are highly detailed and disclosed and represent fairly its financial position is more likely to get funds from the suppliers than one whose financial statements are incomplete, poorly disclosed, and not truly reflective of its financial position. In many cases, companies are not allowed to sell stock or float bonds unless their statements meet certain standards and formats. This is true for any company seeking to sell its shares on the New York Stock Exchange, for example.

Even when strict uniformity is not required, such as in the Eurodollar or Eurobond market, companies have found it necessary to provide financial statements in forms comparable to those of major U.S.- and UK-based multinationals. This does not mean there is international consensus that U.S./UK accounting is the best. But it does reflect the fact that the United States and United Kirgdom have the largest financial markets and their companies are the largest borrowers and investors on a global scale; hence they tend to set the standards. It also reflects the influence of the major international accounting firms, which typically provide the independent audit before a major international funding is attempted. As noted earlier, these accounting firms have their roots in the United Kingdom or the United States, and, as a consequence, they tend to force a certain harmonization of accounting reports along U.S./UK lines.

The same increased need for capital pushes countries toward harmonization in order to obtain funding for large-scale national or regional projects such as infrastructure developments. They, too, must compete for funds with multinationals and other governments seeking funds. Organizations such as the International Bank for Reconstruction and Development generally require a certain uniform format and underlying accounting system in order for a proposal to be considered.

Other pressures for harmonization come from international political bodies, such as the UN, OECD, and the EC. As might be expected, their desires are typically politically inspired and, in turn, are usually driven by the desires of their various political constituencies to obtain greater information from companies in a more standardized form. Their activities are discussed in greater detail later in this chapter.

Impediments to Harmonization

What all this means is that environmental forces, both economic and political, have exerted significant pressures for harmonization. Combined with the earlier cited advantages of harmonization, they offer what appears to be a compelling argument in favor of harmonization.

All well and good, you say. So why hasn't it happened? Who would stand in the way of achieving such a desirable condition? The answer lies in the differences in environments and predilections of the countries of the world. The same environmental differences that cause each country's accounting system to be different also act as impediments to eliminating the differences in accounting. Differences in levels of industrialization, education, societal goals, and aspirations pose significant difficulties in achieving consensus on accounting standards and their feasibility of adoption.

Nationalism, egotism, and pride also impede progress: the French would like to have the new global system patterned after the French system, the Germans after the German system, the Americans after the American systems. Each country believes its system is the best and is reluctant to adopt a system it perceives to be inferior or unsuitable. Some countries, companies, and individuals prefer to retain the imperfections and inefficiencies caused by the differences in accounting in order to take advantage of them. The secrecy offered by the Swiss banking and accounting is one example.

It is difficult to imagine one single, uniform system of accounting for all companies of all countries. After all, the U.S. accounting profession has argued since its inception that uniformity is not desirable or possible even within the United States alone. Flexibility and adaptability, the cornerstones of this line of reasoning, are not totally illogical. Therefore, what is likely to develop is blocs of accounting uniformity. That is, certain groups of nations will establish uniform, highly harmonized accounting standards for their members—for example, regional economic groups and resource cartels.

Yet regardless of the level at which harmonization is desirable and feasible, attaining it requires specific action. Some organizations or groups must lay the groundwork, do the homework, lobby for the change and implementation, and provide the necessary skills and knowledge. It is to these groups that we now shift our attention.

The Actors and the Action

Even a partial list of the actors in this evolving drama of international accounting harmonization looks like a bowl of alphabet soup: ICCAP, IFAC, IASC, AFA, ICAC, AISG, IAA, UEC, CAPA. Many of these organizations have fairly similar objectives; however, their motivations are often different. Other differences can be found in the scope and scale of their efforts, their successes to date and the likelihood of their success in the future. To help simplify the discussion of harmonization efforts, it is useful to categorize the various organizations into several groups, as suggested by Daley and Mueller.[16] One group is composed of international political bodies who seek to formulate accounting reporting requirements in a political organization. The other group consists of private, nonpolitical organizations, which has basically two subgroups. The first subgroup is composed of accounting standard-setting organizations whose representation is from national professional accounting bodies, and whose primary purpose is to set international financial reporting standards. The other subgroup is composed of international professional accounting organizations that deal with professional issues such as auditing standards, education requirements, and ethical standards for the profession—all in an international setting. These two private groups will be discussed together after the international political groups.

International Political Bodies

The major organizations in this group involved in accounting harmonization efforts are the United Nations (UN), the Organizational for Economic Development and Cooperation (OECD), the EC, and the African Accounting Council (AAC). Representation on their accounting committees is established primarily by political considerations rather than accounting expertise. For example, the U.S. representative on the UN and OECD efforts is the State Department.

---

[16]See Lane Daley and Gerhard Mueller, "Accounting in the Arena of World Politics," *Journal of Accountancy*, February 1982, pp. 40–50.

The United Nations. The UN is the organization with the largest geographic spread and representation. Through its Commission on Transnationals and its Ad-Hoc Intergovernmental Working Group of Experts on International Standards of Accounting and Reporting (hereafter referred to as the Ad-Hoc Group of Experts), several objectives have been pursued since the mid-1970s.

The Commission on Transnationals has sought to secure effective international arrangements for operations of MNEs and to further understanding of the nature and effects of MNE activities. To date, their main work has been devoted to establishing a "code of conduct" for MNEs, covering all aspects of their operations including trade, finance, exploitation of natural resources, labor relations and marketing policies, R&D, and transfer pricing. One small part of the code of conduct concerning disclosure requirements is shown in Exhibit 10.1. For the most part, the code's recommendations for minimal disclosure in corporate annual reports are based on U.S. accounting standards for consolidation and segment reporting, but they also include new suggestions for disclosing nonfinancial information in such areas as organizational structure, environmental impacts, production levels, planned investments, and labor and employment.

The Ad-Hoc Group of Experts was composed of 32 nations: 9 from Africa, 6 from Asia, 6 from South and Central America, 2 from North America, and 9 from Europe. Of these 32, 20 were also members of the International Federation of Accountants, 16 were members of the International Accounting Standards Committee, 10 belonged to the OECD, 5 to the EC, 4 to the African Accounting Council, 6 to the Union Europienne des Experts Comptables Economiques and Financiers (UEC), 6 to the Conference of Asian and Pacific Accountants (CAPA), 9 to the Associacion Interamerica de Contabilidad (AIC), and 1 to the ASIAN Federation of Accountants (AFA). In their deliberations about what the UN should do (if anything) regarding accounting standards, the Ad-Hoc Group divided sharply, largely along geographic and economic development lines. The Western industrial group did not believe the UN was the appropriate organization to set standards, sought to reduce the scope of proposed standards, and sought to make the form of recommendation be only illustrative of "best practice" rather than be mandatory. The other group, composed essentially of developing nations in South and Central America, Africa, and Asia, wanted the standards to be wide ranging and mandatory.

Thus, the UN's efforts have become polarized along north–south, developed–less developed political lines, with little chance for reconciliation or agreement.[17]

---

[17]For more details on the workings, deliberations, and progress of these UN efforts, see James Carty, "Accounting Standards in the United Nations," *World Accounting Report*, Special Feature, September 1982, pp. 1–15.

The OECD.   Like the UN, the OECD has also proposed a code of conduct for multinational enterprises, which deals in part with accounting. More specifically, one provision of the code contains guidelines for financial disclosure. The major elements of this provision are listed below.

- Enterprises should publish within reasonable time limits, on a regular basis, but at least annually, financial statements and other pertinent information relating to the enterprise as a whole, comprising in particular:
- the structure of the enterprise, showing the name and location of the parent company, its main affiliates, its percentage ownership, direct and indirect, in these affiliates, including shareholdings between them;
- the geographical areas where operations are carried out and the principal activities carried on therein by the parent company and the main affiliates;
- the operating results and sales by geographical area and the sales in the major lines of business for the enterprise as a whole;
- significant new capital investment by geographical area and, as far as practicable, by major lines of business for the enterprise as a whole;
- a statement of the sources and uses of funds by the enterprise as a whole;
- the average number of employees in each geographical area;
- research and development expenditure for the enterprise as a whole;
- the policies followed in respect of intra-group pricing;
- the accounting policies, including those on consolidation, observed in compiling the published information.[18]

Comparing the recommendations of the UN and OECD, it is evident that the OECD takes a less negative view of MNEs and tends to ignore the recommendations of the UN to significantly expand disclosure standards beyond what is already common practice among OECD member nations. Thus, no new ground is being broken by the OECD, and its recommendations are largely distillations of existing national standards. These differences are primarily attributable to the different compositions of the two international organizations. The OECD is often referred to as "the rich man's club" because its members are industrialized nations and the home of most of the world's MNEs. The UN represents a much broader spectrum of countries and is significantly influenced by developing nations, especially in its General Assembly and committees (with the exception of the Security Council), many if not most of whom are antagonistic toward MNEs.

It should be pointed out that both the UN and OECD codes are suggestive. Company and country compliance with them is voluntary, and neither organization has any real power to enforce adoption or adherence. Nevertheless, these two international organizations do carry a certain amount of clout and powers of suasion not found in most other international groups. This fact, and the fact that both groups tend to be more

[18]Organization for Economic Cooperation and Development, "Declaration on International Investment and Multinational Enterprises," *OECD Observer*, No. 82, July–August 1976, p. 14.

Exhibit 10.1 Accounting Requirements Contained in the Code of Conduct for Transnational Corporations

43.   Transnational corporations should disclose to the public in the countries in which they operate by appropriate means of communication, clear, full and comprehensible information on the structure, policies, activities and operations of the transnational corporation as a whole. The information should include financial as well as non-financial items and should be made available on a regular annual basis, normally within six months and in any case not later than twelve months from the end of the financial year of the corporation. In addition, during the financial year, transnational corporations should wherever appropriate make available a semi-annual summary of financial information.

The financial information to be disclosed annually should be provided where appropriate on a consolidated basis, together with suitable explanatory notes and should include, inter alia, the following:

(1)   a balance sheet;
(2)   an income statement, including operating results and sales;
(3)   a statement of allocation of net profits or net income;
(4)   a statement of the sources and uses of funds;
(5)   significant new long-term capital investment;
(6)   research and development expenditure.

The non-financial information referred to in the first paragraph should include, inter alia, the following:

(1)   the structure of the transnational corporation, showing the name and location of the parent company, its main entities, its percentage ownership, direct and indirect, in these entities, including shareholdings between them;
(2)   the main activity of its entities;
(3)   employment information including average number of employees;
(4)   accounting policies used in compiling and consolidating the information published;
(5)   policies applied in respect of transfer pricing.

The information provided for the transnational as a whole should as far as practicable be broken down:

—by geographical area or country, as appropriate, with regard to the activities of its main entities, sales, operating results, significant new investments and numbers of employees;
—by major line of business as regards sales and significant new investment.

The method of breakdown as well as details of information provided should/shall be determined by the nature, scale and interrelationships of the transnational corporations' operations, with due regard to their significance for the areas or countries concerned.

The extent, detail and frequency of the information provided should take into account the nature and size of the transnational corporation as a whole, the require-

Exhibit 10.1 *Continued*

ments of confidentiality and effects on the transnational corporation's competitive position, as well as the cost involved in producing the information.

The information herein required should, as necessary, be in addition to information required by national laws, regulations and administrative practices of the countries in which transnational corporations operate.

Source: United Nations Commission on Transnational Corporations, proposal for a Code of Conduct.

political than accounting in nature and composition, has caused some alarm in national professional accounting groups. Yet, until the latter groups can make more substantial progress on their own or collectively toward international accounting harmonization, the UN and OECD are certain to persist in their respective courses of action.

The EC. Even more active and with even greater prospects for being effective in achieving regional accounting harmonization is the EC. The EC has moved toward full economic and political integration of its member countries along a planned schedule. Significant strides have already been made by eliminating internal trade restrictions and establishing an EC parliament. The parliament has also made progress toward establishing EC-wide laws, including business law, and several steps have been taken by an EC commission to harmonize the accounting systems of the member countries. More specifically, as shown in Table 10.4, the commission has worked on a number of directives regarding the presentation and content of limited liability companies' annual reports or financial statements, the

Table 10.4 EC Directives Related to Accounting

Directive	Subject	Date of Initial Draft	Date Adopted
First	Ultra-vivre rules	1964	1968
Second	Minimum capital limitations on distributions and interim dividends, separation of public from private companies	1970	1976
Third	Mergers	1970	1978
Fourth	Statement formats, accounting rules	1971	1978
Fifth	Structure, management, and audit of companies	1972	
Sixth	Prospectuses	1972	1980
Seventh	Consolidations	1976	1983
Eighth	Qualifications and work of auditors	1978	1984

method of valuation and consolidation used to derive them, and their audit and publication. Of the directives issued or proposed by the commission, the Fourth, Fifth, and Seventh Directives most directly concern accounting harmonization.

The Fourth Directive, proposed in 1971, revised and reissued in 1974, was formally adopted in 1978. The main objectives of the Fourth Directive are as follows:[19]

1. To coordinate the numerous national laws governing the publication, presentation, and content of financial statements.
2. To establish throughout the EC minimum requirements for the disclosure of financial information by companies.
3. To establish the underlying principle that financial statements should give a "true and fair" view of a company's financial position and the results of its operations.
4. To protect the interests of third parties such as employees, unions, government bodies, and creditors.

Articles 1 and 2 specify the types of companies covered by the directive (essentially the European equivalents of U.S. corporations) and the general reporting requirements. Articles 3 through 27 pertain to the format of the annual reports, and Articles 28 through 39 concern the rules for valuation. Articles 40 through 43 deal with the content of the notes to the accounts, Articles 44 through 50 deal with publication requirements, and Articles 51 and 52 concern the procedural, statutory changes in national laws that would be necessary for compliance.

The main features of the EC-wide system of financial reporting are the true and fair presentation concept, the going concern and matching concepts, valuation at replacement cost of limited-life tangible fixed assets, disclosure of differences in inventory values determined by FIFO and any other specified method used (if internal), and considerable improvements in disclosure in general, including a great deal of segment reporting.

The Fourth Directive is the most comprehensive set of accounting rules developed and in existence within the EC, and both private and public companies must comply with it. As yet, only a few EC member nations have officially adopted legislation implementing the directive, although most have appropriate legislation pending.

The proposed Fifth Directive deals with the structure, management, and external audits of limited-liability corporations. However, significant difficulties in reaching agreement on this directive caused it to be withdrawn. The major disagreements centered on the management structure of

---

[19]Commission of the European Communities, *Amended Proposal for a Fourth Council Directive for Co-ordination of National Legislation Regarding the Annual Accounts of Limited Liability Companies* (Brussels, 1974).

these companies, which vary significantly among countries. Probably other EC legislation on this topic will be needed before the Fifth Directive will be taken up again.

The Seventh Directive, proposed in 1976 and adopted in 1983, concerns consolidated financial statements—the largest single omission of the Fourth Directive.[20] The first group of articles describes who must prepare consolidated statements, and a few cases are identified that differ from standards in the United States. One of the cases concerns enterprises under central or unified management but not necessarily a controlling degree of ownership—specifically, an enterprise that (a) holds the major part of another enterprise's subscribed capital, (b) controls the majority of votes in another enterprise, and (c) can appoint more than half the members of another enterprise's administrative, managerial, or supervisory body.

There is also a requirement for consolidation of enterprises that are independent of each other but dominated in the sense of any of these three conditions by a common enterprise (e.g., the parent) domiciled outside the EC. For example, General Motors would have to prepare and publish a combined statement limited to but encompassing all its subsidiaries and branches in the EC countries and including any other subsidiaries dominated by its European subsidiaries.

Articles 9 through 20 cover the composition of consolidated accounts and the methods and principles of consolidation. Among other things, these articles specify that acquired assets be valued at fair market value, accounts of enterprises with different year ends be consolidated on the basis of audited interim statements, the same accounting principles used for consolidation be used in preparing the individual annual accounts that were subsequently consolidated, and the equity method of accounting be applied to all intercorporate investments over which significant influence is exercised (more than 20% of ownership). The remaining articles deal with disclosure of items in the notes of consolidated statements and publication rules.

The Eighth Directive, initially proposed in 1978 and adopted in 1984, deals with the professional qualifications of statutory auditors: education, training, examination, formation of professional associations or companies, and professional independence.

In addition to the eight directives listed in Table 10.4, the commission has issued a directive to publish interim financial statements (1982) and has published a number of other unnumbered directives dealing with industry-specific financial statements (e.g., banking, insurance). The Interim Reporting Directive calls for publication of a six-month statement within four months of the end of the accounting period and requires explanatory statements that enable comparisons to the prior year's corresponding peri-

[20]Commission of the European Communities, Proposal for a Seventh Directive Concerning Group Accounts (Brussels, 1976).

od. It applies to all companies listed on stock exchanges in EC countries, whether or not they are European-based companies.

In assessing EC efforts toward accounting harmonization, several things must be kept in mind. First, most of the articles of the directives are devoted to matters of form rather than content. Second, most of the provisions call on member countries to permit companies to comply with the directives rather than require their companies to comply. A major reason for these situations is that these are essentially two dominant, yet opposing, accounting schools of thought within the EC. The first school is that of France and Germany, basically a legalistic and highly codified approach; the other is that of the United Kingdom, Ireland, and the Netherlands, which is essentially a micro, "true and fair" approach. In addition, professional auditing standards vary considerably among the member countries, as do existing accounting principles and, especially, accounting practices. Finally, significant environmental differences remain among the EC nations, and these differences continue to impede both accounting harmonization and full economic and political integration. Thus, the EC's movement toward accounting harmonization still has a long way to go. Nonetheless, the effort is commendable, has achieved some success, and does demonstrate that harmonization is feasible, albeit a slow and tortuous process.

Private Standard-Setting Organizations

Of the half dozen major organizations in this group, the International Accounting Standards Committee (IASC) is certainly one of the most influential and broadly based, and is probably the most successful in achieving harmonization of standards. Founded in 1973, IASC's main objectives have been to formulate standards to be observed in the presentation of audited financial statements, and to promote their acceptance and adherence.

The formal IASC objectives are as follows:

1. To establish and maintain an International Accounting Standards Committee with a membership and powers set out below whose functions are to formulate and publish, in the public interest, standards to be observed in the presentation of audited financial statements and to promote their worldwide acceptance and observance.

2. To support the standards promulgated by the Committee.

3. To use their best endeavors
   a. To ensure that published financial statements comply with these standards or that there is disclosure to the extent to which they do not, and to persuade governments the authorities controlling securities markets, and the industrial and business community that published financial statements should comply with these standards.
   b. To ensure (1) that the auditors satisfy themselves that the financial statements comply with these standards or, if the financial statements do not comply with these standards, that the fact of non-compliance is dis-

closed in the financial statements, (2) that in the event of non-disclosure reference to non-compliance is made in the audit report.

   c. To ensure that, as soon as practicable, appropriate action is taken in respect of auditors whose audit reports do not meet the requirements of (b) above.

4. To seek to secure similar general acceptance and observance of these standards internationally.[21]

The actual workings of the IASC are similar to those of the Financial Accounting Standards Board of the United States. Both organizations conduct research studies, make exposure drafts, do interim studies, and promulgate standards. As of 1984, the IASC had adopted 19 standards, and had 5 exposure drafts outstanding. Table 10.5 lists the topics these standards and exposure drafts are concerned with.

The founding members of the IASC were Australia, Canada, France, Japan, Mexico, the Netherlands, the United Kingdom, Ireland, the United States, and West Germany. Currently over 88 organizations from 62 countries are members. On a comparative basis, the IASC has been successful. However, it is evident that adherence to the existing standards, even by the founding member countries, has been far from complete or comprehensive. In his now classic article on international accounting standards, Sir Henry Benson, former president of the Institute of Chartered Accountants in England and Wales, summarized some of the major reasons.

> It is one step to write international Standards; it is another step forward for professional bodies to notify their members that they are to observe them. The ultimate goal is to make reasonable efforts to see that the members do, in fact, observe them. Although progress is being made here and in other countries, I am sure that no other accountancy body anywhere in the world has yet done enough to ensure that either its own local Standards or international Standards are, in fact, being applied by its members in the conduct of their professional practice or in their capacity as directors of business enterprises.[22]

As but one example, the FASB, has no official role in, nor does it routinely consider or take positions on, IASC standards. Ralph Walters, a former member of FASB, has said that the FASB's attitude toward the IASC has been a mixture of unofficial encouragement, moral support, and benign neglect.[23] Yet the United States, primarily through the AICPA, which is a member of the IASC, does essentially encourage its accounting profession to adhere to IASC standards, which is more than can be said of all IASC members. Thus, although there has been explicit formal acceptance of the

[21]International Accounting Standards Committee, *Work and Purpose of the International Accounting Standards Committee* (London: IASC, 1973).

[22]Sir Henry Benson, "The Story of International Accounting Standards," *Accountancy*, July 1976, pp. 34–39.

[23]Ralph Walters, *DH&S Week in Review*, 6 April, 1984, p. 1.

Table 10.5 Standards and Exposure Drafts of the IASC as of March 1983

Definitive Standards	
IAS-1	Disclosure of Accounting Policies
IAS-2	Valuation and Presentation of Inventories in the Context of the Historical Cost System
IAS-3	Consolidated Financial Statements
IAS-4	Depreciation Accounting
IAS-5	Information to Be Disclosed in Financial Statements
IAS-6	Accounting Responses to Changing Prices
IAS-7	Statement of Changes in Financial Position
IAS-8	Unusual and Prior Period Items and Changes in Accounting Policies
IAS-9	Accounting for Research and Development Activities
IAS-10	Contingencies and Events Occurring after the Balance Sheet Data
IAS-11	Accounting for Construction Contracts
IAS-12	Accounting for Taxes on Income
IAS-13	Presentation of Current Assets and Liabilities
IAS-14	Reporting Financial Information by Segment
IAS-15	Information for Reflecting the Effects of Changing Prices
IAS-16	Accounting for Property, Plant, and Equipment
IAS-17	Accounting for Leases
IAS-18	Revenue Recognition
IAS-19	Accounting for Retirement Benefits in the Financial Statements of Employers

Exposure Drafts Outstanding	
E-21	Accounting for Goverment Grants and Disclosure of Government Assistance
E-22	Accounting for Business Combinations
E-23	Accounting for the Effects of Changes in Foreign Exchange Rates
E-24	Capitalization of Borrowing Costs
E-25	Disclosure of Related Party Transactions

Source: Jeffrey S. Arpan and Dhia D. AlHashim, *International Dimensions of Accounting* (Boston, Mass.: Kent Publishers, 1984), p. 53.

IASC Standards, considerable discrepancy remains between what some countries say they do and what they actually do.

The other broadly based international organization is the International Federation of Accountants (IFAC), whose membership of 87 accountancy bodies from more than 60 countries represents over 75,000 accountants. As was discussed in Chapter 9, IFAC is primarily concerned with auditing standards. Its Auditing Practices Committee has issued a dozen Definitive Standards and is working on more than a dozen exposure drafts, its Education Committee has issued three guidelines, and its Ethics Committee has issued numerous guidelines and statements of guidance. (The reader can refer to Chapter 9, pp. 309 to 312, for a more detailed discussion of IFAC.)

In addition to these broadly based organizations, there are a number of regional associations dealing with the auditing standards/profession and still others dealing with general accounting standards. These groups' concerns, by definition and practice, are oriented toward harmonization on a regional rather than international basis.

In the African region there is the Association of Accountancy Bodies in West Africa (ABWA). Established in 1981 by professional accounting bodies in Ghana and Nigeria, ABWA membership is open to other West African countries. There is also the African Accounting Council (AAC), but it is more of a political organization than a private one.

In the Western Hemisphere, there is the Association Interamericana de Contabilidad (AIC), also known as the Inter-American Accounting Association, established in 1949. In addition to organizing conferences, the AIC has several standing committees that issue periodic reports on a wide range of accounting topics, a preponderance of which deal with accounting in Spanish-speaking countries and problems of accounting development.

In the Asian Pacific regions, there are the Confederation of Asia and Pacific Accountant's (CAPA) and the Association of Southeast Asian Nations Federation of Accountants (AFA). CAPA's origin was in 1957 and it has held ten regional conferences. CAPA aims at developing a coordinated regional accounting profession among its membership of roughly 30 professional accounting organizations from some 20 countries. The AFA, established in 1977, is composed of only five member nations: Indonesia, Malaysia, the Philippines, Singapore, and Thailand. It has standing committees on Accounting Principles and Standards, Auditing, Education, and Professional Development. As could be expected, there are considerable overlaps between AFA and CAPA in objectives and membership.

In Europe, there is the UEC. By far the most active of the private regional organizations, the UEC represents a much broader base of European countries than the EC, as its 25 member organizations come from 19 nations. The UEC conducts congresses every three to four years, operates five standing committees (Auditing, Education, Ethics, Lexicology, and Technical Research), and issues a wide variety of publications including professional statements, research studies, special reports, occasional papers, a quarterly newsletter, and an accounting dictionary. Other details of UEC's organizations and activities related to auditing harmonization have already been discussed in Chapter 9.

In Scandinavia, there is the Nordic Federation of Accountants (NFA), the "grandfather" of all regional organizations, having been founded in 1931. The NFA's membership is composed of all accounting organizations in Denmark, Finland, Iceland, Norway, and Sweden, representing over 4000 practicing accountants.

Exhibit 10.2 Selected Representation on International Standard-Setting Bodies by Individual Country[a]

Country	AAC	AFA	CAPA	EEC	UEC	AIC	IASC	IFAC	OECD	UN[b]
6 Group Representation										
Canada	—	—	X	—	—	X	X	X	X	X
France	—	—	—	X	X	—	X	X	X	X
Germany	—	—	—	X	X	—	X	X	X	X
Italy	—	—	—	X	X	—	X	X	X	X
Netherlands	—	—	—	X	X	—	X	X	X	X
Great Britain	—	—	—	X	X	—	X	X	X	X
United States	—	—	X	—	—	X	X	X	X	X
5 Group Representation										
Belgium	—	—	—	X	X	—	X	X	X	—
Denmark	—	—	—	X	X	—	X	X	X	—
Ireland	—	—	X	X	X	—	X	X	X	—
Japan	—	—	—	—	—	—	X	X	X	X
Luxembourg	—	—	—	X	X	—	X	X	X	—
Norway	—	—	—	—	X	—	X	X	X	X
Philippines	—	X	X	—	—	—	X	X	—	X
4 Group Representation										
Australia	—	—	X	—	—	—	X	X	X	—
Brazil	—	—	—	—	—	X	X	X	—	X
Finland	—	—	—	—	X	—	X	X	X	—
Greece	—	—	—	—	X	—	—	X	X	—
India	—	X	X	—	—	—	X	X	—	X
Malaysia	—	X	X	—	—	—	X	X	—	—
Mexico	—	—	—	—	—	X	X	X	—	X

	4 Group Representation				3 Group Representation					
New Zealand	—	X	X	X	—	—	—	X	—	X
Nigeria	X	—	X	X	—	—	—	—	—	—
Panama	X	—	X	X	X	—	—	X	—	—
Pakistan	X	—	X	X	—	X	—	X	X	—
Portugal	—	X	X	X	—	—	—	—	—	—
Singapore	—	—	X	X	—	X	—	—	—	—
Spain	—	X	X	X	—	X	—	X	—	—
Sweden	—	X	X	X	—	X	—	X	X	—
Argentina	X	—	X	—	X	—	—	—	—	—
Bangladesh	—	—	X	X	—	—	—	X	—	—
Cyprus	X	—	X	X	X	—	—	—	—	—
Dominican Republic	X	—	X	—	—	X	—	X	—	—
Fiji	—	X	X	X	—	—	—	—	—	—
Iceland	—	—	X	—	—	—	—	X	X	—
Sri Lanka	—	—	X	X	—	—	—	X	—	X
Thailand	—	—	X	—	—	—	—	X	X	—
Representatives	19	21	37	32	7	16	9	14	5	1
Total number of representations in body	30	23	53	42	21	18	9	18	5	23

[a] Adapted from United Nations Report E/C.10/AC.3/7 of 9 September 1980. Second session of the Ad-Hoc Intergovernmental Working Group on International Standards of Accounting and Reporting–Commission on Transnational Corporations–UN Economic and Social Council.

[b] Member of the UN intergovernmental working group.

Source: Lane Daley and Gerhard Mueller, "Accounting in the Arena of World Politics," *Journal of Accountancy*, February 1982, p. 43.

Exhibit 10.3 Interrepresentation among Major International Standard-Setting Bodies[a]

Body	AAC	AFA	CAPA	EEC	UEC	AIC	IASC	IFAC	OECD	UN[b]
AAC	23	—	—	—	—	—	1	1	—	3
AFA	—	5	5	—	—	—	3	5	—	1
CAPA	—	5	18	—	—	2	13	16	5	5
EEC	—	—	—	9	9	—	9	9	9	5
UEC	—	—	—	9	18	—	16	16	17	5
AIC	—	—	2	—	—	21	5	11	2	7
IASC	1	3	13	9	16	5	42	39	20	17
IFAC	1	5	16	9	16	11	39	53	22	21
OECD	—	—	5	9	17	2	20	22	23	8
UN[b]	3	1	5	5	5	7	17	21	8	30

[a]Adapted from United Nations Report E/C.10/AC.3/7 of 9 September 1980. Second session of the Ad-Hoc Intergovernmental Working Group on International Standards of Accounting and Reporting–Commission on Transnational Corporations–UN Economic and Social Council.
[b]Member of the UN intergovernmental working group.
Source: Daley and Mueller, *Journal of Accountancy*, February 1983, p. 44.

Interrelationships

Despite the plethora of political and private organizations working toward harmonization, there are significant interrelationships among them. As Daley and Mueller observed, within the ten major Organizations (AAC, AFA, AIC, CAPA, EC, VEC, IASC, IFAC, OECD and the UN), thirty-seven countries have memberships in at least three international/regional bodies.[24] And as shown in Exhibit 10.2, the countries with the most representation (in six of the ten organizations) are all Western industrialized nations, and none are Middle Eastern. Exhibit 10.3 shows the cross-representation among several of the major international accounting organizations. It can be seen that the UEC is almost completely represented in the OECD, IASC, and IFAC; the IASC and IFAC represent almost every OECD country; and the IASC is essentially a subset of the IFAC. This high degree of cross-representation facilitiates the process of international interaction and accounting harmonization as efforts on regional levels are quickly communicated to more global organizations, and vice versa.

Supporting Roles

In addition to the harmonization activities of the major international and regional organizations described above, many other groups are involved directly or indirectly in the harmonization effort. Some take essentially a

[24]Daley and Mueller, "Accounting in the Arena of World Politics."

lobbyist role, such as the International Chamber of Commerce, the National Foreign Trade Council, and the FASB. Others provide forums of interaction for accounting practitioners, researchers, and educators, such as the International Congress of Accountants, the International Accounting Education Conference, the American Accounting Association, the Canadian Association of Academic Accountants, the European Accounting Association, the Japanese Accounting Association, the Association of University Instructors in Accounting (United Kingdom, Australia, New Zealand), and on a broader, interdisciplinary basis, the Academy of International Business and the European International Business Association.

Several major universities have also played supporting roles in harmonization by establishing centers and institutes of international accounting education and research, such as the University of Illinois, the University of Washington (Seattle), the University of Texas at Dallas, California State University at Northridge, the University of Connecticut, and in the United Kingdom, the University of Lancaster.

More on the practitioner side, various associations and federations of financial analysts and financial executives also conduct research, seminars, and operate task forces dealing with international accounting issues. Virtually all national professional accounting institutes have international sections, divisions, or committees that deal with international accounting practices and seek to inform their memberships of new developments as well as respond to exposure drafts of international accounting organizations. Similarly, the World Federation of Stock Exchanges, and individually most of its members, is also involved in the accounting harmonization efforts.

Last but not least are the major international accounting firms. To provide accounting services to clients with international activities, the larger accounting firms followed their clients abroad, opening offices in many countries. Other firms established formal relationships with local accounting firms in other countries. Regardless of the methods followed in expanding internationally, they had to establish some uniformity in the work they performed, or had performed for them, around the world. This uniformity was necessary, so that the accounting firm could be confident in the work's quality, reliability, and verfiability.

As most of the international accounting firms discovered, a great deal of work was necessary before this desired uniformity could be achieved: their employees had to be trained in the idiosyncrasies of other countries' accounting practices and the intricacies of international accounting. The foreign employees also had to become knowledgeable about U.S. or UK accounting practices and procedures, and so forth.

To solve these problems, the large international accounting firms embarked on a series of programs involving international exchanges of personnel and international training seminars. Through these programs, their employees in the countries where they had representation acquired the background, perspective, and experience necessary to perform international accounting services on a much higher level of uniformity, consistency, and sophistication. These efforts were not oriented primarily toward achieving international harmonization, but the exchange of information, personnel, and experience resulted indirectly in an atmosphere more conducive to harmonization.

Yet when all is said and done, despite numerous efforts of numerous organizations at national, regional, and global levels, the degree of harmonization remains fairly low. And even though, as Choi and Bavishi observed in their recent study of corporate balance sheets and explanatory notes of 1000 companies from 23 different countries, fundamental differences were not as extensive as expected, significant differences still existed even among the largest firms of industrialized countries.[25] Even greater differences remain between industrial and developing nations and among developing nations.

Thus, despite the growing economic and political forces pushing for harmonization, other environmental factors continue to impede its progress. So, like the person in Robert Frost's poem "The Road Not Taken," the process of harmonization has many miles to go before it sleeps.

SUMMARY

- Major differences remain in the way accounting standards are developed in each country.

- Some countries' governments dictate accounting standards, others partially regulate them; and in only a few countries does the accounting profession play a major role in their development.

- Differences in the standard-setting processes evolve from differences in many environmental characteristics, but most significantly the degree of economic control desired by the government and the size, sophistication, and power of the accounting profession. The greater the former and the lesser the latter, the more standards are likely to be government-developed and regulated.

- Wide variations also exist among accountants in different countries in terms of their stature or status, sophistication, and the qualifications required to become a "certified public accountant" or its equivalent.

- Despite numerous differences in accounting standards and professions, certain nations exhibit enough common similarities sufficient to identify and cluster these nations into rather distinct groups. Differences within each group are less than the differences between groups.

- Two major pressures behind efforts to eliminate or significantly lessen differences (harmonize) in accounting systems are the increase in inter-

[25]Frederick Choi and Vinod Bavishi, "International Accounting Standards: Issues Needing Attention," *Journal of Accountancy*, March 1983, pp. 62–68.

national business competition, and the increased need to raise capital, particularly in international capital markets.

- The major impediments to harmonization are differences in national environmental characteristics, nationalism, and lack of agreement on which (whose) system is best.
- Many groups have pursued harmonization, but few have had any major successes, at least on a truly international scale. Most successes have been, and are likely to remain, on a subglobal, regional scale.

Study Questions

10-1. Although each nation has different environmental characteristics and accounting standards, several groups of nations have fairly similar accounting systems and standards. Why?

10-2. Discuss the major differences in the accounting standard-setting process in the United States, France, Brazil, and the Netherlands.

10-3. What impact does the size and sophistication of a nation's accounting profession have on the manner in which accounting standards are established?

10-4. What is the essential difference between accounting standardization and accounting harmonization?

10-5. Identify and discuss the major arguments for and against the international harmonization of accounting systems and standards.

10-6. Identify and explain the major forces behind the movement toward harmonization and those that are impeding its progress.

10-7. Identify the major international political organizations working for accounting harmonization. What is the major objective of each and what success has each had?

10-8. Discuss the major reasons why some regional groups have been more successful than others in achieving harmonization.

10-9. Could it be argued that harmonization would be easier to achieve at the principles level than at procedural or practices level? Why or why not?

10-10. Discuss the role that the major international accounting firms have played in moving the world toward greater harmonization of accounting standards and practices.

10-11. Discuss how international accounting courses, conferences, and exchange programs might affect the process of harmonization.

10-12. How might multinational enterprises cause pressures for governments to seek harmonization of accounting systems?

10-13. How might the multinational enterprise itself be an instrument for accounting harmonization?

10-14. How would you assess the prospects for achieving global harmonization in the next decade? What about regional harmonization?

Case

The Presentation

Roy Burgher, a junior staff member of one of the large international accounting firms, had been given a rush assignment. The senior partner of his firm had been asked to present a paper on the progress of international accounting harmonization to a group of accountants from several countries who would be visiting the city in a few days. The presentation was to cover the origins of the harmonization efforts, the problems it had encountered, and what prospects there were for success any time soon. In a quick trip to the local university's library Roy had swept together a potpourri of information about the topic but nothing that outlined in any systematic form the details sought by his boss. Roy knew that he did not have much time to prepare a suitable presentation, but as a junior staff member he knew he had better come up fast with something good.

Assignment

Write a two-page description and analysis of the major efforts to harmonize differences in international accounting that Roy's boss could use for his presentation.

INDEX